Roman Catholic Hegemony and Religious Freedom

Dr. Edwin Cook

Frontispiece: "The Triumph of Truth" statue of a woman trampling upon Protestants. The writings of Calvin, Luther, and Zwingli are being destroyed by a cherub. The Church of Jesus (Jesuits), Rome, Italy.

Copyright © 2012 Edwin Cook

All rights reserved.

ISBN: 0-615-66117-3
ISBN-13: 978-0-615-66117-9

DEDICATION

To my mother, who instilled within me a sense of justice and an obligation to duty; and to my sister Catheryn and her family who supported me during the long process of writing this book

CONTENTS

	Foreword	v
	List of Figures and Tables	vii
	Acknowledgments	viii
1	*Dignitatis Humanae*: 1965-2012	1
2	*Dignitatis Humanae* and Roman Catholics	48
3	*Dignitatis Humanae*, Conscience, and Coercion	101
4	*Dignitatis Humanae* and Seventh-day Adventists	174
5	*Dignitatis Humanae* and Religious Freedom in Spain	230
6	*Dignitatis Humanae* and Religious Freedom in Mexico	259
7	*Dignitatis Humanae* and the Future of Religious Freedom	278
	APPENDIX A, *Dignitatis Humanae*	307
	APPENDIX B, New States in the European Union	322
	BIBLIOGRAPHY	325
	INDEX	371

FOREWARD

With the publication of *Dignitatis Humanae*, the year 1965 marked a revolution in Roman Catholic thought regarding the issue of religious freedom. The predominant author of the text, Fr. John Courtney-Murray, had been addressing the issue of Roman Catholicism and religious freedom, especially as it had been addressed in the American context. Courtney-Murray believed that it was possible for Roman Catholic social thought to evolve to the modern age where tolerance of religious belief without church or state coercion was possible, *based on the teachings of the Roman Catholic Church*. The result was the Vatican II document put forth by Pope Paul VI. While the teachings of *Dignitatis Humanae* marked a watershed in Roman Catholic social thought regarding religious freedom, for many the document did not go far enough in granting complete religious freedom. Courtney-Murray, himself, believed that more was to be done.

While some have argued that *Dignitatis Humanae* marks a radical break with Roman Catholic social thought as promoted by Pope Leo XIII, Dr. Edwin Cook demonstrates in this work that there is a continuation in philosophy with Pope Leo XIII's thought and Vatican II. Through his discussion both with conservative and moderate Roman Catholics, he shows that there is a latent tendency towards hegemony on the part of Roman Catholicism, especially as understood by religious minorities such as Seventh-day Adventists.

Cook presents a fascinating study of the text from a Seventh-day Adventist perspective. In his analysis of the document, Cook demonstrates some of the weaknesses of the argument put forward by Courtney-Murray and the Fathers of the Council by arguing that the text does not go far enough in allowing for religious freedom, especially for minority religions in countries where a predominant Roman Catholic culture retains its hegemony. This, he argues, is the Catholic hegemony thesis, whereby the Roman Catholic Church continues to desire a hegemonic relationship with the society in which it has traditionally had such a relationship. In this regard, Cook examines Spain and Mexico to test his thesis.

What Cook realizes is that there is the latent possibility for the perpetuation of Catholic hegemony, even within *Dignitatis Humanae* both philosophically as well as through its interpretation and implementation in regards to the relationships engendered by the Vatican with nation-states. Although it is becoming an increasingly secularized nation, Spain has continued a cultural Catholic hegemony in relationship to religious minorities, particularly Seventh-day Adventists. However, despite Vatican attempts to establish Concordats with Mexico, it has fought to remain a neutral and secular state in how it relates to religious minorities.

Cook's argument and analysis of *Dignitatis Humanae* from a religious minority perspective shines new light on this very important document in Roman Catholic social thought. While Vatican II did not go as far as some, especially Protestants, would have liked in acknowledging their status as churches, the papacy in *Dignitatis Humanae* did attempt to bring Roman Catholicism into a *rapprochement* with the modern world. Through the respect of others, although from the Roman Catholic perspective they are in spiritual error, the Church can tolerate them and live peacefully with other religions and faiths. What is needed, according to Cook, is additional work by the papacy in promoting religious freedom and toleration for all faiths and religions. While the Roman Catholic Church is not at this time about to recognize other Christian denominations as churches, the Church can learn to exist, and must learn to exist, in the world alongside these other faith groups as a servant, rather than hegemonic lord.

I commend Dr. Cook's work for studies on *Dignitatis Humanae* as well as for studies on Roman Catholicism and religious minorities. His work makes a valuable contribution to this field of studies.

Fr. Daniel P. Payne, Ph.D.
Baylor University
September, 2012

LIST OF FIGURES AND TABLES

Fig. 2.1 Paternalistic Church Model	59
Fig. 2.2 Secular Church Model of John of Paris	72
Fig. 2.3 Public Church Model	73
Fig. 2.4 Madisonian Separationist Model	97
Fig. 3.1 Old Testament Theocratic Model	118
Fig. 3.2 New Testament Apolitical Model	119
Fig. 3.3 Coercive Church Model	130
Fig. 3.4 Four Models of Church-State Relations	166
Fig. 3.5 Societal Construct with Latent Power to Coerce	169
Fig. 3.6 Protestant and Catholic Concepts of Religious Freedom	170
Fig. 4.1 The "Times" of *Dignitatis Humanae*	225
Table 3.1 Protestant and Catholic Concepts of Religious Freedom, 1529	140
Table 3.2 Catholic Concepts of Religious Freedom, 1529 and 1965	142
Table 4.1 The Year-Day Principle	211
Table 4.2 An Interpretation of Daniel 7	212

ACKNOWLEDGMENTS

I am thankful to Dr. Daniel Payne, who challenged my thinking about many portions of this manuscript and without whose faithful dedication to the review process, it would not reflect the level of scholarship that it now does. I am grateful as well to the staff of the J. M. Dawson Institute, Baylor University, for their helpfulness during my years of research there. In particular, I wish to thank Dr. Bill Pitts, Dr. Victor Hinojosa, Dr. Jerold Waltman, and Dr. Lizbeth Souza-Fuertes, each of whom provided insightful comments and spent hours of time reviewing this literary work for accuracy.

I wish to thank Dr. Rafael Calonge, director of the Public Affairs and Religious Liberty department for the Spain Conference of Seventh-day Adventists. He and his office staff received me as a brother and provided excellent support in my research efforts there. In particular, I wish to also thank Toñi and the Fleidner Foundation, Madrid, Spain, for the invaluable assistance given me in obtaining information from news articles related to Vatican II and the promulgation of *Dignitatis Humanae*, which reflect the prevailing sentiments of that time period toward the Document on Religious Freedom.

I extend gratitude to Elizabeth B. Mandujano Alanuza, Director of Minister of Worship, Secretary of Government, in Distrito Federal, Mexico for the gracious way she and the other staff of the Mexican government received me into their offices and treated me as royalty. In particular, I thank them for the invaluable gifts of books dealing with church-state relations, religion and society, and the history of Mexico, all of which have served as useful tools toward the completion of this literary work.

I would be remiss in giving honor where honor is due if I failed to mention my gratitude to members of my faith community living in Waco, Texas, both English and Hispanic, many of whom often lifted me up in prayer and supported me in a variety of ways while I worked to finish this monograph. Thank-you! Gracias!

A heartfelt acknowledgment to Mr. Ben Rogers, Director of W. R. Poage Legislative Library, Baylor University, for those moments he took to listen to some of my ideas and insights, as well as challenge them, which now find fruition in the pages of this work. "It is now done!!"

DIGNITATIS HUMANAE: 1965-2012

"Roman Catholic Hegemony and Religious Freedom" examines the Document on Religious Freedom, also known as *Dignitatis Humanae*, that was promulgated by the Roman Catholic Church in December, 1965. The thesis of this book is Catholic Hegemony, which argues that the Church applies *Dignitatis Humanae* in different ways, depending upon extant political and religious conditions in a given country – in some cases to maintain its hegemony, and in others, to establish its hegemony over time. Hegemony, as used here, does not refer to singular dominance, as demonstrated by the Church during the medieval era. Rather, it refers to the Church seeking and maintaining a place of preeminence among other religious groups within a pluralistic society founded upon a constitutional democracy. The idea of the Catholic Church as a preeminent religious entity among other religious bodies, and holding a more influential position, allows for other religious groups to join in the national public policy councils.[1] "Catholic Hegemony and Religious Freedom" will contribute to scholarly discussion among the Catholic Church and Protestant groups, among civil libertarians, and in debates on shaping public policy. Chapter One introduces the issues related to *Dignitatis Humanae* and Catholic hegemony, and provides an overview of following chapters.

The year 1963 was significant for both Seventh-day Adventists and Catholics in the area of religious freedom. For the former group, the case of *Sherbert v. Verner*, decided on June 17, 1963, marked an important legal victory protecting the free exercise rights of Adelle Sherbert to observe the biblical Sabbath, Saturday, without incurring monetary losses.[2] For the

---

[1] The thesis of "Catholic Hegemony" as defined here is original to the

[2] J. Brennan, *Sherbert v. Verner*, in Cornell University Law School, Legal Information Institute, http://www.law.cornell.edu/supct/html/historics/USSC_CR_0374_0398_ZO. html (accessed June 6, 2011). This case was pivotal in

latter group, "the first schema (or draft-text) on religious freedom was presented to the conciliar Fathers on November 19, 1963,"[3] which was a stalwart defense against the incessant criticisms that the Catholic Church lacked consideration for the religious views and rights of other groups.

Religious freedom plays a central role in the beliefs of both groups. However, the type of religious freedom advocated by each group deserves further investigation. Shortly after *Dignitatis Humanae* was promulgated in its final form on December 7, 1965, its principal author, John Courtney Murray, S.J., entertained questions from his audience after a short address upon the meaning and significance of the conciliar document (also referred to by him as "the Declaration [on Religious Freedom]"). In particular, the dialogue between him and his interlocutor, Smith,[4] raises honest questions about the type of religious freedom inherent to *Dignitatis Humanae*:

> SMITH: Father Murray, you state that the protection and vindication of the rights named in the Declaration of Independence is to be carried out by government in accord with the principles of equality before the law, and this principle forbids classification of citizens according to their religious beliefs or the lack thereof. I recall two cases before the Supreme Court: the Everson and Sherbert cases. The New Jersey law in the Everson case, the bus transportation law, was written to benefit the children in Catholic parochial schools. If you recall Justice Jackson was opposed to the law on that ground. That was a case of classification according to religion in vindication of free exercise and the protection of children on the streets.
>
> The Sherbert case, more recently, is completely distinct. It was directed that the South Carolina Social Security Commission should pay social security benefits to Mrs. Sherbert, who is a Seventh-day Adventist and had refused to work on her Sabbath, Saturday. She was singled out for this benefit, because her reasons for refusing to work on that day were religious, and it was expressly stated that if her reasons had had to do with family care that the case

---

establishing the right of employees to have legal recourse for dismissal from work, or denial of benefits, for the observance of a religious day of worship, in this case Saturday.

[3] John Courtney Murray, S. J., *Religious Liberty: an End and a Beginning* (New York: The Macmillan Co., 1966), 15.

[4] This is the only name given to Murray's interlocutor in this source.

would not have gone favorably to her. The second and more telling instance of classification according to religion in vindication of free exercise [sic].

Now, my question is: Does your principle stand when it applies to the vindication of free exercise, so that it favors religion, and not stand when the case is opposite?

MURRAY: First of all, my recollections of the Everson case are vague. It was in 1947 that it was decided. I seem to recall that one of the lawyers was trying to make the point that the law should be struck down, precisely because it was an unreasonable classification according to religious beliefs. The court decided to play it the other way: that not to admit Catholic children to enjoy these benefits, transportation by buses, would have been to classify them out on grounds of religion. *I would want my principle to hold in full universality.*

SMITH: Professor Kurland has argued this same point: classification according to religion should never be done, and that would have meant that Mrs. Sherbert would have been out of work and out of social security because her religious principles forbade her to work on her Sabbath day. So the court went against that general counsel contained in this principle in order to vindicate her freedom of exercise against the indirect pressure of denial of unemployment compensation.

MURRAY: The problem of classification is a delicate and needed one, in its thrust, in its direction, and then of course in verifying the famous adjective that goes with it, "reasonable" classification. *You are saying then that if this principle were to be held with full universality, then the Court was wrong in the second case that you are mentioning. Is this right?*

SMITH: I think this is the impression I would draw. I myself think that maybe we ought to go this far: the universality of this rule can be broken when a free exercise matter is in question. But that also is a delicate matter.

MURRAY: Yes, very delicate at the moment in American courts, because it is not entirely clear whether or not the presumption today does stand for free exercise, or for no aid to religion.[5]

---

[5] John Courtney Murray, S. J., "Session XIV: The Declaration on Religious Freedom," in *Vatican II: An Interfaith Appraisal*, ed. John H. Miller (Notre Dame, IN: Univ. of Notre Dame Press, 1966), 578-579 [italics mine].

Murray's response in this dialogue is that the religious convictions of an individual or group should not be allowed to render judgment in his favor, arguing instead for "equality" before the law that should hold in "full universality." In the case of *Everson*, Catholic children received the same transportation benefits as all other public school children. The reason the Court did not strike down this law was because they looked beyond the religious orientation of the children and viewed them on an equal par as children attending public schools. In the case of *Sherbert*, the Court ruled in her favor because of her religious convictions and ordered the Unemployment Commission to pay her just compensation for the time during which she was not employed. Murray's principle supports the former case, but questions the latter.

There are several weaknesses in Murray's rationale. First, he fails to distinguish between an establishment clause case, *Everson*,[6] and a free exercise case, *Sherbert*.[7] In *Everson*, the issue in question revolved around whether or not the Board of Education of the township of Ewing, New Jersey, had violated the First Amendment Establishment Clause.[8] A New Jersey statute allowed for local school districts to reimburse parents for the cost of public transportation to take their children to school. The difficulty arose when some children attended Catholic parochial schools, and Everson, a tax payer questioned their reimbursement as a violation of the Establishment Clause. In contrast, the case of *Sherbert* did not present the

---

[6] *Everson* is classified as "Establishment of Religion," see for example, Robert T. Miller and Ronald B. Flowers, *Toward Benevolent Neutrality: Church, State, and the Supreme Court*, 5th ed., 2 vols. (Waco, TX: Baylor University Press, 1996), 1:iv, under the section "The Establishment of Religion," sub-heading "Government Aid to Church-Related Schools."

[7] Ibid., 2:v, under the section "The Free Exercise of Religion," sub-heading "Religion and the Right to Work."

[8] Justice Black delivered the opinion of the Court, "The only contention here is that the state statute and the resolution, insofar as they authorized reimbursement to parents of children attending parochial schools, violate the Federal Constitution [including by] forc[ing] inhabitants to pay taxes to help support and maintain schools which are dedicated to, and which regularly teach, the Catholic Faith. This is alleged to be a use of state power to support church schools contrary to the prohibition of the First Amendment which the Fourteenth Amendment made applicable to the states." *Everson v. Board of Education*, 330 U.S. 1, 67 S. Ct. 504, 91L. Ed. 711 (1947) as cited in Kathleen M. Sullivan and Gerald Gunther, *First Amendment Law* (New York: Foundation Press, 1999), 531.

potential to establish Seventh-day Adventism as a state religion through recognizing and paying unemployment benefits to Mrs. Sherbert.[9]

On the flip side of the question, seeing it from a free exercise perspective, *Everson* did not involve the free exercise rights of Catholic children because it is not part of Catholic dogma (doctrine) to *require* Catholic children to attend a Catholic school.[10] However, it is part of Catholic dogma that the State should aid Catholic education,[11] which may

---

[9] Justice Brennan, delivering the opinion of the Court, stated, "In holding as we do, plainly we are not fostering the 'establishment' of the Seventh-day Adventist religion in South Carolina, for the extension of unemployment benefits to Sabbatarians in common with Sunday worshippers reflects nothing more than the governmental obligation of neutrality in the face of religious differences, and does not represent that involvement of religious with secular institutions which it is the object of the Establishment Clause to forestall." *Sherbert v. Verner*, 374 U.S. 398, 83 S. Ct. 1790, 10 L. Ed. 2d. 965 (1963), as cited in Sullivan and Gunther, *First Amendment Law*, 478.

[10] "Parents and those who take their place are bound by the obligation and possess the right of educating their offspring. Catholic parents also have the duty and right of choosing those means and institutions through which they can provide more suitably for the Catholic education of their children, according to local circumstances." The Code of Canon Law, Book III, The Teaching Function of the Church, Title III, Catholic Education, Canon 793, Art. 1, http://www.vatican.va/archive/ENG1104/_INDEX.HTM (accessed August 4, 2011). The phrase "according to local circumstances" allows for situations where there is no Catholic school available; additionally, see footnote 11, which acknowledges "the right of parents to make a genuinely free choice of schools."

[11] "Government, in consequence, must acknowledge the right of parents to make a genuinely free choice of schools and of other means of education, and the use of this freedom of choice is not to be made a reason for imposing unjust burdens on parents, whether directly or indirectly. Besides, the rights of parents are violated, if their children are forced to attend lessons or instructions which are not in agreement with their religious beliefs, or if a single system of education, from which all religious formation is excluded, is imposed upon all." *Dignitatis Humanae*, Article 5. The statement "and the use of this freedom of choice is not to be made a reason for imposing unjust burdens on parents," opens the door wide for Catholics to claim that the payment of taxes to support a secular, public educational system, which does not teach the Catholic faith, is an "unjust burden" upon them since they must also pay parochial school tuition. From this argument, a great shift has taken place in favor of school vouchers in the United States, which indirectly support religious educational institutions. In addition, the Roman Catholic Code of Canon Law, states, "Parents also have the right to that assistance, to be furnished by civil society, which they need to secure the Catholic education of their children." Book III, The Teaching Function of the Church, Title III, Catholic Education,

be why Murray supported this decision. In the case of *Sherbert*, it indeed was a direct violation of her free exercise rights, the Court inquiring "whether the disqualification for benefits imposes any burden on the free exercise of appellant's religion," and finding that "it is clear that it does."[12] The Court further argued, "The ruling forces her to choose between following the precepts of her religion and forfeiting benefits, on the one hand, and abandoning one of the precepts of her religion in order to accept work, on the other hand."[13] Considering these differences, Murray's argument seems to hint at a very subtle type of Catholic hegemony: *Everson* being upheld, thus indirectly aiding Catholic educational efforts, and *Sherbert* being overturned, thus directly denying Sabbatarians,[14] in this case a Seventh-day Adventist, any shelter from religious discrimination.

Additionally, Murray's "equality before the law" argument, whereby courts should not refer to the religious convictions of appellants in deciding cases, seems to portray the confusing idea of a veterinarian's office that posts a sign which says "No pets allowed." He desires to place *Sherbert* in the rubric of "equality before the law" without appeal to the religious convictions of the individual, which is a contradiction of the very intent of the free exercise clause. In order for the Court to uphold the free exercise rights of the individual (or group), it must consider what are those religious convictions. Under Murray's rubric, Catholic children would be favored by state aid and Seventh-day Adventists would not have recourse for appeal regarding violations of their conscientious convictions with respect to Sabbath observance.

Scrutinizing the argument more closely, Murray's "equality before the law" principle falls far short of the mark when compared to the principle of *benevolent neutrality* used among church-state scholars, which originated in the opinion of the U. S. Supreme Court in *Waltz v. Tax Commission*.[15] Murray's

---

Canon 793, Art. 2, http://www.vatican.va/archive/ENG1104/ _INDEX.HTM (accessed August 4, 2011).

[12] Justice Brennan, delivering the opinion of the Court, in *Sherbert v. Verner*, 374 U.S. 398, 83 S. Ct. 1790, 10 L. Ed. 2d. 965 (1963), as cited in Sullivan and Gunther, *First Amendment Law*, 477.

[13] Ibid.

[14] Sabbatarians include Seventh-day Adventists, Jews who observe the Sabbath, Seventh-day Baptists, the Church of God (7th day), the Worldwide Church of God (Sabbath observing), and various Pentecostal groups.

[15] ". . . there is room for play in the joints [of the First Amendment religion clauses] productive of a benevolent neutrality which will permit religious

principle reveals disparity between Catholics and Seventh-day Adventists, whereas *benevolent neutrality* argues in this fashion: the real principle involved in both cases is that of ensuring that an individual (or group) is not harmed due to his religious convictions, or government follows the principle of *bene volonte* (good will) toward religion by remaining neutral, neither harming nor directly favoring it.[16] Following this principle, the Catholic children are not penalized for being Catholic and thus, should receive the same benefits as public school children. In the same way, Adelle Sherbert should not be penalized for following her faith and should be entitled to the same benefits as anyone else who should become unemployed. Thus, Murray's "equality before the law" argument reveals great flaws in the area of religious freedom jurisprudence.

From this brief overview regarding the religious freedom views of a leading Catholic scholar, who was a *periti* (expert) and the principal drafter of *Dignitatis Humanae* at Vatican II, and how such views, if adopted as jurisprudence, could result in detrimental consequences for Seventh-day Adventists (and possibly other religious groups), it is appropriate to investigate as fully as possible certain of the religious freedom concepts contained in the conciliar document *Dignitatis Humanae*.

The Importance of This Study

This study examines *Dignitatis Humanae* from a Seventh-day Adventist understanding of religious freedom. Among Seventh-day Adventists, such

---

exercise to exist without sponsorship and without interference." Chief Justice Warren Burger, *Waltz v. Tax Commission* (397 U. S. 664, 669) as cited in Miller and Flowers, *Toward Benevolent Neutrality*, 1:xi.

[16] This is not the same principle as "non-preferentialism", which is gaining influence among religious groups, especially evangelical Protestants and Catholics, and which argues that as long as all religious groups are aided by government, with no preference being given to any particular group, then there is no violation of the establishment clause. The problem with this rationale is that it falsely assumes that all religious groups hold the same basic beliefs and, thus, when all are treated "equally" under the law, they will all benefit "equally." As is evidenced by Murray's views on *Everson* and *Sherbert*, not all religious groups benefit "equally" under law when using a supposedly "non-preferentialist" approach. Cf. Douglas Laycock, "Religion and the State: Article: The Origins of the Religion Clauses of the Constitution: 'Non-preferential' aid to religion: A False Claim about Original Intent," *William and Mary Law Review*, 27 (Summer, 1986), 875, in which Laycock refutes the "non-preferentialist" theory espoused by Philip Kurland, et al., by showing it is not historically founded by the relevant writings of the Framers.

an evaluation is yet lacking.[17] Historically, Seventh-day Adventists and the Roman Catholic hierarchy have viewed one another with a large degree of suspicion.[18] Based on eschatological interpretations, the former regard the latter as the fulfillment of the Beast power in Revelation 13, including all of its persecuting activity.[19] To say the least, the document *Dignitatis Humanae*

---

[17] At the time of its promulgation, Bert Beach, a long-time veteran of church-state issues in Europe for the Seventh-day Adventist Church, commented favorably toward the document, but also noted some areas for investigation, Koshy, *Religious Freedom in a Changing World* (Genevea, Switzerland: WCC Publications, 1992), 89-90. Since then, several Adventist scholars have either cited the document and included a cursory analysis of it, or have referred to its impact in the area of religious liberty: Marvin Moore, *Could It Really Happen? Revelation 13 in the light of history and current events* (Nampa, ID: Pacific Press, 2007), 87-94; Marvin Moore, *Challenges to the Remnant* (Nampa, ID: Pacific Press, 2008), 35-37; Christa Reinach and Alan J. Reinach, eds., *Politics and Prophecy* (Nampa, ID: Pacific Press, 2007); V. Norskov Olsen, *Supremacia Papal y Libertad Religiosa* (Miami, FL: Asociacion Publicadora Interamericana, 1992), 162-168; Bert B. Beach, *Bright Candle of Courage* (Boise, ID: Pacific Press, 1989), 73-99; Douglas Morgan, *Adventism and the American Republic: The Public Involvement of a Major Apocalyptic Movement* (Knoxville, TN: University of Tennessee Press, 2001), 131, 133-134, 185-187; et al. Of these, the only author to approximate an incisive, in-depth treatment of the subject is Bert Beach, in *Bright Candle of Courage*, and he even suggests areas for further analysis by stating, "How permanent is the new religious liberty teaching?. . . Does it represent only a juridical and historical response to contemporary conditions and pressures, or does it represent unconditional doctrinal truth, which once acquired cannot be abandoned?"

[18] The primary rationale for which the former hold this view is based on their belief that they constitute a continuation of the Protestant Reformation. Marvin Moore, *Challenges to the Remnant* (Nampa, ID: Pacific Press, 2008), 172-185; *Seventh-day Adventists Believe: A Biblical exposition of 27 fundamental doctrines* (Washington, D.C: Ministerial Association, General Conference of Seventh-day Adventists, 1988), Chapter 12, "The Remnant and Its Mission," 152-169.

[19] "[J. N.] Andrews [an early Seventh-day Adventist pioneer] identified the beast of Rev. 14:9-11 as the beast of Rev. 13:1-10, the latter of which was identified with the fourth beast of Dan. 7. The identification of the first beast of Rev. 13 with the fourth of Dan. 7 he based on the fact that (1) in John's time three of the beasts (empires) had passed away, making it logical that only Daniel's fourth beast was shown to John; (2) both beasts ascended out of the sea. He concluded that the beast of Rev. 13 "is evidently the Papal form of the fourth beast, for it receives its seat and dominion from the dragon [Rev. 13:2], Rome Pagan. The seat is Rome, which was given him at the same time that his power was given." P. Gerard Damsteegt, *Foundations of the Seventh-day Adventist Message and Mission* (Berrien Springs, MI: Andrews University Press, 1995), 195; cf., "The papal church will never relinquish her claim to infallibility. All that she has done in her persecution

has posed significant challenges to Seventh-day Adventist eschatology.[20] Essentially, there are two groups among Adventists on this issue: the first group adopts a stereotypical view of the Catholic Church, believing that it is merely using *Dignitatis Humanae* to gain the favor of the world while retaining its pre-Vatican II position regarding religious freedom; the second group recognizes validity in the document, but is facing an *impasse* regarding how to uphold this view and at the same time conceptualize the Catholic Church within the historic, traditional Adventist interpretation of Bible prophecy. As a Seventh-day Adventist, I expect the conclusions drawn from this book to aid both groups: for the former, to recognize the positive impact *Dignitatis Humanae* has had in some countries toward promoting religious freedom; for the latter, to provide an Adventist concept of religious freedom by which to evaluate *Dignitatis Humanae* and thereby remove the *impasse* that the document presents, or at minimum, to provide principles by which both groups can better understand each other's positions.

Additionally, Roman Catholics can benefit from the conclusions of this book in the following areas: 1) clarifying the views of Catholic scholars who were uncertain of its intent at the time it was promulgated[21]; 2) offering

---

of those who reject her dogmas she holds to be right; and would she not repeat the same acts, should the opportunity be presented? Let the restraints now imposed by secular governments be removed and Rome be reinstated in her former power, and there would speedily be a revival of her tyranny and persecution." Ellen G. White, *The Great Controversy* (Nampa, ID: Pacific Press Publishing, 2005), 564.

[20] "This book provides an occasion for Adventists to wrestle with whether this classic perspective on Catholicism is essential to Adventism. Does the belief that the Catholic Church is the beast of prophecy serve as the mark of authentic Adventism? If so, why didn't Jesus preach a single sermon on the topic? . . . is this belief excluded from the 28 Fundamental Beliefs precisely because it is not fundamental to Adventism? How should conscientious Adventists interpret this intentional silence?" David A. Pendleton, "A Review of Marvin Moore's *Challenge to the Remnant*," *Spectrum*, September 19, 2009, http://www.spectrummagazine.org/reviews/book_reviews/2008/09/19/review_marvin_moore%E2%80%99s_challenges_remnant, paragraphs 18-20 (accessed September 20, 2009); cf. Douglas Morgan, *Adventism and the American Republic: The Public Involvement of a Major Apocalyptic Movement* (Knoxville, TN: University of Tennessee Press, 2001), Chapter 6: "A Pluralistic Remnant, 1976-2000".

[21] "Among the progressive theologians who have admitted the difficulty of proving a legitimate development between the traditional teaching and that of Vatican II are five Council *periti* (experts) whose testimony is of the very highest importance – the first two being the experts most influential in drafting the text of the Declaration itself. These experts are Father John Courtney Murray, S.J., Msgr. Pietro Pavan, Father Yves Congar, O.P., Father Hans Kung, and Father Joseph

insights that may help solve some of the present-day confusion among Catholics regarding how to correctly interpret the document[22]; 3) providing a reasonable explanation with respect to the practical application of the document in various countries where Roman Catholics form a significant part of the population, thereby helping to resolve some of the dissonance among Catholics regarding its application[23]; 4) contributing to the current dialogue about the document by Catholic scholars, which has taken on an international dimension with scholars submitting interpretations in a variety

---

Ratzinger." Michael Davies, *The Second Vatican Council and Religious Liberty* (Long Prairie, MN: The Neumann Press, 1992), 199.

[22] Peter W. Miller, "Differing from Other Councils. . .", *Seattle Catholic*, Jan. 3, 2003, http://www.seattlecatholic.com/article_20030103_Differing_from _Other_Councils.html, (accessed March 18, 2007). Also, in mid-October, 2009, a special dialogue between the Vatican and the Society of Saint Pius X (SSPX) happened that centered on the issue of religious freedom as espoused by *Dignitatis Huamanae* and the pre-Vatican II position of the same, http://acatholiclife. blogspot.com/2009/09/talks-between-sspx-and-rome-will-occur.html (accessed September 17, 2009).

[23] Examples of dissonance of application include the Church respecting the rights of non-Catholics, such as: In many Latin American countries, such as Paraguay, Peru, Bolivia, and Mexico, church leadership changed its proselytism strategies, showing greater respect and latitude for indigenous religious practices, in accord with the Church's position taken at Vatican II. See, Edward L. Cleary and Timothy J. Stegenga, *Resurgent Voices in Latin America: Indigenous Peoples, Political Mobilization, and Religious Change* (New Jersey: Rutgers, 2004), 9, 19, 45, 68, et al. But in other examples, the Church does not demonstrate that respect for religious diversity: In Croatia, a national Sunday law took effect on January 1, 2009. Although supported by the majority of the populace who are Catholic, it nonetheless creates economic hardships upon other minority religious groups such as Seventh-day Adventists who observe Saturday, rather than Sunday, as a day of worship, http://abcnews.go.com/ International/wireStory?id=5378375 (accessed August 27, 2008). In 2006, Pope Benedict XVI made a public statement, "The Unicity of Salvation," affirming the traditional stance of the Church that *nunc potestis salus ex-ecclesia* (outside of the Church there is no salvation), which caused much uproar among some Protestant groups. Historically, this statement carried an overtly coercive tone, since man's end was God and the Church's mission was to aid man in achieving his ultimate end, thus, justifying almost any means to that end. *Dignitatis Humanae*, taken in light of Benedict's statement, would seem to imply that its guarantees of religious freedom really mean that one must seek the Catholic faith until one is convinced of it and embraces it.

of languages.[24]

Dignitatis Humanae, Latin for "Of human dignity," follows in the Catholic tradition of using the first few significant words at the beginning of a document promulgated by the Church by which to refer to it. This book follows the same practice, as well as using two other terms that are used interchangeably by Catholic scholars to refer to it, which are "the Declaration,"[25] and "the Declaration on Religious Freedom."[26]

---

[24] E.g., books alone include, in Latin: Francisco Gil Hellin, *Declaratio de Libertate Religiosa – Dignitatis Humanae* (Roma: Pontificia Universitas Sanctae Crucis, 2008); in French: *La liberté religieuse dans l'enseignement des Papes* (Abbaye Saint-Pierre de Solesmes, 1989); Dominique Gonnet, S.J., *La liberté religieuse à Vatican II: La contribution de John Courtney Murray* (Paris: Les editions du Cerf, 1994); Fr. Basile, O.S.B., *Le droit à la liberté religieuse dans la Tradition de l'Eglise: Un cas de developpement doctrinal homogene par le magistere authentique* (Editions Sainte-Madeleine, 2005); Francois Bosquet, *Pour Une Conscience Vive et Libre: "Dignitatis Humanae" – Une declaration prophetique de Vatican II* (Editions Parole et Silence, 2006); in German: Lukas Vischer, "*Dignitatis Humanae*: Zur Notwendigkeit eines kirchlichen Menschenrechtsprogramms," in *Das Zweite Vatikanische Konzil und Die Zeichen der Zeit Heute*, ed. Herausgegeben von Peter Hunermann, (Freiburg: Herder, 2006), 439-442; Tamara Bloch, *Die Stellungnahmen der romisch-katholischen Amtskirche zur Frage der menschenrechte seit 1215* (Frankfurt am Main: Peter Lang, 2008), 115-136; in English: Michael Davies, *The Second Vatican Council and Religious Liberty* (Long Prairie, MN: The Neumann Press, 1992); John T. Ford, C.S.C., ed., *Religious Liberty: Paul VI and "Dignitatis Humanae"* (Brescia: Istituto Paulo VI, 1995); Herminio Rico, *John Paul II and the Legacy of "Dignitatis Humanae"* (Washington, D.C.: Georgetown University Press, 2002); John T. McGreevy, *Catholicism and American Freedom* (New York: W.W. Norton & Company, Inc., 2003); Kenneth R. Himes, O.f.M, ed., *Modern Catholic Social Teaching: Commentaries and Interpretations* (Washington, D.C.: Georgetown University Press, 2005); Kenneth L Grasso and Robert P. Hunt, eds., *Catholicism and Religious Freedom: Contemporary Reflections on Vatican II's Declaration on Religious Liberty* (New York: Rowman & Littlefield Publishers, 2006); Stephen B. Bevans, SVD and Jeffrey Gros, FSC, *Evangelization and Religious Freedom: Ad Gentes, Dignitatis Humanae* (New York: Paulist Press, 2009); in Spanish: Gerardo del Pozo Abejon, *La Iglesia y la libertad religiosa* (Madrid: Biblioteca de Autores Cristianos, 2007); in Italian: Gabrio Lombardi, *Persecuzioni Laicita, Libertà Religiosa: Dall' Editto di Milano alla "Dignitatis Humanae"* (Roma: Edizioni Studium, 1991); Silvia Scatena, *La Fatica della Libertà: L'elaborazione della dichiarazione "Dignitatis Humanae" sulla Libertà Religiosa del Vaticano II* (Bologna: Societa editrice il Mulino, 2003); Renato Papetti and Rodolfo Rossi, eds., *"Dignitatis Humanae": La Liberta Religiosa in Paolo VI* (Brescia: Istituto Paolo VI, 2004).

[25] John Courtney Murray, "Religious Freedom" Introduction to *Dignitatis Humanae*, in *The Documents of Vatican II*, edited by Walter M. Abbott (New York: The Crossroad Publishing Company, 1989), 672.

The Declaration promotes a strong sense of religious freedom, using such phrases as "immunity from coercion in civil society,"[27] "a right to religious freedom,"[28] and the individual "is not to be forced to act in a manner contrary to his conscience."[29] These phrases aptly reflect the concern of the Council to promote human rights as responsible freedom.[30] Appealing to prior ecclesial documents promulgated by such popes as Pius XI, Pius XII, John XXIII, and Paul VI, the Second Vatican Council built upon prior ecclesial teachings to establish a unique doctrine on religious freedom.[31]

Although it was the most hotly debated document of the Council,[32] Catholic scholars indicate that the greatest issue of contention was how to express the theological continuity from Leo XIII's encyclical *Libertas Praestantissimum* – which denounced separation of church and state, freedom of conscience, and freedom of speech that might contain error[33] – to *Dignitatis Humanae*, which seemed to espouse ideas completely contrary to

---

[26]Pietro Pavan, "Declaration on Religious Freedom," in *Commentary on the Documents of Vatican II*, edited by Herbert Vorgrimler, 5 vols. (New York: The Crossroads Publishing Company, 1989), 4:50.

[27] *Dignitatis Humanae*, Art. 1, par. 4.

[28] *Dignitatis Humanae*, Art. 2, par. 1.

[29] *Dignitatis Humanae*, Art. 3, par. 4.

[30] "Finally, though the Declaration deals only with the minor issue of religious freedom in the technical secular sense, it does affirm a principle of wider import – that the dignity of man consists in his responsible use of freedom." Murray, "Religious Freedom," 674. "In the new schema (draft) this dignity is the basic motif, but it is understood above all as the responsibility of action." Pavan, Declaration, 4:53.

[31] Pavan, Declaration, 4:61.

[32] Murray, "Religious Freedom," 673.

[33] "There now follows a lengthy examination of the Liberty achieved in the new age – that is to say, since 1789 – according to the four principles in which it is commonly summed up, namely, Liberty of Worship; Liberty of Speech and of the Press; Liberty of Teaching; Liberty of Conscience." See section "III. Four Modern 'Liberties' Examined" in Philip Hughes, *The Pope's New Order: A Systematic Summary of the Social Encyclicals and Addresses, from Leo XIII to Pius XII* (New York: The MacMillan Co., 1944), 115-118.

the aforementioned.³⁴ John Courtney Murray acknowledged that (as of 1966) there existed a need to develop this theological continuity.³⁵ From this insight, one may conclude that opposition to the Declaration was not based on rejection of religious freedom *as enunciated in the document*, although there was a minority who were so disposed. Rather, initial opposition was due to a perceived lack of theological continuity.

The contending viewpoints among the conciliar fathers were based on the pre-Vatican II understanding of the role of the Church in relation to the State, which obligated the State to only permit religious truth (i.e., the Church's teachings) in society, and to forbid religious error.³⁶ The only exceptions were instances that might cause greater harm to society, in which case religious error was tolerated.³⁷ Catholics of today still exist who hold these views and they are referred to as Traditionalists in this book. Chapter two, "*Dignitatis Humanae* and Roman Catholicism," explains the pre-Vatican II concept of Church and State, as well as the contentions Traditionalists have with *Dignitatis Humanae*. With like fervor, Modernist Catholics defend *Dignitatis Humanae*, claiming that it is not a break with the tradition of the Church.³⁸ The second half of chapter two reveals their side of the debate.

In light of such furor, what kind of religious freedom, then, is contained in the conciliar document? More than any other concept of religious freedom contained in *Dignitatis Humanae*, the religious freedom of the

---

³⁴ Pavan, Declaration, 4:60, 64.

³⁵ Murray, "Religious Freedom," 673.

³⁶ "Hence, if almost all members of a society or the majority profess the true, that is to say the Catholic, religion, the State, too, has the duty to profess it." Pavan, Declaration, 4:50.

³⁷ "Those citizens who belong to other religions *do not have the right not to be prevented from professing these religions*; however, for the sake of the common good the State may tolerate their profession, both for the sake of the common good of the relevant community and for that of all mankind." Pavan, Declaration, 4:50.

³⁸ "This addition was meant to suggest to these fathers that they should consider not only the doctrine of Leo XIII and his immediate predecessors, but also that of his successors, . . . Such a sober and objective consideration could not but result in the certainty that there had, of course, been a doctrinal development, but that its last phase tended towards what was said in the Council document, if it did not actually agree with it." Pavan, Declaration, 4:61.

Church to fulfill its mission in society is the predominant one.[39] Additionally, the document deals with the religious freedom rights of the individual based on the dignity of the human person and its corresponding constitutional guarantees.[40] It treats the authority of the Church over its members, as well as the rights of parents to determine the religious education of their children.[41] It also delineates the rights of groups of believers to assemble and the corresponding limitation of those rights in society.[42]

However, there are some concepts and phrases that have raised questions among non-Catholic readers of the document. In Article one, paragraph two, not only is the Catholic Church clearly identified as the sole depository of truth, "We believe that this one true religion subsists in the Catholic and Apostolic Church,"[43] but the right to religious freedom for the individual is posited against an objective (Catholic) moral order: "Therefore it leaves untouched traditional Catholic doctrine on the moral duty of men and societies toward the true religion and toward the one Church of Christ."[44] Additionally, such an ambiguous phrase as "This freedom means that all men are to be immune from coercion on the part of . . . any human power,"[45] and the equally nebulous phrase of "Therefore, the right to

---

[39] *Dignitatis Humanae* declares "the theological doctrine of the freedom of the Church as the fundamental principle in what concerns the relations between the Church and the socio-political order." Murray, "Religious Freedom," 673.

[40] The Document declares "the ethical doctrine of religious freedom as a human right (personal and collective)." Murray, "Religious Freedom," 672-673.

[41] "Here [in *Dignitatis Humanae* Article 5] the parents have the duty to order the religious life. They have the right to determine the religious education of their children in accordance with their own religious beliefs; hence they have the right to choose schools and other educational institutions with this end in view. Governments, in consequence, must acknowledge and respect this right." Pavan, Declaration, 4:71.

[42] "The Council wants here to emphasize once more that men are by nature social beings and hence have the natural right to profess their individual religious faith also externally and in a communal form (cf. Article 3, para. 3)." Pavan, Declaration, 4:70.

[43] *Dignitatis Humanae*, Art. 1, par. 2.

[44] *Dignitatis Humanae*, Art. 1, par. 4.

[45] *Dignitatis Humanae*, Art. 2, par. 1.

religious freedom . . . . is not to be impeded, provided that just public order be observed,"[46] leave unclear whether the religious freedom of *Dignitatis Humanae* is founded upon unalterable principles, or whether it is formulated for specific prevailing circumstances in given localities that could favor a predominant religious institution, such as the Catholic Church. Some questions that the above phrases raise are: What about coercion from religious powers claiming more than mere human authority? What about situations occurring in societies of a predominant religious persuasion and in which its citizenry do not wish to be exposed to differing religious viewpoints, thus claiming that the "just public order" is being disturbed? These and other complex issues will be addressed more fully in chapter four, *Seventh-day Adventists and Dignitatis Humanae*. Nonetheless, these issues lead to "the Catholic hegemony thesis," which the reader will find to be a recurring theme in the course of this book. Simply stated, "the Catholic hegemony thesis" argues that the Church applies *Dignitatis Humanae* in different ways, depending upon extant political and religious conditions in a given country, --- in some cases to maintain its hegemony, and in others to establish its hegemony over time.[47]

The Catholic Hegemony Thesis

The issue of Catholic hegemony bears further explanation. In Western Europe, prior to the Protestant Reformation, one could very well argue that the *Corpus Christianum* consisted of only one religion, namely the Roman Catholic Church. Since European society was structured around the Church, historians of that era have identified the two as one.[48] From this

---

[46] *Dignitatis Humanae*, Art. 2, par. 3.

[47] Roman Catholic authors acknowledge that the Church seeks to establish and maintain its hegemony: "Secular powers compete with their rivals for military advantage and economic and territorial gains; the Holy See conducts a different form of diplomacy through competition for influence with rival religious systems – Orthodoxy, Protestantism, Judaism, and Islam." Peter C. Kent and John F. Pollard, eds., *Papal Diplomacy in the Modern Age* (Westport, CT: Praeger Publishing, 1994), 13.

[48] "Each of the two cities [the earthly one, the State, and the City of God, or the Church, in Augustine's *De Civitate Dei*] represents the complete antithesis of the other, but in the present age they remain radically mixed together, the boundaries of each being known only to God." John Tonkin, *The Church and the Secular Order in Reformation Thought* (New York: Columbia University Press, 1971), 7. "For centuries, however, Church and state formed a single body, internally differentiated by two authorities, each of which was thought to share in Christ's triplex munus of priest, prophet, and king." F. Russell Hittinger, "The Declaration

perspective, one cannot rightly say that the Church was challenged in the religious realm concerning its hegemony by another religious power. Rather, European church history is replete with confrontations and arduous struggles occurring between the Church and regal powers, each vying for what it perceived as its rightful sphere of influence in society.[49]

With the advent of the Protestant Reformation, however, the dynamics of the religious sphere changed drastically. Not only was the Church facing the challenge of a reformer such as Martin Luther, but there developed as an outgrowth of the Protestant principles of *Sola Scriptura* and the priesthood of all believers, an ever-widening spectrum of religious leaders and their adherents.[50] From this perspective, one may certainly state that the Church's hegemony was challenged in numerous ways, including defiance toward papal authority, rejection of indulgences, and in time, a variety of doctrines.

Historical developments that involved constitutional, juridical, theological, and political concepts became key elements in the contention for religious hegemony between Protestants and Catholics in the years following Luther's posting of the *95 Theses*. Especially notable are the developments from the Diet of Worms (1521), in which the papal bull *Decet Romanum Pontificem* formally excommunicated Luther and his followers,[51] to the Diet of Speyer (1526), which introduced a concept of religious liberty more akin to modern days.[52] Three years later, the events of the Diet of

---

on Religious Liberty, *Dignitatis Humanae*" in *Vatican II: Renewal within Tradition*, edited by Matthew L. Lamb and Matthew Levering, (New York: Oxford University Press, 2008), 363.

[49] Joseph Lecler, *The Two Sovereignties: The Relationship between Church and State* (London: William Clowes and Sons Limited, 1952), 3.

[50] "Since Luther's protest, hundreds of Protestant denominations and sects have sprung up in the modern world, and new ones continue to appear." Steven Ozment, *Protestants: The Birth of a Revolution* (New York: Doubleday, 1991), x.

[51] J. H. Merle D'Aubigne, *The History of the Reformation of the Sixteenth Century* (Rapidan, VA: Hartland Publications, n.d.; reprinted from 1846 ed., London), 221, fn. 6.

[52] "The estates... agreed at Speyer in 1526 to deal with the religious controversy in such a way 'as everyone hopes and trusts to be accountable before God and his Imperial Majesty.'... the reform minded estates took it as an endorsement of full freedom of action." Herbert Immenkotter, "Augsburg, Peace of" trans. Hans J. Hillerbrand, in *The Oxford Encyclopedia of the Reformation*, ed. Hans J. Hillerbrand, 4 vols. (New York: Oxford University Press, 1996), 1:91.

Speyer II (1529) highlight the religious controversy and struggle for hegemony occurring between Catholics and Protestants.[53] The Catholics claimed that the Protestants had misunderstood and abused the religious liberty from the Diet of Speyer (1526) and that it "had given rise to great disorders" in society.[54] Responding, Protestants contended for the right to freedom of conscience in religious matters and sought civil guarantees to that effect.[55] The outcome of these struggles ultimately culminated in the Peace of Augsburg (1555), which legally allowed for the coexistence of both groups.[56] When studying the world field of today, one finds that not much dissimilarity exists between then and now. Religious freedom and spiritual hegemony are still points of contention among religious groups today.[57]

---

[53] "To inhibit this development [of the Reformation spreading], a proposition was presented by the imperial representative Ferdinand at the beginning of the second Diet of Speyer on 15 March 1529 to repeal the article on religion of 1526 on the grounds of its misuse and erroneous interpretation." Eike Wolgast, "Speyer, Protestation of," trans. Susan M. Sisler, in *The Oxford Encyclopedia of the Reformation*, ed. Hillerbrand, 4:103.

[54] D'Aubigne, 518.

[55] "The protestation received legal status through the appeal that the Protestant princes and imperial cities lodged before two notaries in Speyer on 25 April 1529." Wolgast, "Speyer," in Hillerbrand, *The Oxford Encyclopedia of the Reformation*, 4:104.

[56] "The most important constitutional edict of early modern Germany, the Peace of Augsburg was signed on 25 September 1555. . . Before 1555, the empire had no uniform ecclesiastical law." In essence, the Peace of Augsburg provided "a political peace and the legally guaranteed coexistence of two confessional parties in the empire." Immenkotter, "Augsburg, Peace of," Hans J. Hillerbrand, trans., in Hillerbrand, ed., *The Oxford Encyclopedia of the Reformation*, 4 vols., 1:91, 92

[57] Tension still exists between Protestants and Catholics, despite ecumenical discussions *ad infinitum*, as C. F. Pauwels, Catholic theologian, declares, "This faith of the Catholic Church in her own vocation is in the last analysis the true explanation of the fact we can never afford to forget in discussions on the Catholic work of making converts: that the Catholic Church, from the first centuries of her history has endeavored to make converts of all nations, religions and churches, and that this claim of absoluteness has always been considered an offense and a scandal." C. F. Pauwels, "Ecumenical Theology and Conversions" in *Vatican II: The Theological Dimension*, ed. Anthony D. Lee (USA: The Thomist Press, 1963), 585. "Historically, the Church has sought to expand its resources and power in many countries. It has sought to maximize its wealth and resources and to enact laws and policies that protect it against competitors such as Protestant Christianity and other faiths." Paul Christopher Manuel, Lawrence C. Reardon, and Clyde

From this viewpoint, the document *Dignitatis Humanae* should be examined with great care. Thus, these historical issues dating to the time of the Reformation will be further developed in chapter three, "*Dignitatis Humanae*, Conscience, and Coercion."

The concept of religious hegemony, however, does not end with a mere historical review. More nuanced issues must be investigated, such as establishing a *de jure minimo* of definition for the type of hegemony under investigation in this book. During the Reformation era, the primary manner of determining Catholic or Protestant hegemony was based on territory, or the principle of *cuius regio, eius religio* (whose region, his religion), referring to the power of princes, or territorial rulers, to determine the faith of those living within their realms.[58]

In contrast, the modern, democratic nations of today present a diversity of interconnected issues that can define Catholic hegemony: growth in numbers (membership), increased political clout, more diplomatic ties (concordats), implementation of Catholic social policy in public policy debates, the existence of any control mechanisms to dissuade Catholics who wish to transfer out of the Church, restriction of proselytism by other religious groups, prohibition of religious gatherings, and denial of, or at least minimal allowance, of religious advertising (such as sign displays, media announcements, etc.).[59] Lest one should draw the conclusion that the previous list is prejudicial toward Catholicism because it contains specific reference to the Church, readers should be aware that of all Christian churches, the Catholic Church alone claims not only a spiritual role in society, but also considers itself a political entity; hence, the existence of concordats between it and various governments around the world, which intend "to regulate matters of religious interest concerning them."[60] Although "the Catholic hegemony thesis" will be referred to throughout

---

Wilcox, eds., *The Catholic Church and the Nation-State: Comparative Perspectives* (Washington, D.C.: Georgetown University Press, 2006), 4.

[58] Ozment, *Birth*, 121.

[59] These issues will be examined primarily in chapters five, six, and seven.

[60] Francesco Margiotta Broglio, "Concordat" entry in *The Papacy: An Encyclopedia*, 3 vols., ed. Philippe Levillain (New York: Routledge, 2002), 1:396. "In fact, it [*Gaudium et spes* of Vatican II] recognizes, respectively, the independence and the autonomy of the two societies [the Church and the political community] and hopes for a 'healthy collaboration' between them that takes into account an evolution over time and circumstances." Ibid, 397. Concordats are still ratified in the present time, as will be discussed in chapters five and six.

this book, the aforementioned list will be used predominantly in chapter five, "*Dignitatis Humanae*'s Impact in Spain," chapter six, "*Dignitatis Humanae*'s Impact in Mexico," and chapter seven, "*Dignitatis Humanae* and the Future of Religious Freedom."

A further nuanced perspective of Catholic hegemony must also take into consideration the Church's shift in perspective from a pre-Reformation paternalistic role, by which the Church exercised a more direct guardianship over the spiritual well-being of citizens through the power of the state, to a public church model in harmony with the Vatican Council II document *Gaudium et spes*, which delineates the Church's shift from a direct political player to an influential moral actor among society, seeking to persuade men of transcendental truths and moral claims.[61] Its tools of persuasion primarily include natural law arguments[62] and the social principles brought to light through *Rerum novarum* ("Of new things," i.e., new perspectives on workers' rights in light of Industrialization, and efforts to check the influence of Marxism among the working classes), and which have been developed further through the encyclicals *Quadragesimo Ano* (40 year celebration of *Rerum novarum*) and *Centesimus Ano* (100 year celebration of the same.).[63]

Seeing the stark differences between Reformation society and that of today, noting the marked changes in political systems, and the altered religious landscape, it remains evident that core principles of the Church have not changed through the centuries: its nature of self-preservation, its adherence to naturalistic principles of life, such as those of self-identity and expansion, as well as struggles with contending powers, all define the position of the Church and its statement of religious freedom. With respect to self-preservation, *Dignitatis Humanae* does not allow for conversion of its

---

[61] John T. Pawlikowski, "*Gaudium et spes* and *Dignitatis Humanae*: Are they in conflict: Reflections in light of the current controversy regarding Catholicism and politics," http://www.stthomas.edu/cathstudies/CST/conferences/gaudium/papers/Pawlikowski.pdf. (accessed March 26, 2010).

[62] Stephen J. Pope, "Natural Law in Catholic Social Teachings," in *Modern Catholic Social Teaching*, ed. Kenneth B. Himes (Washington, D.C.: Georgetown University Press, 2004), 41-71.

[63] Michael J. Schuck argues that the roots of modern Catholic social teaching actually preceeds *Rerum Novarum* and came into existence through reform-minded Catholics. Nonetheless, for the sake of brevity, I have listed here the "traditional and simplistic" chronology of its development. Michael J. Schuck, "Early Modern Roman Catholic Social Thought, 1740-1890," in Ibid., 99-124.

members outside of the faith;[64] with respect to self-identity, *Dignitatis Humanae* declares, "Therefore, it leaves untouched traditional Catholic doctrine on the moral duty of men and societies toward the true religion and toward the one Church of Christ"[65]; with respect to expansion (through proselytism), *Dignitatis Humanae* argues "that all men should be at once impelled by nature and also bound by a moral obligation to seek the truth, especially religious truth," implying that this truth is Catholicism;[66] and with respect to struggles with contending powers, *Dignitatis Humanae* unequivocally declares the right of the Church to fulfill its mission in society (*libertas ecclesia*), irrespective of the possible totalitarian nature of some modern regimes.[67] Thus, the religious freedom postulated through *Dignitatis Humanae* is uniquely defined in harmony with a Roman Catholic worldview.

The Evolving Historical Context of Dignitatis Humanae

One facet that contributes to the enduring nature of *Dignitatis Humanae* is its ability to adapt to an evolving historical context. One may describe it as a document for the times, as variable as they may be, within a constitutional democracy. In light of this observation, this section does not

---

[64] *Dignitatis Humanae*, Art. 1, par. 2, "On their part, all men are bound to seek the truth, especially in what concerns God and His Church, and to embrace the truth as they come to know it, *and to hold fast to it*." (Italics mine). Earlier in this paragraph, one finds the statement, "We believe that this one true religion subsists in the Catholic and Apostolic Church."

[65] *Dignitatis Humanae*, Art. 1, par. 4.

[66] *Dignitatis Humanae*, Art. 2, par. 3. "It follows from this that just as there is an obligation to seek for truth and to accept it according to one's certainty, so there is also the obligation to accept and profess the Catholic religion as soon as, and in so far as, it is known. *Hence it is an obligation which concerns and binds the conscience, because truth binds only in virtue of its own light*." Pavan, Declaration, 4:58.

[67] *Dignitatis Humanae*, Art. 3, par. 4, "To deny man the free exercise of religion in society, when the just requirements of public order are observed, is to do an injustice to the human person and to the very order established by God for men." F. Russell Hittinger explains that "the just requirements of public order" are conditioned by Article 7, par. 2, which states "[Government's] actions are to be controlled by juridical norms which are in conformity with the objective moral order." He further states this "qualification was necessary in order to make clear to the communist states that 'public order' cannot be a pretext for overriding basic moral principles." Hittinger, "Declaration on Religious Liberty," 368.

attempt an exhaustive treatment of every category that follows. Rather, it only focuses on the information necessary to suggest the possible hegemonic nature of *Dignitatis Humanae* within the context of changing historical situations.[68]

Several decades prior to, as well as after, Vatican II can be characterized as a political period of totalitarianism. Such political regimes as Communism, Fascism, and Nazism posed serious threats to societal well-being. However, the major threat on today's horizon is that of rampant secularism, especially in the European context.[69] Religious issues also defined the historical context prior to, and following, Vatican II. Protestants complained of Catholic prevarication regarding religious freedom: when Catholics were in a majority, mere religious tolerance was granted to non-Catholic religions; when Catholics were in a minority, the Church argued for full religious freedom, aiding Catholics in their proselytism. Yet another historical context that has evolved regards moral issues and the Church's authority. During the decade of Vatican II, society was convulsed by the sexual revolution, which posed serious challenges to the Church's stance on contraception (*Humanae vitae*, 1965). Nowadays, the Church struggles with a membership that tends to follow its own conscientious convictions on certain moral issues. The ability of *Dignitatis Humanae* to address the changing historical dynamics of society during the last forty-plus years reveal a document that was highly scrutinized and carefully crafted to uphold the foundational character of the Church.

Political Issues

Historically, Catholicism has favored a monarchical order of governance of the state as an ideal, or absolute form, based on the political philosophy of Thomas Aquinas, who adapted much of the political principles of Aristotle to fit a Christian construct of society:[70]

The best regime of a community is government by one

---

[68] For a modern perceptive history of the papacy, see Eamon Duffy, *Saints and Sinners* (U.S.A.: Yale University Press, 2006), 325-368.

[69] David Kerr, "Vatican reveals European evangelization project," *Catholic News Agency*, July 12, 2011, http://www.catholicnewsagency.com/ news/vatican-reveals-european-evangelization-project/ (accessed August 19, 2011).

[70] "St. Thomas follows the Aristotelian doctrine that makes of man a 'political animal,' but he modifies it in accordance with the exigencies of his Christian philosophy." Dino Bigongiari, *The Political Ideas of St. Thomas Aquinas* (New York: Haffner Press, 1953), vii.

person, which is made evident if we recall that the end for which a government exists is the maintenance of peace. Peace and unity of subjects is the goal of the ruler. But unity is more congruently the effect of one than of many.[71]

However, based on practical considerations, Thomas Aquinas favored a mixed government – a monarchical form tempered by limiting the power of the ruler – as more suitable to maintain societal peace and unity, to motivate the citizenry to achieve the best for the common good, and to meet the desires of the populace.[72] Democracy had always been considered as the least favorable to the ordering of society.[73] As Heinrich Rommen summarizes,

> While the monarchical constitution of the Church and the pope's authority of divine law could perhaps be declared a model for the constitution of the secular state, on the other hand the democratic constitution and the principle of popular sovereignty could not be declared a model for the constitution of the Church or for the ecclesiastical states.[74]

Thus, the Church adapted itself to either the monarchical or the mixed form of government, while trying to avoid the democratic form for internal Church governance.

However, the Jesuit theologian and primary drafter of *Dignitatis Humanae*, John Courtney Murray, recognized that democracy, with its

---

[71] Thomas Aquinas, *C. G.* iv. 76, (fn. 4), as cited in Dino Bigongiari, xxvii.

[72] Bigongiari, xxvi – xxxi.

[73] St. Thomas Aquinas, *Regimine Principum* I, Art. 11, p. 178, as cited in fn. 5, Bigongiari, xxiv; cf. Heinrich Rommen describes three primary reasons for which the Church had rejected the democratic form of government: 1) the philosophical foundation, at least of European democracy, was anti-Christian, allowing for pantheistic and atheistic sources for its justification; 2) the libertarian impulse actuating it, resulting in a societal focus upon materialism and secularism, to the detriment of man's spiritual needs; 3) the abuse of this democratic form within the Church by its members who wished to use it to elect their priests, bishops, and even the pope. Heinrich Rommen, *The State in Catholic Thought: A Treatise in Political Philosophy* (St. Louis, MO: B. Herder Book, Co., 1945), 486-493.

[74] Rommen, 490.

counterpart of religious pluralism, was part of the political makeup of the twentieth-century:

> Moreover, it [*Dignitatis Humanae*] will have to be more than a doctrine on "Church and State" in the theological sense of "Church" and in the classical sense of "state." The traditional rubric accurately defined the issue only in the days when the Church was, or was considered to be, conterminous with society, and when a single structure of spiritual authority confronted a single structure of temporal authority. The Council, by its recognition of religious pluralism in the world (in the conciliar sense of "world"), acknowledged that this historical situation no longer exists, if it ever really did exist."[75]

So, by the mid-twentieth century, when faced with the option of democracy or totalitarian political ideologies, the Church opted for supporting democracy. Since to have a singular religion (Catholicism) was not an option, the lesser of two evils was a plurality of religions with Catholicism among them, instead of a government opposed to all religion.[76]

By 1965, Communism was the dominant totalitarian regime posing a threat to the Church. *Dignitatis Humanae* boldly confronts political ideologies that attempt to confine or annihilate religion.[77] It teaches that "injury therefore is done to the human person and to the very order established by God for human life, if the free exercise of religion is denied in society, provided just public order is observed."[78] This statement clearly

---

[75] John Courtney Murray, "The Issue of Church and State at Vatican II," *Theological Studies* 27 (December 1966): 580-606, as re-published in J. Leon Hooper, ed., *Religious Liberty: Catholic Struggles with Pluralism* (Louisville, KY: Westminster/ John Knox Press, 1993), 199-227.

[76] John Paul II, *Centesimus Annus*, encyclical promulgated May 5, 1991, Articles 44-46, http://www.vatican.va/edocs/ENG0214/__P7.HTM (accessed June 4, 2012).

[77] "*Dignitatis Humanae* . . . is intended primarily as a defence [sic] of human rights in general, and religious freedom in particular, against the attentions of Marxist-Leninist regimes." Franz Cardinal Konig, "The Right to Religious Freedom: The Significance of *Dignitatis Humanae*," in *Vatican II, by those who were there*, ed. Alberic Stacpoole (London: Geoffrey Chapman, 1986), 284.

[78] *Dignitatis Humanae*, Art. 3, par. 4.

contends for a societal order that is theistic, as opposed to atheistic. The next paragraph (no. 5) of Article 3 more specifically addresses totalitarian governments that seek to inhibit, or repress religion:

> The religious acts whereby men, in private and in public and out of a sense of personal conviction, direct their lives to God transcend by their very nature the order of terrestrial and temporal affairs. Government therefore ought indeed to take account of the religious life of the citizenry and show it favor, since the function of government is to make provision for the common welfare. However, it would clearly transgress the limits set to its power, were it to presume to command or inhibit acts that are religious.

These pro-religious principles of *Dignitatis Humanae* make up the vast arsenal of theological, ethical, and political weapons[79] at the disposal of the Church as it contends with religious and political powers in the twentieth- and twenty-first centuries.[80]

The power of religion, in the following case Catholicism, to permeate society and eventually destroy any other contenders is an apt demonstration of the principles contained in *Dignitatis Humanae*. It was through the religious solidarity of Catholics in Poland under the coordination of the Vatican[81] and through covert U.S. operations[82] that Pope John Paul II

---

[79] *Dignitatis Humanae* is a mix of "an ethical, a political and a theological doctrine." Konig, 283.

[80] "Secular powers compete with their rivals for military advantage and economic and territorial gains; the Holy See conducts a different form of diplomacy through competition for influence with rival religious systems – Orthodoxy, Protestantism, Judaism, and Islam." Kent and Pollard, *Papal Diplomacy*, 13.

[81] "It was through [William] Casey's contacts, his associates say, that elements of the Socialist International were organized on behalf of Solidarity -- just as the Social Democratic parties of Western Europe had been used as an instrument of American policy by the CIA in helping to create anticommunist governments after the war. And this time the objective was akin to creating a Christian Democratic majority in Poland -- *with the church and the overwhelmingly Catholic membership of Solidarity as the dominant political force in a post-communist Poland.*" (Italics mine). Carl Bernstein, "The Holy Alliance: Ronald Reagan and John Paul II," *Time*, Feb. 24, 1992, page 9, under "The Secret Directive," http://www.time.com/time/magazine/article/ 0,9171,974931,00.html#ixzzlTpmAeoJD (accessed August 1, 2011).

effected the fall of Communism there, causing a domino-effect which spread throughout the then communist-dominated countries of Europe. This history suggests the hegemonic nature of Catholicism, even through the promotion of such a basic human right as the right to worship, or religious freedom. Even Central Intelligence Agency (CIA) analysts recognized the power of the Catholic Church when stressing its right to religious freedom in the Soviet satellite country of Poland. A CIA political analyst submitted the following report, dated October 19, 1978:

> A Polish pope will in particular have a long-term impact on a variety of internal issues between church and state that will ultimately demand Moscow's attention. Polish Catholics have been treated as second-class citizens by the party and have always looked to the church as a political alternative. *Now the church can be expected to stiffen its position on such issues as establishing the legal status of the Roman Catholic Church, permitting greater access to the media for church officials and religious services, and allowing an uncensored church press.* The Pope's support for human rights issues as well as the emphasis by the Polish Catholic church on the country's cultural heritage could increase problems for Edward Gierek as well as the potential for mass discontent. Gierek's reaction to these problems will be watched closely in every Warsaw Pact capital, but none so closely as Moscow.[83]

---

[82] "Less than three weeks before his meeting with the Pope in 1982, the President signed a secret national-security-decision directive (NSDD 32) that authorized a range of economic, diplomatic and covert measures to "neutralize efforts of the U.S.S.R." to maintain its hold on Eastern Europe. In practical terms, the most important covert operations undertaken were those inside Poland. The primary purposes of NSDD 32 were to destabilize the Polish government through covert operations involving propaganda and organizational aid to Solidarity; *the promotion of human rights, particularly those related to the right of worship and the Catholic Church*; economic pressure; and diplomatic isolation of the communist regime." (Italics mine). Ibid, page 7, under "The Secret Directive," http://www.time.com/magazine/article/0,9171, 974931,00.html#ixzzlTpXTUgxZ (accessed August 1, 2011).

[83] CIA political analyst, Memorandum, "The Impact of a Polish Pope on the USSR," Central Intelligence Agency, National Foreign Assessment Center, 19 October, 1978, page 2 (Italics mine), from folder entitled "Pope John Paul II and CIA Files," in The Paperless Archives, The Library Collection, DVD-ROM Disc

The italicized portion of this report echoes the sentiments of *Dignitatis Humanae* with respect to the freedom of the Church to exercise its rights in society.

Not only does *Dignitatis Humanae* challenge totalitarian ideologies, but it also confronts rampant secularism. Within the Document, one finds statements and key phrases that describe a societal order in which government favors and promotes religion: "religious communities should not be prohibited from freely undertaking to show the special value of their doctrine in what concerns the organization of society,"[84] and "therefore, government is to assume the safeguard of the rights of religious freedom of all its citizens."[85] It argues for a society in which religion is not merely an institutionally recognized entity, but one in which government fosters religious sentiments among the citizenry by aiding religious entities in their efforts to disseminate their religious teachings:

> The search for religious truth is innate and necessary to human dignity and flourishing, hence it must be protected by societies and governments. Because it is accomplished in community with others, the religious quest requires protection for communities, whose essence is the public proclamation of what they believe. The good of men and of societies mandates that governments not only protect the right to pursue these matters, but also, as DH puts it, government must 'help create conditions favorable to the fostering of religious life.' (DH#6)[86]

The language of *Dignitatis Humanae* presupposes religion as the keystone to support the wellbeing of society.

Such a societal construct is not only a reflection of the contributions of John Courtney Murray, but also of Jacques Maritain, who was regarded by

---

No. 7 (BACM Research: 1999-2007); available at W. R. Poage Legislative Library, Baylor University, Waco, TX.

[84] *Dignitatis Humanae*, Art. 4, par. 5.

[85] *Dignitatis Humanae*, Art. 6, par. 2.

[86] Thomas F. Farr, "Dignitatis Humanae and Religious Freedom in American Foreign Policy: A Practitioner's Perspective," in *After 40 Years: Vatican Council II's Diverse Legacy*, ed. Kenneth D. Whitehead (South Bend, IN: St. Augustine's Press, 2007), 247.

the 1930s as "the world's most distinguished Catholic philosopher."[87] He also contributed to the thought of several prominent theologians, such as Garrigou-Lagrange and Etienne Gilson,[88] who years later, in 1962, held prominent places among the eminent intellectuals who formulated documents at Vatican II. Maritain's vision for a religious society is well-outlined in his works such as *"Integral Humanism* (1936), *Scholasticism and Politics* (1940), *The Rights of Man and the Natural Law* (1943), and *Man and the State* (1951)."[89] Similar to Murray's analysis, Maritain's societal construct envisioned the Church playing an indirect role in society through the proper formation of the laity. Religion is not privatized; it is central to societal mores through the influence of the laity. Thus, the Church remains distinct from the state and yet influences the common good of society.[90]

Dignitatis Humanae, then, contends with atheistic constructs of society, as well as warring against secularism. Recognizing this point and assessing secularism as the foremost threat to the Church in the beginning of the twenty-first century, the Vatican has taken definitive steps hoping to safeguard its faith. During his trip to Spain in November, 2010, Pope Benedict recognized the staunch Roman Catholicism embedded in Spanish culture for centuries, giving rise to the popular saying among Spaniards that they are "más papista que el Papa" (more papal than the Pope). However, Juan G. Bedoya, a reporter for the daily *El País*, expressed the concern that Pope Benedict has regarding the issue of a growing secularism, not only in Spain, but throughout Europe, with its consequent diminished regard for religious matters:[91]

Secularization, relativism, and atheism are the boars that are devastating the Vatican vineyard in Europe, according

---

[87] John T. McGreevy, *Catholicism and American Freedom* (New York: W.W. Norton & Co., 2003), 189.

[88] Jude P. Dougherty, *Jacques Maritain: An Intellectual Profile* (Washington, D.C.: Catholic University of America, 2003), 2.

[89] Paul E. Sigmund, "Catholicism, Roman," in *The Encyclopedia of Democracy*, 4 vols., ed. Seymour Martin Lipset (Washington, D.C.: Congressional Quarterly, 1995), 1:183.

[90] William T. Cavanaugh, *Torture and the Eucharist* (Malden, MA: Blackwell Publishers, 1998), 137-141.

[91] Daniel P. Payne and Jennifer M. Kent, ""An Alliance of the Sacred: Prospects for a Catholic-Orthodox Partnership against Secularism in Europe," *Journal of Ecumenical Studies* Wntr, 2011.

to the Catholic hierarchy. In order to fight them, Benedict XVI created the Pontifical Council [or Congregation] for the Promotion of the New Evangelization this past October 12 [2010]. It involves a new ministry of the Holy See, with the same rank as the classical congregations. For the sake of promoting evangelization, in areas where churches are newly created and the baptized a minority, Rome counts upon the Congregation for the Evangelization of the Peoples. This other organism has been created to announce the Gospel in nations of ancient Christianity submersed now in a profound crisis.[92]

Benedict concluded his visit with an appeal to the Spanish populace to recover their spiritual heritage. Needless to say, under such a robust support for religious sentiments in society as enunciated and promulgated through *Dignitatis Humanae*, rampant secularism meets a formidable contender for the public square. The battle for the heart of Spain – Catholicism versus secularism – is one of the factors analyzed in more detail within the general context of religious freedom in chapter five, "*Dignitatis Humanae*'s Impact in Spain."

Religious Issues

Prior to Vatican II, the Church faced charges of duplicity, leveled particularly by Protestants, against the Catholic "thesis-hypothesis" of Church-State relations. This doctrine, expounded quite clearly by Cardinal Ottaviani in March, 1953, teaches that,

> only he who is in possession of truth has a right to freedom of practice and expression of his religion: only the Catholic religion is in possession of the truth, all other religions including non-Catholic Christian confessions, containing elements of error; therefore only the Catholic Church and her corporate members have a right to religious freedom. Other faiths are entitled to tolerance and understanding, because it is to be assumed that these beliefs are held sincerely. The state is obliged to acknowledge God and accord him fitting (i.e. Catholic)

---

[92] Juan G. Bedoya, "Report: From the Light of Trent to a Country of Mission[ary Need]," *El Pais*, October 31, 2010, http://www.elpais.com/articulo/reportajes/luz/Trento/pais/mision/elpepusocdmg/20101031elpdmgrep_2/Tes. (accessed July 14, 2011).

worship, (although it was recognized that this was a practical possibility only in countries with a Catholic majority). Where Catholicism is a minority religion the state should recognize Catholic believers' rights to religious freedom on the basis of natural law.[93]

However, at the beginning of deliberations regarding *Dignitatis Humanae*, the council fathers determined to reject this position,[94] leading John Courtney Murray to remark that "a long-standing ambiguity has been cleared up. The Church does not deal with the secular order in terms of a double standard – freedom for the Church when Catholics are a minority, privilege for the Church and intolerance for others when Catholics are a majority."[95]

A natural question for one to ask, especially for Catholics, is why did the council fathers reject a doctrinally supported position that obviously granted outright hegemony to the Church? The history of the development of *Dignitatis Humanae* offers an insightful answer. Originally, it was chapter nine of the schema (draft) of the *Constitution on the Church*, entitled "On Relations between Church and State, or on Religious Tolerance."[96] This section was later dropped from the *Constitution on the Church*. Simultaneously, the Secretariat for the promotion of Christian Unity had drafted a similar document, which shortly thereafter became chapter five of the Decree on Ecumenism.[97] From there, it became an appendix of the same, and finally an independent document that went through five schemas (drafts) before its final form.[98] Considering its origins as a document treating on religious tolerance and defining part of the nature of the Church, then being dropped from this category, and finally being adopted by the Secretariat for Christian Unity, the following observation by Pietro Pavan, who attended Vatican II as an expert, is of no surprise:

---

[93] Konig, 286.

[94] Konig, 283; Pavan, Declaration, 4:50.

[95] Murray, "Religious Freedom," 673.

[96] John E. Linnan, "Declaration on Religious Liberty: Dignitatis Humanae, 7 December, 1965" in *Vatican II and Its Documents: An American Reappraisal*, ed. Timothy E. O'Connell (Wilmington, DE: Michael Glazier, 1986), 168.

[97] Linnan, 168-169.

[98] Konig, 283; Pavan, Declaration, 4:51-62.

> It is said there that many non-Catholics are opposed to the Church or at least suspect it of Machiavellianism, because it demands freedom for itself in those political communities where Catholics are in the minority, while refusing the same freedom to non-Catholics in political communities where Catholics are in the majority. Hence it was essential for the Church to state its view on religious freedom unequivocally. *Unless this was done, a larger and deeper development of the ecumenical movement would be difficult, perhaps even impossible.*[99]

From this first-hand *relatio*, it becomes evident that at least one of the driving factors for a clear statement on religious freedom was directly proportional to ecumenical efforts – how to regain the "separated brethren" (i.e., Protestants) back to the fold of the Church, and how to reach other non-Christian religions.[100] Thus, it seems that the Church gave up overt hegemony in some countries where it had a majority population (confessional states) for the sake of fostering ecumenical relations.

Another factor, apart from fostering ecumenical relations, lies in the changing political spectrum in the international community. Ideally, confessional states function best under a monarchical, or a semi-totalitarian state that favors the Church. Politically speaking, these systems are

---

[99] Pavan, Declaration, 4:51 (Italics mine).

[100] "Nevertheless, our separated brethren, whether considered as individuals or as Communities and Churches, are not blessed with that unity which Jesus Christ wished to bestow on all those whom He has regenerated and vivified into one body and newness of life –that unity which the holy Scriptures and the revered tradition of the Church proclaim. For it is through Christ's Catholic Church alone, which is the all-embracing means of salvation, that the fullness of the means of salvation can be obtained. It was to the apostolic college alone, of which Peter is the head, that we believe our Lord entrusted all the blessings of the New Covenant, in order to establish on earth the one Body of Christ into which all those should be fully incorporated who already belong in any way to God's People." *Unitatis Redintegratio* (Decree on Ecumenism), Article 3, par. 5, in Walter M. Abbot, gen. ed., *The Documents of Vatican II* (New York, NY: The America Press, 1966), 346. "This characteristic of universality which adorns the People of God is a gift from the Lord Himself. By reason of it, the Catholic Church strives energetically and constantly to bring all humanity with all its riches back to Christ its Head in the unity of His Spirit." *Lumen Gentium* (Dogmatic Constitution on the Church), Article 13, par. 2, ibid., 31.

becoming more obsolete.[101] This point is worth noting, especially in light of the fact that from the Cold War era to the present, democracy has become the dominant political system throughout much of the world and that *Dignitatis Humanae* is designed to function best within a constitutional democracy,[102] a point that will be further developed in chapter seven, "Dignitatis Humanae *and the Future of Religious Freedom*."

Indeed, true to its intent, *Dignitatis Humanae* has fostered increased ecumenical relations in the Post-Vatican II context. The atmosphere of enhanced ecumenical relations in America is characterized by ongoing dialogue between the Catholic Church and "the churches traditionally involved in ecumenical dialogue – Orthodox, historic Protestant, [and] Anglican" – with the goal of the "full, visible, sacramental unity of the Church."[103] In America, the Bishops' Committee on Ecumenical and Interreligious Affairs of the National Conference of Catholic Bishops outlines three phases being implemented to achieve their goal of unity: 1) "an emerging vision of full communion;" 2) "reception," meaning openness to "collaboration," leading to the more "intentional commitment to dialogue," which culminates in "the commitment of the churches to unity;" and 3) "ecumenical formation," by which materials are provided to the

---

[101] Kenneth R. Himes argues that is was precisely because some Church leaders did not recognize this shift, "For a variety of reasons, even in the case of secular states that were not hostile but self-limited in their role in pluralistic societies, Catholic leaders failed to grasp the import of the transition from paternalistic monarchies to limited, constitutional republics," that *Dignitatis Humanae* "created the condition for a new kind of Catholicism to develop. . . [and that] broke traditional linkages between Catholicism and the state, thus allowing a reconceptualization of how Catholicism and society might be related." Kenneth R. Himes, "Vatican II and Contemporary Politics," in *The Catholic Church and the Nation-State*, eds. Manuel, Reardon, and Wilcox, 25.

[102] "In order to arrive at the doctrine of the Declaration, according to which all men are granted religious freedom as a basic personal right, it was necessary for people to become more conscious of their own dignity, . . .Since this greater consciousness of the dignity of the person was understood as the claim to inner freedom and freedom from coercion in the exercise of responsibility, it reacted necessarily on the legal organization and the exercise of public authority. This means that the concept of the constitutional State came into existence and was realized, at least to a certain degree and in a certain form." Pavan, Declaration, 4:82, 83.

[103] Lydia Veliko and Jeffrey Gros, eds., *Growing Consensus II: Church Dialogues in the United States, 1992-2004* (Washington, D.C.: United State Conference of Catholic Bishops, 2005), xxii.

churches to orientate their membership to the same ecumenical vision.[104]

With respect to "separated brethren" who have returned to the fold of the Catholic Church, one can begin with the Anglican Church. On January 11, 2011, BBC News UK announced that seven Anglican priests and 300 members from six congregations would be received into the Roman Catholic Church by April, 2011.[105] Among the list of converts to the Catholic Church, one must also include a former Seventh-day Adventist, David Pendleton. A lawyer who formerly served as a pastor in the SDA Church, he served as a state representative for Hawaii, and currently works as a member of the Hawaii Labor and Industrial Relations Appeals Board.[106] In his testimony, Pendleton acknowledged that *Dignitatis Humanae* was directly instrumental to his conversion to Catholicism.[107] Húgo Méndez, a former theology student at an Adventist university, converted to Catholicism and now ardently defends Catholic doctrine, especially *Dignitatis Humanae*. He even uses the document to denounce the historic Seventh-day Adventist position regarding the Catholic Church as a persecuting religio-political power in biblical eschatology.[108]

Striving for a common social goal has united the efforts of evangelical Protestants and Catholics, especially in the United States. The book, *Evangelicals and Catholics Together*, by Chuck Colson, describes their efforts to infuse religious sentiments and morality into society.[109] Such issues as

---

[104] Veliko and Gros, eds., *Growing Consensus II*, xxi – xxxi.

[105] BBC News, "More Anglican priests to join Catholic Church," *BBC News UK*, January 11, 2011, http://www.bbc.co.uk/news/uk-12260569 (accessed August 10, 2011).

[106] *Asian Journal Press*, "David Pendleton: Former Hawaii State Representative, Board Member, Hawaii Labor and Industrial Relations Appeals Board," in *Asian Journal Press*, September 1, 2009, http://www.asianjournal.com/voice-of-fil-america/72-voice-of-fil-america/2786-david-pendleton-former-state-representative-of-hawaii-board-member-hawaii-labor-and-industrial-relations-appeals-board.html (accessed August 14, 2011).

[107] Anna Weaver, "This is where my faith has led me," *Hawaii Catholic Herald*, posted March 21, 2008, http://www.hawaiicatholicherald.com/Home/tabid/256/newsid884/ 1259/Default.aspx (accessed April 10, 2008).

[108] Húgo Méndez, "The Catholic Church and Change," Jan. 5, 2010, http://sda2rc.blogspot.com/2010/01/catholic-church-church.html (accessed January 9, 2010).

[109] Chuck Colson and Richard John Neuhaus, eds., *Evangelicals and Catholics Toward a Common Mission Together* (Dallas, TX: Word Publishing, 1995).

homosexual marriages, abortion, and religion in the public square have proved to be common ground for both groups. In the area of theology, especially notable is the *Joint Declaration on the Doctrine of Justification*, the work of both Catholic and Lutheran scholars who address the topic which was central to the Protestant Reformation – How is one saved? The Lutheran World Federation issued the first version in 1995, which was sent to the 124 member Lutheran denominations to obtain their input. After several revisions, the final document was approved in June, 1998. Consensus on this point alone marked more than a milestone in Catholic efforts to regain their "separated brethren."[110]

Moral Issues and Ecclesial Authority

Since the 1960s, the Church has faced growing challenges regarding some of its moral teachings on such topics as contraception, abortion, divorce and re-marriage, and bioethics. With advanced medical technology, previous moral guidelines are now being challenged and new issues are being raised for debate. Dissent is another problematic internal development the Church faces due to the innovations of Vatican II. To what extent can members of the Church, whether hierarchy or laity, differ

---

[110] David W. Cloud, *Evangelicals and Rome* (Port Huron, MI: Way of Life Literature, 1999), 331-340. On page 335, Cloud cites *Unitatis Redintegratio* (Decree on Ecumenism), Article 4, pars. 2 and 3, "The 'ecumenical movement' means those activities and enterprises which, according to various needs of the Church and opportune occasions, are started and organized for the fostering of unity among Christians. These are: first, every effort to eliminate words, [etc., that] make mutual relations between them more difficult; then, 'dialogue' between competent experts from different Churches and Communities. In their meetings, which are organized in a religious spirit, each explains the teachings of his Communion in greater depth and brings out clearly its distinctive features. . . . When such actions are carried out by the Catholic faithful with prudence, patience, and the vigilance of their spiritual shepherds, . . . The results will be that, little by little, as the obstacles to perfect ecclesiastical communion are overcome, all Christians will be gathered, in a common celebration of the Eucharist, into that unity of the one and only Church which Christ bestowed on His Church from the beginning. This unity, we believe, dwells in the Catholic Church as something she can never lose, and we hope that it will continue to increase until the end of time." Walter M. Abbot, gen. ed., *Documents of Vatican II* (New York, NY: The America Press, 1966), 347, 348. Although the mutual signing of the *Joint Declaration on the Doctrine of Justification* did not make Lutherans into Catholics, or vice-versa, Cloud cites *Unitatis Redintegratio* to point out the steps outlined at Vatican II to achieve an eventual unity between the Church and other Christians.

with prescribed Church teachings? Individuals like Hans Kung, Leonardo Boff, and Charles Curran were all silenced for certain of their teachings that were not considered *nihil obstat* (without objection).

Some Catholic members have interpreted *Dignitatis Humanae* to allow complete freedom of conscience according to one's own convictions. Considering that religious freedom involves some type of freedom for the individual conscience, they have appealed to *Dignitatis Humanae* to either question the Church's stance on, or give outright endorsement of the following issues: reproductive health bills (typically focusing on contraception), abortion, and divorce and re-marriage.

Fr. Joaquin G. Bernas, S. J., argues that *Dignitatis Humanae* justifies the Philippine government in its distribution of contraception pills to the public without regard to whether Catholic or non-Catholic citizens receive them.[111] He also believes that *Dignitatis Humanae* limits the role of pastors in public policy debates when their actions might be "exercised to the detriment of the religious freedom of non-communicants, or even of dissenting communicants. This is a clear implication of Vatican II's 'Dignitatis Humanae.'"[112]

In the face of blatant and ardent opposition by the Catholic Bishops' Conference of the Philippines (CBCP), Elias L. Espinoza also argues that the bishops have no right to oppose the Reproductive Health Bill (RH Bill), because to do so would be to impose Catholic teachings regarding contraception upon non-Catholic citizens in an effort to regulate morality among Catholics.[113] Adding to the complexity of the debate, Eleanor R. Dionisio considers herself a progressive Catholic who sees the unchanging nature of *Humanae Vitae* (against contraception) and its obligation upon Catholics, but who also argues for the application of *Dignitatis Humanae*'s guarantee of freedom of individual conscience. She posits that to resolve

---

[111] Joaquin G. Bernas, S. J., "Religion and the RH Bills," *Philippine Daily Enquirer*, Oct. 25, 2010, under Religion and Belief, Family planning, http://opinion.inquirer.net/inquireropinion/columns/view/20101025-299587/Religion-and-the-RH-bills (accessed Nov. 2, 2010).

[112] Bernas, "A War of Religions," *Philippine Daily Enquirer*, May 2, 2011, under Religion and Belief, Family planning, http://opinion.inquirer.net/inquireropinion/columns/view/20110502-334122/A-war-of-religions (accessed May 3, 2011).

[113] Elias L. Espinoza, "Espinoza: Foul smell from septic waste," *The Sun Star Cebu*, May 19, 2011, under "Free Zone," http://www.sunstar.com.ph/cebu/opinion/2011/05/19/espinoza-foul-smell-septic-waste-156269 (accessed May 19, 2011).

the apparent contradiction of two authoritative documents, there is the need for a moral consensus in society through dialogue. Once this consensus is reached, the principles of *Humanae Vitae* can be implemented for Philippine society without violating the consciences of any of its citizens.[114] Paul Gerard Horrigan further argues that in light of the teaching authority of the Church and the Magisterium, *Humanae Vitae* does not violate the consciences of the faithful; rather, it enlightens their erroneous consciences to bring them into harmony with the "divine, eternal, law."[115]

As one example of the strength of tradition, however, the White Lily Blog carries an article denouncing *Dignitatis Humanae* and Vatican II as the cause of the liberal moral condition prevailing in America – from pro-choice abortion laws and Catholic politicians such as Nancy Pelosi, Joe Biden, Ted Kennedy (deceased), Patrick Leahy, and John Kerry who support such laws – to homosexual marriages. The author specifically faults John Courtney Murray, a Jesuit theologian and primary author of *Dignitatis Humanae*, for the destruction of former Catholic dominated countries through the concept of elevating a secular state to supremacy over the Catholic Church merely for the sake of "humankind's conscience."[116]

More precisely to the point, in 2007, Archbishop Thomas Tobin communicated to Rep. Patrick Kennedy (D-RI) that as a pro-choice politician, he was unworthy of taking Communion and should refrain from doing so.[117] More recently, on July 11, 2011, Cardinal Arinze, "the Vatican's prefect emeritus of the Congregation of Divine Worship and the Discipline of the Sacraments," addressed strong words to pro-choice American Catholic politicians during a "conference entitled 'Dignitatis

---

[114] Eleanor R. Dionisio, "On the Sweet Insidiousness of Dialogue," *The Philippine Daily Inquirer*, July 11, 2011, under "Commentary," http://opinion.inquirer.net/7510/on-the-sweet-insidiousness-of-dialogue (accessed July 13, 2011).

[115] Paul Gerard Horrigan, "Conscience and Contraception," under blog "True Wisdom Comes from God – The Source of all Virtues and Knowledge," http://thesplendorofthechurch.blogspot.com/2010/01/conscience-and-contraceptions-by-dr.html (January 7, 2010).

[116] The White Lily Blog, "The Council Pow-wow and Pro-Life," September 21, 2009, http:// thewhitelilyblog.wordpress.com/2009/09/21/the-council-pow-wow-and-pro-life/ (accessed Sept. 23, 2009). I cite this blog merely to point out how some Catholic members perceive the Document and its effects.

[117] The Associated Press, "R.I. bishop asked Rep. Kennedy to avoid Communion," *USA Today*, November 22, 2009, http://www.usatoday.com/news/religion/2009-11-22-kennedy-communion_ N.htm?obref=obinsite (accessed November 23, 2009).

Humanae: Catholic Teaching on Bioethics' hosted by Christendom College in Virginia." Arinze likened abortion to a violation of the eternal Law of God, or in essence, murder. Addressing the issue of respect for others' consciences, he stated, "Some. . . say, I am personally not in favor of abortion, but I will not impose my views on others. It is like saying, I am personally not in favor of killing you. . . But since some people want to shoot all of you in the Senate and the House of Representatives, I won't impose my views on them, it is pro-choice!"[118] Obviously, the Catholic hierarchy do not interpret *Dignitatis Humanae* as a document giving unrestricted license for one to follow his conscience contrary to the teachings of the Church, nor do they apply it to Catholic politicians who wish to respect the conscientious convictions of their non-Catholic constituents.

The issue of divorce and re-marriage in the Catholic dominated populace of Malta became a heated issue in April, 2011, and during the following months. Malta, approximately ninety-five per cent Catholic (of a 400,000 population), has long been subject to the moral and civic influence of Church leadership dedicated to Catholic social policies.[119] Maltese history reveals a Church hierarchy that used religious forms of coercion to maintain the status quo of a Catholic society – such methods as denying Communion to those who believed in supporting political parties whose platforms were antagonistic toward the Church's teachings.[120] In the current debate, however, Catholic leaders have indicated that members who support divorce legislation will not be denied Communion.[121]

The opposition camp consists of Catholics who believe in respecting the freedom of conscience of their non-Catholic neighbors, but who also believe and practice in their own lives the Church's teachings regarding marriage. They find justification in *Dignitatis Humanae* for passing a new bill

---

[118] Kathleen Gilbert, "Cardinal Arinze to pro-choice pols: law against murder a 'Divine law, not a tennis club regulation,'" July 11, 2011, http://www.lifesitenews.com/news/cardinal-arinze-to-pro-choice-pols-law-against-murder-is-divine-law-not-a-t/ (accessed August 6, 2011).

[119] Mario Cacciottolo, "Divorce in Malta: Referendum causes acrimonious split," BBC News, May 27, 2011 under "Europe," http://www.bbc.co.uk/news/world-europe-13559970 (accessed August 24, 2011).

[120] Martin Scicluna, "Divorce, the Church, and our conscience," *The Malta Independent Online*, posted April 27, 2011, http://www. independent.com.mt/news.asp?newsitemid=124185 (accessed April 28, 2011).

[121] Cacciottolo, "Divorce in Malta."

into law that would allow divorce and re-marriage. These Maltese Catholics have organized themselves into "Kattolica: Iva Ghax Dritt" (Catholic: yes, because it is a right).[122] Their spokesman, Carmel Hili, describes their rationale for organizing:

> All of us Catholics wholeheartedly endorse such a belief. All of us believe in the sanctity of marriage. However, *not all Maltese citizens are Catholics*. While we hold to our beliefs, we Catholics must accept that we have a duty to allow non-Catholics the freedom to contract or dissolve marriages as they see fit. We have no right to expect the State to impose our will and our beliefs on the whole population.[123]

In the press release announcing the launching of their organization, they cite *Dignitatis Humanae* several times, as well as referring to the Catechism of the Catholic Church, in support of their views.[124]

The vigorous opposition of the Church leadership to the proposed bill leads some, like Martin Scicluna, "a member of the IVA Campaign and the lead author of the Report 'For Worse, For Better: Remarriage After Legal Separation,'"[125] to find the leadership acting contrary to the fundamental teaching of *Dignitatis Humanae*, as he interprets it:

> Justice should be an issue for the Church as well, in particular what justice, charity and compassion demand in regard to persons whom the Church may believe to be in error. The relevant aspects of its teachings would appear to be the Vatican Council's declaration of religious liberty (*Dignitatis Humanae*), which asserts that a person must not

---

[122] Carmel Hili, "Launching of Kattolici: Iva Ghax Dritt – 14 May, 2011," under "Press Releases," http://www.ivadritt.org/launching-of-kattolici-iva-ghax-dritt-14th-may-2011/ (accessed May 24, 2011; italics in original).

[123] Carmel Hili, "Catholic Marriage – 18 May, 2011 (English)," under "Press Releases," http://www.ivadritt.org/catholic-marriage-18-may-2011/ (accessed on May 18, 2011; italics in original).

[124] Hili, "Launching of Kattolici."

[125] Martin Scicluna, "Strike a blow for justice, fairness, and your civil rights," http:// www.independent.com.mt/news.asp?newsitemid=125929 (accessed May 27, 2011).

be prevented from acting according to conscience. A law which prohibits a man and a woman from marrying one another despite their belief that they can and should do so comes clearly within the ambit of the Vatican Council's repudiation of coercion, provided only that both the man and the woman are free of contradictory commitments.

In assessing such a law, the determining factor for the Church has to be the requirements of justice (and charity), which apply to all, and not the Church's marriage doctrine, which may be preached to all but forced on none whose conscience it offends.[126]

Scicluna's analysis of *Dignitatis Humanae* and that of the Catholics who are members of Kattolici: Iva Ghax Dritt reveals a dissonance between them and the Maltese leadership of the Church. If the leadership understood *Dignitatis Humanae* as the laity do, there would not be such vigorous opposition in Malta to the proposed divorce legislation.

Each of these case examples present various facets of how the document *Dignitatis Humanae* is understood and applied. In the Philippines, some Catholics have used it to defend the rights of conscience of non-Catholics. Other Catholics have viewed it as an instrument to introduce dialogue, through freedom of conscientiously held convictions, regarding Catholic social teachings, but with the intent of gaining moral consensus in society that will eventually support Catholic social principles. In the United States, Catholic politicians have tried to implement *Dignitatis Humanae*'s principles out of respect for their non-Catholic constituents, but only in the face of strong opposition from bishops and other Church leaders. In Malta, Catholic members have appealed to *Dignitatis Humanae*'s emphasis upon freedom of conscience to pass legislation that would respect the views of non-Catholic Maltese regarding divorce and re-marriage.

The one perspective, however, that has been consistent in each of these cases, is the view of the Church hierarchy regarding the role of *Dignitatis Humanae*: it should not be interpreted to support a freedom of conscience without moral restraints, not even for non-Catholics. Rather, its role has been to promote religious freedom for the sake of dialogue regarding Catholic social and moral principles, not for the sake of respecting the conscientious religious and moral convictions of individuals who are not considering changing their beliefs. In essence, *Dignitatis Humanae* has been used as an instrument to introduce Catholic social and moral teachings into

---

[126] Scicluna, "Divorce, the Church, and our conscience," *Malta Independent*.

society. Such societal permeation, in the long term, is designed to produce a society that more closely approximates a Catholic society until those minority groups (or individuals) eventually become persuaded to adopt the majority moral and religious teachings of their environment, i.e. converting to Catholicism. Seen from this light, *Dignitatis Humanae* certainly suggests a passive, subtle Catholic hegemony, at least from the perspective of the Catholic hierarchy.

While the previous cases have dealt with the Church and its external sphere of influence among non-Catholics, *Dignitatis Humanae* also challenges the internal ecclesial sphere by raising the question of how the hierarchy relates to some of their own leaders, such as theologians and priests, who exercise their consciences to arrive at conclusions not necessarily orthodox. Notable figures within the Church have been silenced in recent years. Silencing refers to orders from the Vatican given to the individual in question to desist from further dissemination, either in writing or speaking, on certain matters considered to be erroneous, thus giving sufficient time for the Congregation for the Doctrine of the Faith to investigate the matters in question.

Leonardo Boff, formerly of the Jesuit order, was silenced by papal leadership regarding his actions to promote Liberation Theology. The Congregation for the Doctrine of the Faith was primarily concerned with some of his views regarding the Holy Spirit and the institutional nature of the Church. The ban of silence was lifted after Boff's material had been reviewed, but it nonetheless raises the question regarding the way the Church handles issues of doctrinal orthodoxy and the rights of conscience of its theologians. Robert McAfee Brown stated, "There is no doubt that the Vatican's image suffered as a consequence of *a punitive action, suited (if at all) to other centuries than our own*, while Boff became an instant folk hero throughout the Third World."[127]

Charles Curran, formerly a professor of moral theology at the Catholic University of America in Washington, D. C., (and now at Springhill College, TX) came under scrutiny for his views on certain moral teachings about sex. Upon reviewing his material, the Congregation for the Doctrine of the Faith removed him from his teaching post, eliciting strong dissent from Archbishop Rembert G. Weakland, of Milwaukee, who said, that in the efforts to maintain doctrinal purity there was also the need "to avoid the fanaticism and small-mindedness that has characterized so many periods of the church in its history – tendencies that lead to much cruelty, suppression

---

[127] Robert McAfee Brown, "Leonardo Boff: Theologian for all Christians," *Christian Century*, July 2-9, 1986, p. 615, http://www.religion-online.org/showarticle.asp?title=1045 (accessed August 30, 2011, italics mine).

of theological creativity and lack of growth."[128] Perhaps the irony of *Dignitatis Humanae* is that its principal author, John Courtney Murray, was also silenced by the Vatican during the 1950s for his views regarding Church-State relations.[129] Although Murray continued to study the issue in earnest, he did not publish anything further on the topic and did not give public lectures either. Then, several years later, during Vatican II, he became a *periti* who aided in much of the drafting of the very document that appears to give more liberty of conscience to his fellow theologians.

The Concrete Concepts of Dignitatis Humanae

As the previous section has demonstrated, although the societal context from 1965 to the present has changed dramatically, *Dignitatis Humanae* has continued to remain contemporary and applicable in a variety of circumstances. Taking into account the morphing political, religious, and societal/moral factors, it becomes evident that *Dignitatis Humanae* contains unchanging concepts that facilitate the response of the Church and aid it in its quest for hegemony. The freedom of the Church, posited as a divine right, is a broad enough concept to give the Church the advantage over any contender, either political or religious. The idea of the juridical authority of the Church is a metaphysical concept based on the transcendental realm. Nevertheless, it assures that the Church always retains its identity, as well as provides the basis for its claims to religious authority, while it interacts with other religious bodies. The two previous concepts combined raise the issue of the role of the Church with respect to the conscience of the individual and the novel idea contained in *Dignitatis Humanae* of immunity from coercion. These three concepts are further elaborated in the next sections.

The Freedom of the Church

By speaking of government obligations to foster the religious life of its people, "Government therefore ought indeed to take account of the religious life of the citizenry and show it favor, since the function of government is to make provision for the common welfare,"[130] *Dignitatis*

---

[128] Joseph Berger, "Leading Archbishop Challenges Vatican on Silencing Dissent," *The New York Times*, September 24, 1986, http://www.nytimes.com/1986/09/24/us/leading-archbishop-challenges-vatican-on-silencing-dissent.html (accessed August 30, 2011); cf. Hans Kung, who was also stripped of his authority to teach in 1979, http://josephsoleary.typepad.com/my_weblog/2007/12/hans-kung-in-fu.html (accessed August 30, 2011).

[129] Hooper, ed., *Religious Liberty: Catholic Struggles with Pluralism*, 32.
[130] *Dignitatis Humanae*, Art. 3, par. 5.

Humanae presents a door to society, the key of which is in the hand of the Church. Such statements establish limits to government intrusion into the religious sphere and also allow for the introduction of Roman Catholic social policy in public policy debates, as demonstrated in the prior case examples from Malta and the Philippines.

The Juridical Authority of the Church

Although the theoretical foundation for the juridical authority of the Church resides in the transcendental realm, it also bridges the temporal realm. The jurisdictional authority, which is symbolized by the keys, represents "the power to bind or loosen, to close or open, granted by Christ to Peter, his vicar on earth. Transmitted to all of Peter's successors, they represent the authority of the pope over the Church and over the world, as well as his power to administer the benefits of the resurrection."[131] It is precisely because the Church views itself as a spiritual entity commissioned with the future, eternal welfare of mankind that it insists on exerting its spiritual influence in the secular, or temporal, realm. Thus, not satisfied with limiting itself to the things of heaven, it takes decisive measures to ensure that it molds public policy.

Dignitatis Humanae, through the language it employs, raises the question, how extensive is the juridical authority of the Church? On one hand, the document declares the freedom of the Church to fulfill its mission, but on the other hand, it also argues for the right to religious freedom and immunity from coercion for the individual as a civil right, "This Vatican Council declares that the human person has a right to religious freedom. This freedom means that all men are to be immune from coercion on the part of individuals or of social groups and of any human power."[132] How should the Church relate to its own members who may deviate from doctrine? If the authority to enforce a teaching is lacking, what significance does it have? Regarding non-Catholics, if the authority of the Church is called into question, how can it effectively evangelize? To what authority can the Church appeal to give validity to its teachings?

An additional factor resides in the nature of Vatican Council II. If it is viewed as merely pastoral in nature, as some Catholics have suggested, then the dogmatic positions of the Council of Trent and Vatican Council I, with their inherent juridical authority, remain in full force. If, however, Vatican

---

[131] Michel Pastoureau, article "Keys," in *The Papacy An Encyclopedia*, 3 vols., ed. Philippe Levillain (New York, NY: Routledge, 2002), 2:891.

[132] *Dignitatis Humanae*, Art. 2, par. 1.

Council II was truly dogmatic in nature, then the juridical authority declared at Trent and Vatican I need to be re-evaluated in the light of Vatican II. So closely is the exercise of the juridical authority of the Church inter-related to the rights of individual conscience, both of its own members, as well as of non-Catholics, that the resulting complexities will be elaborated in chapter three, "*Dignitatis Humanae*, Conscience, and Coercion." However, to address the most basic of questions related to the jurisdictional authority of the Church, the following section discusses the complex issue of conscience and coercion.

Conscience and Immunity from Coercion

The role of the conscience of the individual becomes a central factor in consideration of *Dignitatis Humanae* given that the Church defines its mission as assisting man to achieve his ultimate end, which is God, and given the juridical authority claimed by the Church to fulfill this mission. Pre-Vatican II theory of Church and State allowed for toleration of non-Catholic religions under the premise that those who held such views did so from a sincere conscience. Vatican II posited the idea of immunity from coercion as a civil right of the individual. Some might consider the differences in view as a matter of semantics, but there are deeper implications regarding the latter view as opposed to the former. A more detailed analysis of this point will be given in chapter three, "Dignitatis Humanae, *Conscience, and Coercion*," but the following points help to address some of the principal areas of concern.

Dignitatis Humanae does not refer to a "liberty of conscience" as it is generally understood in the tradition of Enlightenment thought:

> The intellectual framework through which this [modern quest for freedom] and the institutions and practices of democratic government were conceptualized in eighteenth- and nineteenth-century Europe were, for the Church, problematic. Carried to their logical conclusion, the philosophical and theological premises that inform what is sometimes called Enlightenment or Continental Liberalism resulted in a naturalism that denied the existence of a supernatural order of revelation and grace and a radical individualism whose effect was to make each individual a law unto himself, subject to no objective order

of obligations.[133]

Rather, it describes a conscience guided by moral norms of natural law and an objective order.[134] In order to understand the rights of conscience guaranteed through *Dignitatis Humanae*, one must first define man's moral nature. Pope John Paul II and Pope Benedict XVI both elaborated on man's moral nature in many of their writings and public addresses. For the sake of reserving a detailed discussion of these views for a later chapter of this book where they may be addressed more fully, yet, it may be stated that the views of both popes argue for a distinctly religious (Catholic) view of man's nature with an orientation toward God.

Another area for consideration regards toleration versus immunity from coercion. If the pre-Vatican II concept of toleration is now superseded by the Vatican II idea of immunity from coercion, it seems that the latter is more favorable to religious freedom than the former. Is it better for the individual (or group of minority believers) to live in a society that tolerates their religious views, or to live in a society that grants them immunity from coercion? Or, is there a difference? When one investigates the etymology of the terms used in both cases, the latter seems to imply an enhanced power, or hegemony, of the Church in society, which point will be further developed in chapter three.

Roman Catholic Hegemony and Dignitatis Humanae

Seventh-day Adventists have a long historical record as advocates of religious freedom, not only for themselves, but also for all other non-violent religious groups.[135] Roman Catholics, in more recent decades, have

---

[133] Kenneth L. Grasso and Robert P. Hunt, eds., *Catholicism and Religious Freedom* (New York, NY: Rowman and Littlefield Publishers, Inc., 1996), xvi. The issue of Enlightenment thought and its impact on the formulation of modern documents of religious freedom such as the First Amendment religion clauses of the U. S. Constitution and the United Nations Declaration of Human Rights, Article 18 will be addressed in the next chapter. Suffice it to say, though, that Grasso and Hunt overlook the fact that Enlightenment thought offers a generic transcendental realm for ordering government.

[134] "On their part, all men are bound to seek the truth, especially in what concerns God and His Church, and to embrace the truth they come to know, and to hold fast to it." *Dignitatis Humanae*, Art. 1, par. 2; "that all men should be at once impelled by nature and also bound by a moral obligation to seek the truth, especially religious truth." *Dignitatis Humanae*, Art. 2, par. 3.

[135] The International Religious Liberty Association (IRLA) is the oldest such association and was founded by the General Conference of Seventh-day

been recognized as advocates of religious freedom as well. Most notably, the document *Dignitatis Humanae* has proven instrumental in positioning the Church in such favorable light. Much of its language echoes modern concepts of religious freedom. Certain passages seem to imply an almost absolute regard for the rights of individual conscience. Without doubt, the document definitively places a limit upon the constitutional power of government in the arena of religious rights, almost creating a sacred space for the individual through the idea of immunity from coercion. Most assuredly, one may say that freedom of conscience for the sake of pursuing truth through the exchange of ideas, dialogue, and teaching, is foundational to *Dignitatis Humanae*.

Does *Dignitatis Humanae* hint at a subtle type of Catholic hegemony? To begin, one must candidly recognize that the term "hegemony" never once appears in the document. A balanced perspective, however, acknowledges that the religious freedom concepts contained within it are posited against an objective moral order, which does describe the Church as the sole depository of truth. The Church is certainly, and without equivocation, given freedom to accomplish its mission in society, as are other religious groups generally referred to in the document. From this perspective, the document seems to presuppose, and if necessary, to create, a religiously-oriented society. Seen in the light of this societal construct, the language utilized in *Dignitatis Humanae* seems to suggest a subtle, semi-overt form of Catholic hegemony. If all religious groups are aided in society, then Catholicism seems to be aided slightly more so.

Also, the phrases used in *Dignitatis Humanae* are broad enough in description to be adaptable to any given political or religious context. Taking into account the recent past and the current conditions in political trends, it becomes evident that *Dignitatis Humanae* is an ideological document of no small consequences. By reference to the "civic right" to immunity from coercion, *Dignitatis Humanae* is designed for application within a constitutional democratic system of governance, which is precisely the dominant political system of the twentieth- and twenty-first centuries. From this perspective, it has a wide political field to which it is ideally suited. While it contains political sentiments, it is heavily-laden with religious ones as well, and thus it can be used most advantageously by an entity that is both religious and political in nature. Therefore, although it argues for religious freedom in general, it is best suited to the Catholic Church. Wielded as a political weapon, its arguments on behalf of religion challenge any political ideology in opposition to religious sentiments, as the

---

Adventists in 1893. It is dedicated to "the universal and non-sectarian promotion of religious freedom for all people everywhere." http://www.irla.org/354.htm (accessed August 20, 2011).

fall of Communism can well attest. Secularism is the new giant on the field of battle and only time will reveal the outcome of the contest between it and a Church astute in the game of political and ideological warfare.

As a religious document, especially stressing the civil right to freedom from coercion and seeming to imply respect for the individual conscience, it finds ready acceptance among religious groups. Former barriers to ecumenism have tumbled in light of its advocacy of religious freedom for all groups in pluralistic societies, such as the United States. Through championing the most fundamental human right, and the one held most closely to the soul – that of religious freedom – the Church has gained ubiquitous favor and recognition as a modern defender of the rights of humanity. In terms of social popularity, one may say the Church has elevated its status significantly in comparison to former years, especially those prior to Vatican II. But its territorial gains do not end here. Not only has the Church gained social status, but also adherents from among those groups formerly considered as its enemies, or at least considered as "separated brethren." Taking these facts into consideration, if one defines hegemony to include societal influence, then it seems plausible to argue that *Dignitatis Humanae* has advanced Roman Catholicism to such a favorable light as to dispel the dark shadows of its history prior to Vatican II.

The foregoing evaluation leads to a more nuanced approach to the idea of Catholic hegemony. With respect to Catholic hegemony and *Dignitatis Humanae*, it is necessary, as well, to acknowledge that a wide spectrum exists when defining the term, from overt, aggressive hegemony to subtle, passive hegemony. F. Russell Hittinger, recognized in academic circles as an erudite Catholic scholar and a Thomist, referred to the liberty of the Church to fulfill its mission among global political powers and stated "The liberty of the Church does not require political hegemony,"[136] alluding to the medieval construct wherein Church and the political power were nearly united as one. However, upon further analysis, it would seem the phrase should be added, "nor does the liberty of the Church deny political hegemony," as the history of Polish nationalism combined with papal claims to religious freedom, precipitating the fall of Communism in Europe, readily shows. One may suggest, then, that *Dignitatis Humanae* is broad enough in scope as to allow the Church to exert an aggressive hegemony, under certain circumstances – such as against an overt enemy like Communism – and on other occasions, to exert a passive hegemony, such as when seeking pre-eminence among other religious groups under the general rubric of religious freedom for all faiths.

A perennial challenge facing any research in the area of Catholic

---

[136] Hittinger, "The Declaration on Religious Liberty," 375.

hegemony, of course, deals with the dual nature of the Church: it exists both as a religious and a political entity. For this reason, Robert A. Graham, S. J., gave the following warning to politicians and historians of the modern era:

> It is so easy to interpret our subject [of Vatican diplomacy in world politics] in purely political terms. For if, in this dual relationship, the state, the civil power, has political and not religious motives and objectives, can the Holy See be denied the right to have purely religious and not political motives in its own actions? It is therefore important to submit that, as a high religious institution – founded, as it claims, by Jesus Christ and endowed by the Saviour with a certain high and imprescriptible mission to evangelize in His name – the Holy See has a right to have its diplomatic activity understood, or comprehended from its own particular point of view. Failure to take this into account, I would say, would risk a complete misunderstanding of what has really happened in history. Politics and religion here confront each other in mega terms. One who does not believe can at his pleasure reject the idea that Christ founded a church, let alone the Catholic Church. But he would be making a deadly mistake, especially if he is in office, say a foreign minister, if he cannot persuade himself that his Vatican counterpart does believe it. The phenomenon we are studying could not have lasted through the centuries, experiencing and surviving the most drastic challenges and setbacks, if it were based on a purely political foundation.[137]

Therefore, in some circumstances, it may be obvious that the Church has lost hegemony from a religious perspective, but it may at the same time have gained hegemony in the political arena. The converse, obviously, is just as true. Thus, the complexity of Catholic hegemony with respect to *Dignitatis Humanae* is that through the context of advancing religious freedom, the Church also builds or maintains political and religious bulwarks.

Perhaps more than any other factor, though, that raises the perplexing question regarding the type of religious freedom advocated by the document, is its application by papal leadership on moral issues that are

---

[137] Robert A. Graham, "Introduction: Reflections on Vatican Diplomacy," in Kent and Pollard, eds., *Papal Diplomacy*, 1, 2.

interwoven in society. Related issues of individual conscience and the juridical authority of the Church, then, become factors for consideration in an evaluation of Catholic hegemony, which later chapters will address.

Having completed a broad overview of the issues related to, and a tentative analysis of, *Dignitatis Humanae*, the next chapter addresses how the document has been received internally by the Roman Catholic Church. By studying the interpretations and analysis of Catholic scholars from both Traditionalist and Progressive groups, some of the questions raised in this chapter perhaps will find clarification.

DIGNITATIS HUMANAE AND ROMAN CATHOLICS

Catholic media sources revealed on September 15-16, 2009 that the long-awaited talks between the Society of Saint Pius X (SSPX) and the Vatican would occur by the middle of the following month.[138] The purpose for the meetings was to clarify certain documents of Vatican II, including *Dignitatis Humanae* (1965). The SSPX was founded by Monsignor Marcel Lefebvre, who had attended Vatican II, but who desired to preserve traditional Catholicism, rather than promote the innovations of Vatican II. Although schismatics (considered to be outside of mainstream Catholicism), members of the society are recognized as staunch, traditional, Roman Catholics, even preserving the Latin Mass and holding some teachings, such as the traditional view of a Catholic confessional state, that are appealing to some Catholics remaining within the Church. Michael Collins states that Lefebvre "was horrified in particular with the *Decree on Religious Freedom*."[139] Such divergent views between the Vatican and the SSPX on religious freedom made this meeting all the more historic. Before the talks began in October, 2009, however, the Jesuit Father Federico Lombardi, director of the Vatican press office, stated clearly "what is not negotiable for the Holy See," which includes "such fundamental

---

[138] Christopher Nowak, "The Vatican and the SSPX: the discussion begins", in *The Grand Rapids Catholic Examiner*, September 16, 20009, http://www.examiner.com/x-20920-Grand-Rapids-Catholic-Examiner~y2009m9d16-The-Vatican-and-the-SSPX-the-discussion-begins (accessed September 17, 2009).

[139] Michael Collins, *Pope Benedict XVI: Successor to Peter* (New York: Paulist Press, 2005), 77.

conclusions of the Second Vatican Council as its position on Judaism, other non-Christian religions, other Christian churches and on religious freedom as a basic human right."[140] These opposing views highlight the conditions existing between Traditionalists and Progressives since Vatican II.

By the 1990s, the impact of *Dignitatis Humanae* within the Church made itself apparent as the two groups from Vatican II – Traditionalists and Progressives – began debating the meaning of the Document. Traditionalists view Vatican II as a deviation from the historic teachings of the Church, and especially consider *Dignitatis Humanae* as a purely modernist construct of religious liberty that has sown confusion and discord among Catholics.[141] They may be characterized as upholding a traditional, historic rendering of the Church's position on religious liberty.[142]

Appealing to natural law theory as espoused by Aquinas and numerous other theologians, philosophers, and popes, Traditionalists argue that the Catholic Church is the one true faith; that all other religions are "erroneous"; that in an ideal state, all such "erroneous" teachings must be suppressed because "error has no rights"; that the state may tolerate "error" for the greater good, or to prevent a greater evil; that such toleration does not in itself concede a "right" to the individual to embrace that which is "erroneous"; that because of man's nature, he is obligated to seek the truth and embrace it when found; and that religious freedom is correctly defined as freedom of *will*, to choose either good or evil, but not as a *right*.[143]

---

[140] Editors, zenit.org news, "Vatican-Pius X Society Talks Set for October," in *Zenit News*, September 15, 2009, http://www.zenit.org/article-26878?l=english (accessed July 19, 2011).

[141] Allen Schreck, a professor of theology at Franciscan University of Steubenville, OH, states, "Michael Davies is only one of many who have vocally dissented from the teaching of Vatican II. For some this may involve only one, two, or a few issues. For others, it is dissent against the council itself." Schreck, *Vatican II: The Crisis and the Promise* (Cincinnati, OH: St. Anthony Messenger Press, 2005), 4-14. Schreck refers to five Catholic authors who challenge *Dignitatis Humanae*: Michael Davies, Atila Sinke Guimaraes, *In The Murky Waters of Vatican II* (1997); Robert Sungenis, "Was God Behind the Ambiguities of Vatican II? A Biblical Answer to an Intriguing Question," *Catholic Family News*, February, 2003; Christopher A. Ferrara and Thomas E. Woods, Jr., *The Great Façade: Vatican II and the Regime of the Novelty in the Roman Catholic Church* (2002).

[142] "Opponents of Vatican II believe that only the true religion (Catholicism) has unrestricted rights to religious freedom." Schreck, 17.

[143] Pietro Pavan, "Declaration on Religious Freedom," in *Commentary on the Documents of Vatican II*, ed. Herbert Vorgrimler (New York: Crossroad Publishing Co., 1989), 50; Franz Cardinal Konig, "The Right to Religious Freedom: The

Widely recognized as a champion of Traditional Catholicism, Lefebvre believed that *Dignitatis Humanae* demonstrated a departure from the traditional, pre-Vatican II stance of the Church. He was so strongly convinced of this that he wrote, *Dubia sur la Déclaration Conciliaire sur la Liberté Religieuse*, (*Doubts about the Conciliar Declaration upon Religious Liberty*) in which he identifies what he believes to be thirty-nine conceptual errors contained in *Dignitatis Humanae*,[144] the major four of which will be presented in the first section of this chapter. Expressing similar sentiments as Lefebvre's critique is a contemporary Traditionalist, Michael Davies, whose views are also presented in section one.

Progressives hold views distinctly different, many of which are at odds with Traditionalist views. The term "Progressive" should not be misconstrued to mean "liberal," because most Progressives uphold the Church's conservative teachings and support the reforms initiated at Vatican II.[145] A more detailed description of their views comprises section two. Section three will evaluate the views of both Traditionalists and Progressives in comparison with two modern documents on religious freedom – the First Amendment religion clauses of the United States Bill of Rights and the United Nations Declaration on Human Rights Article 18 (on religious freedom) – in order to better assess the Roman Catholic Church's stance on religious freedom. The last section addresses Catholic hegemony and how the positions of both groups relate to it.

Traditionalist Catholics and a Pre-Vatican II Concept of Church-State Relations

To understand the areas of conflict between Traditionalists and Progressives, one must first understand the theoretical foundation of their development of Church-State relations, which requires understanding the Church *and* the State from a philosophical and theological foundation.

Significance of *Dignitatis Humanae*" in *Vatican II, by those who were there*, ed. Alberic Stacpoole (London: Geoffrey Chapman, 1986), 286.

[144] Marcel Lefebvre, *Dubia sur la Déclaration Conciliaire sur la Liberté Religieuse* (éditions saint-remi, 1987), 107-143.

[145] Thomas T. Love provides perhaps the best definition of a Catholic Progressive: "By 'progressive' we mean the views of those Catholic writers who also wish to preserve what is considered to be essential in Catholic thought, practice, and pronouncement but who are fundamentally concerned to represent this in a more vital way for the contemporary world." Thomas T. Love, *John Courtney Murray: Contemporary Church-State Theory* (Garden City, NY: Doubleday & Co., Inc., 1965), 19.

Philosophical and Theological Foundations

The "traditional" view of church-state relations was developed from philosophical and theological perspectives that govern the formulation of political philosophy. From natural law observations, Catholic philosophy argues that the family unit is the most basic form of communal existence, which grows until the tribal level is reached, whereupon political government becomes necessary.[146] The philosophical foundation precedes that of the political, and thus the former should govern the latter. Likewise, the Church directs man to his teleological end, and therefore, the Church should direct the political order as it pertains to man's eternal welfare. Thus, the papal perspective on the state (and prior to the Reformation, the empire or kingdom) argues that "The State is an organization of human beings which exists for and is necessary for the welfare of human beings."[147] Its proper objective should be to provide for the common good, or the well-being of the humans who comprise it.[148]

Theologically, Roman Catholicism firmly adheres to the biblical concept of the Church as a divinely created institution, brought into existence by Jesus Christ and, therefore, having prerogatives that outweigh those of any earthly government.[149] Not only is the Church a created entity, but also the state. Relying upon Romans 13:1, "Let every soul be subject unto the higher powers. For there is no power but of God: the powers that be are ordained of God," Catholic scholars have upheld the teaching that the State, under most any type of political system, exercises its authority only as it has been given to it by God.[150] Since the Church has objectives regarding the salvation of mankind, which far outweigh mere temporal objectives of the state regarding its dealings with man, the Church has authority far

---

[146] John A. Ryan and Francis J. Boland, *Catholic Principles of Politics* (New York: The MacMillan Co., 1941), 29-32.

[147] Ibid., 102-103.

[148] Ryan and Boland, 102-107.

[149] "It is the Church, and not the State, that is to be man's guide to Heaven. It is to the Church that God has assigned the charge of seeing to, and legislating for, all that concerns religion. . . of administering freely and without hindrance, in accordance with her own judgment, all matters that fall within her own competence." Pope Leo XIII, encyclical *Immortale Dei* (The Christian Constitution of States), Nov. 1, 1885, as cited in Philip Hughes, *The Popes' New Order* (New York: Macmillan, 1944), 92.

[150] Ryan and Boland, 49.

superior to that of the state. Thus, the public policy of the state must be guided by the theological and philosophical concepts as taught by the Church.[151]

Historically, this arrangement was facilitated by centuries of monarchical political systems in Western Europe that allowed for a much simpler interaction between the Church and empire, or kingdom.[152] The Protestant Reformation, however, changed this arrangement.[153] Beginning with the Peace of Westphalia (1648), sovereign nation states had their beginnings.[154] Under this arrangement, the Church retained its hegemony in those territories where the majority of citizens were Catholics.[155] Such Catholic

---

[151] "It was for the spiritual power, as the directing force of the body of Christendom, to decide what should be done, [and] for the temporal [State] to put the decisions into effect." T. M. Parker, *Christianity & the State in the light of history* (London: Adam and Charles Black, 1955), 111.

[152] "The first model is that of political Christendom. Since the eighth century, the Catholic Church was wedded to Western society in the form of a single, though differentiated, *corpus mysticum*. . . . For centuries, however, Church and state formed a single body, internally differentiated by two authorities, each of which was thought to share in Christ's *triplex munus* of priest, prophet, and king. The king participated in Christ's rule *pedes in terra* (feet on earth), while the Episcopal authority imaged Christ's rule *caput in caelo* (head in heaven)." F. Russell Hittinger, "The Declaration on Religious Liberty: *Dignitatis Humanae*," in *Vatican II: Renewal within Tradition*, eds. Matthew L. Lamb and Matthew Levering (New York: Oxford, 2008), 363.

[153] "The third model has already been mentioned. This is where the status and liberty of the Church are conflated with the status and liberty of the state itself. In modern times, this model goes back to the Peace of Augsburg (1555), which effected a settlement of religious conflict in Germany on the basis of the formula *cuius regio, eius religio* ("whoever rules, his religion"). Far from being a flimsy legal device for a temporary modus Vivendi in Germany, *cuius regio* established itself as a fundamental doctrine of state during the age of absolutism." Hittinger, 364.

[154] *The Economist*, "The Institutional Pillars of Global Order: The Nation-State is Dead; Long Live the Nation-State," (originally titled, "The Nation-State is Dead. Long live the Nation-State," in *The Economist*, Dec 23-Jan 5, 1996) in *The Global Agenda: Issues and Perspectives*, eds. Charles W. Kegley, Jr. and Eugene R. Wittkopf (Boston, MA: McGraw-Hill, 1998), 232, 237-239.

[155] "In the sixteenth and seventeenth centuries [*cuius regio, eius religio*] had meant that the religion of a state and all its citizens was determined by that of its ruler. In the eighteenth and nineteenth centuries the tenet was more liberally interpreted, and tempered by tolerance: the state religion of a country was that of the majority of its citizens; and minority confessions were tolerated in the public

dominance gave rise to the Catholic confessional state as the ideal to be achieved. The various propositions leading to the development of the ideal Catholic state, as well as nuanced definitions governing the relations between the Church and the State, have been written during the centuries from then until Vatican II. Although not drawing upon all encyclicals written during the centuries from the Peace of Westphalia to Vatican II, the following section briefly summarizes the key points from several encyclicals that provide a concise conceptual understanding of the Catholic confessional state.

Papal Encyclicals on Church-State Relations

One essential fact to bear in mind regarding the history of Church-State relations is that they not only trace back to the time of the Catholic Church's nascent organization (2nd century A.D.) when the Church pitted itself against a domineering Empire, but more specifically do they take on a more aggressive nature from the time of the Protestant Reformation because of another religious competitor. Against this religious backdrop, Pope Gregory XVI wrote the encyclical *Mirari vos*, August 15, 1832, in which he condemned the prevalence and teaching of such views as: "that no preference should be shown for any particular form of worship (or, indifferentism, art. 13); that it is right for individuals to form their own personal judgments about religion (art. 13); that each man's conscience is his sole and all-sufficing guide (or, freedom of conscience, art. 14); and that it is lawful for every man to publish his own views (or, freedom to publish, art. 15), . . ."[156] While not employing the specific term "Protestantism," Pope Gregory XVI did allude to it: "Indeed this great mass of calamities had its inception in the heretical societies (Masons) and sects in which all that is sacrilegious, infamous, and blasphemous has gathered as bilge water in a ship's hold. . ." (art. 5).[157] The condemned beliefs include the idea "to separate the church from the state, and to break the mutual concord between temporal authority and the priesthood" (art. 20), highlighting the

---

interest." Konig, "The Right to Religious Freedom" in *Vatican II, by those who were there*, ed. Stacpoole, 286.

[156] Pope Gregory XVI, *Mirari vos*, August 15, 1832, as cited by Pope Leo XIII, *Immortale Dei*, November 1, 1885, and appearing in *Papal Thought on the State: Excerpts from Encyclicals and Other Writings of Recent Popes*, ed. Gerard F. Yates (New York: Appleton-Century-Crofts, Inc., 1958), 23.

[157]Pope Gregory XVI, *Mirari vos*, August 15, 1832, http://www.papalencyclicals.net/Greg16/g16mirar.htm, (accessed December 15, 2011).

underlying contention between Masons, Protestants, and the Church. Such Protestant (and Enlightenment) beliefs as freedom of conscience in religious matters and separation of church and state become the subject of rebuttal in subsequent encyclicals.

Pope Leo XIII is cited on several of the following pages on Church-State relations because he is recognized as the Pope who began "the modern phase" of Catholic social teaching (1891), which includes religious freedom. Thus, his statements that follow actually describe the Traditionalist Catholic view of Church and State, but also provide the foundation for the Progressive view. Pope Leo XIII defined the origin and end of the state in *Diuturnum Illud* (On Civil Government).[158] In the late nineteenth century, the Church was subject to resistance and attacks from civil authority in Italy, Germany, and France. Although occurring primarily in France, yet the term "Gallicanism," refers to "the various currents of resistance to the absolutization of papal primacy." Their ideology consisted of: 1) "autonomy of the political domain with regard to religion, and 2) and constitutional limitation of the Pope's powers."[159]

Additionally, Enlightenment philosophers had posited the nature of the state without any biblical foundation and theorizing the beginnings of society with man in a state of nature with inherent natural rights, moving Pope Leo XIII to declare,

> Those who believe civil society to have risen from the free consent of men, looking for the origin of its authority from the same source, say that each individual has given up something of his right, and that voluntarily every person has put himself into the power of the one man in whose person the whole of those rights has been centered. But it is a great error not to see, what is manifest, that men, as they are not a nomad race, have been created, without their own free will, for a natural community of life. It is plain, moreover, that the agreement which they allege is openly a falsehood and a fiction, and that it has no authority to confer on political power such great force, dignity, and firmness as the safety of the State and the common good of the citizens require. Then only will the

---

[158] George Weigel & Robert Royal, eds., *Building the Free Society: Democracy, Capitalism, and Catholic Social Teaching* (Grand Rapids, MI: Eerdman's, 1993), vii.

[159] Jacques Gres-Gayer, "Gallicanism," in *The Papacy: An Encyclopedia*, 4 vols., ed. Philippe Levillain (New York, NY: Routledge, 2002), 2:615.

government have all those ornaments and guarantees, when it is understood to emanate from God as its august and most sacred source.[160]

Here, Pope Leo XIII clearly argues for a divine origin of the State and, consequently, asserts that the political authority of rulers derives from God. Based on this divine mandate, he argues for the obedience of subjects to their rulers.[161] The only exception being when a ruler commands obedience that is contrary to the will of God as revealed in the divine or natural law.[162] In such cases, Christians should obey God and submissively endure any punishment given them for refusing to obey merely human laws.

Four years later during his pontificate, Pope Leo XIII, promulgated perhaps the most significant encyclical on Church-State relations, *Immortale Dei* (The Christian Constitution of States), on November 1, 1885, which defined the purpose of the state in relation to the Church. After establishing that political authority derives from God, Pope Leo XIII declares, "As a consequence, the State, constituted as it is, is clearly bound to act up to the manifold and weighty duties linking it to God by the public profession of religion."[163] Continuing in this line of thought, Pope Leo XIII draws several logical conclusions:

> Since, then, no one is allowed to be remiss in the service due to God, and since the chief duty of all men is to cling to religion in both its teaching and practice – not such religion as they may have a preference for, but the religion which God enjoins, and which certain and most clear marks show to be the only one true religion – it is a public crime to act as though there were no God. So too is it a sin in the State not to have care for religion, as something beyond its scope, or as of no practical benefit; or out of

---

[160] Pope Leo XIII, *Diuturnum Illud*, par. 10, issued June 29, 1881 (Yates, 4, 5).

[161] Pope Leo XIII, *Diuturnum Illud*, pars. 11, 12 (Yates, 5).

[162] Pope Leo XIII, *Diuturnum Illud*, par. 13 (Yates, 6), "The one only reason which men have for not obeying is when anything is demanded of them which is openly repugnant to the natural or the divine law, for it is equally unlawful to command and to do anything in which the law of nature or the will of God is violated."

[163] Pope Leo XIII, *Immortale Dei*, par. 6, (Yates, 14).

many forms of religion to adopt that one which chimes in with the fancy; for we are bound absolutely to worship God in that way which He has shown to be His will...[164]

Obviously condemning atheism and religious pluralism, Pope Leo XIII argues for the obligation of the State to the one true religion, which he later describes as the Church, or Roman Catholicism, "For the only-begotten Son of God established on earth a society which is called the Church... This society is made up of men, just as civil society is, and yet is supernatural and spiritual, on account of the end for which it was founded."[165] Thus, he argues, "just as the end at which the Church aims [salvation of mankind] is by far the noblest of ends, so is its authority the most exalted of all authority, nor can it be looked upon as inferior to the civil power, or in any manner dependent upon it."[166]

Having subordinated the State to the ultimate authority of the Church, Pope Leo XIII next defines the relationship between the two powers, "The Almighty, therefore, has appointed the charge of the human race between two powers, the ecclesiastical and the divine, the one being set over divine, and the other over human, things."[167] Recognizing that under such a societal construct, man is obligated to two powers, he contends that both powers must work together as ordained of God toward the same common end in order to avoid confusion among the populace,[168] reaching a union similar to that "of the soul and body in man." He further elaborates upon this arrangement,

> One of the two has for its proximate and chief object the well-being of this mortal life; the other the everlasting joys of heaven. Whatever, therefore, in things human is of a sacred character, whatever belongs either of its own nature or by reason of the end to which it is referred, to the salvation of souls, or to the worship of God, is subject to the power and judgment of the Church. Whatever is to be

---

[164] Pope Leo XIII, *Immortale Dei*, par. 6, (Yates, 14).

[165] Pope Leo XIII, *Immortale Dei*, par. 7 (Yates, 15).

[166] Pope Leo XIII, *Immortale Dei*, par. 8 (Yates, 15).

[167] Pope Leo XIII, *Immortale Dei*, par. 10 (Yates, 16). This is similar to the two swords doctrine of Pope Gelasius I (492-496).

[168] Pope Leo XIII, *Immortale Dei*, par. 10 (Yates, 16).

ranged under the civil and political order is rightly subject to the civil authority.[169]

By thus elaborating upon the ideal, harmonious functioning of the State and the Church, Leo XIII reiterated the traditional understanding of the role of both Church and State. From such a construct, it is easy to conclude that Leo XIII should have concerns regarding the American concept of church and state separation.

Addressing the American concept of church-state relations (separationism), also known as "Americanism", Pope Leo XIII promulgated *Testem benevolentiae nostrae* on January 22, 1899 as an expression of concern regarding liberalism and the separation of church and state.[170] In this apostolic letter to Cardinal James Gibbons, Leo XIII voiced uneasiness regarding what he had understood to be existing conditions among the American Catholic churches that reflected church governance operating on democratic principles.

Just seven years later, Pope Pius X, had recourse to Leo XIII's encyclical, *Immortale Dei*, when addressing the French republic regarding the separation of church and state. Pope Pius X issued *Vehementer nos* on February 11, 1906 against the French law separating the two entities.[171] In article 3, Pope Pius X declared, "That the State must be separated from the Church is a thesis absolutely false, a most pernicious error." He lambasted the French government for abrogating the Concordat in 1904, which it had solemnized with the Holy See (arts. 5, 6) and expressed the disgust of the Holy See regarding the odious manner in which the French Law of Separation assigned to "an association of laymen" the responsibility for organizing the worship services of the Church, rather than leaving the sacred constitution of the Church, viz., Bishops appointed by the Vatican

---

[169] Pope Leo XIII, *Immortale Dei*, par. 11 (Yates, 17).

[170] Pope Leo XIII, apostolic letter *Testem benevolentiae nostrae*, January 22, 1899, http://www.papalencyclicals.net/Leo13/l13teste.htm (accessed December 14, 2011). Debate over its real intent is still current within the Church. Traditionalists hold that it condemns American concepts of separationism, liberalism, and democratic principles to govern the Church, while Progressives argue that it was a reaction to an erroneous translation by a liberal-minded, French author of the work by Isaac Hecker in which Hecker describes existing conditions among the American Catholic church.

[171] Pius X, *Vehementer nos*, Feb. 11, 1906, http://www.vatican.va/holy_father/pius_x/encyclicals/documents/hf_p-x_enc_11021906_vehementer-nos_en.html (accessed December 14, 2011).

who oversee the flock, intact (art. 8). Pius X notes a further violation of the Church's rights through the supreme jurisdiction given to the Council of State over each "association of laymen," by reducing freedom of religion to mere public worship, and by denying to the Church's Religious Orders legal recognition (art. 9). Pius X denounced the confiscation of Church property and the transfer of funds used to support Catholic schools to the lay associations (art. 10). He next condemned the denial of financial support to the Catholic clergy (art. 11); argued that by restricting religion, French society would experience disunity and discord (art. 12); and, in article 13, that the French republic had offended God by not recognizing any "public cult" (i.e., legalizing disestablishment).

Traditionalists appeal to this encyclical to argue against any form of separationism, whereas Progressives contend that this encyclical cannot apply to America where such overt anti-clericalism does not exist. Perhaps a balanced perspective on this debate is to recognize the standard, or ideal conditions, enunciated by Pope Leo XIII regarding the proper functioning of the Church with the State (*Immortale Dei*). From this, one may conclude that the conditions in France are overtly against the Church (an anti-clerical, lay state), and the conditions in America, while closer to the Catholic ideal, viz., allowing the Church to manage its internal affairs, still do not harmonize fully with a Catholic State (America being a neutral, but religiously benevolent state). The dissonance between Traditionalist and Progressive's views of American separationism and the religion clauses of the First Amendment will be addressed at the end of this chapter under "Challenges facing both views."

Seeking to reaffirm to Catholics that they must not separate their religious commitments from their civic responsibilities, Pope Pius XI, on December 11, 1925, issued *Quas primas* in which he instituted a feast to Christ as King, both in the heavens and over the earth. He argued theologically that Christ had the authority to declare laws that both individuals and states were obligated to obey. In sum, he declared the Social Kingship of Christ that must exist within society.[172]

From these authoritative encyclicals and one apostolic letter addressing aspects of the Catholic Church in relation to the State, one may conclude that a conceptually-based diagram of the pre-Vatican II position would look like that found in Figure 2.1.

---

[172] Pope Pius XI, *Quas primas*, December 11, 1925, as appearing in Hughes, *The Popes' New Order*, 102-107.

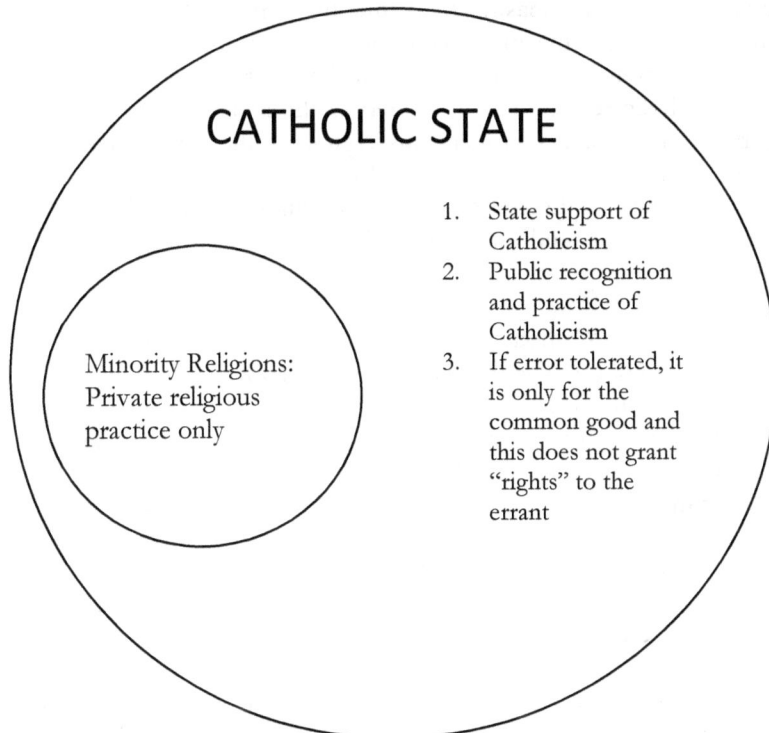

Figure. 2.1. Paternalistic Church Model – used during the centuries when the conscience of humanity was not enlightened regarding its moral responsibilities, requiring the Church to guide and directly influence the State regarding moral norms.

Traditionalist Catholics' Objections to Dignitatis Humanae

Marcel Lefebvre, although signatory to *Dignitatis Humanae* at Vatican II,[173] studied it more extensively after its promulgation, and expressed his doubts regarding its theoretical foundations, as well as its practical application.

No Concept of a "Catholic State"

Lefebvre describes "the Catholic doctrine" of how the Church is

---

[173] Brian W. Harrison, "Marcel Lefebvre: Signatory to Dignitatis Humanae," *CatholicCulture.org* http://www.catholicculture.org/culture/library/view.cfm?id=857&CFID=80441610&CFTOKEN=56631028 (accessed May 10, 2011).

superior to the State inasmuch as the mission of the former (eternal salvation) outweighs the mere temporal considerations of the latter. He then posits how the "the union between the Church and the State implies that the Catholic religion be considered as the religion of the State." He adds that "the Church considers this regime as the *normal state.*"[174] It is precisely because *Dignitatis Humanae* lacks this formula that Michael Davies, a devout follower of Lefebvre's teachings, almost thirty years after it was promulgated at the end of Vatican II, rejects it as reflective of true Catholicism:

> The term 'Catholic State' is not so much as mentioned throughout the entire Declaration. Father Murray had denied any doctrinal basis for the concept of a state-church, or for that concept of Catholicism as the religion of the State. He considered these concepts to be no more than 'an adaptation to a particular historical context.' *Dignitatis Humanae* certainly appears to endorse his position. The terms "Catholic State", "Union of Church and State", or "Religion of the State" do not appear anywhere in the Declaration.[175]

Both Lefebvre, in his day, and Davies, in the twenty-first century, consider this lack to be sufficient grounds to call for a repeal of the Declaration.

No Reference to a "True Religion"

Just as the concept of a "Catholic State" is built upon the premise of religious absolutism, so also is the concept of the "true religion" with reference to Catholicism. Lefebvre argues that, according to traditional Catholic doctrine, "the State, the central organ of civil society, must: Honor God, who is the Author of civil society, and this through worship of the true religion; and by consequence, recognize the Catholic religion as being the religion of the State" against any other form of religion, as well as against "agnosticism and religious indifferentism, as much as (against) laicism."[176]

Echoing Lefebvre's sentiments, Michael Davies argues that "the relevant

---

[174] Lefebvre, *Dubia sur la Declaration*, 85 (emphasis in original).

[175] Michael Davies, *The Second Vatican Council and Religious Liberty* (Longprairie, MN: The Neumann Press, 1992), 177.

[176] Lefebvre, 77.

sections of *Dignitatis Humanae* (notably articles 3 & 4) do not so much as hint at the existence of a true religion, let alone any duty incumbent upon the State to protect it." Recognizing that the concept of a "true religion" also implies a false religion as its antonym, Davies continues arguing that "The term 'doctrinal error' does not occur anywhere within the Declaration."[177] If, as Lefebvre and Davies suggest, *Dignitatis Humanae* does not allow for a Catholic State, and does not mention a "true religion," then the Document must also disallow any concept of the common good.

No Concept of the Common Good

In traditional Catholic doctrine, "the temporal common good is the proper end of civil society and the State. It is principally a moral good. It is never independent of, but to the contrary, intrinsically dependent upon the consideration of an objective, moral and religious order."[178] Lefebvre continues to explain the necessity of a Catholic State in order to achieve the "perfect order" in society:

> The moral and religious order can be a perfect order, which is that which reigns within a Catholic city; it can be an order more or less imperfect and itself only the appearance of an order, according to which a non-Catholic Christian city acts, by which a religiously pluralistic city operates, by which a pagan city, or ultimately, a communist city [functions]. Only the Christian social order is the guarantee of the true common good, as well as of true liberties.[179]

Based on Lefebvre's last sentence, one might plausibly believe he refers to a Christian society, either Catholic, or non-Catholic. However, a little further, he clearly removes all possibility of doubt that he is referring to a Catholic Christian social order: "The religious unanimity of the citizens regarding the true religion is the required corollary for the realization of the perfect, temporal, common good. This is why, within a Catholic nation, the principle of religious unity should be inscribed within the constitution of the State."[180]

---

[177] Davies, 186.

[178] Lefebvre, 71.

[179] Ibid., 71.

[180] Ibid., 71-72.

Taking into account this explanation of the Catholic concept of the common good, Michael Davies points out inconsistencies within the Declaration on Religious Freedom, as well as explains why the term "common good" was replaced by "public order":

> In *Dignitatis Humanae*, however, although the term 'common good' was used in early drafts, it was deliberately removed in deference to Protestant objections, and replaced by 'public order' as the criterion for deciding the 'due limits' within which religious liberty can be exercised. The public order of Vatican II certainly does require some degree of restriction over and above the necessary minimum for the maintenance of public peace. . . but by no possible stretch of the imagination can *Dignitatis Humanae* be said to uphold the traditional position. . .[181]

By pointing out the substitution of terms to acquiesce Protestants, Davies is underscoring that "public order" merely requires the basic minimum of maintaining societal peace, without having the obligation of achieving and upholding the moral, objective, religious order required by reference to the common good. In short, it means that as long as civil society is kept at a peaceful level, it matters not if the citizenry are not guided toward a moral, religious (Catholic) end.

No Moral Concept of Error, or Restrictions of the Same

In the societal order envisioned in *Dignitatis Humanae*, since there is no common good as the end to be achieved, there can be no corresponding moral concept of error, or restrictions of the same. In contrast to this, Lefebvre describes the moral rights that pertain to the State under a traditional Catholic concept, "In order to guarantee, in view of the common good, that [Catholic] religious unity, the State has the duty, and by consequence the right of limiting by legal constraint, public manifestations of other religions, at least when [the State] does not judge it preferable to use tolerance."[182] From this perspective, Michael Davies observes, "The words 'tolerate', 'tolerance', or 'toleration' do not occur anywhere in the Declaration [of Religious Freedom]. The concept that error has no rights, and can be tolerated only in the interest of the common good, has been

---

[181] Davies, 186, 187.

[182] Lefebvre, 72.

abandoned completely."[183]

While the previous four central arguments used by Traditional Catholics against *Dignitatis Humanae* are logical and consistent with traditional teachings, Progressive Catholics have responded to these critiques and have given an explanation for their rationale in the development of the religious freedom espoused in *Dignitatis Humanae*, as the next section demonstrates.

Progressive Catholics: A Vatican II Theory of Religious Freedom

Progressive Catholics are characterized as viewing Vatican II, and especially *Dignitatis Humanae*, as the Church's successful effort to bridge the abyss that once separated it from the modern masses of humanity.[184] They consider *Dignitatis Humanae* not as a rejection of prior teachings of the Church, but instead as the consummation of its teachings regarding religious liberty through the long centuries of its existence.[185] They tend to view *Dignitatis Humanae* as employing conciliatory language and concepts designed to reach those separated from the Church. Some have even interpreted the document to allow a greater freedom of individual conscience in moral matters, such as abortion, contraception, and salvation outside of the Church.[186] Regarding religious liberty, they see *Dignitatis Humanae* as recognizing the sacred, inviolable nature of man's conscience as a *right*, as opposed to merely freedom of the *will*. Under this construct, they believe that the state has the obligation to promote religious freedom, including that of the Church to fulfill her mission in her appointed way.[187] In particular, such religious freedom does not address the moral issue of erroneous beliefs, but instead focuses upon the dignity of the human being,

---

[183] Davies, 188.

[184] "At the Second Vatican Council the Catholic Church took a decisive step forward in its transition from defensiveness, characterized by apologetic, to a much more positive and outgoing attitude towards the world and mankind, characterized by the will to engage in discussion and collaboration." Konig, "The Right to Religious Freedom," in *Vatican II, by those who were there*, ed. Stacpoole, 284.

[185] Enda McDonagh, *The Declaration on Religious Freedom of Vatican Council II: The Text and Commentary* (London: Darton, Longman, & Todd, 1967), 7-11; Fr. Basile, *Le droit à la liberté religieuse dans la Tradition de l'Eglise* (Editions Sainte-Madeleine, 2005).

[186] As noted in chapter one, which gave examples of debate in the Philippines, Malta, and America.

[187] Hittinger, 370-372.

which requires that no coercion should be used to mold his or her conscientious religious convictions.[188]

The most notable advocates of *Dignitatis Humanae* among the Progressive group includes, J. C. Murray, Brian Harrison, Father Most, Dr. William Marshner, Dr. Jeffrey Mirus, Kenneth L. Grasso, Robert P. Hunt, David Hollenbach, and Charles Curran. In recent years, Brian Harrison and Dr. John Mirus have been the more prominent advocates of *Dignitatis Humanae*. Central ideas from these various progressives will be used to explain and support the Catholic, modern concept of religious liberty.

Toward the end of this section dealing with Progressives, Figure 2.2 illustrates the Church-State concepts of John of Paris, a medieval theologian, whose ideas John Courtney Murray adopted in the formulation of *Dignitatis Humanae*. Figure 2.3 depicts Murray's concepts of Church-State relations in a post-Vatican II context in what is referred to among Catholic scholars as the "Public Church Model." The appellation derives from *Gaudium et spes*, which describes the public role of the Church in a religiously-pluralistic, democratic society.

Doctrinal Development the Central Issue of Contention

Various Catholic theologians and historians reiterate that the intent of Vatican II was to promote religious freedom, as well as other ecclesial reforms.[189] They go to great lengths to explain that the debate regarding *Dignitatis Humanae* had nothing to do with whether to accept, or to reject, religious freedom, despite a few scholars who argue the contrary.[190] Instead, the debate regarded the doctrinal development necessary to show the faithful adherence to prior Church teachings and how those could be harmonized with the new teaching of *Dignitatis Humanae*.[191]

---

[188] Pavan, Commentary, 66-67.

[189] John Courtney Murray, "Religious Freedom," in *The Documents of Vatican II*, ed. Walter M. Abbott (New York: Crossroads Publishing Co., 1989), 673; "When Pope John XXIII convened the Second Vatican Council in 1962, most observers understood that the council would need to address the issue of religious liberty in the civil sphere." Hittinger, 359.

[190] "In fact, the tumultuous history of the redaction and approval of *Dignitatis Humanae* indicates that the question of religious freedom represented a particularly grave crisis for the Catholic community in the 1960s." John Conley, "Religious Freedom as Catholic Crisis," in *The Human Person and a Culture of Freedom*, eds. Peter A. Pagan Aguiar and Terese Auer (Washington, D.C.: The Catholic University of America Press, 2009), 226.

Prior Papal Teachings

Prior papal teachings since the time of Leo XIII that support the concept of a Catholic State have been examined in the previous section under Traditional Catholics. From the perspective of Progressive Catholics, however, their intent has been to examine *the same* corpus of material to discover additional insights, as well as a more amplified understanding, of the traditional teaching that would be more applicable to the modern political and social context.

Those Popes, whose pontificates occurred several decades prior to Vatican II, began to mention the need for religious freedom in several of their messages to the faithful. Pope Leo XIII advanced the idea of the freedom of the Church in several of his encyclicals. This laid the foundation for the eventual development of the right to the freedom of the individual.[192]

F. Russell Hittinger identifies the Church's modern teaching on religious liberty as beginning in the 1940s through the pontificate of Pope Pius XII (1939-1958).[193] Especially in his Christmas homilies in 1942 and 1944, Pius XII "represented a significant breakthrough in the Roman estimation of the modern states. It was Pius XII who abandoned the older Roman policy of intransigence toward modern democratic governments and who began the process of making the necessary distinctions for shaping a new approach to Church-state relations."[194] Pope John XXIII echoed the sentiments of Pius XII, supporting religious freedom and human rights, in the encyclical *Pacem in terris* (Peace on Earth), which was promulgated April 11, 1963. During his United Nations General Assembly address delivered on October 4, 1965, Pope Paul VI emphasized the need for religious freedom in the global

---

[191] "Such a sober and objective consideration [of the teachings of recent popes, viz., the successors to Pope Leo XIII, roughly from 1900-1965] could not but result in the certainty that there had, of course, been a doctrinal development, but that its last phase tended towards what was said in the Council document [*Dignitatis Humanae*], if it did not actually agree with it." Pavan, 4:61.

[192] "In his intervention, Cardinal Shehan of Baltimore illustrated how this developmentalist interpretation could be applied to the magisterial patrimony of declarations on religious freedom: '. . . By making the freedom of the church so central, Leo XIII led us to recognize that this freedom included the freedom of the human person.'" Conley (quoting Cardinal Shehan), 233.

[193] Hittinger, 361.

[194] Ibid., 361.

community just two months before *Dignitatis Humanae* was officially promulgated on December 7, 1965.[195] Based on these precedents, the intent, then, of Vatican II was to formally express through a council, the Church's position on various reforms, among them religious freedom. From this perspective, the most influential contributor was John Courtney Murray, S. J.

John Courtney Murray's Contribution

Without rehearsing the biographical history of John Courtney Murray and the events leading up to his role as *periti* at Vatican II, which other authors have done superbly,[196] this section focuses on his specific contributions to a modern Catholic concept of religious freedom. John Courtney Murray, S. J., held a doctorate in sacred theology (1937) and while working at Woodstock College spent several years (1946-1952) studying the issues of church-state relations and society.[197] By 1952, Murray had begun wrestling with broader democratic concepts such as religious pluralism, American Church-State relations, and religious freedom.[198] Murray attempted to reconcile traditional Catholic teaching in these areas with the concepts of the Founding Fathers of America on the same concepts. Given the long history of the "Americanist controversy" – papal denunciations of American civil concepts such as separation of Church and State, freedom to believe or disbelieve, government neutrality toward religion, etc. – Murray had taken on a great challenge.

In short, *Dignitatis Humanae* reveals Murray's contribution as a formulation for religious freedom (the issue of Church-State relations is actually secondary, since it is more fully addressed in *Gaudium et spes*), based

---

[195] "Here indeed We seem to hear the echo of the voice of Our Predecessors, and particularly of Pope John XXIII, whose message of "Pacem in Terris" received so honourable and significant a response among you. You proclaim here the fundamental rights and duties of man, his dignity, his freedom and above all his religious freedom." Pope Paul VI, under section, "Disarmament Essential to Brotherhood," http://www.christusrex.org/ www1/pope/UN-1965.html (accessed December 21, 2011).

[196] Donald E. Pelotte, *John Courtney Murray: Theologian in Conflict* (New York, NY: Paulist Press, 1976); Thomas T. Love, *John Courtney Murray: Contemporary Church-State Theory* (Garden City, NY: Doubleday & Co., Inc., 1965).

[197] Biography page, Spring Hill College, http://www.shc.edu/theolibrary/resources/murray.htm (accessed June 4, 2012).

[198] Pelotte, 34-46.

on the historic model of John of Paris, in which the Church functions compatibly with the State within a constitutional democracy. Under such an arrangement, the Church no longer seeks to directly influence the State. Rather, each has its respective role to fulfill in society. The State has the obligation to guarantee religious freedom so that the Church may fulfill its spiritual mission without hindrance. Likewise, the State attends to its temporal duties. The Church persuades society of its claims, and through the citizenry, indirectly influences public policy. Thus, *Dignitatis Humanae* reflects a combination of juridical, philosophical, theological, and political perspectives that result in a document which parallels modern documents dealing with religious freedom. Rather than formulate a document solely from juridical and theological principles, as Traditionalist Catholics would have done, Murray uses some of those concepts, but balances them with philosophical and political concepts that offer a Catholic understanding of religious freedom within a modern political context. In the following section, Murray's contribution will be examined more closely.

Progressive Catholics' Defense of Dignitatis Humanae

Catholic Progressives agree that *Dignitatis Humanae* does not reflect the "traditional" pre-Vatican II teaching of church and state, but they argue that the "traditional" understanding is not the true Catholic doctrine on this topic, since no pope had declared through his encyclicals the final word on this subject.[199] Instead, they argue that "this doctrine [of religious freedom] develops, as it were, like a seed, which first germinates and then becomes an ever more vigorous plant. As is emphasized in the text, under the influence of the evolving historical situation the Popes have increasingly emphasized the dignity of the human person. . ."[200] Progressives further argue that there is a doctrinal continuity between the "traditional" view and the Vatican II teaching.[201] They assert that papal encyclicals written prior to

---

[199] "Another difficulty of the council fathers has already been mentioned in the Introduction. This concerned the question whether the doctrine of the Declaration contradicted the teaching of the Popes, especially of Leo XIII. *The Council text, however, does not regard this teaching as having been defined by a Pope in its final form once and for all,* but sees it as gradually developing through new papal contributions, especially in our own century." Pavan, 4:64.

[200] Idem.

[201] "Likewise, Pope Benedict XVI, Pope John Paul II, the Extraordinary Synod of 1985 and others have stressed the continuity of the teachings of Vatican II with previous ecumenical councils (and other magisterial teachings), rather than a discontinuity or 'break' with past tradition." Schrek, 36.

Vatican II that seem to contradict *Dignitatis Humanae*, for example, in the area of "freedom of conscience," must be understood in their historical context.[202] As a *periti* (expert, or counselor) at Vatican II, John Courtney Murray's theological contribution addresses the movement within society toward secularism and a "historic consciousness." It also includes Murray's "Americanism," the freedom of the Church, and an appeal to John of Paris's church-state model. Each of these component provide the interrelated, intellectual foundation for the development of Murray's thought on religious freedom in the modern context of democratic, constitutional states.

"Historic Consciousness" as Interpretive Tool

The first theological contribution Murray made at Vatican II addressed the sacrality of society and state moving toward a secular state. As Donald Pelotte comments,

> With the breakup of the sacrality of society and state the nineteenth century saw a movement toward secularity... [By Vatican II] [t]he sacrality of society and state is now transcended and archaic. Its duties and rights do not include the *cura religionis*. The government's function is secular, that is, "It is confined to a care of the free exercise of religion within society, a care therefore of the freedom of the Church and the freedom of the human person in religious affairs."[203]

Murray's contribution on this point was the first significant step toward repositioning the Church in relation to the modern state and society. Murray appealed to the encyclicals of Leo XIII, which he believed not only anticipated this modern development, but also established the foundational structure that could be utilized in the legitimate development of doctrine

---

[202] "There is no question that previous popes condemned 'freedom of conscience' (as well as freedom of speech and of the press), yet they did this because in their historical context these liberties were being promoted with total disregard to the obligations they entail, especially the obligation to seek and submit to the truth." Schreck, 37.

[203] Pelotte quoting John Courtney Murray, 130-131; Murray, "The Declaration on Religious Freedom," *War, Poverty, Freedom: The Christian Response, Concilium*, XV (New York: Paulist Press, 1966), 9.

toward the dual spheres of authority contained in *Dignitatis Humanae*.[204]

Murray's second theological contribution was in response to the movement toward historical consciousness. For Murray, classicism defined society with an orientation toward objective truth. In other words, in religious matters, it viewed society from the divine perspective. A natural corollary to this view is that the Church, therefore, had the moral right to obligate society and state toward that end. Murray recognized, however, a shift toward what he termed "historical consciousness," which does not deny objective truth, but focuses more upon the recognition, understanding, and embracing of such truth by the individual. In other words, it is anthropologically centered and is concerned with man's response to objective truth. Since human beings are religious by nature, they have the corresponding responsibility to search for truth. From this perspective, the Church adopts the role, not of obligating the individual in the paternalistic model of classicism, but of persuading the individual through force of argument and appeal to reason, seeking to arouse the conscience of man.[205] Under this rubric, the need for religious freedom becomes undeniably apparent so that the Church may fulfill its role of instructing society and the individual has the freedom to search for and hear the truth, weigh its arguments, and incorporate its teachings into his or her life through religious practices. For Murray, the specific conditions necessary for such religious freedom were enshrined in the constitutional principles of America, or, as he referred to them, "political Americanism."

Murray's "Americanism"

From a Progressive perspective, the "Americanist" controversy, observes Thomas W. O'Brien, was not really a condemnation of the American concept of religious freedom.[206] Instead, European bishops who incorrectly related the American concept of religious freedom that they had gleaned from their American counterparts caused the Vatican to mistake the American form for the radical forms of liberty associated with subjectivism and liberalism rampant in Europe during the latter part of the nineteenth century. Progressives claim that Leo XIII was condemning European liberalism and that form of religious freedom which produces a lay state, as in France, and that he was not referring to the form of religious

---

[204] Pelotte, 130.

[205] Ibid., 131.

[206] Thomas W. O'Brien, *John Courtney Murray in a Cold War Context* (Dallas: University Press of America, 2004), 6.

freedom nascent in the United States.

In order to better understand Murray's "Americanism," O'Brien distinguishes between "ecclesial Americanism," and "political Americanism," the latter type being the form Murray incorporated within *Dignitatis Humanae*.[207] "Ecclesial Americanism" would suggest that principles of democracy should govern the Church's actions, such as the election of bishops instead of their appointment by the Vatican, etc., for which reason it is condemned by the Church and was not incorporated into *Dignitatis Humanae*. However, "political Americanism," as Murray understood it, suggests concepts of religious freedom as a civil right, the Church in the midst of a religious plurality, and the State as a societal actor, rather than a distinct governing entity. Under such conditions, Murray argued that the Church was free to exercise all of her God-given freedom in fulfilling her appointed mission.

Freedom of the Church the Central Doctrine

Based on the foregoing distinction, Progressive Catholics argue that "ecclesial Americanism" would certainly be a restriction upon the Church's constitutional order. However, "political Americanism" is not. Rather than restricting the freedom of the Church to accomplish her mission, "political Americanism" actually provides the societal freedom the Church needs in order to reach the masses through "free exercise" of religion, which allows the Church to not only govern its internal affairs, but also to freely disseminate its teachings. Such ideal conditions do not prevail in every country, given the existence of totalitarian states during the twentieth-, and into the twenty-first centuries. For this reason, the Church utilizes a more complex argument for the international community.

The root theoretical concept that underlies the freedom of the Church in relation to the several states that make up the global community is based on papal sovereignty:

> State-to-State relations might be termed *horizontal*, or geographical, in the sense that they involve jurisdictions mutually exclusive and clearly marked out by territorial borders. The relations between the State and the Holy See, on the other hand, can be described as *vertical*, or coterminous, in the sense that both the temporal and the religious sovereignty are exercised on the same territory and over the same subjects, even though at different levels of human activity. The State deals with a religious

---

[207] O'Brien, 8, 9.

authority located outside its territory, concerning institutions and persons who, civilly, are within its own jurisdiction. This is a feature not encountered in the pure State-to-State relationship. It is for this reason that the concept of spiritual sovereignty must be looked at not merely as a problem of international law but also as a problem of constitutional law.[208]

From this perspective, Catholic theologians argue that individual nations need to recognize the jurisdictional authority of the Vatican and each should adjust its constitution to reflect this recognition. A *de minimus* recognition would include the freedom of the Church to appoint its own priests at each level of Church governance; legal recognition of Church property, whether fixed assets (land, buildings, etc.) or liquid assets (bank accounts, etc.); and exemption of priests from trial in civil courts.

From a theoretical viewpoint, a concise explanation of the freedom of the Church in relation to individual states is that originally taught by Pope Gelasius I in *Duo Sunt* ("Two they are," 494 A.D.), and according to Catholic historians, which was later taught by John of Paris. It argues for two distinctly separate roles for Church and State in society, as well as placing the divine sphere outside of the societal sphere.

John of Paris's Model of Church-State Relations

John of Paris (1269-1306) was a Dominican professor at the University of Paris. He was considered to hold eclectic views on some doctrines, such as papal sovereignty and the Eucharist. He was put to death in 1306 for his views on the proper method of celebrating the Mass, which was considered to be unorthodox. In the area of church-state relations, he developed the novel idea of separate spheres for each, but included minimal shared power, which he referred to as "accidental," or indirect, power. Paris formulated this theory during the time of papal and regnal tensions, which occurred between Pope Boniface VIII and Philip IV of France. Paris reasoned that both spheres derive their power to rule from God, thus neither is dependent upon, or subordinate to, the other. Both have their respective role to fulfill in society and neither should depend upon the other to achieve this. He also introduced "a notion of corporate authority in which some would find roots of popular sovereignty," arguing that "the authority of the Church was not concentrated in the person of the pope, but was

---

[208] Robert A. Graham, *Vatican Diplomacy: A Study of Church and State on the International Plane* (Princeton, NJ: Princeton University Press, 1959), 247, 248.

suffused throughout all its members."[209] Figure 2.2 illustrates Paris's concept of church-state relations and Figure 2.3 illustrates the societal model that John Courtney Murray envisioned through an application of *Dignitatis Humanae*.

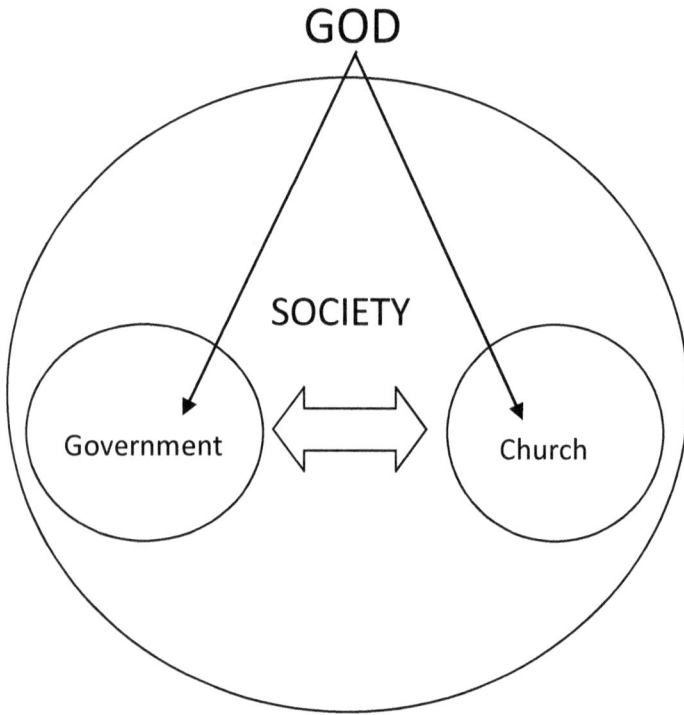

Figure 2.2. Secular State Model based on John of Paris's Theory. "God" is located outside of the sphere of society in order to produce equality of power between government and the Church. Each has indirect influence upon the other and each has its respective role to fulfill in society.

---

[209] Lee Cameron McDonald, *Western Political Theory: Part 1, Ancient and Medieval*, 3 parts (New York: Harcourt, Brace, Jovanovich, 1968), 1:170.

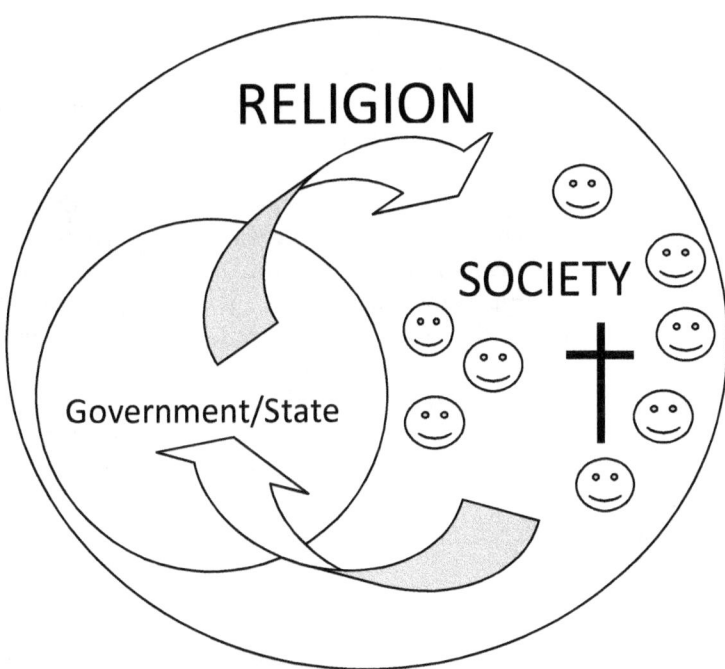

Figure 2.3. Public Church Model based on *Dignitatis Humanae, Gaudium et Spes, Ad Gentes,* and *Nostra Aetate* (The Church indirectly influences State through the "demos" [people], who influence government to legislate religion for society; note that "atheists" do not exist as a group in this model; tolerance for non-Catholic religions is not even addressed in *Dignitatis Humanae*; religion definitely dominates the State in this model). Religion, i.e., "God," is within society, alluding to Church dominance over the State, as opposed to Paris's model where "God" is outside the sphere of society to produce equality between the spheres.

Challenges Facing Both Views

Both Traditionalists and Progressives appeal to authoritative Church documents to sustain their positions. While both use well-developed arguments, each has its weaknesses, as this section points out.

Traditionalists and Democracy

The greatest objection to the Traditionalist position is its incompatibility with democracy. Although Traditionalists can properly appeal to historic sources with more certainty than Progressives, they cannot overcome the difficulties presented by democratic forms of government. Under a Traditionalist rubric of Church-State relations and religious freedom, two points of contention surface immediately: preference for a monarchical political system and the development of a theocratic form of governance.

Catholic concepts of the State and the common good postulate the need for a single, true religion to guide society. The monarchical form of governance has ideally been suited to achieve that end. Deriving their political concepts from Aristotle, as "Christianized" by Thomas Aquinas, Roman Catholic political philosophy recognizes the ideal system, but not the only allowable form, as monarchical rule. With a single political figure, it is much easier to rule the masses. This form lends itself quite well to the support of a single religious creed as well. However, for Traditionalists, the monarchical system of governance is no longer the dominant form in the political global arena. Incompatibility between the Traditionalist model and modern constitutional democracy is the greatest, insurmountable obstacle that makes this model archaic.

The second challenge facing Traditionalists is that of theocratic rule. Although Traditionalists may argue that a Catholic State is not the establishment of a theocracy, the history of Western European church-state relations from the time of Constantine to the middle of the 15th century argues definitively to the contrary. Beginning with Augustine's (354-430) *De Civitate Dei* (The City of God), which posits the Heavenly City as supernatural and the Earthly City as existing within time, the argument of the Church preceding the temporal reign of earthly kings began to develop. Pope Gelasius I (492-496), who conceptualized the dual subordination to each of the two sovereignties (Church and king), argued that the State existed to promote the salvation of its citizens, thus relegating princely power to a sub-authoritative, and supporting role to the superior, spiritual role of the Church. In succeeding centuries, various popes and theologians expounded upon this theory, finally leading to the height of papal supremacy (a spiritual theocracy) during the pontificate of Boniface VIII when he issued the bull *Unam Sanctam* (18 November 1302).[210] Thus, history cogently demonstrates that the Traditionalist model of Church-State relations, when implemented, is destined to produce a theocracy with the state subordinate to the power of the Church. As the next section will demonstrate, Progressive Catholics also have challenges facing their position.

---

[210] Jean Favier, article "Theocracy, Papal, Middle Ages," in Philippe Levillain, gen. ed., *The Papacy: An Encyclopedia*, 3 vols. (New York: Routledge, 2002), 3:1482-1486.

Progressives and Religious Freedom within a Hermeneutic of Doctrinal Continuity

Although Progressives have rallied around the recent teachings of Pope Benedict XVI regarding Vatican II, in which he upholds the authority of Vatican II based upon a "hermeneutic of reform," as opposed to a "hermeneutic of rupture," there are still challenges facing the Declaration on Religious Freedom. Benedict's interpretation alone poses significant issues for some Progressives. Other challenging areas include Murray's interpretation of some papal encyclicals; his interpretive tool of "historic consciousness;" his argument in favor of apolitical Catholicism; and his usage of John of Paris's teaching on regnal and papal power.

Pope Benedict XVI and the interpretation of Vatican II. From the perspective of arguments *internal* to the Catholic Church, perhaps the greatest challenge facing the Progressive position is the doctrinal stance taken by Pope Benedict XVI. Shortly after Vatican II, then Cardinal Ratzinger wrote a commentary on several of the documents, in which he criticized them for their ambiguity. Now, as Pope, he has continued that pursuit by indicating his intentions of challenging the prevailing "hermeneutic of discontinuity and rupture" by issuing a *motu proprio* (literally, his *own initiative*) that will render a minimalist reading of several of the Vatican II documents, among them *Gaudium et spes*, *Dignitatis Humanae*, and *Unitatis redintegratio*.[211] Based on this action by Benedict XVI, it would appear that at least some theological aspects of religious freedom from a pre-Vatican II era are still doctrinally valid for defining the Church's position on the subject.

When one actually reads Benedict's message, it becomes evident that his definition of religious freedom, based on *Dignitatis Humanae*, does not allow for religious indifference (inability to know the truth about God):

> Basic decisions, therefore, continue to be well-grounded, whereas the way they are applied to new contexts can change. Thus, for example, if religious freedom were to be considered an expression of the human inability to discover the truth and thus become a canonization of relativism, then this social and historical necessity is raised

---

[211] "The Holy Father fired a salvo in that direction (toward reinterpretation of Vatican II documents) on 22 December 2005 in his *Christmas Address* to the Roman Curia, in which he challenged the prevailing interpretation of Vatican II as the 'hermeneutic of discontinuity and rupture.'" http://gregorianrite2007.blogspot.com/2009/06/vatican-sspx-recent-ordinations-and.html (accessed June 29, 2009).

inappropriately to the metaphysical level and thus stripped of its true meaning. Consequently, it cannot be accepted by those who believe that the human person is capable of knowing the truth about God and, on the basis of the inner dignity of the truth, is bound to this knowledge.[212]

If indeed Benedict's intent is to give such a narrow rendering of *Dignitatis Humanae*, then some Progressive Catholics will find themselves outside the veil of doctrinal orthodoxy.[213]

Murray's critique of some papal encyclicals. Murray attempts to place Pope Leo XIII's encyclicals on church-state relations in a historic context that may not actually reflect the true facts of history:

> Murray argued that if the polemical element was overlooked in an assessment of Leo's works one could easily misinterpret their teachings and draw erroneous conclusions from them. In contradiction to mainstream theological positions, Murray believed that Leo's statements were historically contingent in that they were addressed to a particular set of circumstances. He argued that it would be inappropriate to take them out of that context and apply them literally and unaltered to the current situation.[214]

For Murray, there were two types of democracy developing in the late eighteenth-century, the first of which he termed "totalitarian democracy," and the second "American democracy." Likewise, there were two types of church-state relations to consider: the first, which corresponded to

---

[212] Benedict XVI, *Christmas Message*, December 22, 2005, http://www.vatican.va/holy_father/benedict_xvi/speeches/2005/december/documents/hf_ben_xvi_spe_20051222_roman-curia_en.html (accessed November 29, 2011) (italics mine).

[213] "I am convinced that the damage that we have incurred in these twenty years is due, not to the 'true' Council, but to the unleashing *within* the Church of latent polemical and centrifugal forces; and *outside* the Church it is due to the confrontation with a cultural revolution in the West. . . [and all Catholics who wish to remain such need] to return to the authentic texts of the original Vatican II." Pope Benedict XVI, during an interview in 1985, as cited in Schreck, 30.

[214] O'Brien, 84.

"totalitarian democracy," was radical and liberal in nature and the second, the American version, which harmonized with the Catholic concept of the two sovereignties of Church and State, allowed each differing roles in society.[215] According to Murray, Pope Leo XIII condemned the first type, but in so doing, did not offer a fixed concept of the Catholic state that would condemn all forms of democracy and church-state separationism, such as the second type. From Murray's nuanced analysis, O'Brien concludes that "Murray manipulated the corpus of Leo XIII" enough to use it " as an authoritative confirmation that official Roman Catholic teaching supported his Americanized understanding of extreme separation of church and state."[216]

Etienne Gilson, a prominent Catholic theologian, who could also be labeled a "progressive" theologian due to his support of the *nouvelle theologie* movement (1920s to 1940s), takes a far different approach to the writings of Leo XIII than Murray, and thus, seems to concur with O'Brien. In *The Church Speaks to the Modern World: The Social Teachings of Leo XIII*, Gilson addresses some of the common interpretational errors committed by those who attempt to re-interpret the teachings of the popes. He notes,

> The teaching of the encyclicals should not be made either broader in scope or narrower than it is. Dealing as it does with a restatement of the Catholic faith as well as with its applications to definite problems, this teaching must be understood as given. Only a Pope has authority to complete the teaching of one of his own encyclicals as well as that of encyclicals of other Popes, since only a Pope has authority to write and to publish such a document.
>
> Another rule to observe is not to yield to the temptation of 'improving' the doctrine of the Popes. In commenting the encyclicals, many consider it their duty either to broaden the meaning of the doctrine or, more often still, to tone it down in the hope that, with a few minor adjustments, it will become more palatable to the modern mind. Generally speaking, this well-intentioned desire to better the teaching of the Popes springs from misinterpretation.[217]

---

[215] Obrien, 84-87.

[216] Ibid., 87.

[217] Etienne Gilson, *The Church Speaks to the Modern World: The Social Teachings of Leo XIII* (Garden City, NY: Image Books, 1954), 21, 22.

Gilson's hermeneutic seems to suggest that Murray may have passed legitimate bounds of interpretation, especially in light of the notable dissonance between Leo XIII's writings and Murray's interpretation when one reads both documents, or when one diagrammatically illustrates the concepts of each position (contrast Figure 2.1 with 2.2 and 2.3).

Murray's hermeneutic of doctrinal development and its internal weakness. Murray adopted the hermeneutic of doctrinal development that was first conceptualized by Henry Cardinal Newman, *Essay on the Development of Doctrine*, which postulated that,

> It was necessary to situate the doctrinal declarations of the magisterium in an historical process of progressive clarification, maturation, and adaptation as the Church proclaimed the gospel across the centuries. According to this developmentalist perspective, changes in doctrinal texts follow two complementary rules: one of continuity and one of change.[218]

Based on this hermeneutic, Murray was able to situate encyclicals such as those of Leo XIII within the larger historical context of recent popes (Leo's successors) and evaluate Leo's writings so as to balance them with the writings of his contemporaries.

Scholars pursuing the path that Murray laid out have contributed to the discussion through examining a given historic context, as well as re-evaluating foundational premises. Jeannine Hill Fletcher, in "Responding to Religious Difference: Conciliar Perspectives," adds to this discussion by noting what appear to be distinct differences in regard to salvation when comparing the Council of Trent with the Vatican II Council.[219] The former argued for *extra ecclesiam nulla salus* ("outside of the Church there is no salvation"), whereas the latter seems to adopt an inclusivist stance. She explains these apparent differences by elaborating upon what she understands are five theses for consideration.

First, through the discovery of the New World, a shift began to take place from colonization to globalization, demanding of the Church a new response to other religions with which it more frequently came into contact

---

[218] Conley, 232.

[219] Jeannine Hill Fletcher, "Responding to Religious Difference: Conciliar Perspectives," in *From Trent to Vatican II: Historical and Theological Investigations*, eds. Raymond F. Bulman and Frederick J. Parrella (New York: Oxford University Press, 2006), 267-281.

through its missionary activity. Second, by the twentieth-century, the Church had entered new territories beyond European boundaries and thus had official representatives from those countries who were present at Vatican II, and who shared their native perspectives regarding the mission of the Church among other religions. Third, due to Enlightenment emphasis upon the individual, Vatican II documents reflect concern for the dignity of the human person, with a focus upon Christian anthropology. Fletcher states, "Commitment to the dignity of the human person and recognition of historical consciousness support the document's defense of the individual's search for ultimate meaning, even when it is conditioned by a distinctive culture and its attendant religious tradition."[220] Fourth, the Church became more engaged with the world, thus demanding that salvation be viewed from a more integral approach. Fifth, just as a hard-line stance by the Church at Trent regarding intra-Church differences (i.e., Protestant views of salvation, etc.) resulted in an even more definitive stance against non-Christian religions concerning salvation, so also at Vatican II, the Church's efforts to repair the breach within Christianity has resulted in a more openness toward non-Christian religions.

Fletcher's summary of historical events is accurate, but her conclusions actually underscore the differences, not the continuity, between the period of Trent and Vatican II. Her conclusions are a prime example of what John Conley, a Jesuit scholar, refers to in his article, "Religious Freedom as Catholic Crisis":

> Despite its declared intention to develop pontifical teaching (*DH* no. 1), the declaration cites sources that fall into two distinct eras of ecclesiastic history: the pontifical writings since Leo XIII, especially since Pius IX (*DH* no. 26), and the writings of the New Testament and the early fathers of the Church (*DH* no. 33). These margins of the text are ecclesiastic history (namely, the Middle Ages and the modern period) in the reflection on religious freedom. Obviously one cannot easily integrate the pontifical condemnations of the nineteenth century in a declaration that appears to reverse the major tenor of these texts. Moreover, a contextualist reading of these condemnations risks an unconvincing interpretation of these texts that simply occults the serious ruptures in ecclesiastic teaching. If the condemnation of Pius IX aimed at the anticlerical liberals of the period, they also censured a Montalember

---

[220] Fletcher, 274, 275.

and a Lacordaire, ancestors of the Church's contemporary teaching on religious freedom. If the condemnations of Pius IX denounced subjectivism, they also clearly denounced the general principle of freedom of worship and related religious liberties.[221]

Conley identifies the central issue of weakness regarding the doctrinal development hermeneutic, *viz.*, the integral nature of the documents in question. Conley points out that if one portion of an encyclical denounces a certain error, then the other portions of the encyclical must also denounce related errors. Applying this understanding to Jeanine-Hill Fletcher's views of the Council of Trent and that of Vatican II, one concludes that they stand in distinct contrast, not harmony. Likewise, it is difficult for one to accept Murray's rationale that Pope Leo XIII only had in mind to denounce certain forms of democracy and church-state relations *without specifically stating which ones*. Thus, it would seem proper to take Leo XIII's writings as integral documents of general application, rather than specific application, as Murray suggests.

Murray's concept of apolitical Catholicism. Murray argues that Catholicism is apolitical, being able to function under any system of political governance and not having any particular one considered as ideal. From this perspective, Murray is able to develop a concept of religious freedom based on the civil right of the individual to pursue religious truth, rather than arguing from the solitary perspective of a Catholic confessional state. Murray finds support for this teaching based on Leo XIII's encyclical, *Diuturnum* (June 29, 1881) in which the pope states in article 7,

> There is no question here respecting forms of government, for there is no reason why the Church should not approve of the chief power being held by one man or by more, provided only it be just, and that it tend to the common advantage. Wherefore, so long as justice be respected, the people are not hindered from choosing for themselves that form of government which suits best either their own disposition, or the institutions and customs of their ancestors.[222]

---

[221] Conley, 235.

[222] Pope Leo XIII, *Diuturnum Illud* (June 29, 1881) as printed in Gilson, 143.

Catholic scholars even before Vatican II, such as John Ryan and Francis Boland, referred to the passage above by Pope Leo XIII, to explain how Catholicism was compatible with democracy. However, Pope Leo XIII does refute the idea common to democracy that the power of government resides in the people themselves when he denounces so-called philosophers who say "that those who exercise [power] in the State do so not as their own, but as delegated to them by the people, and that, by this rule, it can be revoked by the will of the very people by whom it was delegated. But from these Catholics dissent, who affirm that the right to rule is from God, as from a natural and necessary principle."[223]

The "so-called philosophers" to whom Leo XIII refers are such political philosophers as Hobbes, Rousseau, and Locke. In their theoretical foundation for the state, they do not include power derived from God; rather they argue from man's state of nature, which out of necessity leads him to unite with others to form a community, or *polis*. From this theory, the power comes from the people who opt to unite under a social contract.

Thus, the dilemma facing Catholicism is how to truly reconcile the concept of divine authority for political rule being invested in a political leader under a democratic form of government, and at the same time recognizing that in a democracy, it is the people who elect their political leader. Does the divine authority flow from God to the people who elect their leader? And, upon election, is that authority conferred to their leader? If it has been conferred, cannot it be revoked? Two erudite Catholic scholars – Jacques Maritain,[224] and John Courtney Murray[225] – had dedicated laborious study to the dilemma posed by such a political theory.

Although the issue of the source of political authority does not seem to

---

[223] Pope Leo XIII, *Diuturnum Illud*, par. 5 (Yates, 3).

[224] Although Jacques Maritain died in 1973, he left a legacy of books that apply Thomist principles to democracy, such as, "*Integral Humanism* (1936), *Scholasticism and Politics* (1940), *The Rights of Man and the Natural Law* (1943), and *Man and the State* (1951)." Paul E. Sigmund, "Christian Democracy," in Seymour Martin Lipset, ed., *The Encyclopedia of Democracy*, 4 vols. (Washington, D.C.: Congressional Quarterly, 1995), 1:212.

[225] John Courtney Murray's particular emphasis was upon religious plurality in a democratic modern state: "Separation of Church and State," *America* 76 (December 7, 1946), 261-263; "Separation of Church and State: True and False Concepts," *America* 76 (February 15, 1947), 541-545; cf., http://woodstock. georgetown.edu/library/Murray/0_murraybib.html for a complete on-line reference to his works.

be directly related to the issue of religious liberty in a modern democracy,[226] it actually becomes one of the central factors under consideration because of related issues of separation of church and state, religious pluralism, and a pre-determined religious moral order. With respect to separation of church and state, if divine authority comes from God to the people who elect their leaders, then some obligation rests upon those leaders in collective capacity as "government," or "state," to acknowledge at least religion, if not the Church. Regarding religious pluralism, if divine authority has been given to the collective leaders elected to office, then there must either be one true religion through which they derive their authority to rule, or some type of civil religion that embraces all religions within the state. Considering a pre-determined moral order, if elected officials in collective capacity derive their authority to rule from deity, there can be no public space for any ideology other than a religious one. Thus, despite the efforts of Murray and other Catholic scholars, a distinct dissonance remains between the historical theoretical foundations for the modern nation state and the epistemological foundations they propose in order to support the type of religious freedom espoused in *Dignitatis Humanae*.

Murray's appeal to John of Paris. Murray appeals to the model of church-state relations as written by John of Paris in *De potestate regia et papali* (*On Kingly and Papal Power*, 1302), which describes both entities with their respective spheres of responsibility. Lee Cameron McDonald summarizes the key concepts in Paris's thought:

> [Paris] defended the Aristotelian idea of the political community as the highest form of natural society, a society that could be perfected outside the sanctification of the Church. The *regnum* does not require the *sacerdotum*, even though the latter is morally superior, for the two pertain to different levels of existence.[227]

According to Paris, both derive their authority from God, and both have causality (purpose), thus making neither superior to the other.[228] From this,

---

[226] Joseph J. Baierl, *The Catholic Church and the Modern State* (Rochester, NY: St. Bernard's Seminary, 1955), 213-218.

[227] McDonald, 1:169.

[228] "In accepting the logical concept of unity as explanatory of plurality, he locates the unity outside this world, in God Himself. This enables him to give to the spheres of the temporal and spiritual positions of hierarchical equality rather than of subordination and superiority to one another. In this world the two

he concludes that each has authority within its respective sphere, and each has indirect power over the other in certain areas.[229] For example, a king, who rightly rules, can appeal to his subjects to depose a Pope who abuses his spiritual power.[230]

Based on the foregoing, Murray's appeal to John of Paris overlooks several points, which weaken his argument. First, the historic context of 1302, when Paris wrote his treatise, was when Philip of France was resisting papal demands regarding taxation and undermining subsequent papal decrees to French priests. Paris wrote his treatise in support of both royal and papal power, not solely papal power,[231] as *Dignitatis Humanae* tends to do with its focus on the right of the Church to religious freedom. In addition, Paris wrote on a topic, viz., of papal supremacy versus conciliarism, which has tended to be controversial in the history of the Church, as well as one which has not received majority support.[232] For

---

spheres are not subordinate one to the other; they are on the same plane 'causally' in that both are derivative directly from God, and not from one another." Introductory comment by Arthur P. Monahan, trans., in John of Paris, *On Royal and Papal Power* (New York: Columbia University Press, 1974), xxix.

[229] Monahan describes how John of Paris viewed civil cases in which the priesthood could judge only the rightness or wrongness of a matter, whether it was a sin or not, and had no further jurisdiction over the temporal affair in question. Monahan, Introduction, xxxiv and John of Paris, *De Potestate Regia et Papali*, chapter 13, "Jurisdiction of Prelates," article 4, 64-65.

[230] Monahan, Introduction, xxxv and John of Paris, *De Potestate Regia et Papali*, chapter 13, "Jurisdiction of Prelates," article 4, 66-69.

[231] Paris's title alone, *De Potestate Regia et Papali*, reveals something of this idea, not to mention those portions in which he cogently argues that both derive authority from God and exist causally, neither deriving authority from the other.

[232] "If these solemn decisions [of the decree *Haec sancta*, 1415] had been applied thereafter, the face of the Church would have been transformed, but the roman Curia carried on a subtle and persistent effort to render them fruitless. A new council opened in Basel in 1431. It marked the high point of the confrontation between the council and the pope. . . [After the Council of Basel], the papacy, however, rapidly took the situation in hand. It sought and obtained the support of the princes, thanks to concordats, especially on the question of benefices, and rendered the Curia more efficacious by making it a direct instrument of the government of the universal Church. Pius II (formerly a conciliarist at Basel), formulated an explicit condemnation of conciliarism through the Bull *Exsecrabilis* of 18 January, 1460. From then on papal condemnations followed one another. . ." Aldo Landi, "Conciliar Movement," in *The Papacy: An Encyclopedia*, 3 vols., ed. Philippe Levillain (New York: Routledge, 2002), 1:391.

Paris's views regarding the indirect power of the State (*regnum*) in some ecclesial affairs to stand, the subordinate papal role to a conciliar body must be conceded.

Murray's analysis, also, is one-sided, since he does not include Paris's teaching that a temporal ruler has indirect ("accidental") power over the spiritual power (the Pope), even to the point of being able to have him deposed by a conciliar council.[233] Additionally, the Church's historical record shows not a single instance of Paris's model being used whereby a Pope conceded to the indirect power of a temporal ruler.[234] Some may argue that the Emperor Constantine had jurisdiction in ecclesial affairs and, while true, history points out that it was he who assumed this power as Roman Emperor since it was his actions that conceded legal recognition to Christianity and the church in Rome.[235] Thus, the Church never conceded this power to him. Additionally, in the decades following Constantine's rule, the Church began to develop and exert the petrine doctrine of papal primacy with specific reference to the church in Rome, thereby demonstrating the Church's intent at superiority.[236]

The Challenge of Two Modern Documents on Religious Freedom

Perhaps the most challenging issue facing Progressives is how to reconcile a Roman Catholic concept of religious freedom with that of modern democratic nations, especially one like the United States of America. Murray, in his day, claimed that the two concepts were

---

[233] Anyone who reads *Dignitatis Humanae* will certainly not find this teaching in it!!

[234] Readers acquainted with European history will acknowledge this point. Although Paris refers to the two popes, Constantine II who "was deposed by the princes," and John XII who "was deposed by emperor and clergy," in neither case did these popes recognize the royal authority, and history records that later papal prelates condemned such royal presumptions, as well as conciliarism. Paris, 68. Cf., fn. 95.

[235] Walter Ullmann, *A Short History of the Papacy in the Middle Ages* (London: Methuen and Co., 1972), 5-12. Also, T. M. Parker points out that Constantine's involvement in most ecclesial affairs was merely as a figurehead, since "he was apt to listen to personal advisers among the bishops, such as Hosius, and later Eusebius of Nicomedia, and to enforce decisions arrived at by their advice." Parker, 53.

[236] Ullmann, 13-27.

compatible,[237] and other Catholic scholars claim the same, of which two are cited here: 1) Alan Schreck states that the religious freedom of *Dignitatis Humanae* "embodies the ideal of religious freedom very similar to that enumerated in the United States Constitution, including the very phrase concerning the 'free exercise of religion' that is found in the First Amendment."[238] 2) James Carrol, a Catholic scholar in residence at Suffolk University and columnist for the Boston *Globe*, believes that Murray achieved this reconciliation through *Dignitatis Humanae*:

> This Enlightenment impulse took flight in America, where "these truths" were held to be "self-evident." Such emphasis on the individual, together with corollaries like inbred rights, religious pluralism, and separation of church and state, led the Catholic Church to lump such ideas together and label them as heresy; the heresy, indeed, of "Americanism," which the Vatican condemned in 1899. . . It is not too much to say that Dignitatis Humanae was the Catholic embrace of Americanism.[239]

While Carrol makes the broad assertion for compatibility between "Americanism" and *Dignitatis Humanae*, his statement also reveals a core issue – the influence of Enlightenment thought upon the American Founding – for which another Catholic scholar, Michael Sean Winters, contends the two are incompatible.

Winters clearly identifies the central difficulty inherent to such an endeavor as allowing freedom of conscience in religious matters – with the resulting possibility of atheism, or agnosticism – and avoiding the (inevitable?) development of laicism. He states:

---

[237] "Murray, in fact, affirmed that Vatican II's *Declaration on Religious Liberty* came unambiguously from the same political tradition as the American Constitution and the First Amendment. 'It [the Vatican II *Declaration on Religious Liberty*] is an important endorsement, therefore, of the Anglo-Saxon political tradition which is the tradition of the United States.'" O'Brien quoting John Courtney Murray, 18.

[238] Schreck, 221.

[239] James Carrol, "The Americanist heresy: When should dogma bow to experience?" in the Boston *Globe*, http://www.boston.com/bostonglobe/ideas/articles/2009/04/19/the_american_heresy/? page=1 (and 2 and 3), (accessed April 20, 2009).

The (Vatican II) Council fathers were concerned about laicism, a concern that obviously did not animate the founding fathers (of America), steeped as they were in decidedly anti-Catholic ideas about religion and its relationship to the state. And, John Courtney Murray, great though he was, could not achieve for the Enlightenment what Aquinas achieved for Aristotle, a synthesis that resolved the difficult issues. No one has yet done so. I readily confess that it will take a greater mind than mine to forge such a synthesis. But, I think sufficient time has passed that we must ask the question whether or not the failure to achieve a synthesis might be because no such synthesis can be achieved.[240]

Not only does Winter's candid evaluation of *Dignitatis Humanae* pose one of the central issues (inability to synthesize them), but also one must consider five other areas that justify why this book adopts the position of incompatibility between *Dignitatis Humanae* and the religion clauses of the First Amendment to the American Constitution, a position that is not alone in the realm of academia.[241]

---

[240] Michael Sean Winters, "MSW replies to Fr. Komonchak," *National Catholic Reporter*, Sept. 21, 2011, http://ncronline.org/blogs/distinctly-catholic/msw-replies-fr-komonchak (accessed November 12, 2011).

[241] "On more than one occasion Murray seems to misread the intellectual history of Western culture. One example of this misreading is Murray's problematic notion that American political philosophy was in continuity with what he referred to as the 'Christian tradition of civility.' Recently, some Murray scholars, like Peter Augustine Lawler, have been critical of Murray's belief that the American founders were devotees of a Thomistic natural law. Murray made this assertion on the grounds of certain references in the Declaration of Independence to "Nature's God" and "the Creator." However, according to Lawler, "'Nature's God,' interpreted in the light of Jefferson's thought as a whole, is actually the God of the secular philosophers. The phrase has an antirevelationist and even anticreationist connotation." Lawler's observations are indispensable to understanding the problematic nature of Murray's misreading of history because they effectively invalidate one of Murray's important 'proofs from the historical record.'" O'Brien, 15, 16; Peter Augustine Lawler, "Murray's Natural-Law Articulation of the American Proposition," in *John Courtney Murray and the American Civil Conversation*, eds. Robert P. Hunt and Kenneth L. Grasso (Grand Rapids, MI: Eerdman's, 1992), 116-134; David T. Mason, "Animadversions on John Courtney Murray's Political Ontology," ibid., 135-163.

Distinct foundational principles. There are several foundational principles that mark distinct differences between Murray's *Dignitatis Humanae* and the First Amendment religion clauses. The foundational document to which the First Amendment has been added, the Constitution, has no transcendental point of reference.[242] While mentioning "religion" in Article 6, the intent behind this article is to emphasize the civil nature of congressional office, without taking into account a candidate's religious background.[243] Thus, rather than endorsing religion, Article 6 adopts a neutral stance: whether a candidate is religious or irreligious should not be of significance since the office is a secular, or civil, one.

The reference to "religion" in the First Amendment is generic in nature, not being derived from any particular religion. Although Baptists were influential in the formulation of Madison's thoughts regarding both clauses,[244] Madison was also influenced by Jefferson, who was a nominal Anglican, Unitarian in belief, and a *philosophe*, or "free-thinker" (deist).[245] When one examines the intellectual and philosophical influences that contributed to Jefferson's thoughts on religious freedom, five French philosophers – Pierre Bayle, Charles Louis Montesquieu, Jean Jacques Rousseau, Marie Jean de Condorcet, and Francois Marie de Voltaire – made the most significant impact.[246] Bayle argued passionately for freedom of

---

[242] "Charles A. Beard, the American historian, says: 'The Constitution is a purely *secular* document. It does not confer upon the federal government any power whatever to deal with religion in any form or manner.' The Constitution contains no invocation to God, nor even mention of God; and the only mention of religion in it is to forbid Congress to establish it by law or to interfere with its free exercise." Joseph Martin Dawson, *America's Way in Church, State, and Society* (New York: Macmillan, 1953), 22.

[243] Ronald B. Flowers, *That Godless Court? Supreme Court decisions on Church-State Relationships* (Louisville, KY: Westminster John Knox Press, 2005), 16.

[244] "The absence of protection for religious freedom was particularly noted. The Baptist General Committee, for example, announced opposition to the proposed Constitution solely because it had not 'made sufficient provision for the secure enjoyment of religious liberty.'" Michael W. McConnell, John H. Garvey, and Thomas C. Berg, *Religion and the Constitution* (New York: Aspen Publishers, 2002), 72.

[245] Edwin S. Gaustad, *Sworn on the Altar of God* (Grand Rapids, MI: Eerdmans, 1996), 25.

[246] Anson Phelps Stokes, *Church and State in the United States*, 3 vols. (New York: Harper & Bros., 1950), 1:134-136.

thought for all men, going so far as to utilize skepticism to erode religious dogma for the sake of promoting toleration.[247] Ruth Whelan describes his views on "toleration" as "the most radical of his day, surpassing those of Locke, for example, in their commitment to a constitutionally guaranteed freedom of conscience without exception and, by implication, a plurality of institutions held together by reciprocal toleration."[248]

John Locke was the most notable Enlightenment philosopher who influenced the thought of James Madison and Thomas Jefferson.[249] He argued for religious toleration, but also denied the same toward Catholics and atheists.[250] This raises the question, then, how did Madison formulate the "free exercise" clause with the intent to provide legal guarantees to freedom of conscience – for religionists, as well as non-religionists – a position similar to that of Bayle?[251] It could not have been from Locke, as noted above. History shows that Jefferson's Bill for Establishing Religious Freedom (1777), which was not passed at the time, found later expression through Madison's *Memorial and Remonstrance* (1785).[252] It would seem that Jefferson, who had been influenced by the French *philosophes*, had shared some of his views with Madison.[253]

---

[247] Ruth Whelan, article "Bayle, Pierre," in Alan Charles Kors, ed. in chief, *Encyclopedia of the Enlightenment*, 4 vols. (New York: Oxford University Press, 2003), 1:123-124.

[248] Ibid., 124.

[249] Stokes, 1:141.

[250] Ibid., 1:145, citing John Locke, *Letters Concerning Toleration* (1765), 58-60.

[251] Madison's original proposal stated, "Congress shall make no law establishing religion, or prohibiting the free exercise thereof; nor shall the rights of conscience be infringed." The Senate modified the wording and struck the final phrase, producing what finally became the religion clauses of the First Amendment. Robert S. Alley, ed., *The Constitution and Religion* (Amherst, NY: Prometheus Books, 1999), 25. Madison's original wording distinguishes between religion and "the rights of conscience," suggesting an appeal to the "free-thinking" French philosophers of the Enlightenment tradition (see fn. 253).

[252] Gaustad, 55-59.

[253] Edwin Gaustad notes that while Jefferson was in France as an emissary in 1785, he bought books for Madison on a variety of subjects dealing with "all treatises on the ancient or modern federal republics, 'on the law of nations, and the history natural and political of the New World.'" Views of the French *philosophes*,

From this historic background, the First Amendment religion clauses reflect more of an emphasis upon philosophical guarantees to religious freedom based upon Enlightenment thought, as well as political practicalities, rather than transcendental guarantees, such as that found in *Dignitatis Humanae*, which describes religious freedom from a specifically Roman Catholic moral order.[254]

Government not to pro-actively support religion. The historic background to the Bill of Rights indicates that the intent behind its passage was to restrict the power of government (Congress), rather than empowering it in religious matters.[255] Regarding the First Amendment religion clauses, Congress was neither to pass legislation establishing religion, or prohibiting its free exercise. Madison formulated those clauses with a parallel to the principles in his *Memorial and Remonstrance*, which played a central role in the debate for religious freedom in Virginia before the General Assembly, and which laid the foundation for the American concept of Church-State separation and religious freedom.[256] F. Russell Hittinger, a Catholic scholar, contrasts Madison's *Memorial and Remonstrance* with *Dignitatis Humanae*:

---

who appealed to "nature and reason," are echoed in Madison's arguments in support of the *Memorial and Remonstrance* (1785), as Gaustad remarks, "Like his Monticello neighbor, Madison found succor and support in the appeal to Reason and to Nature. Religion can be 'directed only by reason and conviction, not by force or violence.' The right of every person to exercise his or her conscience in this realm 'is in its nature an unalienable right.'" Gaustad, 19, 59.

[254] *Dignitatis Humanae*, Article 3; Cf., Philip S. Denenfeld declared, "At this point it may be necessary for me to state that I am not criticizing the Vatican Council declaration for failing to do what it never intended to do, agree with the Bill of Rights. It is, after all, a statement of one faith, not all, and directed to an entire world, not a single nation. My concern, rather, is that its impact on American life, Catholic and non-Catholic, could be divisive because of what I think is its basic contradiction of our concept of religious freedom." "The Conciliar Declaration and the American Declaration," in *Religious Liberty: an End and a Beginning*, ed. John Courtney Murray (New York: Macmillan, 1966), 123.

[255] Flowers, 16; Leo Pfeffer, "Religious Liberty," in *The First Amendment: Selections from the Encyclopedia of the American Constitution*, eds. Leonard W. Levy, Kenneth L. Karst, and Dennis J. Mahoney (New York: MacMillan, 1990), 440.

[256] "The struggle which took place in Virginia in its last days as a colony and its early days as a state needs special attention, as it influenced the American theories of Church-State separation and religious freedom more than any other historical factor." Stokes, 1:366.

In his *Memorial and Remonstrance*, for example, James Madison insisted that 'Religion is wholly exempt from its [government's] cognizance.' *Dignitatis Humanae*, articles 5-6, on the other hand, contends that government has an obligation to promote the free exercise of religion.[257]

Hittinger correctly assesses the difference between both documents, but fails to mention that *Dignitatis Humanae*, however, obligates government to pro-actively support religion, *with a special regard for Roman Catholicism*.[258]

Broader rights to religion versus narrower rights. In general, the First Amendment religion clauses do not place a restriction upon religion. As the Supreme Court has adjudicated religious cases, there is the obvious restraint upon religious action that is deemed harmful to society, but no restriction upon religious belief.[259] The latter point bears particularly upon the sharp distinction between the "free exercise" clause and *Dignitatis Humanae*, which does not allow for freedom of conscience apart from a religious mooring. *Dignitatis Humanae* grants religious freedom with its corresponding obligation to "seek for religious truth," and once finding it, "to adhere to it."[260] In addition, *Dignitatis Humanae* does not address the issue of an "erroneous conscience,"[261] i.e., one that does not accept Roman Catholicism. By virtue of its silence regarding an "erroneous conscience," and in light of its clear declaration regarding the rights of a religiously-

---

[257] Hittinger, 367.

[258] "Even if the Church warmly salutes the defense of religious freedom in international accords (DH no. 15), the articulation, the foundations, the limits, and the practical implications of this right in *Dignitatis Humanae* remain specifically Christian and Catholic." Conley, 236.

[259] "Although the First Amendment's mandate that 'Congress shall make no law respecting an establishment of religion, or prohibiting the free exercise thereof' is expressed in unconditional language, religious liberty, insofar as it extends beyond belief, is not an absolute right. The First Amendment, the Supreme Court said in *Cantwell v. Connecticut* (1940), 'embraces two concepts – freedom to believe and freedom to act. The first is absolute but, in the nature of things, the second cannot be. Conduct remains subject to regulation of society." Pfeffer, "Religious Liberty," 439.

[260] *Dignitatis Humanae*, Art. 2, par. 3.

[261] "Thus it is clear that the problems of the true or the erroneous conscience are not touched on at all in the document." Pavan, Commentary, 66.

oriented conscience, it is obvious that *Dignitatis Humanae* does not uphold freedom of conscience apart from a religious orientation (i.e., freedom to disbelieve), as John Courtney Murray points out:

> It is worth noting that the Declaration does not base the right to the free exercise of religion on "freedom of conscience." Nowhere does this phrase occur. And the Declaration nowhere lends its authority to the theory for which the phrase frequently stands, namely, that I have the right to do what my conscience tells me to do, simply because my conscience tells me to do it. This is a perilous theory. Its particular peril is subjectivism – the notion that, in the end, it is my conscience, and not the objective truth, which determines what is right or wrong, true or false.[262]

Murray's description of "freedom of conscience," against which he argues, seems to distort the historic context of the free exercise clause. Madison formulated it with the intent to protect the "freedom of conscience" of the individual, which was based on convictions derived from religious sources, as well as Deistic notions regarding God.[263] From this historical perspective, it would be wholly proper for one to follow one's conscience *freely*, in belief and action, as one was convicted to do, even if this should be expressed as disbelief.[264]

---

[262] Murray, comments on *Dignitatis Humanae*, art. 2, regarding the "right to religious freedom" in *The Documents of Vatican II*, ed. Abbot, 679.

[263] "Between the third and fourth paragraphs of Article I, section 9, [Madison] proposed to add the following provisions: 'The civil rights of none shall be abridged on account of religious belief or worship, nor shall any national religion be established, *nor shall the full and equal rights of conscience be in any manner, or on any pretext, infringed.*'" "Madison proposed adding between the first and second paragraphs of Article I, section 10, *a provision prohibiting the states from violating the equal rights of conscience*, the freedom of the press, or the right of trial by jury in criminal cases." (italics mine) Richard L. Perry, ed., *Sources of Our Liberties: Documentary Origins of Individual Liberties in the United States Constitution and Bill of Rights* (Chicago: American Bar Foundation, 1978), 422, 423. Although this exact phrasing was not incorporated into the "free exercise" clause, Madison's intent becomes obvious.

[264] "The Supreme Court has consistently held that freedom of religious belief is absolutely protected by the free exercise clause and that this protection extends to disbelief as well. Thus, the government is categorically precluded from mandating, prohibiting, or regulating religious or irreligious beliefs as such. In *Torcaso v. Watkins* (1961), for example, the Supreme Court invalidated a religious

The scope of application. The First Amendment religion clauses grant a much broader guarantee of religious freedom since they do not address the individual as the primary agent. Rather, government is the focal point, and it is a restriction of its power. The individual is only the corollary recipient of government restriction. This leaves religious organizations and individuals free to pursue (or not) religious truths as their conscience dictates (provided such pursuits do not lead to violations of the law). In contrast, since *Dignitatis Humanae* focuses upon the civil rights of the individual, specifying such rights as the right to seek religious truth, to embrace it, and making reference to "the one true religion subsisting in the Roman Catholic Church," it is much narrower in its application. It seems to imply that the individual has the right to pursue religious truth with the end objective of becoming Roman Catholic.[265]

The presupposition of an entity with authority to coerce. The restrictions placed upon government under the religion clauses of the First Amendment do not assume that government is coercive in nature, generally speaking (apart from those instances when religious practice is harmful to society). The First Amendment religion clauses state, "Congress shall make no law respecting an establishment of religion, or prohibiting the free exercise thereof." Madison initially did not want to even include the Bill of Rights, of which the religion clauses were originally the third amendment and not

---

oath requirement for state office holders, thereby reading the free exercise clause to mirror Article 6 of the original Constitution, which explicitly bans such religious tests, but only for federal offices. "[N]either a State nor the Federal Government," wrote the Court, "can constitutionally force a person 'to profess a belief or disbelief in any religion.'" As *Torcaso* suggests, the free exercise clause protects not only the right to hold religious or irreligious beliefs, but also the right to state them publicly or, conversely, to refuse to do so." Daniel O. Conkle, article "Free Exercise Clause," in *Encyclopedia of Religious Freedom*, ed. Catharine Cookson (New York: Routledge, 2003), 137.

[265] Pietro Pavan distinguishes between the transcendental sphere, upon which the traditional Catholic doctrine of religious freedom was based, and the civil right to religious freedom, as contained in *Dignitatis Humanae*, which is religious freedom only among people in society. He notes that, with this distinction, the traditional Catholic doctrine remains unchanged: "According to the schema under consideration God has revealed that the way to salvation is to be found in the only true religion which is the Catholic Church... It follows from this that just as there is an obligation to seek for truth and to accept it according to one's certainty, so there is also the obligation to accept and profess the Catholic religion as soon as, and in so far as, it is known. *Hence it is an obligation which concerns and binds the conscience, because truth binds only in virtue of its own light.*" Pavan, 58.

the first,[266] because he feared that by an enumeration of restricted powers, one might infer that Congress had other non-enumerated powers.[267] After lengthy correspondence between Madison and Jefferson, who was in France at the time of the ratification of the Constitution, Madison conceded to Jefferson's insistence that the Bill of Rights should be included in the Constitution.[268] Although both political erudites initially differed on the inclusion of the Bill of Rights, their underlying rationale was the same: Madison did not wish to give the impression of Congress having certain powers beyond those which had been enumerated, and Jefferson wished to leave no doubts regarding the limitations resting upon the powers of Congress through the explicit enumeration of such limitations.[269] Therefore, one may conclude that for Madison, Congress had no powers in religious matters, and therefore any enumerations of restrictions were unnecessary. Jefferson, whose emphasis upon democratic principles reflected his concerns "of tyrannical infection in centralized power" (Congress),[270] certainly did not believe in conceding powers in religious matters to Congress.[271] He did not operate from the premise that Congress had powers in religious matters and, thus, needed the Bill of Rights to restrain it. Rather, he feared a corruption of Congress, which could lead to religious oppression. For this reason, he firmly insisted on a Bill of Rights that would clearly identify the rights of the people, even in the event that Congress should become corrupt. Thus, one cannot argue, or presume that

---

[266] Alley, 24.

[267] Lenni Brenner, ed., *Jefferson and Madison on Separation of Church and State: Writings on Religion and Secularism* (Fort Lee, NJ: Barricade Books Inc., 2004), 67. Cf. Alexander Hamilton, The Federalist No. 84, "I go further, and affirm that bills of rights, in the sense and in the extent in which they are contended for, are not only unnecessary to the proposed constitution, but would even be dangerous. They would contain various exceptions to powers which are not granted; and on this very account, would afford a colourable pretext to claim more than were granted. For why declare that things shall not be done which there is no power to do?" as cited in John P. Kaminski and Richard Leffler, *Creating the Constitution* (Action, MA: Copley Publishing Group, 1999), 232.

[268] Adrienne Koch, *Jefferson & Madison: The Great Collaboration* (London: Oxford University Press, 1976), 33-61.

[269] Ibid., 40, 41, 54, 55.

[270] Ibid., 44.

[271] Gaustad, 181-209.

Madison or Jefferson conceptualized of a *properly* functioning Congress that had powers to coerce in religious matters.

By contrast, Murray viewed these clauses as "immunities from coercion." From this interpretation, he incorporated the same view into *Dignitatis Humanae* attempting to pattern what he believed to be the teaching in those clauses.[272] However, by the phrase used in *Dignitatis Humanae*, "immunity from coercion," the implication is that government, or some entity, has the power to coerce. Thus, the individual needs a civil right by which he is granted immunity from that coercive power. The implications of Murray's views on this point will be explored in detail in chapter three.

Based on the foregoing five points, it becomes evident that Murray either tended to interpret the First Amendment religion clauses from a Catholic perspective, or that he understood them from their correct historical perspective as a product of Enlightenment thought, but failed to fully synthesize them with a Catholic, objective, moral order. Whichever the case may be, the religious freedom guarantees as reflected in *Dignitatis Humanae* do not pattern the true intent behind the First Amendment religion clauses.

Another modern document on religious freedom that does not resonate with *Dignitatis Humanae* is the U.N. Declaration of Human Rights (hereafter, UNDHR), which was crafted through the contributions of Catholicism, Communism, Hinduism, Greek Orthodoxy, and Confucianism.[273] Since its intent was to be a universal declaration, it appropriately needed to reflect the contributions of a multi-cultural world. To achieve this end, the drafters of the U. N. Declaration opted for certain ideas of Enlightenment thought. Especially in a sensitive area such as religion and belief, the drafters of Article 18 sought to provide as broad a platform as possible for accommodating the variety of world religions and ideologies. Thus, dependence upon Enlightenment ideas of morality[274] is reflected not only in

---

[272] "In guaranteeing the free exercise of religion, the First Amendment guarantees to the American citizen immunity from all coercion in matters religious." Murray, comments on the Declaration of Religious Freedom, in *The Documents of Vatican II*, ed. Abbott, 678.

[273] Paul Marshall, "Religious Freedom and the United Nations' Universal Declaration of Human Rights," in *Fifty Years After the Declaration: The United Nations' Record on Human Rights*, eds. Teresa Wagner and Leslie Carbone (Lanham, MD: University Press of America, 2001), 2.

[274] Johannes Morsink, *The Universal Declaration of Human Rights: Origins, Drafting, and Intent* (Philadelphia, PA: University of Pennsylvania Press, 1999), 281-282.

Article 18 ("Everyone has the right to freedom of thought, conscience and religion"), but also in the first recital of the preamble ("inherent dignity. . . equal and inalienable rights. . .") and Article 1 ("All human beings are born free and equal in dignity and rights. They are endowed with reason and conscience. . ."). Identification of the link between Enlightenment thought and the UNDHR facilitates the most accurate understanding of the term "conscience" as used in Article 18.

Perhaps the greatest contribution of Enlightenment thought was the formulation of a schema for a universal morality that at the same time was secular.[275] Such a novel idea was ideal when considered against the backdrop of the bloody religious wars that had resulted from a more integral association of religion and morality for the ordering of society. In Enlightenment thought, the idea of the Creator-God who was somewhat distant from His creation, yet who chose to reveal Himself through Nature and Reason, provided a more appealing, less dogmatic schema for societal governance. Those who drafted the U. N. Declaration adopted this philosophic schema, but advanced it a step further.

Recognizing that some of the world's population was atheistic (Communist countries), those formulating the UNDHR chose not to use any term with reference to deity, such as God or Creator as were common in Enlightenment thought. They also broadened the traditional idea of religious protection to include the terms "conscience" and "thought." This decision was much more inclusive and allowed conservative religionists to view conscience in Article 18 as conscientious convictions they held and, at the same time, atheists could affirm it while being assured of equal protection.

Another fundamental shift that occurred in the drafting of the UNDHR was in the concept of natural law. In its medieval conception, natural law emphasized the obligations of man in an objective moral order, much like that envisioned by Thomas Aquinas. Under this system, the state took on a paternalistic attitude toward its citizens, even to the point of concerning itself with their eternal welfare. However, Enlightenment thinkers of the eighteenth-century, such as John Locke,[276] altered the concept of natural law to one that stressed the rights of man and individual conscience. The state, through a social contract, then became merely an agent of its

---

[275] Morsink, 282.

[276] Wilson Ober Clough, *Intellectual Origins of American National Thought: Pages from the Books Our Founding Fathers Read* (New York, NY: Corinth Books, 1961), 148.

citizens.[277] Locke referred to this concept as "the law of nature" rather than the former natural law tradition. Under this system, the rights of the individual citizen were protected from an oppressive state on the one hand, and from the moral dogmatism of religion on the other.[278]

The formulation of the UNDHR took Locke's concept one step further.[279] Rather than employing the term "natural rights" as Locke did, they opted for the term "human rights." Their rationale was based on the need to distance their concept from the deistic element that formed a subtle part of Enlightenment thought. In order to embrace the atheistic element of the world community, they grounded "human rights" in "the dignity of the human person." Thus, the UNDHR may correctly be viewed as a secular document that seeks to neither endorse, nor deny the existence of God. It is a document that offers grounds for the protection of the individual who either adopts a theistic worldview, or a non-theistic worldview.[280]

Due to the influence of Enlightenment thought upon the religion clauses of the First Amendment to the U. S. Constitution, and upon the UNDHR Art. 18, there exist distinct areas of incompatibility between these modern documents on religious freedom and the religious freedom espoused in *Dignitatis Humanae*. To further highlight those differences, the Madisonian Separatist Model, based upon the points that have been given to establish Madison's intent behind the religion clauses of the First Amendment (Madison's concept of Church-State relations), is best illustrated in Figure 2.4 below. When one compares this Model with the Catholic Traditionalist Model (Paternalistic Model) in Figure 2.1, and with the Vatican II Model of *Dignitatis Humanae* (Public Church Model) in Figure 2.3, the obvious differences become apparent.

---

[277] John Mclaren and Harold Coward, eds., *Religious Conscience, the State, and the Law: Historical Contexts and Contemporary Significance* (New York, NY: State University of New York Press, 1999), 46-47.

[278] Ernst Cassirer, *The Philosophy of the Enlightenment* (Boston, MA: Beacon Press, 1962), 239.

[279] Morsink, section 8.1, "A Bargain About God and Nature," 283-290.

[280] Bahiyyih G. Tahzib, *Freedom of Religion or Belief: Ensuring Effective International Legal Protection* (The Hague, Netherlands: Martinus Nijhoff Publishers, 1996), 3.

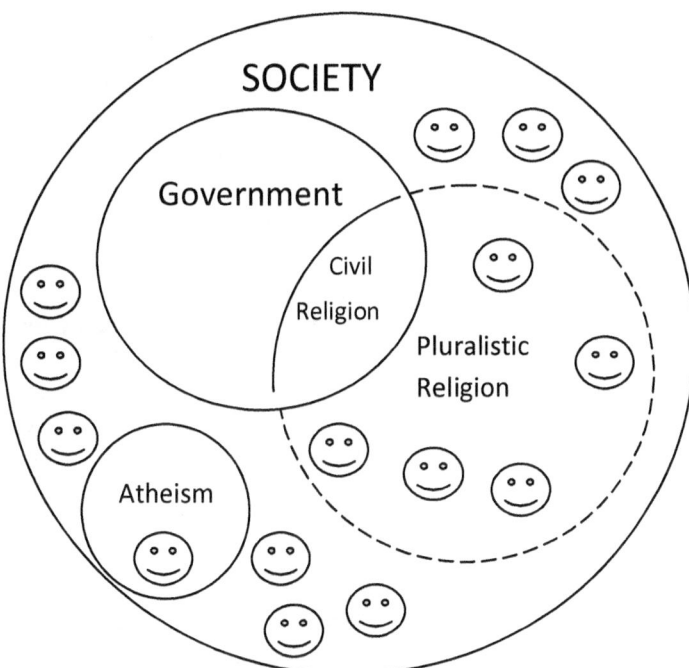

Figure 2.4. Pluralistically Separatist Model (Madisonian Model) – Religion is symbolized with a permeable sphere to indicate that it can interact within society, but it is not mandated by government.

1. Religion has no direct impact on government. Neither does government directly support religion, patterned more upon a "separationist" model. Areas of overlap, such as congressional chaplains, national days of prayer, etc., may be considered as "civil religion."
2. Atheism is symbolized with a non-permeable sphere because the First Amendment is pre-disposed to religion, *but is not pro-actively religious*, thus allowing non-believers to exist and express their views in society.
3. Government serves as a Neutral Arbiter among religious groups.
4. Thus, a religiously pre-disposed society under law is created based on religious pluralism and freedom of conscience (free to not believe).
5. Tolerance for any religious group, including atheists, is not even an issue since all are guaranteed the freedom of conscience to believe according to the dictates of conscience, or to not believe.

Roman Catholic Hegemony and Internal Debate

Although both Traditionalists and Progressives existed in the Church at the time of Vatican II, it has only been since the 1990s that the intensity of debate has increased enough for scholars to examine the document in light of contemporary circumstances. Their conclusions demonstrate that the least that can be said about *Dignitatis Humanae* is that it has produced change within the Church – whether for good or bad, depends upon the group making the evaluation. Perhaps the most notable change evident from the document is that it disallowed outright Catholic hegemony under the current preponderance of democracy in many countries of the world. The traditional, historic position, without doubt, aggressively established Catholicism as the religion of the state, with the state being subject to the Church. Under that system, there was no question as to the hegemonic nature of the Church.

However, how does the current debate within the Church on the topic of Catholicism and religious freedom within the context of a pluralistic democracy reflect upon the issue of hegemony? From the perspective of Traditionalists, their stance clearly reveals *that hegemonic sentiments still exist within the Church*. Based on their position, democratic society ultimately cannot exist without religion, and must therefore reject all forms of liberalism and laicism. Hypothetically, from their viewpoint, if given the opportunity, every country should become a Catholic confessional state.

From the Progressive's perspective, there have been numerous public statements by the Vatican hierarchy, as well as by the various popes since 1965 – Pope John XXIII, Pope Paul VI, Pope John Paul II, and Pope Benedict XVI – arguing for religious freedom, even to the point of being unwilling to negate, refute, or deny the religious freedom promulgated by the Church in *Dignitatis Humanae*. If one assumes that the type of religious freedom inherent to the Document is the same, or similar, to that contained in the First Amendment to the U.S. Constitution, or to that declared in Article 18 of the U. N. Declaration of Human Rights, then one may conclude that the Church is truly a modern champion of religious freedom.

However, since both the First Amendment and Article 18 are based upon Enlightenment concepts of the law of nature, the dissonant relationship between them and *Dignitatis Humanae* becomes apparent. Historically speaking, the First Amendment resonates with Jeffersonian Deistic undertones, and Article 18 advanced those Enlightenment deistic concepts to the next level in order to embrace the widest possible sphere of religious diversity spanning the globe, making the Article acceptable to the large majority of religious and atheistic groups who formulated it.

In contrast to Enlightenment deistic notions, *Dignitatis Humanae* is established upon a particular religious viewpoint reflecting a Catholic, objective, moral order. Although Murray masterfully designed *Dignitatis Humanae* to pattern, at least in some respects, the First Amendment religion clauses, he fell short of truly reconciling a Catholic concept of religious freedom with that of Enlightenment thought. Not only a lay Catholic, Michael Sean Winters, but also two Catholic scholars, Kenneth L. Grasso and Robert P. Hunt, openly acknowledge that *Dignitatis Humanae* is not founded upon Enlightenment thought.[281] Rather, *Dignitatis Humanae* rejects such notions of freedom of conscience that would allow one to disbelieve, which are inherent to Enlightenment thought of the French *philosophes* tradition. The worldview of *Dignitatis Humanae* is overtly religious in nature, clearly defining the parameters of conscience within the realm of belief in deity, and more specifically, identifying the one true religion as that of the Roman Catholic Church. Thus, when addressing the concept of Catholic hegemony, based upon the dissonance between *Dignitatis Humanae* and modern documents of religious freedom, it can be argued that *Dignitatis Humanae* is indeed hegemonic in nature.

Perhaps a more overt indication of Catholic hegemony is illustrated by Murray's appeal to the model of John of Paris. Murray is selective regarding which parts of Paris's model to emphasize in the Public Church model birthed from Vatican II. Paris argued for a concept of exclusivist power belonging to two entities, Church and State, which also included a minimalist "accidental/indirect" power by which each could influence the other. Murray only presents half of this dynamic, focusing upon the responsibility of the State to promote the spiritual mission of the Church, and the Church proclaiming its freedom of religion to fulfill that mission. He does not include the indirect power of the State to influence ecclesial affairs, resulting in a definite demonstration of Catholic hegemony.

Another dimension of the debate regarding Catholic hegemony and the contentious views of both Traditionalists and Progressives needs consideration. Under the Pre-Vatican II concept of Church-State relations, the Church focused its efforts at control of the state through the argument of the state's divine origin. Consequently, the Church easily justified its influence over the state, identifying itself as a divine institution with more civil clout due to its salvific mission, which had transcendental, eternal results.

In the modern political age, the preponderance of democracy demands of the Church a change in its approach, but not a change in its hegemonic nature. Under a democratic system, the nexus of power lies with the people. Naturally, the Church shifts its focus from direct control of the

---

[281] Kenneth L. Grasso and Robert P. Hunt, eds., *Catholicism and Religious Freedom: Contemporary Reflections on Vatican II's Declaration on Religious Liberty* (New York: Rowman and Littlefield Publishers, Inc., 2006), xvi.

state, to the agents who drive it. Thus, the Vatican II approach reveals the Public Church Model, in harmony with *Gaudium et spes*, by which the Church does not become directly involved in politics, as European history so vividly records; rather, the Church now seeks to influence public opinion through reasoning, rational arguments, and the influence of natural law theory. The Church persuades the moral consciences of men, now living in an enlightened period of conscientiousness, and through these political agents, eventually molds public policy to reflect a Catholic moral order. Through this approach, there is no need for direct control of the state, since the citizenry, being enlightened, form political action coalitions, lobbying groups, and turn out for vote on moral issues.

Under this rubric, *Dignitatis Humanae* is ideally crafted to grant religious freedom to the Church to teach and declare moral truth within society, or "the public square," to quote the late Richard John Neuhaus. The Document undercuts any notion of liberal, atheistic elements by arguing for a governmentally-sponsored, pro-active support of religion, bearing in mind that among religious bodies, the Church must be preeminent. Should this societal construct ever dominate a given nation, there remains the underlying question within the sphere of religious freedom regarding the role of the Church toward the conscientious convictions of rejecters of religion, non-Catholic Christians, non-Christians, and dissenting Catholics. The following chapter, thus, addresses "*Dignitatis Humanae*, Conscience, and Coercion."

DIGNITATIS HUMANAE, CONSCIENCE, AND COERCION

During the Presidential election of 2004, the Democratic candidate was Senator John Kerry. While on campaign, he was asked regarding his stance on abortion by the Dubuque (Iowa) *Telegraph Herald*, on July 4. He responded, "I oppose abortion, personally. I don't like abortion. I believe that life does begin at conception. I can't take my Catholic belief, my article of faith, and legislate it on a Protestant, or a Jew, or an atheist." For such a response, he "received an official warning to be excommunicated for heresy, but never actually was."[282] Regarding discussion of the issue by some of the leading Roman Catholic Bishops in America, Monsignor McElroy commented,

> *The denial of the Eucharist to political leaders who support abortion legislation will inevitably be perceived by Americans, Catholic and non-Catholic alike, as coercive.* . . . *It does not matter that eucharistic sanctions would be fully within the legitimate moral and civil rights of the church to adopt, and that those who have attacked them as a violation of the separation of church and state are totally in error in their understanding of the constitutional tradition of the United States.* What does matter enormously is that Americans will in general recoil from the use of the Eucharist as a political weapon, and will reassess their overall opinion of the

---

[282] From website dedicated to John Kerry's political views, under section four, "Stance on Social Issues," sub-section 4.1, "Abortion," http://www.rtbot.net/John_Kerry_presidential_campaign,_2004 #Abortion (accessed March 11, 2012).

church's role in the political order. Not only will sanctions not increase support for pro-life legislation; they will also undermine support for the church's entire effort to bring Gospel values to the structures and policies of American government and society.[283]

Msrg. McElroy indicates by this statement that Eucharistic sanctions, in principle, are fully valid within the moral and civil rights of the Church, but as a matter of expediency, they should not be enforced. Stated otherwise, the ecclesial authority of the Church over its members, through Eucharistic sanctions, while wholly valid, should not be exercised in order to avoid damage to the public appearance of the Church in the American context.

Although the debate on this issue has diminished since that election cycle, the issue nonetheless highlights an area of concern regarding the role of the Catholic Church in those countries that function under a constitutional democracy which protects religious freedom and which advocates for separation of church and state. This chapter will examine the delicate interaction between conscience, religious and irreligious conviction, and coercion within the complexity of religious freedom advocated in *Dignitatis Humanae*. The first section develops a biblical concept of conscience and toleration as the standard by which to evaluate the interaction of both ideas, such as the act of belief in God, as well as the development of conscientious convictions, and toleration of the same. Protestant and Catholic ideas of conscience and toleration have some similarities, but also notable differences, which will be explored in sections two and three of this chapter. The final section is dedicated to analysis of the differences between the pre-Vatican II concept of toleration and the Vatican II idea of "immunity from coercion."

A Biblical Concept of Conscience[284] *and Toleration*

The Greek term for "conscience" (συνείδησις) derives from the two Greek words σύν (meaning "together with") and οἶδα (meaning "I know").

---

[283] Msgr. Robert W. McElroy, "Prudence and Eucharistic Sanctions," *America*, January 31, 2005, http://www.americamagazine.org/content/article.cfm?article_id=3982 (accessed December 8, 2010), second set of italics are mine. Other Bishops said they would refuse to offer Communion to Kerry.

[284] The portion of this section that deals with conscience first appeared in an article I wrote. Edwin Cook, "Conscience in the New Testament," in *Journal of the Adventist Theological Society*, 15/1 (Spring 2004): 142–158; http://www.atsjats.org/publication_file.php?pub_id=12&journal=1&type=pdf.

Thus, the term συνείδησις literally means "I know together with".[285] As used in Greek society, it usually was limited in application to those cases that involved civic or societal relationships and was rarely used in reference to an individual alone.[286]

Despite the limited application found in non-biblical Greek literature, the usage of the term συνείδησις as found in the New Testament allows for a more comprehensive application, especially in relation to the believer and God. *Significantly, Paul's usage of the term emphasizes the individual.* The term "conscience" is used 30 times in the New Testament and the verb form (σύνοιδα), meaning "I know together with," is used four times. For the purposes of this chapter, only select passages employing the term "conscience" will be used which have a direct bearing on its role in the act of faith and the development of religious freedom concepts.

Acts 23:1

"And Paul, earnestly beholding the council, said, Men and brethren, I have lived in all good conscience before God until this day."

In order to better understand the significance of Acts 23:1, it is necessary to briefly recount the events that preceded it. The historical context of this occasion[287] reveals that Paul had entered the temple the day before, to complete the days of purification according to Jewish law. Several of the Jews from Asia had roused other Jews and brought the charge against Paul that he had been teaching men in opposition to Jews, to the law, and to the temple. In response, Paul obtained permission of the Roman chief captain to speak to the Jews that had gathered before the temple. Paul gave his testimony in Hebrew, bearing testimony in favor of Christ and the Christian way. The whole city responded in an uproar and the Roman chief captain brought Paul into the castle for protection. The following day, Paul appeared before the Sanhedrin (συνέδριον), which was

---

[285] Helen Costigane, "A History of the Western Idea of Conscience," in *Conscience in World Religions*, ed. Jayne Hoose, (Notre Dame, IN: University of Notre Dame Press, 1999): 3;, Roy B. Zuck, "The Doctrine of Conscience," *Bibliotheca Sacra* 126, no. 504 (Oct- Dec, 1969): 329; Wayne Barton, "The Christian Conscience in an Age of Crisis," *Southwestern Journal of Theology* 4, no. 2 (April, 1962): 101; Paul W. Gooch, "'Conscience' in 1 Corinthians 8 and 10," *New Testament Studies* 33, no. 2 (April 1987): 244.

[286] Costigane, 6.

[287] Acts 21:15-22:30.

the highest Jewish council in civil and religious matters.[288]

The context of this verse reveals several elements related to the idea of "conscience." First, Paul relates the Greek verb, πολιτεύομαι (to live, to conduct one's life[289]), to the term συνείδησις (conscience) when he states, "I have lived in all good conscience." The textual idea brought forth from the Scripture implies that the role of "conscience" is in *relation to the conduct of one's life*. Ernesto Borghi elaborates further by stating, "The syntax πάση συνειδήσει ἀγαθη ("in all good conscience") explicitly reveals the individual faculty of discernment between good and evil."[290]

Furthermore, Paul introduces another element into this understanding. Not only is "conscience" related to how one lives, but it is also *how one lives "before God."* In this phrase, there is the subtle hint that links the conscience to the divine sphere. This is not to say that the conscience is a divine element in man, nor the voice of God,[291] but it suggests that since God is the Creator of man, then He is the Originator of the conscience in man as well.[292] As Allen Verhey consistently argues from a philosophical

---

[288] Kurt Aland and others, eds., *The Greek New Testament*, (third corrected edition with Greek dictionary, Federal Republic of Germany: Biblia-Druck GmbH Stuttgart, 1983), 172.

[289] Ibid., 146; "πολιτεύομαι," 3rd entry in Walter Bauer, William Arndt, Wilbur Gingrich, and Frederick Danker, *A Greek-English Lexicon of the New Testament* 2nd ed. (Chicago: Univ. of Chicago Press, 1979), 686. (hereafter, BAGD, from authors' names)

[290] Ernesto Borghi states, "le syntagme πάση συνειδήσει ἀγαθη explicite pleinement la faculte de descernement personnel du bien et du mal," (Ernesto Borghi, "La notion de conscience dans le Nouveau Testament." *Filologia Neotestamentaria* 10 (Mayo-Noviembre, 1997): 90; BAGD, 2nd entry, 786.

[291] Larry Gates states, "It is a psychological truth that conscience is perceived by many as the voice of God. The faithful take inner moral imperatives as divine and consider them to be more important than any merely human wishes [Larry Gates, "Conscience as the Voice of God: A Jungian View," *Journal of Religion and Health* 31, no. 4 (Winter 1992): 282]." In contrast, Alfred M. Rehwinkel states, "That the voice of conscience stands in some relation to God is true," but if conscience were the voice of God then "conscience would have to be infallible," *The Voice of Conscience* (St. Louis: Concordia Publishing House, 1956), 7, cited in Barton, 101; Zuck (331) concurs with Rehwinkel and Barton.

[292] Barton, 99; Don E. Marietta, Jr., describes how, even among non-biblical literature, the conscience was referred to as being divine in origin [Don E. Marietta, Jr., "Conscience in Greek Stoicism," *Numen* 17 (Dec., 1970): 181].

perspective, "A person's conscience is the product of the inescapability of God."[293]

Moreover, since the context of this verse reflects the *conflict* between a group of men recognized as having authority to judge in religious and civil matters and an *individual* (Paul), the idea is introduced of *individual accountability before God.* Paul here demonstrates that it is to God alone that the individual must answer for the conduct of his life. Significantly, this passage clearly establishes that in matters of belief, and especially of conduct based on those beliefs, that *the ultimate arbiter is God in relation to the individual,* without any intermediary agency such as the State or a religious body, both of which, civil and religious, were combined in the Sanhedrin in this particular case.

Last, and perhaps the one insight that strikes most strongly upon the subject of "conscience," is that in this instance, Paul was confronted by those with whom he had at a previous time associated. At one time, he had believed, advocated, and zealously defended the traditions and teachings of his Jewish upbringing.[294] However, once having met Christ on the road to Damascus, he became an apostle of Jesus. This conversion experience of Saul of Tarsus into Paul the Apostle offers insights on the subject of "conscience." Consider for a moment, based on Paul's conversion, the following points: 1) Conscience can be a faulty guide. His experience teaches that one can sincerely follow one's conscience and yet be sincerely wrong in God's view.[295] Saul thought he was sincerely serving God when

---

[293] Allen Verhey, "The Person as a Moral Agent," *Calvin Theological Journal* 13, no. 1 (April, 1978): 12. James A. Knight (133), commenting on "conscience" from a theological point of view, states "Conscience is the voice of moral man speaking to himself as a moral being and making moral judgments. This voice was placed by God in man at his creation, and man cannot rid himself of it. . . . God created man to be a moral being. Thus, he endowed him with the faculty to be moral"; Barton (101) likewise, states, "Whereas we secure the content of conscience from various sources, it was God who created this capacity for self-knowledge." J. Olbert Kempson concurs, "It appears, however, that conscience can be defined as a God-given capacity, which, when developed in an adequate, healthy manner, can enable the individual to choose a course of direction in achieving a degree of wholeness [Kempson, "Comments on Structure of the Conscience," *The Saint Luke's Journal of Theology* 4, no. 1 (Lent, 1961): 15]."

[294] Galatians 1:13, 14; Philippians 3:4-6.

[295] Barton (106) argues that one can be true to oneself by following one's conscience, and yet be false with God and one's fellow man. Additionally, Frank Mobbs posits that one can even sincerely follow one's conscience and still be wrong. He states, "If I have good reasons for my belief, then it is true. Now all sorts of reasons can make a belief true. But of one thing I can be certain – *the fact*

he persecuted Christians.²⁹⁶ As John M. Espy comments on Paul's conversion, "Full consciousness of sin came only on the Damascus road, where the charge of persecuting God's people, and the Son of God Himself, brought him face to face with his rebelliousness against God – and, after a fashion, with the Law."²⁹⁷ 2) An educated conscience does not necessarily mean a converted conscience. Paul had received a formal education in the rabbinical schools and had even been taught by Gamaliel,²⁹⁸ one of the most prominent religious leaders among the Jews in Paul's day,²⁹⁹ yet he did not know Jesus.³⁰⁰ 3) It is the role of the Holy Spirit through the Word of God to convict the conscience, as when Jesus spoke to Paul, saying, "It is hard for thee to kick against the *pricks* (Gk., κέντρον, literally "goads," but translated as "pricks" in KJV)." When one compares the term "goads" of Acts 9:5 and 26:14 with the "goads" of Ecclesiastes 12:11 ("The words of the wise are as goads"), it teaches that the writings of Scripture serve to instruct the wise. From these verses, the Bible teaches that the Holy Spirit was convicting Saul from the Scriptures of his wayward course, but he was stubbornly resisting such promptings. 4) In defining religious freedom, one is obligated to concede that the conscience must be free to investigate and search for religious truth. If not, Saul would not have become Paul and he would not have been one of Christianity's most ardent defenders as well as one of its most brilliant advocates. Additionally, Paul's Damascus road experience reveals that religious freedom includes the right to convert out of one's previous faith and to follow one's conscientious convictions based on God's Word.

---

that I believe something is not a reason that makes it true [Frank Mobbs, "Conscience and Christian Morality," *St. Mark's Review* 160 (Summer 1995): 33 (italics his)];" Jeong Woo Lee further notes, "Conscience, of course, is not the ultimate standard of righteousness [Jeong Woo (James) Lee, "To every man's conscience in the sight of God," *Kerux: A Journal of Biblical-Theological Preaching* 15, no. 3 (Dec., 2000): 17]."

[296] Acts 26:9-12.

[297] John M. Espy, "Paul's 'Robust Conscience' Re-Examined," *New Testament Studies* 31 (1985): 175.

[298] Acts 22:3.

[299] Acts 5:34.

[300] Acts 9:5; 22:8; 26:15.

Acts 24:16

"And herein do I exercise myself, to have always a conscience void of offence toward God, and toward men."

Acts 24:16 is a continuation of Paul's previous defense. By the usage of the Greek term ἀσκῶ ("to endeavor, to do one's best;"[301] KJV "I do exercise"), the concept of the "will" is introduced as the volitional force that follows the dictates of "conscience." From this verse, it is evident that the "will" is not to be confused with the "conscience," yet the two are interrelated. The conscience is the "bull's eye" to which the "arrow" of the will must fly. Paul states that he "endeavors", or "does his best" to have always an ἀπροσκοπον (blameless, faultless; inoffensive; clear [of conscience][302]) συνείδησιν. Roy B. Zuck comments on Paul's statement, "*Disciplining himself* he *strived deliberately* and continually to avoid known sin."[303]

By introducing the concept of the "will," the corollary of "choice" also enters the discussion of "conscience," which in turn involves the action of rationalization, or reason. Realization of this point aids in establishing that, from the Scriptures studied thus far, the conscience is linked to both the will and the rational faculty within man. Of further significance, this understanding is foundational to the vindication of God's judgment of each person. Since man is created with not only reasoning ability, but also with the moral faculty of conscience, he is therefore accountable for the life he lives and God is justified in the judgment rendered toward each person.

Additionally, when Paul states "to have always a conscience void of offence toward God, and *toward* men," the spectrum of the "conscience" is broadened to include not only a man's relation to God, but also to his fellow men. The implications of this point are significant in the formulation of "conscience," especially from the perspective of ecclesiology (the individual Christian in relation to his community of fellow believers) and individual religious liberty.

Furthermore, as Paul uses the term "conscience void of offense", or "blameless" (ἀπρόσκοπον συνείδησιν), the text implies that "conscience" fulfills *a role of judgment* toward the individual. Roy B. Zuck even goes as far as defining one function of the conscience as "that of a judge."[304] When

---

[301] Aland, 27.

[302] Ibid., 24.

[303] Zuck, 340 (italics mine).

[304] Ibid., 333.

one lives in harmony with one's conscience, one may state that he is "without blame." Contrariwise, if one lives in opposition to one's conscience, then he is worthy of blame.

Romans 2:12-16

"12. For as many as have sinned without law shall also perish without law: and as many as have sinned in the law shall be judged by the law; 13. (For not the hearers of the law are just before God, but the doers of the law shall be justified. 14. For when the Gentiles, which have not the law, do by nature the things contained in the law, these, having not the law, are a law unto themselves: 15. Which shew the work of the law written in their hearts, their conscience also bearing witness, and their thoughts the mean while accusing or else excusing one another;) 16. In the day when God shall judge the secrets of men by Jesus Christ according to my gospel."

For the purpose of this chapter, focus will be placed only on verses 14 and 15 of this passage since they deal with the concept of Gentiles and "law." In verse 14, several issues must be addressed[305]: 1) the term "Gentiles". . . Does it refer to Gentile converts to Christianity, or does it refer to unbelievers? 2) the term "law" . . . Does it refer to "the Law" (Decalogue), or to "a general law"? 3) the term "nature" . . . Does it refer to Gentiles "not having the law," or to Gentiles who "do the works of the law"?

Answering each of the previous points, one finds: 1) the term "Gentile," from the context of the passage, is referring to those who are "unbelievers," because Paul contrasts them with those Jewish converts to Christianity who had claimed prior knowledge of the Decalogue as their basis of justification before God. 2) and 3) In the original Greek, the passage from verses 12-16 uses both the arthrous (with "the") and the anarthrous (without "the") forms of "law," indicating reference being made to both "the Law" and "a (general) law." The arthrous forms appear only in verse 14 ("the things of the Law they do") and in verse 15 ("the works of the Law written"). All other references to "law" in verses 12-16 are anarthrous. For our purposes, focus will be upon verses 14 and 15 with respect to structural parallelism:

v.14 "For when Gentiles, *not having law* by nature, the things *of the Law* do, these, *not having law*, are law unto themselves."
v. 15 "Which [these] show the work *of the Law* written in their heart," "*their conscience* also bearing witness"

---

[305] The Greek exegesis which follows is mine.

From this grammatical construction, one may conclude that Gentiles (unbelievers) who do not have any (general) law, much less the Law, by nature (i.e., by special revelation, Scripture)[306] and yet do the requirements of the Law in principle, show by their own actions[307] the work of the Law upon their hearts. This explains how even atheists can be morally upright citizens. Just because one does not believe in God, it does not negate God's prevenient grace made available to all in Eden and His abundant grace poured out at Calvary.

The issue of those without the Law being "a law unto themselves" introduces the concept of natural law theory. This exegesis suggests the Law (eternal and God-given) and a law of nature to which all men have access. Based on the grammatical construction in verse 15, the idea of *the Law in relation to "conscience"* is introduced. This observation implies a standard, the Law[308], to which the conscience of the individual is oriented.[309] Elaborating this point further, Douglas Straton refers to the

---

[306] Philip Maertens, "Une étude de Rm. 2.12-16," *New Testament Studies*, 46 no. 4 (Oct. 2000): 509-511; Lamp, 46; J. C. Yates, "The Judgment of the Heathen: The Interpretation of Article XVIII and Romans 2:12-16," *Churchman*, 100 no. 3 (1986): 220-230.

[307] I am not here advocating Pelagianism, because it is obvious that "those who do (obey) law are justified," verse 13, indicating passivity – in other words, God is doing this work in them.

[308] Jeffrey Lamp argues that Paul here refers to the Law given to the Jews and which, according to Jewish tradition, had been disseminated among the nations. Thus, while not having the written commandment, Gentiles still had a knowledge of the just requirements of the Law through a quasi-specific revelation by means of oral transmission (Jeffrey S. Lamp, "Paul, the Law, Jews, and Gentiles: A Contextual and Exegetical Reading of Romans 2:12-16," *Journal of the Evangelical Theological Society*, vol. 42:1 (Mar 1999): 44-46.

[309] Zuck, 333; William E. May, "The natural law, conscience, and developmental psychology," *Communio* (Spring, 1975): 10; John Coulson cogently argues, "To disobey the moral law is to disobey our natures, since they are created by God, the author of that law, and this is perhaps how the metaphor of conscience as an inner voice or dialogue arises." He further contends (157), "To admit the claims of conscience is to admit the existence of a law which has conditioned that conscience and of a law-giver, the author of that law" [John Coulson, "The Authority of Conscience," *The Downside Review* 77, no. 248 (Spring, 1959): 151];" Verhey (5, 6) argues the same point; Rodgers even refers to the relationship, in non-biblical literature, between the gods and men, and [divine] law and men's uneasiness when approaching death for not having kept it [V. A. Rodgers, "Συνείδησις and the Expression of Conscience," *Greek-Roman-and Byzantine-Studies* 10, no. 3 (Autumn, 1969): 248].

primary principles of conduct that are found "in all of the major cultures of mankind, Hindu, Buddhist, Confucian, Zoroastrian, Greek, Judeo-Christian, [and] Islamic." He concludes by stating,

> Finding the main content, then, of *the last five of Moses' commandments*, the ethical "laws," or close parallels to them, widely throughout human civilization, constitutes strong historical or empirical evidence *that basic qualities of conscience, or ideas of moral law, are similar or native to mature human life on a universal scale.*[310]

Roy B. Zuck succinctly concludes, "Therefore, based on ethnology and New Testament usage, the conscience can be defined as 'the inner knowledge or awareness of, and sensitivity to, some moral standard.'"[311] Zuck's statement, "some moral standard," combined with Straton's observation about the last five of Moses' commandments produce specific content of natural law for civil society composed of believers as well as unbelievers.

From the perspective of civil society, a distinction must be made regarding the first four commandments and the last six. The first four commandments deal with an individual's relationship to his God.[312] The last six deal with an individual's relationship toward his fellow man, and thus properly can fall under the category of civil jurisdiction. Martin Luther, as opposed to John Calvin, recognized the limits of civil jurisdiction as applying only to the last six commandments.[313] Roger Williams argued the same point when he advocated liberty of conscience in the religious sphere.[314] In order to properly acknowledge the concept of freedom of

---

[310] Douglas Straton, "The Meaning of Moral Law," *Andover Newton Quarterly*, (January, 1965): 31 (italics mine).

[311] Zuck, 331.

[312] While it is true that ancient Israel fulfilled their covenant to God as a people (community), it is equally true that Abraham, as an *individual* first responded to God's call and covenant, which later produced the nation of Israel. In addition, even within the community of believers, one must individually respond to God, even if others do not. Thus, individual accountability is present while alone and while in community.

[313] William A. Mueller, *Church and State in Luther and Calvin* (Nashville, TN: Broadman Press, 1952), 128.

conscience as advocated by such Founding Fathers in America as Thomas Jefferson and James Madison, who largely formulated the First Amendment guarantees, this distinction between at least the first four and last six commandments must be recognized and applied to the limits of civil jurisdiction.[315] Furthermore, it must be recognized that of the last six commandments, only the sixth, the eighth, and the ninth currently form part of civil law because of the complexity of legislating such other commandments as children honoring their parents (5th), not committing adultery (7th),[316] and not coveting (10th).

Exploring the concept of natural law theory from a theological viewpoint must take into account some differences among Protestant and Catholic theologians. The former group emphasizes the consequences of Adam's fall upon his posterity (referred to as "total depravity," and thus affecting man's mental and moral faculties to the extent that he needs the divine revelation of God as an act of grace and mercy to make known the divine will),[317] and the latter group contends for a concept of "natural law," by which they argue that all men have the ability to discover the righteous claims of God's law through reason alone (apart from divine revelation through the Scriptures and the Holy Spirit).[318] A more detailed deliberation

---

[314] Evarts B. Green, *Religion and the State: The Making and Testing of an American Tradition* (New York: New York University Press, 1941), 43, 47-49.

[315] Elwyn A. Smith, *Religious Liberty in the United States* (Philadelphia, PA: Fortress Press, 1972), 28, 29, 36-39.

[316] In early American history, colonies, and later, some states, used to legislate adultery, but no longer do so.

[317] Raymond E. Peterson, "Jeremy Taylor on Conscience and Law," *Anglican Theological Review* 48 (July, 1966): 250-253; T. James Kodera, "Reshaping of Conscience: Religion, Education, and Multiculturalism," *Anglican Theological Review* 78, no. 3 (Summer 1996): 475, 476; George F. Thomas identifies five areas for consideration regarding divine revelation: "1) principles of authoritative revelation are found in the Bible, not in moral philosophy; 2) biblical revelation requires a Christian to 'use reason fully in determining its meaning and implications for his life'; 3) revelation is 'mediated through their moral experience'; 4) 'Christian ethics is inseparable from the Christian faith that God has revealed His will in Christ'; and 5) in examining the facts of moral consciousness 'the Bible must be accorded a privileged position [George F. Thomas, *Christian Ethics and Moral Philosophy*, 373-375 quoted in "A Forum for Conscience," *Scottish Journal of Theology* 22 (March 1969): 65, 66, by I. G. Whitchurch].

[318] May, 5, 6.

that would set forth both views more fully is beyond the scope of this chapter[319] and would be tangential to its purpose, but suffice to say, for the purpose of this section, that both groups concur that all men have a conscience that is amenable to God's law,[320] whether it be through revelation of the Holy Spirit, or whether through reason alone.

Furthermore, the "conscience" is here referred to in a way that distinguishes it from the individual. Paul states "their conscience also bearing witness," not "they bear witness," inferring that while the conscience is a part of the individual, yet it is not the individual *en toto*. Rather, "it integrates a whole range of mental operations" including such mental faculties as reason, emotion, and will.[321] While "conscience" is not to be equated with the individual, it should not be viewed as autonomous, or as an absolute authority unto itself either.[322]

Moreover, "conscience" is also distinguished from the "thoughts" of the individual, since Paul refers to them separately.[323] Thus, "conscience" cannot be the memory, although there is a direct relationship between the

---

[319] For a comprehensive comparison and analysis of both views, see Robert M. Zins, *On the Edge of Apostasy: Evangelical Romance with Rome* (Huntsville, AL: White Horse Publications, 1998), 31-65, 82-87; James G. McCarthy, *The Gospel According to Rome*, (Eugene, OR: Harvest House Publishers, 1995), 21-121; James R. White, *The Roman Catholic Controversy* (Minneapolis, MN: Bethany House Publishers, 1996), 39-44, 130-138; William Cathcart, *The Papal System* (Watertown, WI: Baptist Heritage Press, 1989; originally published in Philadelphia by Ferguson and Woodburn, 1872), 261-262; John Armstrong, *The Catholic Mystery* (Eugene, OR: Harvest House Publishers, 1999), 42-43; John Armstrong, *Roman Catholicism: Evangelical Protestants Analyze What Divides and Unites Us*, (Chicago: Moody Press, 1984), 76-77; and "Original Sin," and "Of Justification" in J.A. Wylie, *Papacy* (London: Hamilton, Adam, and Co., 1867), 271-285; 286-293.

[320] Jan Stepien, "Syneidesis: La Conscience dans L'Anthropologie de Saint Paul," *Revue D'Histoire et de Philosophie Religieuses* 60, no. 1 (Jan – Mar 1980): 11, 12; Marcelino Zalba, "Papel de la conciencia en la calificación de los actos morales," *Gregorianum* 62, no. 1 (1981): 142, 143; Harold J. Berman, "Conscience and Law: The Lutheran Reformation and the Western Legal Tradition," *The Journal of Law and Religion* 5, no. 1 (1987): 181-182.

[321] William C. Spohn, "Conscience and Moral Development," *Theological Studies* 61, no. 1 (March 2000): 123.

[322] Stepien, 10; Gooch, 246; r.e. "conscience" developed in community, see pp. 129-130.

[323] Zuck (333) observes that the Greek does not equate the conscience with the condemning or approving thoughts.

memory and "conscience," since they are both associated in the role of accusing or excusing the individual. Exploring the relationship between thoughts and the role of "conscience" to a further degree, Page Lee adds that "conscience" embraces not only activity regarding past actions, but also is active with respect to *future, contemplated actions not yet performed*.[324] William C. Spohn describes the same idea, but with different terms when he states, "The term is used in two senses: 'anterior conscience' for all the searching and deliberation that leads up to a moral decision, and 'subsequent conscience' that reflects back on decisions we have made."[325]

1 Corinthians 8:7, 10, 12

"7. Howbeit there is not in every man that knowledge: for some with conscience of the idol unto this hour eat it as a thing offered unto an idol; and their conscience being weak is defiled. 10. For if any man see thee which hast knowledge sit at meat in the idol's temple, shall not the conscience of him which is weak be emboldened to eat those things which are offered to idols; 11. And through thy knowledge shall the weak brother perish, for whom Christ died? 12. But when ye sin so against the brethren, and wound their weak conscience, ye sin against Christ."

The central idea reflected in 1 Cor. 8:7, 10, 12 is that of Christian influence among believers with special emphasis upon concern for those newly converted whose "conscience" is weak. Those believers who have the knowledge that there is only one true God can eat food sacrificed unto idols without their conscience becoming guilt stricken. When those believers who don't have this knowledge, referred to as having a "weak conscience,"[326] eat food sacrificed unto idols, their conscience is defiled because they think they have worshipped other gods.

From the perspective of "conscience," the two most solemn points that this passage teaches is that it is a sin to lead another person to violate his conscience ("when you sin so against the brethren") and that the individual conscience in relation to God is a sacred relationship. Since only one of the scholarly works consulted for this passage addressed this issue,[327] it is

---

[324]Page Lee, "'Conscience' In Romans 13:5," *Faith and Mission* 8, no. 1 (Fall 1990): 88; Borghi (91) concurs.

[325] Spohn, 122.

[326] Zuck (338) refers to the "weak conscience" as "one that is over scrupulous or oversensitive."

[327] Paul W. Gooch (248, 249) argues that the passage does not refer to an issue of "moral conscience," since the unenlightened brother is the one who "has a

proper to develop it further. By the usage of the term "sin," the concept of "conscience" is moved from the area of *human* ethics to *divine* ethics. *Realization of this truth establishes the sacredness of the relationship between God and each person, a relationship so sacred that no other person should intrude into this inner sanctuary (foro interno).* From the context of this passage, *this biblical principle has application even to those whose conscience is based on erroneous information, viz., those who hold erroneous beliefs about God and His moral requirements.*

Additionally, this passage introduces the idea of "an informed conscience." Paul refers to those believers who had knowledge about the one true God in contrast to those who did not. Not only does this reiterate the relationship existing between "conscience" and reason, but it establishes how a "weak conscience" may be made strong. Since the knowledge that Paul refers to is about God, and thus based on the Scriptures, the Bible plays a central role in strengthening the conscience of the believer.[328]

When Paul speaks of an "emboldened conscience," the term used is οἰκοδομηθήσεται (from οἰκοδομέω, "to build up, to edify, to encourage").[329] From the context of this passage, it seems that Paul teaches that a person's "conscience" can be influenced by *external factors*, such as the practices of a fellow believer. This insight affords an even broader understanding of "conscience" than developed in this section thus far. While it is evident from the passage that Paul admonishes those "with

---

defective apprehension of Christian moral principles which requires alteration." While this observation is true, it nonetheless overlooks the stated fact in Scripture that such action by the enlightened brother is termed "sin." In order to resolve this apparent paradox, it seems that while the issue in this passage does relate to an "over scrupulous" brother who needs correction by knowledge of the truth, Paul is primarily concerned with the *timing* of when such correction should occur. Until I have informed my brother of the knowledge I have that allows me more liberty than he practices, I should refrain from any course of action that would encourage him to act in violation of his conscience. This interpretation is more in harmony with Paul's emphasis upon "charity [love] that edifies" rather than "knowledge that puffs up (Borghi, 89-90)." Thus, the central point brought forth in this chapter is still valid: the conscience of an individual in relation to God is so sacred that not only a correct knowledge of the truth should be shared with him, but also the proper timing regarding when to do so should so modify my practices that I do not "wound" his "weak conscience."

[328] Zuck, 338. Just because non-believers do not acknowledge God does not mean that He does not instruct them through life's experiences, through others, etc. The primary point noted here is that believers have special, direct revelation through the Bible and does not imply that unbelievers have no source.

[329] Aland, 124.

knowledge" to accommodate those "without knowledge" by not living according to the liberating truths they know, yet the idea is introduced regarding how the Holy Spirit can effect transformation in the life of fellow believers. When a Christian takes the time to become informed about biblical truth and lives by it, the Holy Spirit can influence the life of another believer to search out the truth for himself so that he may not have a "wounded" conscience. Of course, in harmony with Paul's counsel, one must act at the proper time (i.e. – adapting my lifestyle practices to the beliefs of another believer until I have had time to inform him of the knowledge I possess).

1 Corinthians 10:25, 27-29

"25. Whatsoever is sold in the shambles, that eat, asking no question for conscience sake: 27. If any of them that believe not bid you to a feast, and ye be disposed to go; whatsoever is set before you, eat, asking no question for conscience sake. 28. But if any man says unto you, This is offered in sacrifice unto idols, eat not for his sake that shewed it, and for conscience sake: for the earth is the Lord's, and the fullness thereof: 29. Conscience, I say, not thine own, but of the other: for why is my liberty judged of another man's conscience?"

Since 1 Corinthians 10:25, 27-29 is a continuation of the issues set forth in 1 Corinthians 8,[330] only two other points will be addressed here. First, the passage raises the idea of differing levels of growth regarding "conscience" among believers.[331] Basing the interpretation of this passage on 1 Corinthians 8, Paul offers practical ideas of how to deal with issues that could be viewed differently among fellow believers. Perhaps the comment of O. Hallesby is appropriate here: "conscience is an individual matter. Conscience sits in judgment on oneself and ought not therefore properly to sit in judgment on anyone else."[332]

Second, Paul addresses the issue of Christian contact with non-believers. The practical counsel he gives teaches that the best method of "enlightening the conscience" of non-believers is to wait for them to make a statement that opens for discussion matters of Christian faith. Additionally, the passage plainly establishes the need for believers to adhere

---

[330] Zuck, 338.

[331] In the Greek text, the plural tense is used when referring to "you" in verse 27: "and if ye (plural) be disposed to go," or "and if all of you desire to go."

[332] O. Hallesby, *Conscience* (London: Inter-Varsity Fellowship, 1950), 30, cited by Barton, 101.

steadfastly to the truth once it is introduced. Once the issue in question is evident to the non-believer, Paul admonishes, "Eat not for his sake that showed it." In addition, this passage alludes to ideas of toleration among Christians and between Christians and non-believers.

The New Testament Teaching on Toleration

The terms "toleration," "tolerance" and "tolerate" do not appear in the Koine Greek of the New Testament.[333] There are two Greek words that convey the meaning of "toleration," which are ἀφίημι, translated as "to let, let go, tolerate"[334] and the negative of κωλύω, translated as "[not] to hinder, prevent, forbid."[335] Although occurring a limited number of times in reference to toleration, those instances reveal a broader concept of toleration than normally assumed, even suggesting in some instances, a definition synonymous with modern concepts of religious freedom.

The first biblical passage dealing with religious toleration uses the negative of κωλύω in the gospel of Mark 9:38-40, where Jesus' disciples question Him regarding another man who was casting out devils in Christ's name, but who was not part of Jesus' group of disciples. Obviously concerned about this man's activities, Jesus' disciples forbade (ἐκωλύομεν) him. Jesus rebuked them by saying "Forbid him not (Μὴ κωλύετε αὐτον): for there is no man which shall do a miracle in my name, that can lightly speak evil of me. For he that is not against us is on our part." In essence, even though this man was not part of his group of disciples, Christ said, "Do not hinder [or forbid, or prevent] him from casting out devils in my name." The idea conveyed here is one of *Christian religious pluralism* and Christ's acceptance of it. A parallel passage in Luke 9:49, 50 (the second instance of religious toleration) does not add to the passage in Mark 9.

Later, on His way to Jerusalem during the Passover week, Luke records the third instance of religious toleration shown by Christ (Luke 9:51-56).

---

[333] The Greek word, ἀνεκτότερον, "tolerable," appears only six times: Mt. 10:15; 11:22, 24; Mk. 6:11; Lk. 10:12, 14. In each case, the phrase is: "it will be more tolerable for Sodom and Gomorrah," indicating more of the idea of clemency, rather than "toleration" as it relates to holding different religious convictions.

[334] Fourth entry under "ἀφίημι," in Walter Bauer, William Arndt, F. Gingrich, and Frederick Danker, *A Greek-English Lexicon of the New Testament and Other Early Christian Literature* (Chicago: The University of Chicago, 2nd ed., 1979), 126.

[335] First entry under κωλύω, Bauer *et al.* (BAGD), 461.

After sending messengers ahead of Him, they returned with the news that a Samaritan village refused to receive Him as He was on His way to Jerusalem. The animosity between the Jews and Samaritans had existed to the point of hatred and open hostility, eliciting the response of Jesus's disciples, "Lord, wilt thou that we command fire to come down from heaven, and consume them, even as Elias did?" Taking the opportunity to instruct them, Jesus gently rebuked them, explaining that they did not know *the evil spirit that actuated them*, because the Son of Man had come to save men's lives rather than destroy them. One may speculate that racism was a motivating factor for which the Samaritans had rejected Jesus, which is highly likely, but there is no question that this situation also involved religious differences, since the Samaritans worshipped differently than the Jews.[336] Thus, Jesus condemned any manner of coercion among religious groups.

The fourth instance raising the question of religious toleration employs ἀφίημι (John 11:46-53), which records a dialogue among the religious leaders regarding Jesus and His public ministry. After some Jews had reported Christ's miracles to the Pharisees, these gathered with the chief priests and began to discuss how best to address the situation. Sensing Christ's growing influence among the crowds, they said, "What do we? For this man doeth many miracles. If we let him thus alone (ἐὰν ἀφῶμεν αὐτὸν οὕτως), all men will believe on him: and the Romans shall come and take away both our place and nation." Caiaphas proposed that it was better for one man to die than for the whole nation to perish, revealing the murder plot taken against Christ. Although in definite contrast to Christ's own example of toleration, the Jewish religious leaders cannot be wholly faulted for their course of action. YHWH had clearly commanded the death of anyone who should attempt to lead His people astray from the true faith of Judaism (Deut. 13:1-18). Their error was in not understanding how Christ came as the prophetic fulfillment of numerous Old Testament passages concerning the Messiah.

Regarding religious toleration, this passage in John 11 raises several complex issues, among them being the speculative nature of fully understanding God's revealed will and the shift from a theocracy to an apolitical, global, religious movement as YHWH's chosen medium to fulfill His will regarding humanity's salvation. Addressing the first of these two issues and as an argument in favor of religious toleration, one must concede that not everyone interprets the Scriptures in exactly the same way. The Jewish leaders could easily justify their actions based on God's Word, as mentioned previously. However, also based on God's Word, the prophecies concerning the Messiah could be sufficient basis to judge their

---

[336] John 4:19-26.

actions taken against Christ as erroneous and egregious. Those of us who read this passage *after the fact* can readily adopt the latter view instead of the former. However, for the Jewish leaders of Christ's day, they could not have known absolutely that they should not have crucified Christ.[337]

Regarding a shift in YHWH's chosen medium for fulfilling His will, the Old Testament theocratic model operated much like a centripetal action, i.e., nations came to Israel to learn about their faith and the teachings of YHWH. Such a theocratic model united the civil authority with the religious sphere. Under such a model, especially with YHWH as its visible Leader,[338] religious intolerance was the norm (see Figure 3.1).

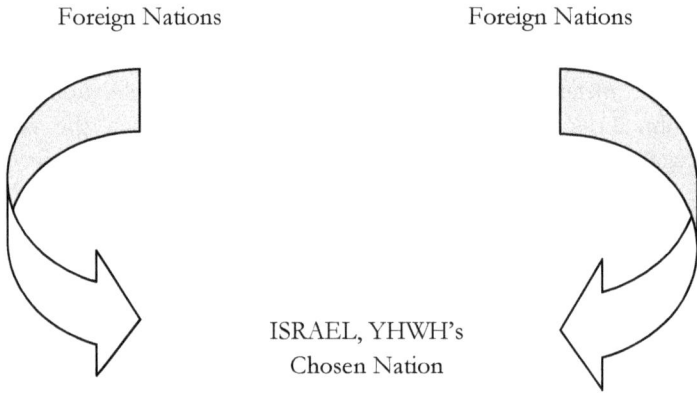

Figure 3.1. Old Testament Theocratic Model – YHWH was the Leader of His chosen nation, Israel. Foreign nations *came to* Israel to learn about YHWH (centripetal action). This model was intolerant toward other religions since it was founded on monotheistic beliefs; YHWH was its divine Sovereign; and it united the civil and religious spheres (theocratic); Numbers 15:32-36.

---

[337] Paul states in 1 Corinthians 2:7, 8, "But we speak the wisdom of God in a mystery, even the hidden wisdom, which God ordained before the world unto our glory: which none of the princes of this world knew: for had they know it, they would not have crucified the Lord of glory." In Luke 23:34, Jesus also stated, "Father, forgive them; for they know not what they do."

[338] YHWH appeared various times: veiled in clouds amid Mt. Sinai (Ex. 19) and covered with the cloud that hovered above the Tabernacle (Ex. 40:33-38). He even intervened on Moses' behalf during the rebellion of the people when the spies brought back a negative report (Num. 14) and when Miriam opposed Moses (Num. 12). Even in later periods of Israel's history, the LORD manifested His presence directly to prophets, or through the miracles He enabled them to do.

In the New Testament, however, the Christian movement utilizes the apolitical model that operates much like a centrifugal action, i.e., the church sends forth disciples, to reach the nations of the world. Under such a model, the church engages with nations, which represent a variety of political systems for governance, without favoring any particular one. Under this model, YHWH does not operate as the visible Leader over a religious nation, as in the Old Testament; rather, the church penetrates society and gains adherents who then become members having two spheres of responsibility – both to Caesar and to God, as citizen and Christian.[339] Under this system, religious toleration (freedom) is the proper norm for His church. Since the church operates within societies, some having religious pluralism, and others with political diversity, the apolitical model is the ideal mode of operation for the church to achieve its objectives (see Figure 3.2).

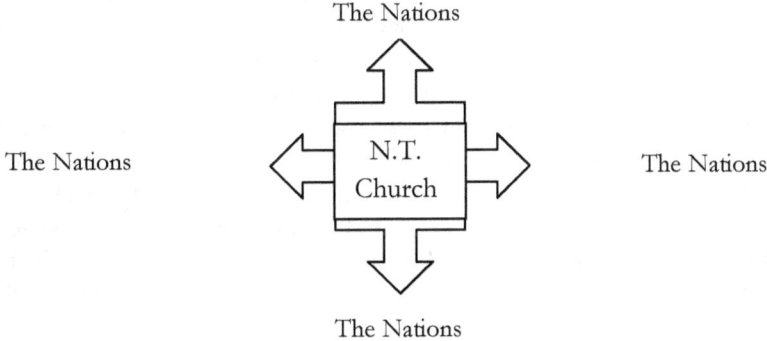

Figure 3.2. New Testament Apolitical Model – Jesus is the Head of the Church, His body. The church *sends forth* missionaries (centrifugal action) to evangelize the nations of the world. The church operates within a multitude of societies, each with its own political system. The church encounters religious pluralism, and following the example of her Lord, practices religious freedom without supporting any particular political system (apolitical).

Taking into account this shift from the theocratic model to the apolitical model reveals that the persecutive spirit of the Jewish religious leaders in John 11 is unacceptable for believers, whether Jewish or Christian, living in the New Testament era. Such a position in favor of toleration harmonizes with the New Testament teaching that one's conscience can be fallible and

---

[339] In Matthew 22:21, Jesus said, "Render therefore unto Caesar the things which are Caesar's; and unto God the things that are God's."

hence the need for at least religious toleration, if not religious freedom. Moreover, when one considers all of the New Testament teachings on the subject, especially Christ's example, then religious toleration, if not freedom, becomes the norm for Christ's followers.

The fifth instance of religious toleration occurred after Christ's resurrection and ascension, when His disciples began to perform miracles among their Jewish fellow-citizens,[340] which caused the high priest and the Sadducees to arrest and imprison them. After a miraculous escape by the angel of the Lord, Peter and the other disciples continued preaching in the temple the following morning. Upon receiving this news, the temple officers brought them before the high priest and the council.[341] The high priest reminded them that they had been solemnly warned not to preach in Christ's name, to which Peter responded, "We ought to obey God rather than men. . . Jesus whom ye slew and hanged on a tree, Him hath God exalted with his right hand. . . and we are his witnesses."[342] At this point, the council was ready to slay them, had not Gamaliel, a council member and doctor of the law, intervened to spare them. After recounting some recent events of a similar nature, he admonished them, "And now I say unto you, Refrain from these men, and let them alone (καὶ ἄφετε αὐτούς): for if this counsel or this work be of men, it will come to nought: but if it be of God, ye cannot overthrow it; lest haply ye be found even to fight against God."[343] Thereupon, the apostles were beaten and warned solemnly not to preach in Christ's name anymore. Upon leaving the council, they rejoiced in their sufferings for Christ and did not cease to teach and to preach Christ daily in the temple and in every house.

This incident reveals a type of toleration that borders on religious freedom. The response of Gamaliel demonstrates a solid philosophical basis for any true concept of toleration, or religious freedom. It recognizes the limited, finite nature of man to judge his fellow man in matters of religious convictions. It also emphasizes how mighty God is, and how capable He is to sustain His truth. Further, it demonstrates magnanimity on behalf of Gamaliel, one who was learned enough in Judaism to be a doctor of the law, but one who also had no difficulty in conceding the

---

[340] Acts 5:12-16.

[341] Acts 5:17-28

[342] Acts 5:29-32.

[343] Acts 5:33-40.

possibility of the new Christian[344] movement being inspired and led by God. Such a concept of religious freedom gave the necessary liberty for the fledgling movement to grow into a community of believers having established churches. It was a similar concept of religious freedom that enabled the Protestant Reformation to take root and become an established movement, as will be noted later in this chapter.

As Christianity grew during the first century, the biblical counsel regarding toleration takes on a more restrictive meaning. However, this counsel should be understood as *intra-ecclesial, that is to say, pertaining only to those within the church*. By the end of the first century, the beloved disciple, John, wrote the apocalyptic book of Revelation, which contains a single usage of ἀφίημι as counsel to the church of Thyatira: "Nevertheless, I have a few things against thee, because thou sufferest (ἀφίημι, tolerate, allow) that woman Jezebel... to teach and seduce my servants."[345] The biblical symbolism of Jezebel used here by John is an allusion to how the historical Jezebel married the Jewish king Ahab and introduced heretical teachings among the Israelites. On that occasion the Lord sent Elijah the prophet to challenge the false prophets of Jezebel. John draws upon those lessons and applies them to the spiritual adultery, i.e., false teachings, that endangered the Church and which should not be tolerated.[346]

Not only John the beloved disciple, but also Paul the Apostle gave clear counsel to the church regarding the need to maintain purity of doctrine. In his letter to Timothy, Paul admonished him, "Take heed unto thyself, and unto the doctrine; continue in them: for in doing this thou shalt both save thyself, and them that hear thee."[347] He also counseled Titus, "A man that is an heretic after the first and second admonition reject."[348] The Greek word translated as "reject" (παραιτοῦ) means "to have nothing to do with," or "to avoid," which is a far different meaning than "to deliver" a heretic into the hands of secular powers to face a death penalty, as will be

---

[344] I use the term "Christian movement" here to indicate the beginnings of the Christian church, although I realize that the "disciples were called Christians first in Antioch," (Acts 11:26) a period of time after this incident with Gamaliel. Nonetheless, by whatever name their movement was given at this time, their teachings were still very radical to Orthodox Judaism of that time, which highlights rather than weakens the argument of biblical religious freedom advocated here.

[345] Revelation 2:20.

[346] 1 Kings 18; cf., 16:29-34.

[347] 1 Timothy 4:16; et al.

[348] Titus 3:10.

described in the next section dealing with the Inquisition.

The apostle Paul had also counseled the church regarding how to deal with a member living in violation of biblical principles – "to deliver such an one unto Satan for the destruction of the flesh, that the spirit may be saved in the day of the Lord Jesus."[349] Paul did not mean the literal destruction of such an offender, as by death or burning at the stake, because, after sufficient time for repentance, he counseled that the former member should be re-instated into fellowship.[350] The latter interpretation seems consistent with the counsel of Christ in Matthew 18:15-18 regarding members who have sinned against a brother, but who are unrepentant and refuse to heed the counsel of the church – they are to be treated as "heathen," i.e., as unconverted, or outside of the fellowship of the church. Nowhere does the New Testament teaching encourage or support using physical force, coercive measures, or manipulative tactics to secure compliance from believers regarding biblical teachings.

Some may argue, as does Thomas Aquinas,[351] that Luke 14:16-24, which describes the invitation to the Great Banquet, actually authorizes Christ's followers "to compel" others to accept the invitation to join the Banquet so that the Master's "house may be filled" (v.23). To the contrary, this passage is not referring to the use of physical force or coercive measures to gain Christian adherents, as the following exegesis shows. The Greek word used here, ἀναγκάζω, signifies "invite (urgently), urge (strongly)."[352] As used in Luke 14:23, it is in the imperative voice, as a command to Christ's followers to compel others to attend the Banquet. However, the idea is that of presenting the Gospel claims so persuasively that one's hearers are compelled, or moved voluntarily, to accept those claims. In Acts 28:19

---

[349] 1 Corinthians 5:5.

[350] 2 Corinthians 2:5-11.

[351] Thomas Aquinas, "It is written: 'Go out into the highways and hedges and compel them to come in.' Now, men enter into the house of God, i.e., into Holy Church, by faith. Therefore, some ought to be compelled to the faith. . . . On the other hand, there are unbelievers who at some time have accepted the faith and professed it, such as heretics and all apostates; such should be submitted even to bodily compulsion, that they may fulfill what they have promised and hold what they, at one time, undertook." Baumgarth, ed., *Saint Thomas Aquinas on Law, Morality, and Politics* (Indianapolis, IN: Hackett Publishing Company, 1988), 249, 250.

[352] "ἀναγκάζω," 2nd entry, BAGD, 52. The first entry gives the meaning "compel, force of inner and outer compulsion," but is not associated with the passage in question, Luke 14:23. The second entry reflects the weaker form of this verb, *viz.*, "to invite urgently."

Paul describes how he "was constrained" (KJV, also using ἀναγκάζω) to appeal to Caesar since the Jews objected to his release from prison. *No one physically forced Paul to appeal to Caesar. It was a voluntary and volitional act of his own.* Paul, having no other options due to the Jews' objections, "was compelled," or "was constrained" to petition for Caesar's intervention. This seems to suggest that Paul would not have needed to appeal to Caesar except *that all other options for his possible release were not available to him.* If seen in this light, comparing Acts 28:19 with Luke 14:23, the command becomes, "Go out into the highways and hedges, and *give them such persuasive arguments for Christianity that they have no other option* but to accept the invitation to the Banquet." Interpreted this way, both passages harmonize not only with each other, but with the other New Testament passages examined in this section that deal with toleration.

Additionally, such an interpretation of Luke 14:23 harmonizes with Paul's description of gospel ministry in 2 Corinthians 5:20, "Now then we are ambassadors for Christ as though God did beseech you by us: we pray you in Christ's stead, be ye reconciled to God." The "beseeching" (παρακαλέω) here means "to appeal to, urge, exhort, encourage, invite"[353] one's hearers "to be reconciled (καταλλάσσω) to God."[354] Paul emphasizes, "We pray (δέομαι, "to ask, beg, pray, implore"[355]) you, be reconciled to God," which demonstrates such a depth of love for one's hearers that there can be no mistaken notion of physical force or coercive measures that Paul might be endorsing here.

In summary of this section, the New Testament teaching on "conscience" stresses the inviolability of individual conscience in relation to God. No religious body – provided one opts not to adhere to it – and no civil authority, or any combination of the two have any jurisdiction in the realm of individual conscience and religious convictions. While it is true that the New Testament teaching regarding the *ecclesia* (Church) defines it as a community of believers, *the individual experience with God always precedes this.*

Conscience is the medium through which God communicates moral imperatives to man. Thus, conscience, whether for the believer or the unbeliever, is always in reference to law – either the Law for the former, or natural law for the latter. The specificity of natural law cannot tread into the first four of the Ten Commandments, viz., the first table of the Law, which deals with one's religious beliefs and practices. The content, then, of

---

[353] "παρακαλέω" 2nd entry, BAGD, 617.

[354] "καταλλάσσω" 2nd entry, (passive, *be reconciled*), a. of man's relation to God, BAGD, 414..

[355] "δέομαι" 3rd entry, BAGD, 175.

natural law being limited to the second table of the Law provides sufficient moral parameters for ordering society. *The distinction between the first and second tables of the moral law is crucial because it underscores that civil authority has no jurisdiction over the religious convictions of the individual.*

Religious convictions developed through conscience and education, however sincerely held, can be faulty. Individuals newly converted to the Christian faith can have weak consciences due to not having as complete an education as members of longer standing within the church. Those members with weaker consciences must always be treated so as to not lead them into doubt, unbelief, or confusion regarding the Christian faith, which is termed sinning against Christ. Since the conscience of a fellow believer should be treated with such sanctity, how much greater should the conscience of those without the church be treated likewise with sacredness? Thus, the need for religious freedom – defined as the freedom to search for religious truth, to convert out of a previously held religious tradition, to practice one's faith, to proselytize, and to acknowledge that conscience is not infallible – becomes central to the conscientious religious experience of the individual.

Likewise, in the civil sphere, there is also the need for toleration toward those who hold varying forms of Christianity and even those differing in faith from Christianity. Such was Christ's example to His disciples. He never once used coercive measures to gain compliance with divine truths. The Scriptures reveal that toleration, far from being a mere permission for private worship in one's home, is "bearing with," or "putting up with," or "letting continue" the proclamation and proselytism activities of the one in question, as in the case of Peter and John. Biblical toleration is based on the belief that God is greater than any religious body and well-able to defend His truth. Thus, New Testament religious toleration approximates what is commonly called religious freedom in the modern era, viz., individuals who hold conscientious convictions and who propagate them without civil restrictions.

Toleration within the faith, however, takes on a more restrictive sense as biblical counsel contains an implied rebuke to the church for tolerating the evils of spiritual adultery (i.e., mingling truth with false teachings). Those who have erred in faith or who have backslidden in their lifestyle, are to be admonished with humbleness and love, seeking their repentance. However, if these efforts avail no change, then the offending member must be disciplined by action of the church. Members under such circumstances have no grounds for claiming a violation, or coercion, of conscience. Church membership is voluntary and is based on an individual's free choice to commit to such teachings and lifestyle. Conversely, one caveat remains to be stated here, namely, that when an individual decides to leave a former religious group and rejects its teachings, he or she should be allowed to freely go and join another religious group, i.e., voluntarily and without restrictions. This is not to say that God will not ultimately judge the rightness or wrongness of such a decision, and mete out judgment accordingly, but it is to emphasize the limited nature of man to fully understand, or control, the inner workings of conscience, religious convictions, and the Holy Spirit.

Having established from the New Testament theological principles defining "conscience" and its relation to religious truths, as well as toleration (religious freedom), the next two sections examine how the Catholic Church deviated from these biblical teachings during the Inquisition, as well as the historical and legal developments during the Protestant Reformation which established civil guarantees for religious freedom.

The Inquisition and the Coercive Nature of the Church

Some may raise the valid observation that Pope John Paul II had asked forgiveness of the Inquisition in the twilight of his papacy. While true, one must recognize that his apology was not for the Church, which is "holy and immaculate," but for the "sons and daughters of the Church" who had erred; that he was not asking forgiveness of those who had been wronged, but of God, "who only can forgive;"[356] and that his confession was "generic in nature," and not intended to ask forgiveness of specific sins.[357] From such statements, the paragraph alluding to crimes of the Inquisition contained in *Dignitatis Humanae* takes on a different meaning:

> In the life of the People of God, as it has made its pilgrim way through the vicissitudes of human history, there has at times appeared a way of acting that was hardly in accord with the spirit of the Gospel or even opposed to it. Nevertheless, the doctrine of the Church that no one is to be coerced into faith has always stood firm.[358]

---

[356] Rory Carroll, "Pope says sorry for sins of Church," *The Guardian*, March 13, 2000, http://www.guardian.co.uk/world/2000/mar/13/catholicism.religion (accessed February 28, 2012).

[357] Miles O'Brien and Jim Bittermann, "Pope John Paul II Makes Unprecedented Apology for Sins of Catholic Church," Sunday Morning News, aired March 12, 2000, http://transcripts.cnn.com/TRANSCRIPTS/0003/12/sm.06.html (accessed February 28, 2012).

[358] *Dignitatis Humanae*, Art. 12, par. 1.

This statement does not condemn such wrongs. It merely acknowledges that the *praxis* (actions) of some Catholics during the history of the Church has not harmonized with the official δόγμα (doctrine) of the Church. Understanding that the Church of today does not forthrightly condemn the crimes of the Inquisition leads one to question what type of religious freedom is inherent to *Dignitatis Humanae* and focuses upon the central investigation of this chapter, namely the Church and its use of coercion.[359]

T. M. Parker traces the origins of the idea of the coercive power of the secular arm on behalf of the Church as beginning in the time of Constantine:

> An even more significant point in this letter [*Aeterna et religiosa*, from Constantine and addressed to the bishops of Arles] is the threat of force against recalcitrants. This was in fact implemented against the Donatists, though without much success. Its importance lies in the fact that as early as 314 there had begun that tradition of persecution in the interests of orthodox conformity which was to mark the Christian Roman Empire and therefore its successor states, the medieval nations.[360]

The medieval nations, operating under this concept, upheld the right of the Church to enforce religious orthodoxy, which was the foundation for the establishment of the Inquisition.[361]

---

[359] John Conley, S.J., concludes his analysis of *Dignitatis Humanae* with this statement, "Finally, the simple distinction between the blameless, orthodox Church and her erring, violent members in the area of religious freedom only dulls the Church's necessary examination of conscience regarding her long complicity with the use of civic coercion in religious matters. The prim demarcation between the sinless Church and her sinful members cannot render justice to the enigma of the holy wars, the tortures, and the executions carried out in the name of the merciful cross." John Conley, "Religious Freedom as Catholic Crisis," in Peter A. Pagan Aguiar and Terese Auer, eds., *The Human Person and a Culture of Freedom* (Washington, D.C.: The Catholic University of America Press, 2009), 241.

[360] T. M. Parker, *Christianity & the State in the Light of History* (London: Adam and Charles Black, 1955), 57.

[361] This erroneous idea was based on the Donation of Constantine and prevailed until the time of the Renaissance when Lorenzo Valla exposed the Donation as a forgery. G. R. Evans, *The Roots of the Reformation: Tradition, Emergence, and Rupture* (Downer's Grove, IL: InterVarsity Press, 2012), 117-118.

For the purposes of this chapter, only relevant aspects of the Inquisition will be analyzed which relate to the coercive power of the Church. Originating in the eleventh-century, the Inquisition was established first in Rome to investigate heresy.[362] The relationship between the Church and the secular power during the Inquisitions was intricately designed, as pointed out in *The New Schaff-Herzog Encyclopedia of Religious Knowledge*:

> The unconditional support of the secular arm for the papal inquisition was invoked by virtue of the Veronese agreement (though this was not properly made for that end). The secular arm was "executor" or "minister" of the inquisition. The popes constantly strove to get the cooperation of the secular powers embodied in state laws, municipal statutes, and the like.[363]

The significance of embodying through legal documents the aid given by secular powers to support the Inquisition cannot be overstressed here. It presupposes the idea of the divine sphere penetrating and uniting with the secular sphere to produce the *Corpus Christianum* (Christian Commonwealth). Moreover, it reveals the jurisdictional authority of the Church to mandate secular laws, bringing them into conformity with divine laws, as understood by the Church. Also, it is one of the key elements in properly understanding the phrase "immunity from coercion" in *Dignitatis Humanae*, as will be noted in the last section of this chapter.

The papal bull, *Ad extirpanda* ("Of Uprooting [heresy]"), issued in 1252 by Pope Innocent IV, contains instructions for the structural organization of the Inquisition.[364] It contains thirty-eight laws, among which several notable ones demonstrate the coercive nature of the Church with respect to heresy and heretics. The bull does not provide any methodology for

---

[362] K. Benrath, "The Inquisition, I. In the Older Church," *The New Schaff-Herzog Encyclopedia of Religious Knowledge* (Grand Rapids, MI: Baker Book House, 1977), 6:1-4, http://www.ccel.org/ccel/schaff/encyc06/ Page_1.html, (accessed March 30, 2012).

[363] K. Benrath, "The Inquisition, II. The Inquisition in the Middle Ages, 2. Relation to Secular Powers," in Ibid., 6:2, http://www.ccel.org/ccel/schaff/encyc06/Page_2.html (accessed March 16, 2012).

[364] San Francisco State University, "Ad Extirpanda," http://userwww.sfsu.edu/~draker/ history/Ad_Extirpanda.html, (accessed February 21, 2012).

determining whether one suspected of heresy is actually a heretic.[365] Rather, it *de facto* assumes heresy on behalf of the one in question and proceeds to outline how such a one should be treated in order to satisfy all just requirements of Church canon law. In this regard, it left full authority with the local bishop to determine who was heretical, and thus subject to the procedures outlined in the bull. It imposed severe penalties upon heretics and those suspected of aiding them, or furthering their teachings – such as loss of possessions and property; loss of any inheritance from condemned heretics; and loss of life itself by burning at the stake.[366]

The most striking element of *Ad extirpanda*, and the point which is most germane to this book, is the jurisdictional authority assumed by the bull. It was written when the papal power began to ascend to the height of its grandiosity and during a time when Church and state had been united for many centuries to produce the *Corpus Christianum* (Christian Commonwealth). Its extent of application was just as far as the Church had representation, regardless of the country, or its distance from Rome. History records the Inquisition, and it's tragic operation, occurring in Goa, India;[367] in Lima, Peru;[368] in Chile;[369] in Mexico;[370] in Portugal;[371] in Sicily,

---

[365] Philip Limborch notes the same attitude of suspicion without proof, "Upon this, in the Year 1542 Pope Paul III by a Constitution beginning *Licet ab initio*, deputed six Cardinals, Inquisitors General of heretical Pravity, in all Christian Nations whatsoever, as well on one Side as the other of the Alps, and gave them Authority to proceed without the Ordinaries, against all Hereticks, *and suspected of Heresy*, and their Accomplices and Abettors. . ." Philip A. Limborch, *The History of the Inquisition*, trans. Samuel Chandler, 2 vols. (London: J. Gray, 1731; reproduced by Eighteenth Century Collections Online Print Editions), 1:151 (italics mine).

[366] Limborch, 2:25-27. Here Limborch cites the common passages used by inquisitors to justify their death decrees: 2 Kings 23, "where Ozias commanded the Bones of the heretical Priests to be burnt; and from the Words of our Lord, John 15:6, 'If a man abide not in me, he is cast forth as a Branch, and is withered, and Men gather them, and cast them into the Fire, and they are burned.'" He includes arguments by inquisitors who try to diminish the barbarity of such punishment and by others who attempt to justify its use by appealing to Jesus' disciples who desired to call fire down from heaven upon the Samaritans (Luke 9:51-56). For refutations of such erroneous interpretations, see the first section of this chapter on toleration.

[367] A. K. Priolkar, *The Terrible Tribunal for the East: The Goa Inquisition* (New Delhi, India: Voice of India, second reprint, 1998).

[368] Jose Toribio Medina, *Historia del Tribunal del Santo Oficio de la Inquisicion de Lima*, 2 vols. (Santiago: Gutenburg Press, 1887; reprinted by Nabu Public Domain Reprints, n.d.).

Sardinia, and Milan;[372] in France and Germany;[373] in Rome, Italy;[374] in Spain;[375] in the Low Countries;[376] and attempts to establish it in England.[377] It was regarded as the single most effective means of maintaining the Catholic faith in its purity[378] and the most successful method of exterminating Protestantism from formerly Catholic lands, as demonstrated in Italy where Protestantism was virtually non-existent by the time of Pope Pius V (1566-1572).[379] It not only authorized the state to exterminate heretics, but also obligated it to do so. It twice mentions the faithfulness of Emperor Frederick, whom Henry Charles Lea describes as enforcing the decrees of the Church and fully supporting her in her work of

---

[369] Jose Toribio Medina, *Historia del Tribunal del Santo Oficio de la Inquisicion en Chile*, 2 vols. (Santiago, Chile: Fondo Histórico y Bibliográfico Medina, 1952).

[370] Jose Toribio Medina, *Historia del Tribunal del Santo Oficio de la Inquisicion en Mexico* (Mexico: Miguel Angel Porrua, Grupo Editorial, 1998).

[371] Limborch, 1:131-142

[372] Limborch, 1:144-147.

[373] Limborch, 1:147-150; Celestin Louis Tanon, *Histoire des Tribunaux de L'Inquisition en France* (Paris, France: Larose & Forcel, 1893; reprinted by Nabu Public Domain Reprints, n.d.).

[374] Limborch, 1:150-156

[375] Limborch, 1:119-131, 156-159

[376] Limborch, 1:160-161

[377] "During the period before the Reformation, England was less affected by the Inquisition. It first became active against the Lollards (q.v.). In 1401, Henry IV had parliament confirm the statute *De haeretico comburendo*." K. Benrath, "The Inquisition, II. The Inquisition in the Middle Ages, 6. Germany, the Netherlands, and England", http://www.ccel.org/ccel/schaff/encyc06/Page_3.html (accessed March 30, 2012).

[378] Juan Manuel Orti y Lara, *La Inquisición* (Madrid: Imprenta de la Viuda e Hijo de Aguado, 1877; reprinted by Nabu Public Domain Reprints), xi, xii; B. J. Kidd, *The Counter-Reformation: 1550-1600* (London: SPCK, 1963), 39.

[379] K. Benrath, "The Inquisition and the Counter-Reformation," in *The New Schaff-Herzog Encyclopedia of Religious Knowledge*, http://www.ccel.org/ccel/schaff/encyc06/Page_3.html (accessed March 30, 2012).

extermination.[380]

The interaction between the coercive power of the Church, the obligation resting upon the state as the secular arm (or, "minister")[381] of the Church, and the fateful end of heretics is illustrated by the Coercive Church Model, as shown in Figure 3.3. It was against such a formidable force supporting religious compliance that Luther and other Protestant Reformers had to square off in their struggle for freedom of conscience.

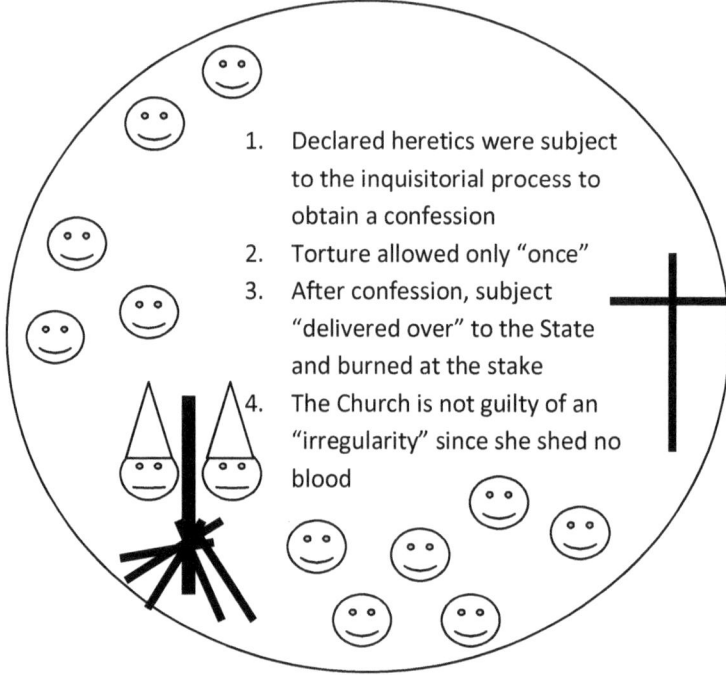

Figure 3.3. The Coercive Church Model – Since Church and State were nearly synonymous in the Medieval Era, the State was considered the "secular arm" of the Church and under obligation to deal with heretics within eight days of their being "delivered over" to its jurisdiction by the Church.

---

[380] Pope Innocent IV, *Ad extirpanda*, Law 20 in Henry Charles Lea, *A History of the Inquisition of the Middle Ages*, 3 vols. (New York: Russel & Russel, 1958; orig. pub. 1887), 1:225.

[381] "[The coercive power of the Church] was applied from the highest to the lowest, and the Church made every dignitary feel that his station was an office in a universal theocracy wherein all interests were subordinate to the great duty of maintaining the purity of the faith." Lea, 1:225.

The Protestant Reformation and Struggles for Freedom of Conscience

While there are numerous events associated with the Protestant Reformation, each of fascination to the reader of religious history, this section will limit itself to those events germane to the focus of this book, namely, the specific Diets (national, secular councils); edicts ensuing from those diets; ecclesiastical councils; and papal bulls related to the issue of conscientious religious convictions, perceived heresy, and ecclesiastical as well as secular mandates regarding the same.

Little did anyone guess that such a simple act of tacking biblical theses to the door of the Wittenburg church in October 31, 1517, would produce the civil unrest and German rallying cries to throw off the yoke of papal bondage. With such an aroused populace, by June 15, 1520, Luther had so infuriated Pope Leo X that he,

> issued a bull, *Exsurge Domine*, which condemned forty-one statements by Luther, ordered the burning of the writings in which these had appeared, and exhorted Luther to abjure his errors and return to the fold. After sixty days of further refusal to come to Rome and make a public recantation, he was to be cut off from Christendom by excommunication, he was to be shunned as a heretic by all the faithful, all places where he stayed were to suspend religious services, and all secular authorities were to banish him from their dominions or deliver him to Rome.[382]

In the months following, Johann Eck and Jerome Aleander began promulgating the bull throughout Germany. Encountering support for the Church on some of those occasions, they also observed the burning of many of Luther's works. Elsewhere, however, Luther and some of his supporters entertained doubts regarding the authenticity of the bull as having come from Pope Leo X, and thus, dismissed its authoritative pronouncements. In the opinion of Erasmus, the lack of clemency in the bull did not reflect the amiableness of the Pope, and he further argued that "Papal bulls are weighty, but scholars attach more weight to books with good arguments drawn from the testimony of divine Scripture, which does

---

[382] Will Durant, *The Reformation* (New York: Simon and Schuster, 1957), 352; Hans J. Hillerbrand, *The Division of Christendom: Christianity in the Sixteenth Century* (Louisville, KY: Westminster John Knox Press, 2007), 50.

not coerce but instructs."[383] In response, on December 10, Luther invited the youth from Wittenburg to observe his burning of the papal bull, thus symbolizing in one act, "his rejection of canon law, of Aquinas's philosophy, and of any coercive authority of the Church."[384]

Upon analysis of the bull, *Exsurge Domine*, Pope Leo X implores the apostles Peter and Paul, as well as Jerome, to stand witness to the need of the Church to resist the errors of Luther. After listing forty-one of Luther's theses, and declaring them to be utterly condemned and reprobate, the bull declares that any person, male or female, who defends such views, or who reads, publishes, proclaims, and disseminates them shall be excommunicated. Leo then proceeds against Luther, fully declaring him to be a heretic, not worthy of appealing to an ecclesiastical council, and not responding to several appeals by the Church leadership. Leo then astutely changes tone to indicate that the papacy shall take an attitude of clemency toward Luther if he will recant, being legally attested to before witnesses. Some translations end the bull at this point.

However, Hans J. Hillerbrand reveals that an additional portion of the bull, not commonly published, indicates a solemn warning to Luther and his adherents:

> And even though the love of righteousness and virtue did not take him away from sin and the hope of forgiveness did not lead him to penance, perhaps the terror of the pain of punishment may move him... Furthermore, this Martin is to recant perpetually such errors and views. He is to inform us of such recantation through an open document, sealed by two prelates, which we should receive within another sixty days. Or he should personally, with safe conduct, inform us of his recantation by coming to Rome. We would prefer this latter way in order that no doubt remain of his sincere obedience.
>
> If, however, this Martin, his supporters, adherents and accomplices, much to our regret, should stubbornly not comply with the mentioned stipulations within the mentioned period, we shall, following the teaching of the holy Apostle Paul, who teaches us to avoid a heretic after having admonished him for a first and a second time, condemn this Martin, his supporters, adherents and

---

[383] Roland Bainton, *Here I Stand: A Life of Martin Luther* (New York, NY: The New American Library, Inc., 1950), 121-122.

[384] Durant, 354-357; Hillerbrand, 55.

accomplices as barren vines which are not in Christ, preaching an offensive doctrine contrary to the Christian faith and offend the divine majesty, to the damage and shame of the entire Christian Church, and diminish the keys of the Church as stubborn and public heretics.[385]

In the previous portions of the bull, there is no mention of how Luther should be punished if unrepentant, but only an intimation that God is not pleased "with the death of the sinner," desiring rather that he should repent and live, which is also the Church's desire for Luther. However, when one takes into consideration that 1520 was in the midst of the centuries of the Inquisition in numerous European, Western Asian, North and South American countries, it requires no guesswork to understand the papal intention of condemning Luther and his followers to be burned at the stake "as public heretics." Not only the historical context aids in such a conclusion, but also the very symbolic language used at the end of the bull suggests the same. Alluding to them as "barren vines which are not in Christ," derived from the Gospel of John, chapter 15:1-8, where Jesus describes those who do not abide in Him as "dry branches" which should be gathered and "cast into the fire," further supports such a conclusion.

Perhaps the strongest argument that can be put forth regarding the papal intention of silencing Luther through the *auto de fe* (burning at the stake) is noted by Yale professor, Roland Bainton, in a letter from Aleander, one of the papal *nuncios* who was entrusted with proclaiming the bull. When the question arose regarding whether Luther should be tried by secular or ecclesiastical courts, Aleander's decisive and quick response was "never" before a secular court, since the Church had already condemned him, necessitating that "the laity should simply implement the Church's decision and not re-examine the grounds of condemnation."[386] Initially, the emperor had issued an invitation for Luther to present his case at the Diet of Worms, but in December, 1520, the invitation was rescinded, due in part to Aleander's persuasive arguments sent by letter to the emperor and which contained, in part, the following:

> The only competent judge is the pope. How can the Church be called the ship of Peter if Peter is not at the

---

[385] Hans J. Hillerbrand, ed. and trans., *The Reformation in its own Words* (London: SCM Prestt, Ltd., 1964), 80-84. Hillerbrand is perhaps the most respected and widely recognized Reformation scholar of the present day.

[386] Bainton, 131; Hillerbrand, 56.

helm? How can she be the ark of Noah if Noah is not the captain? If Luther wants to be heard, he can have a safe conduct to Rome. Or His majesty might send him to the inquisitors in Spain. He can perfectly well recant where he is and then come to the diet to be forgiven.[387]

To satisfy the demands of the laity who comprised the secular, national council (the Diet), Aleander was willing to allow Luther to appear before them, but only after he had presented himself before the ecclesial authorities in Rome or Spain, both locations known for their fervent devotion to the Church, and where inquisitorial practices had occurred. More strikingly evident to Luther's mind must have been the Inquisition in Germany, which, although repulsed by the populace in 1233, still managed to establish itself in some areas, especially northern Germany, by 1484.[388]

Indecision by Charles V as to whether Luther should be allowed to explain his views, or whether he should appear before the Diet merely to recant, – as well as whether the emperor would take full responsibility for Luther's safe passage – caused further delay in the proceedings against Luther. However, the emperor finally agreed to assume responsibility for his passage, so the initial invitation was granted again, resulting in Luther's appearance at the Diet of Worms, in April, 1521.[389]

The Diet of Worms, 1521

During the months of anti-Lutheran propaganda, political developments were taking place that would profoundly affect the future of Protestantism. On October 23, 1520, Charles V was crowned as Emperor of the Holy Roman Empire. Well-favored in Spain, but lacking robust support of the Germans, Charles V faced the dilemma of how best to address the concerns of the Church regarding Luther. The Spanish clergy were expecting a speedy resolution to the problems presented by the heretical monk, while to the German electors, Charles had also given the promise that no German would ever be condemned without a fair trial.[390] Charles V

---

[387] Bainton, 134.

[388] Article, "The Inquisition, II. The Inquisition in the Middle Ages, 6. Germany, the Netherlands, and England" in *The New Schaff-Herzog Encyclopedia of Religious Knowledge*, http://www.ccel.org/ccel/schaff/ encyc06/Page_3.html (accessed February 27, 2012).

[389] Bainton, 135-139; Hillerbrand, 57.

[390] Durant, 358; Hillerbrand, 56.

needed the support of the papacy, not only to enforce morality throughout the empire, but also to direct efforts against the Turkish invasion. With such concerns in mind, Charles V convened and presided over the Diet of Worms, rather than convening it out of concern for a "refractory monk."[391]

The Diet of Worms officially convened on January 27, 1521, but it was not until April 16 that Luther arrived at Worms, and upon the following two days appeared before the Diet. On April 18, he declared his famous statement regarding the rights of individual conscience:

> Unless I am convicted by the testimony of Sacred Scripture or by evident reason (I do not accept the authority of popes and councils, for they have contradicted each other), my conscience is captive to the Word of God. I cannot and will not recant anything, for to go against my conscience is neither right nor safe. God help me. Amen.[392]

By May 6, Aleander had prepared the draft of the "Edict of Worms," which Charles V presented to the Diet. After describing the heretical activities of Luther, the edict states, "We have labored with him, but he recognizes only the authority of Scripture, which he interprets in his own sense. We have given him twenty-one days, dating from April 15 . . . When the time is up, no one is to harbor him. His followers also are to be condemned. His books are to be eradicated from the memory of man."[393]

The Emperor kept his word regarding Luther's safe conduct after the Diet and he was escorted by soldiers on his return home. Out of concern that Luther would not truly be kept safe during the journey, the Elector of Saxony ordered men to capture Luther, under the pretense of being highwaymen, and take him to Wartburg castle where he was protected and wrote much.[394] During the next five years, many events occurred in Germany related to the spread of Luther's teachings, some of which led to the natural animosity and conflict between Luther's followers and Catholics. Such conditions demanded an agreement between the parties regarding mutual respect and understanding, leading to the Diet of Speyer.

---

[391] Durant, 359.

[392] Roger E. Olson, *The Story of Christian Theology: Twenty Centuries of Tradition and Reform* (Downer's Grove, IL: InterVarsity Press, 1999), 378.

[393] Durant, 363.

[394] Hillerbrand, 63.

The Diet of Speyer, 1526

In June, 1526, a group of German princes, prelates, and burghers met to discuss how best to address the religious dissensions that had plagued Germany in prior years. The central issue, which led to the novel idea of religious liberty, was the inability to enforce or repeal the Diet of Worms.[395] The Catholics were insisting that the Diet of Worms be enforced, thus outlawing all of Luther's teachings and re-establishing Catholicism throughout Germany. Luther's followers opined the need for religious freedom until a general council could be convened under German auspices to adjudicate the matter. J. A. Wylie describes the accord finally reached, that until a National Council could be convened, "all shall so behave themselves in their several provinces as that they may be able to render an account of their doings both to God and the emperor"[396] – that is, every State was to be free to act in religion upon its own judgment."[397] The Protestants understood this to mean "sanctioning the establishment of Lutheran churches, the religious autonomy of each territorial prince, and the prohibition of the Mass in Lutheran areas," while "the Catholics rejected these assumptions."[398]

It was precisely due to this initial impasse, and the subsequent solution of religious liberty that gave the fledgling reformation movement an opportunity to establish itself more thoroughly during the next three and one-half years before it faced the threat of the Catholic hierarchy who desired to extirpate it at the Diet of Speyer II, convened in 1529. In addition, "it was . . . the first legal establishment of the Reformation,"[399] an action that would prove to be far more beneficial to the Reformation in the near future than any would have anticipated at the time.

---

[395] J. H. Merle D'Aubigné, *History of the Reformation of the Sixteenth Century*, 8 vols. (New York: Robert Carter and Brothers, 1872), 4:11-12; Hillerbrand, 157-158.

[396] Sleidan, bk. vi., p. 104, cited in J. A. Wylie, *The History of Protestantism*, 2 vols. (Carginagh, Kilkeel, Co. Down, N. Ireland: Mourne Missionary Trust, 1985), 1:530.

[397] Wylie, 1:530.

[398] Durant, 442; Hillerbrand (157) adds that the Catholic estates "felt tricked or at least misunderstood."

[399] Wylie, 1:549.

The Diet of Speyer II, 1529

After reconciling himself with Pope Clement, Charles V called for the reconvening of the Diet of Speyer on February 1, 1529. According to the historian, J. A. Wylie, the only reason for which the Diet was convened was to overturn the decision taken at the Diet of Speyer, 1526, and thus leave in force the Diet of Worms, 1521.[400] He describes the far-reaching implications of such a move:

> Religious freedom, then, so far as enjoyed in Germany, the Diet was now asked to abolish. But this was not all. The edict of 1526 suspended legally the execution of the Edict of Worms of 1521, which proscribed Luther and condemned the Reformation. Abolish the edict of 1526, and the edict of 1521 would come into operation; Luther must be put to death; the Reformed opinions must be rooted out of all the countries where they had taken root; in short, the floodgates of a measureless persecution would be opened in Germany. . . . The sending of such a message even was a violation of the constitutional rights of the several States, and an assumption of power which no former emperor had dared to make. The message, if passed into law, would have laid the rights of conscience, the independence of the Diet, and the liberties of Germany, all three in the dust.[401]

Nevertheless, the papal members of the Diet argued for the repeal of the Edict of Speyer (1526), but met stiff opposition from the reformed members, who pointed out that it was now part of the constitution of the Empire and to make such a sweeping repeal would be to violate not only that national document, but also to usurp the rights of the individual States to decide regarding religious matters. Such a move would introduce "a new spiritual order of things" and be tantamount to civil war and revolt.[402]

Recognizing these dangers, the papal members decided "they would

---

[400] Wylie, 1:548; cf. D'Aubigné, 52; Hillerbrand (160) adds that due to "the Turkish Ottoman threat," the emperor's brother, Ferdinand, "called on all estates to do away with religious disagreements," meaning to "return to the Catholic fold."

[401] Wylie, 1:548, 549.

[402] Wylie, 1:549; cf. D'Aubigne, 54; Hillerbrand, 161.

neither abolish nor enforce the edict of 1526." In those States where the Edict of Worms regulated religious affairs, - viz., the preaching of the Gospel was forbidden and its professors were burned – such practice would continue. In others, where the Edict of Speyer governed affairs (i.e., religious freedom prevailed), the papal members proposed that the *status quo* remain, with "very important modifications . . . that the Popish hierarchy should be re-established, that the celebration of the mass should be permitted, and that no one should be allowed to abjure Popery and embrace Lutheranism till such time as a Council had met and framed a general arrangement."[403]

Recognizing that maintaining the *status quo* and agreeing to no proselytism endangered the fledgling movement, the reformed members rejected the proposal. They realized that the principle of religious freedom was at stake, as well as the Reformation. How could they deny to others the same privilege they had enjoyed to embrace the reformed movement?[404] On April 19, 1529, they nobly took their stand in "protest," hence deriving the name "Protestants"[405] and argued that "in matters of conscience, the majority has no power."[406] The Protestant principles – viz., conscience

---

[403] Wylie, 1:549, Wylie's footnote 1: "Pallavicino, lib. ii., cap. 18. Sleidan, bk. vi., p. 118. Seckendorf, lib. ii., sec. 14, p. 127. The edict contained other articles, such as that Sacramentarians or Zwinglians should be banished from all the lands of the Empire, and that Anabaptists should be punished with death. (Pallavicino, lib. ii., cap. 18); D'Aubigne, 53, 54; Eike Wolgast includes these points, but adds two others: that no new innovative teachings regarding the Eucharist, such as what Zwingli advocated, would be allowed and that the postulate of majority rule in matters of faith, all of which met with protest by the Reformers. Eike Wolgast, "Speyer, Protestation of", trans. Susan M. Sisler, in *The Oxford Encyclopedia of the Reformation*, 4 vols., ed. Hans J. Hillerbrand, (New York: Oxford University Press, 1996), 4:104.

[404] D'Aubigne, 53-55; Wylie, 1:549.

[405] D'Aubigne, 60; Hillerbrand, 161.

[406] D'Aubigne, 55; Wolgast, "Speyer, Protestation of", in *The Oxford Encyclopedia of the Reformation*, ed. Hillerbrand, 4:104. "The protestation received legal status through the appeal that the Protestant princes and imperial cities lodged before two notaries in Speyer on 25 April, 1529. This appeal contained a report on the proceedings between majority and minority and all important documents. . . .The appeal thwarted the execution of the recess of the diet. It was to be of great significance for the future of the constitution of the empire and the negotiations at future diets that in 1529 the individual conscience was established for the first time as a norm of decisions not to be outvoted in political negotiations. Against the positive law was set the conformity of the evangelical teachings to the scriptures;

above the magistrate; the Word of God above the visible church; and, proselytism[407] – gained for modern times "liberty of thought and independence of faith."[408]

At this point in the unfolding of the Protestant struggles for freedom of conscience, great care should be exercised in examining the differences between the Protestant concept of religious freedom and that of the Roman Catholic Church. For Protestants, religious freedom is defined as the liberty to follow one's conscientious convictions based on religious truth from the Word of God. The majority is not to rule over the minority in matters of religious faith and, therefore, each should recognize and respect the rights of the other, while the rights of all should be guaranteed by law. For Catholics, religious freedom meant that Protestants were not forced to renounce their faith, but neither were they allowed to propagate it. In addition, it meant the freedom of the Church (*libertas ecclesiastica*) to maintain the jurisdictional authority of the papal hierarchy (episcopacy), the right to celebrate the mass in Lutheran territory, and the denial of any Catholic to convert to Lutheranism. It also granted a temporary suspension (an immunity) of the use of either force or coercion in the religious sphere.[409] Once Protestantism was well-established and had its own schools by 1544, financial support was guaranteed to all, both Protestant and Catholic.[410]

---

the legal act of protestation presupposed a religious decision. Clearly, the protesting estates intended no political separation."

[407] D'Aubigne, 60-61. "We cannot abandon this proselytism without abandoning the protestant principle." Cf., Peter G. Wallace, *The Long European Reformation* (New York, NY: Palgrave Macmillan, 2004), 97.

[408] D'Aubigne, 55.

[409] The Diet of Speyer, 1526, granted a temporary suspension of the Edict of Worms (1521) due to differences regarding how to settle the religious question. By 1529, at the Diet of Speyer II, the Reformers "protested" the decision taken there to annul the temporary suspension taken in 1526. On November 19, 1530, at the Diet of Augsburg, Emperor Charles V signed into imperial law that "all phases of Protestantism were condemned; the Edict of Worms was to be enforced." He granted them "six months to adjust to the will of the Diet," until April 15, 1531, during which time they were offered "immunity from the Edict of Worms." Durant, 442-444.

[410] At the Diet of Speyer (1544), "The enjoyment of ecclesiastical revenues was guaranteed to all, hence even Protestant holders of benefices. Provided these revenues were applied to such purposes as the founding of schools and so forth, Protestants might retain them: all previous dispositions in this respect were to remain valid." Hubert Jedin, *A History of the Council of Trent*, trans. Dom Ernest

Thus, it weighs heavily as an overt form of Catholic hegemony. Table 3.1 lists the differences between Protestant and Catholic definitions of religious freedom.

Table 3.1: Differences between Protestant and Catholic Concepts of Religious Freedom, Diet of Speyer II, 1529. The hegemonic nature of the Catholic Church is obvious, as well as its intent to stagnate the Protestant Reformation.

Protestant Definition of Religious Freedom	Catholic Definition of Religious Freedom
1. Liberty to follow one's convictions	1. Protestants not forced to renounce faith
2. Convictions based on God's Word	2. No propagation of non-Catholic teachings
3. Majority not to rule over minorities	3. Catholic jurisdictional authority retained
4. Each is to respect the other	4. Celebration of Mass in Lutheran territory
5. Rights of all guaranteed by law	5. No Catholic allowed to convert
	6. Suspension (an immunity) of force or coercion

Such a hegemonic form of Catholic ideas of religious freedom echoes the ideas inherent to *Dignitatis Humanae*. Its central teaching is the *libertas ecclesiastica* (freedom of the Church) to fulfill its mission.[411] It argues for the

Graf, O.S.B., 2 vols. (St. Louis, MO: B. Herder Book Co., English version, 1957), 1:496.

[411] "Whereas *Dignitatis Humanae* proceeds cautiously on other questions, the wording here at article 13 is decisive: 'the most outstanding surely is that the Church enjoy that freedom of action which her responsibility for the salvation of men requires.' Such freedom is called "sacred" (*libertas sacra est*) because it is endowed by Christ.... This history is indisputably the background of *Dignitatis Humanae*, article 13, ... [which] recites practically verbatim important sentences of Leo XIII's letter, *Officio sancissimo*, to the Church in Bavaria, ... 'Of the rights of the

"one true religion" which is "the Roman Catholic Church"[412] and maintains the obligation of men to seek the truth "and once finding it to embrace it."[413] Its language does not teach the freedom to propagate error,[414] nor does it grant any Catholic the right to convert to another faith.[415] Regarding recognition of the papal hierarchy, such is implicitly acknowledged and accepted by those governments that adopt the principles of *Dignitatis Humanae*. Albeit, the language of *Dignitatis Humanae* does not strike the reader as an overt form of Catholic hegemony, but its intent becomes nonetheless evident upon historical analysis and comparison. Table 3.2 shows parallels between Catholic concepts of religious freedom from the Diet of Speyer II and those from *Dignitatis Humanae* (Vatican II).

Church that it is Our duty everywhere and always to maintain and defend against all injustice, the first is certainly that of enjoying the full freedom of action she may need in working for the salvation of souls. This is a divine liberty, having as its author the only Son of God, Who, by shedding of blood, gave birth to the Church.'" Russel Hittinger, "The Declaration on Religious Liberty," in *Vatican II: Renewal within Tradition*, eds. Matthew L. Lamb and Matthew Levering (New York: Oxford University Press, 2008), 370.

[412] *Dignitatis Humanae*, Art. 2, par. 1.

[413] *Dignitatis Humanae*, Art. 2, par. 1.

[414] "Certainly, freedom from coercion in the religious sphere can be realized badly, if errors are professed and propagated, whether in good or in bad faith. But the abuse of a right does not destroy it; at most it may make it advisable to prevent the exercise of this right according to appropriate criteria." Pietro Pavan, "Commentary," in *Commentary on the Documents of Vatican II*, 4 vols. (New York, NY: Crossroad Publishing, 1989), 4:66 .

[415] "In his comments on the Vatican Declaration on Religious Freedom, Carrillo De Albornoz expresses regret 'that the Vatican Declaration does not expressly proclaim the freedom to change one's religion.'" As quoted by V. Norskov Olsen, *Christian Faith and Religious Freedom* (Brushton, NY: TEACH Services, 1996), 77, and originally appearing in A. E. Carrillo De Albornoz, "The Ecumenical and World Significance of the Vatican Declaration on Religious Liberty" in *The Ecumenical Review*, vol. xviii (1966), 61, 63. A. F. Carrillo De Albornoz was an Anglican who served as secretary to the Secretariat for Religious Liberty at Vatican II and was an international jurist who held Ph.D.s in philosophy and theology.

Table 3.2: Parallels between Catholic Concepts of Religious Freedom, Diet of Speyer II (1529) and *Dignitatis Humanae* of Vatican II (1965). The exact, or nearly so, parallels between the two historic time periods with respect to religious freedom suggests that the Catholic Church has not changed its hegemonic nature, only its method of achieving hegemony. Additionally, it strongly suggests that the Church's efforts to arrest and counteract the Protestant Reformation (and any other religion) are far from being buried in the past.

Catholic Religious Freedom – Diet of Speyer II	Religious Freedom in *Dignitatis Humanae*, Vatican Council II
1. Protestants not forced to renounce	1. Does not deny or endorse religious plurality
2. No teaching of non-Catholic faith	2. Does not authorize erroneous teaching
3. Catholic jurisdictional authority retained	3. Catholic jurisdictional authority implicit
4. Celebration of Catholic Mass in Lutheran territories	4. *Libertas ecclesiastica* to fulfill mission anywhere in the world
5. No Catholic conversions	5. No Catholic conversions allowed
6. Suspension (an immunity) of force or coercion	6. Immunity from coercion as civil right

There remains one other highly significant point to consider from the Diet of Speyer II that presents a formidable challenge to Catholic notions of religious freedom. In *A History of the Council of Trent*, Hubert Jedin recounts the political bargaining that led to the legal tolerance extended to Protestants. From his account, it becomes evident that such tolerance was the desire of the Emperor, at least for political reasons. However, the Papacy objected entirely to raising the religious question (tolerance for Protestants) at the Council. *If granted, the Papacy intended to change this legal standing in the future in order to reverse tolerance toward Protestants, thus revealing tolerance not as a principle, but merely a concession:*

The annulment of the previous recesses (Diets) practically amounted to a declaration of toleration. However, all these concessions were only temporary; a final settlement would be made by the new Diet by means of a "reformation" worked out without the Pope's concurrence. . . . All the Curia's efforts to keep the religious question out of the agenda of the Diet of Speyer, or at least to make sure that it would not be discussed without its participation through its delegate, had been in vain. Whereas at Ratisbon the Emperor had given up important Catholic positions in deepest secrecy, he now yielded them openly and in due legal form for the sake of a momentary political success. He lent himself to an arbitrary settlement of the ecclesiastical situation at some future date which, in view of the state of things, might easily lead – was perhaps bound to lead – to the whole of Germany becoming Protestant.[416]

Once the Papacy became aware of this situation, the Pope issued a brief, outlining the relations between the temporal and ecclesiastical spheres, and concluding with specific demands:

> *The Emperor must refrain from encroaching on the ecclesiastical sphere, from discussing religious questions at the Diet and from disposing of Church property.* If peace cannot be brought about by any other means he must accept the arbitration of the Council. *The concessions made to the Protestants must be revoked.* In the event of the Emperor refusing to comply with these demands he will be sternly dealt with.[417]

Although history records that the Protestants stood firmly in defense of religious freedom, the papal record indicates that the religious freedom granted was merely due to political expediencies beyond its ability to control and that the papal intent was to deny such religious freedom. Thus, with respect to *Dignitatis Humanae*, the question of whether it is a revocable concession or an unchanging principle will be addressed more fully in the last section of this chapter. Nonetheless, the jurisdictional authority of the Church was evident during the Reformation and the next section addresses how much of that authority is still recognized by the Church today.

---

[416] Jedin, 1:496-497.

[417] Jedin, 1:498-499 (italics mine).

The Council of Trent and the Jurisdictional Authority of the Church

In a highly evocative paper entitled, "What is the Catholic doctrine of religious liberty?" Thomas Pink proposes that many modern Catholics have applied *Dignitatis Humanae* with a person-centered focus, resulting in justification of liberal practices that actually contradict Church teachings.[418] He further asserts that a jurisdictional-centered view dates back to the Council of Trent and is even more conservative than the nineteenth-century traditional concept of religious freedom.[419] Pink argues:

> But nevertheless, the jurisdiction-centered view may not only be a central feature of the Church's past; it may still be binding on modern Catholics. For if Vatican II appears, at least on a conventional understanding of *Dignitatis Humanae*, to endorse a person-centered view, it will become evident that the Council of Trent clearly endorsed a jurisdiction-centered view.[420]

From this assertion, Pink explores the philosophical and metaphysical arguments set forth by Suarez for which he believes the Church is justified in applying coercion upon its members. What he wrestles with, as well, is the metaphysical argument of "the freedom of the will in the act of faith," and the Church's posture toward those outside of its fold, i.e., those outside of its jurisdiction.[421]

Relying upon Suarez's arguments, Pink describes how the "freedom of the will in the act of faith" is always a free choice, whether one is subject to direct or indirect coercion. The human being always has a free will to make choices for or against any religious beliefs. Even when under coercion, the will is still free, viz., at the command of the individual, to make a choice to retain his own beliefs and suffer ongoing torture, to falsify acceptance of

---

[418] Thomas Pink, "What is the Catholic doctrine of religious liberty?", page 3, http://kcl.academia.edu/ThomasPink/Papers/647475/What_is_the_Catholic_doctrine_of_religious_liberty (accessed November 23, 2011). No date is given as to when this article was originally posted. However, on the webpage, footnote 1 on page 1 reveals that Pink developed his thoughts between 2008 and 2010, with many Catholic scholars giving him their input.

[419] Pink, 4.

[420] Pink, 4.

[421] Pink, 6, 7.

beliefs other than his own, or to relinquish his beliefs in favor of the dominant religion. He posits the case of not only religious acts, but even religious ideas being subject to subtle forms of coercion. He gives the example such as when an individual, or small group of believers, must daily live within a society which is ordered by beliefs contrary to theirs and in which they hear daily propaganda in favor of the dominant religion. Through such *indirect coercion* over time, some minorities give up their previously held beliefs, and others, through prohibitions against proselytism, fail to pass on their faith to their descendants. In any of these examples, the will of the individual is always free and under his own control. Thus, the freedom of the will in the act of faith will always be free *by nature*. Such an insightful perspective on Catholic metaphysical dimensions of faith facilitates a deeper analysis of certain phrases in *Dignitatis Humanae* which refer to the individual having the civil right to "immunity from coercion,"[422] since "the act of faith" must always be free.[423] It suggests that an individual is not being forced into the faith, whether coerced subtly or directly, since the will of the individual is still free to accept or reject the proffered faith.

Pink presents Suarez's teaching that the act of faith must be free from all coercion. But, once an individual makes such a decision, it places him as a now baptized Catholic under the jurisdiction of the Church. The individual does not have the right to leave the Church, according to Suarez, and the Church actually has the jurisdictional authority to compel the individual to keep faithful to his commitment.[424] Through coercive measures both external acts and internal belief can be coerced and still not violate the metaphysical dimension of the freedom of the will in the act of faith.[425] Not only can members of the Church be coerced, but also heretics,

---

[422] *Dignitatis Humanae*, Art. 2, par. 1, "This Vatican Council declares that the human person has a right to religious freedom. This freedom means that all men are to be immune from coercion on the part of individuals or of social groups and of any human power, in such wise that no one is to be forced to act in a manner contrary to his own beliefs, whether privately or publicly, whether alone or in association with others within due limits."

[423] *Dignitatis Humanae*, Art. 10, par. 1, "It is one of the major tenets of Catholic doctrine that man's response to God in faith must be free: no one therefore is to be forced to embrace the Christian faith against his own will. This doctrine is contained in the word of God and it was constantly proclaimed by the Fathers of the Church. The act of faith is of its very nature a free act."

[424] Pink, 5.

[425] Pink, 7, 8.

since both can benefit spiritually, and neither will be deprived of their metaphysical freedom. However, Suarez does not end here – even those who are born into heresy (i.e., Protestants) fall under the jurisdiction of the Church if they have been validly baptized. Suarez's position harmonizes with the position of the Church taken at Vatican II regarding those validly baptized, but in other churches, resulting in the term adopted in Vatican II documents referring to non-Catholic Christians as "separated brethren."[426]

Pink's conclusions drawn from Suarez's works echo similar sentiments by other Catholic scholars who see Vatican II as a continuation of the Council of Trent, albeit with a different focus. Jeanine Hill Fletcher argues that the councils stand in continuity, but only with "a different emphasis in light of changed conditions."[427] What kind of changed emphasis does Vatican II offer compared to Trent? Joseph Komonchak explains:

> Because Trent had not thought it necessary to reaffirm what Protestants had not denied, the theology constructed in its wake also tended to neglect these dimensions in favor of emphasis upon the ones Reformers had denied. Vatican II sought to overcome this polemical slant and to recover the broader and deeper vision of earlier ages of Christian thought, particularly the patristic period. *There is no point at which Vatican II departs from any dogmatic teaching of the council of Trent, but at Vatican II, Trent and its problematic ceased to serve as the supreme touchstone of faith. The tradition was no longer read in the light of Trent; Trent was read in the light of the tradition.* This is visible in what Vatican II has to say about the common priesthood of the faithful, the Eucharist, and the ministerial priesthood: the teaching of Trent is neither denied nor passed over in silence; it is integrated into a larger whole. As Jedin put it, Trent was not revised, it was expanded.[428]

---

[426] For further discussion, see chapter one, page 30, fn. 100.

[427] Jeannine Hill Fletcher, "Responding to Religious Difference: Conciliar Perspective," in *From Trent to Vatican II: Historical and Theological Investigations*, eds. Raymond F. Bulman and Frederich J. Parrella (New York: Oxford, 2006), 280. Jeannine Hill Fletcher holds a Th. D. from Harvard, specializes in systematic theology, and is an assistant professor at Fordham University.

[428] Joseph A. Komonchak, "The Council of Trent at the Second Vatican Council," in *From Trent to Vatican II: Historical and Theological Investigations*, eds. Bulman and Parrella, 76. Komonchak is a specialist in the history and theology of

For religious freedom, this means that the practices of the Church in dealing with heretics and its use of coercive authority are not the norm, but only part of the tradition of the Church. Viewed in this light, the phrase "immunity from coercion" in *Dignitatis Humanae* is more readily understood to mean that the Church retains its coercive authority in religious matters, but due to present conditions refrains from exercising it. Thus, the Church gives such a directive to the modern states of today through *Dignitatis Humanae*, that the individual citizen has a "right to religious freedom," a guarantee to be "immune from coercion on the part of . . . any human power,"[429] which is a position similar in sentiment to that adopted by the Church at the Diet of Speyer, 1526, temporarily suspending the use of physical force or coercion in religious matters.

A Roman Catholic Concept of Toleration and Immunity from Coercion

In the area of religious freedom, terminology and nuanced expressions carry much weight in determining practical applications, especially when declarations are made with reference to the juridical order. The phrases in question here, "toleration" and "immunity from coercion," reflect differing reference points, as well as differing subjects upon whom obligations rest. This section addresses those differences and other related factors.

Pre-Vatican II: Tolerance for Non-Catholic Minority Faiths

The Pre-Vatican II concept of tolerance toward non-Catholic minority faiths is best explained by Thomas Aquinas in *Summa Theologica* Book II-II, the Eleventh Article, "Ought the Rites of Unbelievers to be Tolerated?" He presents three objections that argue in favor of non-tolerance and then reasons for conditional tolerance in this fashion:

> *I answer that* Human government is derived from the divine government and should imitate it. Now, although God is all-powerful and supremely good, nevertheless He allows certain evils to take place in the universe which He might prevent, lest without them greater goods might be forfeited or greater evils ensue. Accordingly, in human government also, those who are in authority rightly tolerate certain evils, lest certain goods be lost or certain

---

Vatican II, holding a Ph.D. in Theology and having taught at the Catholic University of America.

[429] *Dignitatis Humanae*, Art. 2, par. 1.

greater evils be incurred; thus Augustine says, "If you do away with harlots, the world will be convulsed with lust." Hence, though unbelievers sin in their rites, they may be tolerated either on account of some good that ensues therefrom or because of some evil avoided. Thus, from the fact that the Jews observe their rites, which of old foreshadowed the truth of the faith which we hold, there follows this good – that our very enemies bear witness to our faith, and that our faith is represented in a figure, so to speak. For this reason, they are tolerated in observance of their rites.

On the other hand, the rites of other unbelievers, which are neither truthful nor profitable, are by no means to be tolerated, except perchance in order to avoid an evil, e.g., the scandal or disturbance that might ensue or some hindrance to the salvation of those who, if they were unmolested, might gradually be converted to the faith. For this reason, the Church at times has tolerated the rites even of heretics and pagans when unbelievers were very numerous.[430]

From this reasoning, one may summarize the Church's centuries-long position toward unbelievers as "tolerance to achieve a greater good, or to avoid a greater evil."[431] Additionally, the traditional formula for religious freedom argued for full religious freedom for Catholics when they should be in the minority, but only tolerance toward non-Catholics who should be the minority faith among a dominant Catholic populace.

However, the Church's stance toward heretics (former members of the

---

[430] Thomas Aquinas, *Summa Theologica*, Book II-II, Question 10, "Of Unbelief in General," Article Eleven, "Ought the Rites of Unbelievers to be Tolerated?" in *Saint Thomas Aquinas: On Law, Morality, and Politics*, eds. William P. Baumgarth and Richard J. Regan (Indianapolis, IN: Hackett Publishing Co., 1988), 254-255.

[431] John Courtney Murray, referring to the pre-Vatican II stance of the Church, explains tolerance in this fashion: "Error has no rights. Therefore error is to be suppressed whenever and wherever possible; intolerance is the rule. Error, however, may be tolerated when tolerance is necessary by reason of circumstances, that is, when intolerance is impossible; tolerance remains the exception. Tolerance therefore is 'hypothesis,' a concession to a factual situation, a lesser evil." Cited by William Reiser, "Roman Catholic Understanding of Religious Tolerance in Modern Times," in *Religious Tolerance in World Religions*, eds. Jacob Neusner and Bruce Chilton (West Conshohocken, PA: Templeton Foundation, 2008), 160.

Church) is much more severe, as Aquinas elaborates in *Summa Theologica*, Book II-II, Question 11, "Of Heresy," Article Three, "Ought Heretics to be Tolerated?" He first argues from analogy as to why heretics should be put to death, reasoning that "it is a much graver matter to corrupt faith, which quickens the soul, than to forge money, which supports temporal life," and concluding that "if forgers of money and other evildoers are forthwith condemned to death by the secular authority, much more reason is there for heretics, as soon as they are convicted of heresy, to be not only excommunicated but even put to death."[432] The role of the Church in dealing with heretics is to show clemency with the intent of their conversion by not condemning until "after the first and second admonition, as the Apostle directs." But after this, "if he is yet stubborn, the Church, no longer hoping for his conversion, looks to the salvation of others by excommunicating him and separating him from the Church, and furthermore delivers him to the secular tribunal to be exterminated thereby from the world by death."[433]

Anticipating an objection by some of his readers who might refer to Christ's teaching about not plucking up the tares (some versions, cockles, viz., heretics) until the end of the harvest (the end of the world), and thus, argue that heretics should be tolerated, Aquinas distinguishes between being excommunicated and "uprooted":

> *Reply to Obj. 3.* According to the *Decretum*, "to be excommunicated is not to be uprooted." A man is excommunicated, as the Apostle says, that his "spirit may be saved in the day of Our Lord." Yet if heretics be altogether uprooted by death, this is not contrary to Our Lord's command, which is to be understood as referring to the case when the cockle cannot be plucked up without plucking up the wheat, as we explained above when treating of unbelievers in general.[434]

An explanation for the sake of clarification is in order. Aquinas applies Jesus' parable of the wheat and tares (Matt. 13:24-30) to society in general, which may be comprised of unbelievers along with Catholics. This seems to be a correct interpretation, thus far, since Jesus defined the "field" in the

---

[432] Thomas Aquinas, Question 11, "Of Heresy," Article Three, "Ought Heretics to Be Tolerated?" in Baumgarth, 256.

[433] Ibid., 256.

[434] Baumgarth, 257.

parable as "the world."⁴³⁵ Thus, Aquinas' explanation of tolerance toward the non-Catholics in society applies – "tolerance to avoid a greater evil, or to obtain a greater good." The other passage Aquinas quotes from is found in 1 Corinthians 5:5, written by the Apostle Paul, which refers to the church's obligation to "cast out" (v. 13) the immoral members (in the particular case in question in Corinth, the man who had a sexual relationship with his father's wife). Aquinas does not equate the Apostle Paul's counsel "to deliver such an one unto Satan for the destruction of the flesh" with the "plucking up" of Jesus' parable. Thus, in his *Reply to Obj. 3*, Aquinas argues that it "is not contrary to our Lord's command" not to pluck up the tares "if heretics be altogether uprooted by death," as he interprets the Apostle Paul's counsel literally.

Upon closer study of the Scriptures, Aquinas's position seems contrary to the Scriptures for several reasons.⁴³⁶ First, the Apostle's counsel to "cast out" the immoral member does not refer to removing them from this world by death.⁴³⁷ Second, in order to give the benefit of the doubt to Aquinas, one must consider the linguistic factors that might be at work here. There are two Greek words that differ only by one letter, yet both have widely different meanings: ἐξαιρέω and ἐξαίρω. The first term means "to take out," or "to tear out" as "one's eye."⁴³⁸ The second term means "to remove," or "to drive away."⁴³⁹ The second term is used in 1 Corinthians

---

⁴³⁵ Matthew 13:38.

⁴³⁶ Obviously, Aquinas's teaching was not explicitly clear to others: "Froude comments on how the Word of God had "become dead in the droning of the Vulgate," and how Erasmus' Greek New Testament had provided Luther with the original source to translate from, thus restoring "life and meaning" to those words. Froude gives an example, "What meaning the monks had got out of the Vulgate, Erasmus illustrates with a hundred instances. He was present once when some of them were arguing whether it was right to put heretics to death. A learned friar quoted from St. Paul, "Haereticum devita." He had conceived that by "de vita" St. Paul had meant an order *de vita tollere* (tolerate the life of)." James Anthony Froude, *Lectures on the Council of Trent* (New York: Charles Scribner's Sons, 1896), 56-57. Froude was an English historian, novelist, biographer, and editor of *Fraser's* magazine.

⁴³⁷ See exegesis of this passage, 1 Corinthians 5:5, 13, at the beginning of this chapter under "Tolerance," p. 122.

⁴³⁸ First entry under ἐξαιρέω in Walter Bauer, William F. Arndt, and F. Wilbur Gingrich, *A Greek-English Lexicon of the New Testament* (Chicago: University of Chicago Press, 1979), 271.

⁴³⁹ Ibid., under ἐξαίρω, 272.

5:13, "to cast out" the immoral man from the congregation. If scribes had erred in copying from an original manuscript by adding the "ἑ," the whole meaning is changed to "tearing out the immoral man from among you," from which Aquinas could have derived the "uprooting" of heretics."[440] From his own statement, he seems to indicate that he understands some parallelism between 1 Corinthians 5:13 and Matthew 13:24-30, at least enough to try and clarify why he believes they are not contradictory.

The application, of course, of Aquinas's teaching regarding toleration toward unbelievers and persecution of heretics has a varied history in the Church. During the Inquisition, as noted previously, there was little to no toleration shown to heretics. In later centuries, especially by the eighteenth-century, general toleration was shown to all non-Catholics through the "thesis/hypothesis" formula. By the twentieth-century, societal demands for human rights had increased enough to cause the Church to reformulate its position on religious freedom during Vatican Council II (1965).

Vatican II: Immunity from Coercion for Non-Catholic Minority Faiths

John Courtney Murray was determined to revolutionize the "thesis/hypothesis" formula through a systematic, theological development of religious freedom that harmonized with traditional teaching. The central element of Murray's idea in this regard includes "immunity from coercion" for all people, based on the dignity of the human person, which is to be enacted as a civil right. The first part of this section, then, sets forth Murray's rationale in developing this view. The second part scrutinizes some aspects of Murray's novel concept of religious freedom, such as investigating the philosophical rationale sustaining it and analyzing the distinct differences between the linguistic meanings of "tolerance" and "immunity from coercion." Then, an analysis of how such ideas should find application in a constitutional democracy will be presented to conclude.

Murray defined religious freedom as "immunity from coercion" because he recognized that in order to posit it as a civil right, one must draw a fine distinction between "a right as empowerment, and a right as immunity from coercion."[441] Without this distinction, religious freedom could easily be

---

[440] There are other areas for investigation, such as the Latin text used by Aquinas and the Greek words used for "root up."

[441] "[T]here was a need to elucidate the distinction between the notion of "right" as an empowerment and as an immunity. He pointed out that in the Declaration religious freedom is called a right in the sense of an immunity from all coercion. On the ground of this distinction the charge of religious indifferentism is nullified, and the assertion can be made that the Church does not hold that all men

mistaken for complete liberty of conscience as a right before God to choose whichever religion appealed to one's conscience. Thus, by only limiting the right to religious freedom as "immunity from coercion," Murray argued for the freedom of the individual to seek for religious truth in fulfillment of his obligation before God, and not as a right to religious indifferentism. The further benefit was that "immunity from coercion" harmonized with the Church's teaching that "the act of faith" must always be free.

Murray conceptualized of this societal construct based on his perception that the state in modern times had achieved an almost absolute power. He also based it on what he viewed as humanity's growth in consciousness toward human dignity:

> Recall that Murray bases his case for religious liberty as an immunity on the belief that while "illiterate masses" require a paternalistic form of government, the new consciousness persons have of their dignity requires a state that does not interfere in the regular conduct of their religious lives. Murray's argument, therefore, depends on a particular historiography: Leo XIII retrieves Hilderbrand's concept of diarchy from obscurity. . . . Murray's emphasis on the case for diarchy reflects the preoccupying problem of the time: to find a third alternative to the unpalatable choice between state churches and the state suppression of all religions.[442]

From this perspective, one may correctly interpret *Dignitatis Humanae* as being written primarily to the state (or government), with a focus upon the freedom of the Church (*libertas ecclesiastica*) and the rights of the individual based upon his human dignity. This societal construct produces several results: the state becomes limited in its (coercive) power; the Church is free to fulfill its mission; there is limited interaction between both state and Church; the Church has indirect influence upon the state, relying more upon persuading the individual, who in turn can direct public policy

---

are equally empowered by God, or conscience, to practice any religion they choose." Donald E. Pelotte, *John Courtney Murray: Theologian in Conflict* (New York: Paulist Press, 1976), 93.

[442] Todd David Whitmore, "Immunity or Empowerment?: John Courtney Murray and the Question of Religious Liberty," in *John Courtney Murray and the Growth of Tradition*, eds. J. Leon Hooper and Todd David Whitmore (Kansas City, MO: Sheed & Ward, 1996), 161-162.

through elected officials; and, "the spiritual power is limited to spiritual matters and terminates at the conscience of the individual believer."[443] Although reflecting modern concepts, there are some aspects of Murray's innovative approach to religious freedom which merit scrutiny, especially when compared to the pre-Vatican II stance of toleration.

Under the Pre-Vatican II concept, the Church granted tolerance to unbelievers, heretics, and pagans, depending upon the circumstances of each situation. At Vatican II, the idea of religious freedom, defined as one's responsibility to pursue religious truth without coercion, was promulgated as a development of doctrine in harmony with previous teachings. In Article seven, paragraph three, *Dignitatis Humanae* recognizes the right of the individual to religious freedom, even when that right may be abused. The Council fathers argued that the abuse of religious freedom does not abolish it, nor give government the right to suppress it, except "within due limits" in cases that might harm individuals or society. The rationale they used to arrive at this conclusion was based upon the Allocution of 6 December, 1953, given by Pope Pius XII:

> Can God, who could easily suppress error and moral aberrations, nevertheless choose in some cases the *non impedire* without prejudice to his infinite perfection? May he, in certain circumstances, give no command, impose no duty, indeed give no right to men to hinder and suppress what is erroneous and false? One glance at reality compels an affirmative answer. It shows that there is a great deal of error and sin in the world. God rejects them, nevertheless he allows them to continue. Hence the thesis that religious and moral aberration must be hindered whenever possible because its toleration is in itself immoral, is not absolutely and unconditionally valid. On the other hand, God has not given human authority such an absolute and universal commandment, neither in the sphere of faith nor in the sphere of morals. Neither general human conviction nor Christian consciousness nor the sources of revelation or the practice of the Church are aware of such a command.[444]

Pavan indicates that this Allocution formed the basis of the answer given by

---

[443] Pelotte, 125.

[444] Pope Pius XII, Allocution of 6 December, 1953, quoted by Pietro Pavan, Commentary, 73.

the Council fathers regarding whether religious freedom should be granted to religious groups whose activities might pose a threat to society – i.e., since God allowed sin and error in the world, should not *religious freedom* also be granted to those groups who might abuse it?[445] However, this is the same answer used by Thomas Aquinas in response to the question, Ought the Rites of Unbelievers to Be Tolerated? in which he argues that *conditional toleration* be given to unbelievers, heretics, and pagans:

> *I answer that* Human government is derived from the divine government and should imitate it. Now, although God is all-powerful and supremely good, nevertheless He allows certain evils to take place in the universe which He might prevent, lest without them greater goods might be forfeited or greater evils ensue. Accordingly, in human government also, those who are in authority rightly tolerate certain evils, lest certain goods be lost or certain greater evils be incurred; thus Augustine says, "If you do away with harlots, the world will be convulsed with lust." Hence, though unbelievers sin in their rites, they may be tolerated either on account of some good that ensues therefrom or because of some evil avoided. Thus, from the fact that the Jews observe their rites, which of old foreshadowed the truth of the faith which we hold, there follows this good – that our very enemies bear witness to our faith, and that our faith is represented in a figure, so to speak. For this reason, they are tolerated in observance of their rites.[446]

The above comparison seems to suggest that *Dignitatis Humanae* represents a re-worded idea of toleration, rather than a novel concept of religious freedom. A definition of both terms aids in further analysis of this possible conclusion.

Anson Phelps Stokes, of the prestigious Yale University, aptly describes the distinction between toleration and freedom:

> "Toleration" is notably different from freedom, for it

---

[445] Pavan, Commentary, 73.

[446] Thomas Aquinas, *Summa theologia*, II-II, Eleventh Article: Ought the Rites of Unbelievers to Be Tolerated?, in *Saint Thomas Aquinas On Law, Morality, and Politics*, eds. Baumgarth and Regan, 254-255.

generally carries with it the idea that the person, opinion, or institution tolerated is a departure from what is normally right and is not considered entirely satisfactory from the standpoint of the powers that be. It is the "allowance of that which is not wholly approved." Similarly, Murray's *English Dictionary* defines it in connection with religion, as "allowance (with or without limitations) by the ruling power, of the exercise of religion otherwise than in the form officially established or recognized." It is thus often used with the idea of concession, or of indifferentism, without recognition of the importance of allowing for differences of deep conviction. In contrast to complete "liberty," it "connotes that whatever immunity is enjoyed is regarded merely as a revocable concession rather than as a defensible right, implies not only the existence of an established (or favored) church but the denial of complete equality to certain or all of the dissenting religions."[447]

Stokes defines one aspect of toleration as connoting "that whatever immunity is enjoyed is regarded merely as a revocable concession rather than as a defensible right." From this definition, one must ask the question, is the "immunity from coercion" promulgated in *Dignitatis Humanae* a revocable concession (i.e., a modern form of toleration), or a defensible right (i.e., religious freedom as a principle)?

Dignitatis Humanae, Article two, paragraph one uses the language of rights to define its concept of religious freedom:

> This Vatican Council declares that the human person has a right to religious freedom. This freedom means that all men are to be immune from coercion on the part of individuals or of social groups and of any human power, in such wise that no one is to be forced to act in a manner contrary to his own beliefs, whether privately or publicly, whether alone or in association with others within due limits.

Dignitatis Humanae centers the right to religious freedom in the dignity of the human person. However, there is a fundamental difference between the

---

[447] Anson Phelps Stokes, *Church and State in the United States*, 3 vols. (New York: Harper and Brothers, 1950), 1:22.

"civil right" to religious freedom of *Dignitatis Humanae* and what is customarily understood as civil rights. From a Catholic perspective, religious freedom can be defined as "universal, inviolable, inalienable, and imprescriptible" when it is considered in and of itself and from a speculative perspective. But, when it is considered from a practical, concrete viewpoint, then it can be prescribed by law, and even the subject of coercive action by the state.[448]

Yves Congar was one of the *periti* (experts) invited to Vatican Council II and he offers very insightful comments, both from historical and contemporary sources when explaining the usage of the term "right" in reference to freedom of conscience as contained in *Dignitatis Humanae*.[449] He clarifies that it does not refer to the issue of an erroneous conscience (someone who holds "error" as defined by the Church). The document leaves this question completely untouched and instead uses "right" to mean an individual has the "right" to the exercise of his conscience in following conviction; whether such exercise is "erroneous" or "upright" is left to the juridical conditions prevailing in a given constitutional context.[450] From these definitions of "the right" to religious freedom by leading Catholic scholars, it would seem to be more accurate to describe the "right" to religious freedom in *Dignitatis Humanae* as "a Catholic understanding of the right to religious freedom." Another area of scrutiny involves the linguistic differences between "toleration" and "immunity from coercion" in religious matters.

In the pre-Vatican II structure of society, the keyword regarding non-Catholic faiths was "toleration." This implied no right to the errors they held, but they were tolerated in order to avoid a worse societal evil, such as anarchy if they were coerced to embrace Catholicism. The etymological roots of "toleration" come from the Latin word *tollere*, "to bear, to carry," and hence, in colloquial English, "to put up with."[451] It implied no concept of civic duties, and actually placed the burden of restraint upon those of the

---

[448] Enrique Valcarce, *El Concilio y la ONU en la libertad religiosa de los pueblos* (Madrid, Spain: Talleres Afrodisio Aguado, 1966), 39.

[449] Yves Congar, *La liberté religieuse* (Paris: Les Editions du Cerf, 1967).

[450] Ibid., 85.

[451] See word entry "tolerate," Collins English Dictionary (William Collins & Sons Ltd, 2009), http://www.collinsdictionary.com/dictionary/english/ tolerate (accessed April 11, 2012); cognate to *tollere* is "thole" (def. no. 2), from Old English *thola*, Norse, *tholian*, "to endure," http://www.collinsdictionary.com/english/thole (accessed April 11, 2012).

majority faith, in this case, Catholics. They were to "bear, or carry" (or, put up with) the erroneous teachings (in their view), of non-Catholics for the stability of society. Such terminology varies significantly from that of Murray's "immunity from coercion."

"Immunity" derives from the Latin *immunitatem*, which is a combination of *im* ("not") and *munis* ("performing services," cf. municipal), thus, rendering "exemption from performing public service, or charge."[452] A general definition is "exemption from any natural or usual liability," whereas a definition from a legal perspective is "exemption from obligation, service, duty, or liability to taxation, jurisdiction, etc."[453] When one understands the Catholic worldview that man's natural end and obligation is God; and, that the Church has the authority of moral judgment and coercion, then the exemption herein implied becomes obvious -- viz., one is exempt from the moral (and coercive) jurisdiction of the Church. The most alarming point, however, is in relation to the differences between "toleration" and "immunity." The former term has no direct relation to obligations or duties from which one is exempt; the latter term, however, overtly directs one's attention to obligations that should be performed, but from which one is exempt. The former term has no direct implication regarding the power to enforce compliance with any natural obligations, whereas the latter term is colored with overtones of latent power to enforce and to expect compliance. Thus far, scrutiny of some concepts of *Dignitatis Humanae* reveals a document that uses the same philosophical rationale as the pre-Vatican II concept of "toleration," but which also differs from it through the use of language that conveys more subtle overtones of moral obligations to religious compliance in the face of coercive elements.

A societal construct that alludes to coercive elements, while reflecting a modernized Catholic position toward the realities of the current political order, elicits concern in some areas. First, it assumes that government has the power to coerce in religious matters, since the granting of "immunity from coercion" implies the power to coerce. Indeed, it is such a perspective that was "the chief locus for conciliar clarification" according to Murray.[454] He recognized that the theological and ethical dimensions of

---

[452]See word entry "immunity," Online Etymological Dictionary (Douglas Harper, 2010), http://www.etymonline.com/index.php?allowed_in_frame=0&search=immunity&searchmode=none (accessed November 16, 2011).

[453] Dictionary.com Unabridged, based on Random House Dictionary, 2011, http://dictionary.reference.com/browse/immunity?s=t (accessed November 16, 2011).

[454] Pelotte, 91.

religious freedom found consensus not only among Catholics, but also an ecumenical consensus. "The area of confusion and controversy, where a new clarification is needed, is political and legal – that is, in the question of the competence of the public powers *en re religiosa* (in religious matters)."[455] Marcel Lefebvre argues for the right of government to have a general authority to coerce in order to produce compliance among its citizens with its laws.[456] Similarly, *Dignitatis Humanae* recognizes the need for government to have coercive power in religious matters in order to maintain the "just requirements of public order."[457] At the same time, Murray recognized the all-powerful State of the twentieth-century and sought to curtail its unnecessary intrusion into religious matters. The net effect posited by *Dignitatis Humanae* then is a societal construct in which government has the authority to coerce in religious matters, which is curtailed through the "civil right to religious freedom" contained in the Document.

If this position were not enough to cause some concern for defenders of religious freedom, then interpretations of the Document's statements on coercion, which seem to exempt the Church from such restrictions, certainly should be:

> Religious freedom, in turn, which men demand as necessary to fulfill their duty to worship God, has to do with immunity from coercion in civil society. Therefore it leaves untouched traditional Catholic doctrine on the moral duty of men and societies toward the true religion and toward the one Church of Christ.[458]

---

[455] John Courtney Murray, cited by Pelotte, 91.

[456] Marcel Lefebvre, *Dubia sur la Déclaration Conciliare sur la Liberté Religieuse* (Editions Saint-Remi, n.d.), 18-20. Lefebvre distinguishes between purely internal acts of the soul and internal acts of the soul that also have corresponding external actions done by the body. He argues that the latter case is wholly subject to coercion, since the internal actions of the soul are linked to outward actions. For this reason, he argues that laws exist to govern the external actions of individuals toward one another.

[457] *Dignitatis Humanae*, Art. 4, par. 2, and Murray's comments on the same in "The Declaration on Religious Freedom," in *The Documents of Vatican II*, ed. Abbott, 682.

[458] *Dignitatis Humanae*, Art. 1, par. 4.

> This Vatican Council declares that the human person has a right to religious freedom. This freedom means that all men are to be immune from coercion on the part of individuals or of social groups and *of any human power*, in such wise that no one is to be forced to act in a manner contrary to his own beliefs, whether privately or publicly, whether alone or in association with others within due limits.[459]

The phrase "any human power" deserves further analysis. From a juridical perspective, Joaquin Lopez de Prado, argues that mankind has no right to religious liberty (choosing among a variety of religions) before God, and those baptized into the Catholic Church, have no right to religious liberty before the Church; for this reason, *Dignitatis Humanae* "refers to religious liberty that one can invoke before purely human powers."[460] Such an interpretation of the Decree implies that the Church still retains its absolutistic self-identity, as well as its accompanying belief that all people should become Catholic.

Perhaps an historic understanding of Roman law will help to illuminate the jurisprudence in question since concepts of Roman law are interwoven into Catholic jurisprudence. Accordingly, an individual living under such governance was required to show the existence of a law that granted him the right to perform a particular activity in question. In other words, it was a societal construct which assumed the right of the governing body over its citizens, with the exception of narrowly constructed rights based on enacted laws. Thus, the burden of proof rested upon the individual whose activity was in question. T. M. Parker elucidates this concept when explaining why Christians were frequently persecuted by the Roman Empire in the early centuries as criminals without the existence of any specific anti-Christian legislation:

> We are so well accustomed to the English constitutional principle that what the law does not specifically forbid, it allows, that we forget that not all legal systems work this way. An English citizen has a right to do anything he wishes, unless a specific law forbidding it can be produced.

---

[459] *Dignitatis Humanae*, Art. 2, par. 1 (italics mine).

[460] Joaquín López de Prado, "Análisis Jurídico," in *La Libertad Religiosa: Análisis de la Declaración 'Dignitatis Humanae'*, eds. Carlos Corral, S.J., Jose M. Díez-Alegría, S.J., Jose M. Fondevila, S.J., et al (Madrid: Editorial Razón y Fe, S.A., 1966), 235.

Roman law, it is almost true to say, proceeded from the opposite assumption. To prove an absolute right the citizen must produce a law authorizing it: failing this, the State can punish him for any activities it considers undesirable or anti-social. So, under their legal power of *coercitio*, the right to compel obedience to what they considered proper, Roman magistrates possessed a very wide measure of discretion. 'This *coercitio*,' says E. G. Hardy, '. . . was for the state an extraordinary means of self-defence: it was not restricted to the regular rule of procedure: the offences or misdemeanours with which it interfered were not defined by any technical nomenclature, and the punishments which it inflicted were, if not arbitrary, at least not specified with any undeviating precision.' It was Mommsen who first drew attention to the non-specific nature of much Roman criminal law as the probable explanation of persecution of Christians going on without any specific anti-Christian legislation, and subsequent study has done nothing to shake his view.[461]

Thus, in order for Christians to legally practice and propagate their faith, they would have had to present a law granting them such permission. Without it, they were considered as common criminals. Understanding Roman law in this fashion sheds light on the meaning of religious freedom as "immunity from coercion" contained in *Dignitatis Humanae*.

From this perspective, the "civil right to immunity from coercion" contained in *Dignitatis Humanae* becomes very disturbing. It teaches that the societal construct, in which religious freedom is granted, is actually coercive in nature, or has latent authority to coerce *en re religiosa* (in religious matters). The "civil right to immunity from coercion," then is merely granted as an exemption from the rule. Stated otherwise, it does not reflect the Lockean concept of "inalienable rights" to religious freedom, or *rights inherent to the individual*.[462] Rather, the source of the "civil right" resides in the Church

---

[461] Parker, *Christianity & the State in the Light of History*, 30, 31.

[462] Murray addresses this point in his comments by stating, "The Declaration states first the moral norm – the principle of personal and social responsibility. Its restraints, of course, are self-imposed. More difficult is the question of the juridical norm which should control the action of government in limiting or inhibiting the exercise of the right to religious freedom. (Note that the right itself is always inalienable, never to be denied; only the exercise of the right is subject to control in particular instances.)" Murray, "Declaration on Religious Freedom," in *The Documents of Vatican II*, ed. Abbott 686. While Murray's point is

who is obligating the governing authority in society to grant an immunity to the individual. As a corollary argument, then, if the "immunity from coercion" were withdrawn, it would leave the formerly sheltered individual (or religious group) subject to its coercive authority. The individual would be obligated to embrace "the one true faith," i.e., Catholicism and would not be allowed to freely search for truth, nor freely propagate his beliefs.

Historically, the Church relied upon the State as its minister to uphold its decrees, as shown through the history of the Inquisition and as noted in that section of this chapter. *Ad extirpanda* and *Exsurge Domine* are both prime examples of how the Church solicited secular support of its religious orthodoxy project. Thus, *Dignitatis Humanae* presupposes the modern State to be at its disposition – not to enforce its dogmas, as during the Inquisition – but to grant an "immunity from coercion" to the individual, which is to become a "civil right." By decreeing this "civil right," the individual has legal recourse to which he can appeal, demonstrating that, as in the context of Roman law, a decree exists which upholds his right to not be coerced in religious matters. This Decree on Religious Freedom very astutely implies that those governments which adopt it with the intent of establishing religious freedom, are inadvertently acknowledging the authority of the Church, as well as their own power of *coercitio*, which is merely suspended by the Church under the current political exigencies.[463]

---

accurately stated – i.e., government has a certain right to restrain the exercise of religious beliefs considered harmful to the community – the issue raised here deals with the source of the inalienable right and the context in which it is recognized. The Declaration of Independence, as the philosophical norm, and the First Amendment religion clauses, as the juridical norm, both posit the inalienable right to religious freedom within a context of recognition of a government, properly functioning, that has no power to coerce in religious matters (see the end of chapter two). *Dignitatis Humanae*, however, posits a societal construct in which coercion is the norm from which the individual is granted an immunity, or exemption, through a document promulgated by the Church. Murray would argue that *Dignitatis Humanae* counteracts the coercive power of totalitarian governments, such as Communist ones, from prohibiting religious activity, but would be silent regarding any other application. The Founding Fathers would argue that the First Amendment imposes a self-restraint upon government and any other group, whether religious, political, etc. from restricting religious activity.

[463] It would be well to remember that in a Catholic society, technically, heretics do not have civil protections, or rights, as the trial of John Huss so well exemplifies. On that occasion, "the council persuaded the emperor that, as a heretic, Huss was beyond civil protection." LeRoy Edwin Froom, *The Prophetic Faith of Our Fathers*, 4 vols. (Washington, D.C.: Review and Herald Publishing Association, 1948), 2:114. Knowing this, Martin Luther was fearful that emperor Charles V might rescind his safe-conduct pledge after Luther had arrived at

But, if that is the case, then what types of religious laws are in force of which one is exempt under *Dignitatis Humanae?*

It follows that the authority of the Church, when she pronounces on moral questions, in no way undermines the freedom of consciences of Christians. *This is so not only because freedom of conscience is never freedom 'from' the truth but always and only freedom 'in' the truth, but also because the Magisterium does not bring to the Christian conscience truths which are extraneous to it; rather it brings to light the truths which it ought already to possess, developing them from the starting point of the primordial act of faith.* The Church puts herself always and only at the service of conscience, helping it to avoid being tossed to and fro by every wind of doctrine proposed by human deceit (cf. Eph 4:14), and helping it not to swerve from the truth about the good of man, but rather, especially in more difficult questions, to attain the truth with certainty and to abide in it."[464]

Pope John Paul II indicates that the moral teachings of the Magisterium are the norms for society declared by the Church.[465] The faithful Christian (or, perhaps Catholic is more accurate) accepts the teachings of the Church, i.e., his role as *Christianum* (Christian), and seeks to implement them in the societal order through a democratic process, i.e., his role as *civis* (citizen). This conclusion harmonizes with the argument set forth previously in this chapter that *Dignitatis Humanae* is a declaratory document in that it sets forth the pro-active governmental, religious (Catholic) society as the societal ideal to be achieved.[466] Through *Dignitatis Humanae* a Catholic moral order is

---

Worms. From this perspective, the "civil right to immunity from coercion" as guaranteed in *Dignitatis Humanae* amounts to very little, if any, legal protections for those who at some future time should be deemed heretical.

[464] John Paul II, *Veritatis Splendor* , Art. 64, http://www.vatican.va/holy_ father/john_paul_ii/encyclicals/documents/ hf_jp-ii_enc_06081993_veritatis-spendor_en.html, (January 7, 2010; italics mine).

[465] Pope John Paul II was an advocate for human rights. David Hollenbach, *The Global Face of Public Faith* (Washington, D.C.: Georgetown University Press, 2003), 27. This statement does not question that. Rather, it merely describes the Magisterial teachings should a Catholic society prevail.

[466] "*Dignitatis Humanae* therefore declares: (1) that the Church ought to be free to be about its business, which includes the obligation of the laity to sacralize

posited as the "common good" of which all non-Catholics are (temporarily) exempt until such a time that the societal conscience has become "Christianized" enough to enact the moral teachings of the Church into positive law. What then would become of the idea of religious freedom defined as "immunity from coercion"?

Catholic Responses to the Church's Potential to Coercive Power

Russell Hittinger argues that religious freedom would remain in effect for all and uses the term "everyone" based on *Dignitatis Humanae*, article 6,

> [which] insists that the duty to respect involves "individual citizens, social groups, civil authorities, the Church and other religious communities." I take this to mean that, whatever relationship might obtain between the Church and civil society, and regardless of what the state does or does not do, everyone must respect liberty against external coercion in matters religious. That includes the imaginary scenario of a culture successfully evangelized. The Church declares itself to be a claimant and a supporter of this order of liberty with respect to the duties of the state and to the wider and deeper order of human society.[467]

Although a commendable statement, in the previous paragraph, Hittinger delimits *Dignitatis Humanae* by pointing out that it did not attempt to solve the dilemma of how "religious liberty and confession of religious truth"

> on the part of civil society might be synthesized in a distinctly contemporary mode – one in which democratic institutions prevail, the civil liberties of all are duly honored, and Christianization or rechristianization has progressed to the point that the essence of the Gospel has worked its way into a fully public manifestation. . . *Just as* Dignitatis Humanae *does not revisit all of the past problems, it refuses to project its teaching, by way of hypothesis, into the distant future.*[468]

---

culture, . . ." Russell F. Hittinger, "The Declaration on Religious Liberty, *Dignitatis Humanae*," in *Vatican II: Renewal within Tradition*, eds. Lamb and Levering, 366.

[467] Ibid., 366.

[468] Ibid., 366.

It would seem that Hittinger presents the "teaching" of *Dignitatis Humanae* as conditional upon time and circumstances. The very subject of the "times" of *Dignitatis Humanae* and the teachings of the Catholic Church will be discussed more fully in chapter four.

Contrary to Hittinger, John Courtney Murray viewed the teachings of *Dignitatis Humanae* as more permanently valid for all times. He posits the question as to whether any constitutional deviation from its teachings (i.e., a confessional state, or a constitutional order in which religious freedom is curtailed) should not be looked upon as an exception to the rule "prompted by expediency," and not as an established rule "warranted by theological and political doctrine":

> For the theologian, the basic question concerns that constitutional situation itself—is it or is it not the theologically necessary, permanently valid, unalterably ideal realization of Catholic principles on Church-state relationships, in such wise that any constitutional situation which deviates from it can be the object only of "toleration," not of approval in principle—a concession to the exigencies of an "hypothesis," prompted by expediency, and not the embodiment of a "thesis," warranted by theological and political doctrine. In other words, the question is whether the concept of *libertas ecclesiastica* by intrinsic exigence requires political embodiment in the concept of "the religion of the state," with the "logical and juridical consequences" that have historically followed from that concept.[469]

Murray states, "Surely the answer must be no." He explains that his answer is based on a "prospective, not a retrospective sense," that is to say, "it is not a judgment on past or present constitutional situations, but simply a theological answer to the question itself." Murray implies that *Dignitatis Humanae* contains self-inherent principles that deny, even to the Catholic Church, any right to be an established religion of the state. Differing from Hittinger's analysis regarding the "times" of its application, Murray nonetheless reaches the same conclusion as Hittinger, and other Catholic scholars, that *Dignitatis Humanae* even places restrictions of coercive activity upon the Church.

---

[469] John Courtney Murray, (ms. 1949b), "Contemporary Orientations of Catholic Thought on Church and State in the Light of History," *Theological Studies*, 10 (June): 229, http://woodstock.georgetown.edu/library/Murray/ 1949b.htm (accessed April 1, 2012).

Regarding Murray's idea of self-inherent principles in *Dignitatis Humanae* that would limit the Church's dominance in society, he explains elsewhere the foundational principles to the Church's freedom that differ from that of any other religious group:

> The freedoms listed here (*Dignitatis Humanae*, Article 4, par. 2) are those which the Catholic Church claims for herself. The Declaration likewise claims them for all Churches and religious Communities. Lest there be misunderstanding, however, it is necessary to recall here the distinction between the content or object of the right and its foundation. The content or object always remains freedom from coercion in what concerns religious belief, worship, practice or observance, and public testimony. Hence the content of the right is the same both for the Catholic Church and for other religious bodies. In this sense, the church claims nothing for herself which she does not also claim for them. The matter is different, however, with regard to the foundation of the right. *The Catholic Church claims freedom from coercive interference in her ministry and life on grounds of the divine mandate laid upon her by Christ Himself. It is Catholic faith that no other Church or Community may claim to possess this mandate in all its fullness. In this sense, the freedom of the Church is unique, proper to herself alone, by reason of its foundation. In the case of other religious Communities, the foundations of the right is the dignity of the human person, which requires that men be kept free from coercion*, when they act in community, gathered into Churches, as well as when they act alone.[470]

Viewed in this light, one may say that the teachings of *Dignitatis Humanae* have two different foundations: for the Church, upon a divine mandate, and for humanity, upon the mandate of the Church in *Dignitatis Humanae*, which bases religious freedom upon "the dignity of the human person," but defines it as "immunity from coercion" to pursue religious truth under a government that pro-actively supports Christianity (Catholicism?). For enlightening parallels and contrasts regarding this societal construct see Figure 3.4.

---

[470] Murray, "Declaration on Religious Freedom," in *The Documents of Vatican II*, ed. Abbott, 682 (italics mine).

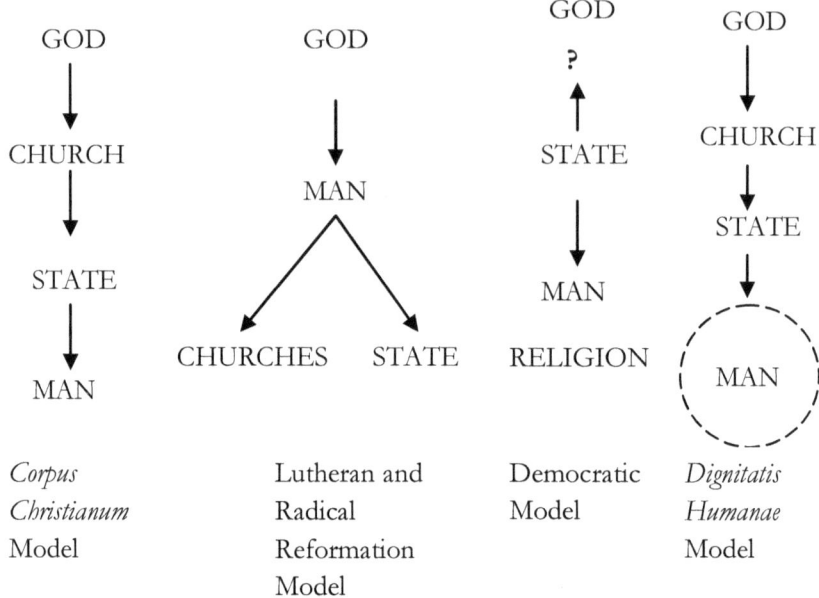

Figure 3.4. Four Church-State Models. In the *Corpus Christianum* Model, the Church made divine pronouncements to guide the State, as its secular arm, in relation to man, resulting in torture and death of heretics. Under the Reformation Model, man enjoys direct communion with God and has a dual citizenship – that of the citizen and Christian. In the Democratic Model, God is portrayed as distant, or not manifest in the affairs of state, while man encounters a variety of religions; there is also a "separation" between religion and state. However, the *Dignitatis Humanae* Model involves the Church declaring to the State its obligation to grant "immunity from coercion" as a civil right. This order of societal actors patterns the *Corpus Christianum* Model except that the use of coercion and force has been suspended.

Another Catholic response to the potentially coercive power of the Church is to argue for the freedom of the citizen. Murray's construct of *sacerdotium* and *civis idem christianum* (priesthood and the citizen who is also a Christian) claims the right to religious freedom for the individual citizen, as declared in *Dignitatis Humanae*. However, closer analysis reveals that the real liberty argued for here is *for that of the Christian conscience which is subject to the authority and teachings of the Church*. John Courtney Murray admits this point outright:

First of all, it is through the freedom of the citizen (in the modern sense) that the freedom of the Church (in the medieval sense) is effectively assured—her right to exercise her spiritual sovereignty over her subjects and to reach those elements of human affairs which are "quoquo modo sacrum.". . . *There is first the free obedience of the Christian conscience to the magisterial and jurisdictional authority of the Church; there is secondly the free participation of the citizen, as a Christian, in the institutions whereby all the processes of temporal life are directed to their proper ends*. . . . This, I take it, is the Catholic thesis in its application to democratic society.[471]

Observing this schematic through historical lenses, one may say that the Medieval Church influenced the conscience of the Christian prince, even through the use of spiritual sanctions, just as the Modern Church now influences the *civis* through persuasion and moral arguments, with a latent power to coerce that is not exercised because it is not politically expedient.

James Sweeney is another author who joins Hittinger and Murray in defending *Dignitatis Humanae* as a document through which the Church now advocates religious freedom. Referring to the lack of morality in societal practices, such as divorce, homosexual unions, and abortion, he raises the question, "What of those who accept them (such practices)? Does the Church concede to those it considers in social or moral error the right to pursue their own way?"[472] He does not directly answer, but emphasizes the need of society to know "Christ as Saviour in the social and political order" and mentions that this "might require a *Dignitatis Humanae* part two."

By such a response, Sweeney seems to indicate, as Hittinger and Murray, that *Dignitatis Humanae* is a document that focuses upon the rights of the Church to fulfill its mission without hindrance, part of which is to Christianize (or, Catholicize?) society. They also agree that if such a societal construct should prevail, then the issues it would raise – such as how to incorporate moral teachings into societal norms without violating the rights of those who do not see through Christian (or, Catholic?) lenses, or how to deal with the erroneous conscience – would require at least a re-evaluation, since *Dignitatis Humanae* is silent on these issues. The underlying concern as set forth in this book, however, underscores that very point since *Dignitatis*

---

[471] Murray, "Contemporary Orientations of Catholic Thought on Church and State in the Light of History" (ms. 1949b), 223-24, http://woodstock.georgetown.edu/library/Murray/1949b.htm. (accessed April 1, 2012; italics mine).

[472] James Sweeney, "Catholicism and Freedom: *Dignitatis Humanae* – the Text and its Reception," in *Reading Religion in Context*, eds. Elisabeth Arweck and Peter Collins (Burlington, VT: Ashgate Publishing, 2006), 29.

Humanae is not silent about "immunity from coercion," which also implies an entity with the power to coerce. Figure 3.5 illustrates a societal construct which has a latent power to coerce. By comparing this model with the Public Church Model of Figure 2.3, one notes that the only difference is the "immunity from coercion" granted to those who differ in belief or practice from the norms established by society. Such a comparison shows the progressive development from a Public Church Model to a Societal Construct with Latent Power to Coerce.

Additionally, the efforts of mainline Protestants have coalesced with the Catholic Church to establish moral values in society, even to the neglect of historical Protestant concepts of religious freedom, as both groups march toward their goal of Christianizing society. Differing historical contexts offer explanations of such phenomena. In Reformation society, Christianity was interwoven in the fabric of society and religious differences were the issues to be resolved. In the modern context, a secular society prevails which threatens religion. Thus, while the efforts to counteract an immoral, secular society can be lauded from a Christian perspective, one must also bear in mind the concerns that minority Christian groups have, especially in light of Reformation history during which both Catholics and Magisterial Reformation Protestant groups persecuted minority Radical Reformation groups, such as Anabaptists. Figure 3.6 offers a contrast and comparison of Protestant and Catholic historical developments related to religious freedom.

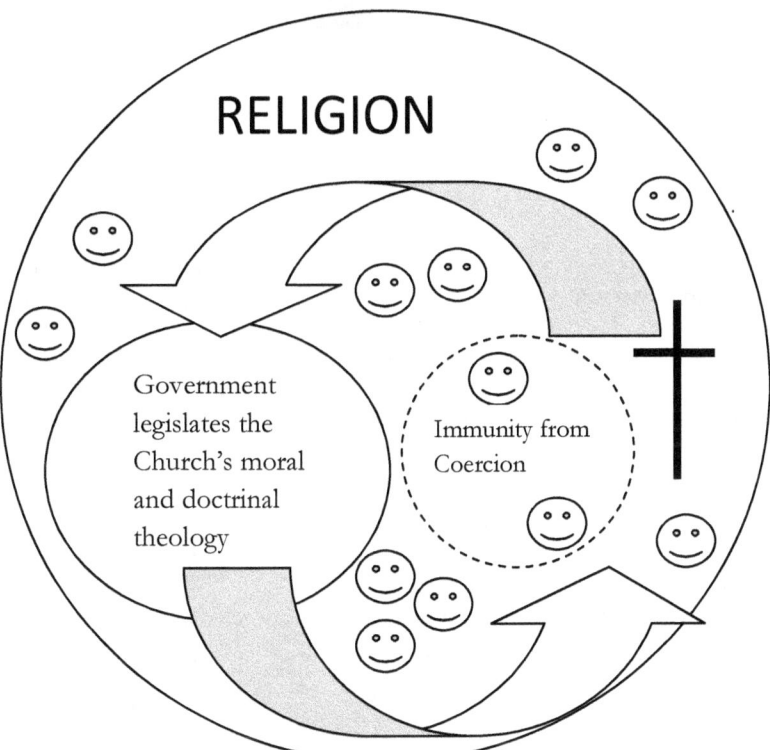

Figure 3.5. Societal Construct with Latent Power to Coerce, based on *Gaudium et Spes, Ad Gentes, Nostra Aetate,* and *Dignitatis Humanae,* in which the Church influences the "demos" (people) in society through its moral arguments based on natural law. The "demos" in turn influence government to enact moral laws based on the Church's rationale. Several points are worth noting:

1. The current priority of the Church is to combat secularism. It does this through a pro-active religious stance, depending upon government support.
2. Once government concedes to the Church's moral arguments on social issues through enacted legislation, the way is opened for government to enact the Church's theological dogma.
3. "Immunity from coercion" is currently a part of the teaching of *Dignitatis Humanae*. However, the phrase also implies a latent power to coerce. Thus, when government concedes to such "immunity from coercion," it by default concedes to the Church's power to coerce. "Immunity from coercion" is one step away from coercion. Thus, the circle of "immunity from coercion" is a dashed line, indicating a fluctuating concept rather than a fixed principle.
4. Two primary challenges to religious orthodoxy are secularism/indifferentism, and religious pluralism. Once addressing the issue of secularism, might not the Church focus upon the threat of religious pluralism?

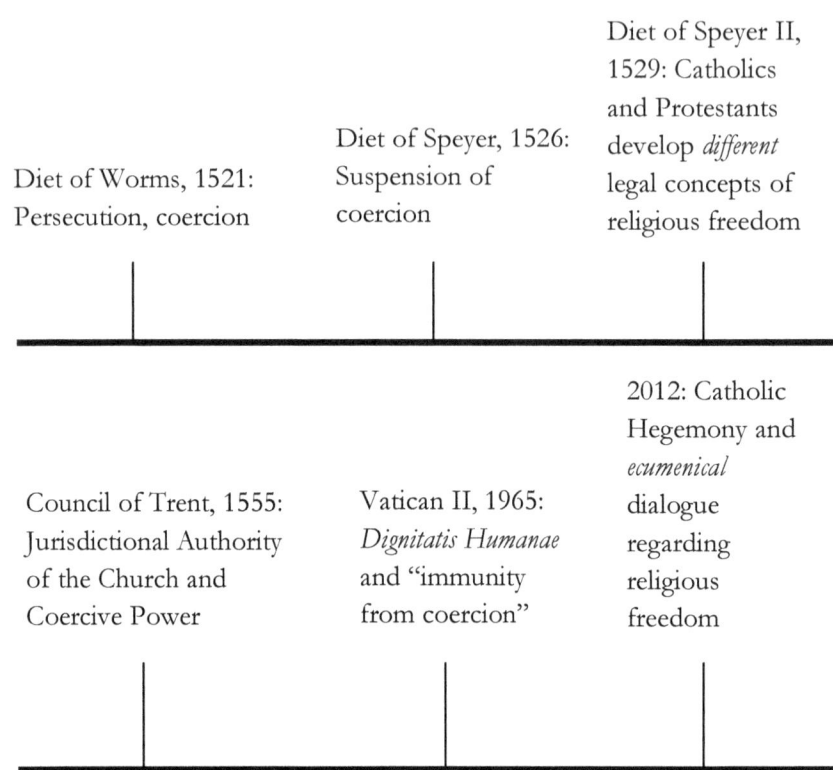

Figure 3.6. Historical Graphs showing the parallels and differences between Roman Catholic and Protestant Concepts of religious freedom. In 1529, both groups held *different* concepts that were legally recognized, but in the modern context, there is a trend toward *ecumenical*, or similar, concepts of religious freedom. Since *Dignitatis Humanae* contains Roman Catholic concepts of religious freedom that parallel those it held during the Reformation Era, one may conclude that the hegemonic nature of the Church has not changed, whereas Protestant concepts have begun to alter. Additionally, the Church has adapted her methods to the political exigencies of modern times.

Catholic Hegemony, Conscience and Coercion

Albeit *Dignitatis Humanae* contains sections that advocate strongly for religious freedom, even to the point of declaring that each person has a right to "immunity from coercion" to follow his convictions in religious matters, there are other portions of the document that argue for a distinctly Catholic type of religious freedom (i.e., freedom to become Catholic). This apparent internal contradiction reflects a document that can be applied in a variety of ways, and according to a given political situation.

The central question, however, that this dichotomy raises, is to what extent the Church retains its former coercive power, whether in relation to its own adherents, or those outside of its fold? To the reasonable individual, it is fair to argue that the Roman Catholic Church has jurisdictional authority over its members, even as far as deciding how to administer ecclesial discipline. For scholars, the Church has always employed "silencing," and in extreme cases, whether for laity or priest, it has resorted to anathema. Such exercises of authority are acceptable for any religious organization and necessary to maintain order and orthodoxy, although each religious body may differ regarding the exact manner of administering its discipline (i.e., disfellowshipping versus anathema). *However, none should believe they have the right to torture, coerce, or take the lives of their adherents for nonconformity with established beliefs.*

Several Catholic scholars mentioned in this chapter, such as Yves Congar, Enrique Valcarce, and Thomas Pink, seem to conclude that *Dignitatis Humanae* can be interpreted to concede to the Church its coercive power. Other scholars, such as Murray, Hittinger, and Sweeney indicate that the language of *Dignitatis Humanae* specifically denies to any entity, including the Church, the power to coerce. They argue from tradition, demonstrating that such preeminent scholars as Augustine contended for the freedom of the will in the act of faith. Such an argument, however, overlooks the metaphysical dimension of the freedom of the will – viz., the individual *by nature* always exercises free control over his own will, whether under coercion or not, as Suarez brings out in his writings.

The papal instructions to the secular power during the time of the Inquisition, and especially in response to the Reformation, were that the state, as an institution having a divine source, had the obligation to restrict freedom of religion *with the intent of maintaining a Catholic commonwealth*. Now, the political environment has changed from considering the state as divine in origin to postulating it as a social contract and secular in nature. In light of the modern political construct of the secular state, the Church, through *Dignitatis Humanae*, obligates secular powers to ensure freedom of religion – both for the Church to fulfill her divine mission, and for the individual to seek religious truth *with the intent of becoming Catholic, viz., producing a Catholic society*. Viewed from this perspective, not only the hegemonic nature of *Dignitatis Humanae* becomes evident, but also the unchanging nature of the Church. She has only adapted her approach to conform to the modern political exigencies of the times.

The historical account of the Protestant Reformation regarding the issue of conscience and religious freedom demonstrates that the Diet of Speyer II, 1529, was the most pivotal and decisive moment that introduced, as well as guaranteed legally, the freedom of conscience of the individual, which cannot be subject to the majority religious views, nor to political expediencies. This history reveals, as well, the determined efforts of the Roman Catholic Church to restrict the spread of Protestantism by denying states the religious freedom to convert to Protestantism, while at the same time arguing for the Church's right to continue practicing the Mass, *et al.*, in those areas where Protestantism had already gained a foothold. Thus, the Church had developed its position which it maintained for centuries afterwards – religious freedom for the Church whenever and wherever it was a minority religious group, and religious restrictions for other religious groups whenever and wherever it was the dominant religious group.

From this historical perspective, the question is raised, with respect to Catholic hegemony and individual conscience, what changes has *Dignitatis Humanae* implemented in the Church's position? In this Document, the Church argues for the civil right of the individual to seek truth, understood to be Roman Catholicism as the one true faith, and once finding it, to embrace it. *Dignitatis Humanae* argues for the religious freedom of the individual to become a Catholic, but does not even mention the possibility of the freedom of the individual who desires to leave the Catholic faith.[473] In other words, it does not allow for proselytism of Catholics. At the same time, it does argue for the right of the Church to proclaim and teach its doctrine in society, whether secular or religious, again with the overall intent that individuals should become Roman Catholic. In this respect, it does not differ much from the same position it adopted during the time of the Diet of Speyer II (1529).

While *Dignitatis Humanae* does argue for the *civil right* of the individual to religious freedom, it leaves unaddressed the *moral sphere*.[474] The Document

---

[473] "It follows that a wrong is done when government imposes upon its people, by force or fear or other means, the profession or repudiation of any religion, or when it hinders men from joining or leaving a religious community." *Dignitatis Humanae*, Art. 6, par. 6. For those who cite this part of the Document to argue the contrary, it is important to note that this paragraph refers to *government*, not the Church, preventing a person from joining or leaving a religious community.

[474] The moral sphere here mentioned is that which the Church refers to as "indirect power," or its right to intervene in the temporal sphere for purely spiritual interests. Cf. Jacques Maritain, *The Things That Are Not Caesar's*, xii; William T. Cavanaugh, *Torture and the Eucharist* (Malden, MA: Blackwell Publishers, 1998), 159-161. *Dignitatis Humanae* does not address this issue, but neither does it deny it.

does not mention the erroneous conscience of the individual who rejects Catholicism, or who adheres to another faith, or who denies belief in Deity outright. By taking a stance neither against nor in favor of the individual in the moral sphere, "the Church leaves intact its former teaching"[475] – (i.e., the power to coerce) – in other words, it has laid aside, temporarily, its moral authority to coerce in light of the current political construct of constitutional democracies which focus on the rights of the individual.

The Church defends this construct due to Murray's idea of a re-positioning of the state in modern democracies. By shifting the State from a role of supreme authority to a mere societal player among others, it places the role of moral authority upon society – i.e., the *demos* (the people), who in turn influence the state. Under this construct, the state no longer serves as neutral arbiter among religious bodies. Thus, there exists the potential that if political winds should shift, and if the general populace should so consider it necessary to establish a singular religion, such as Christianity, then the state must bend to its wishes. From this perspective, it becomes quite clear why the Church has in recent decades emphasized its social ethics agenda and why the Church has sought to weaken, if not wholly remove the concept of separation between church and state. By building a broad coalition of Christian groups, "separated brethren" (the language of Vatican II, i.e., Protestants), the Church intends to present a formidable line of defense against what it views as rampant secularism and aggressive atheism.

The real question resulting from this chapter, however, is how will the Church relate to those religious groups that it now considers as its allies when a religious (Christian) societal construct shall have been produced? Once there is no longer a threat from atheism, or secularism, -- and given the unchanging, hegemonic nature of the Church – how will all non-Catholic religious groups fare? The next chapter, "*Dignitatis Humanae* and Seventh-day Adventists," explores possible answers to this question.

---

[475] *Dignitatis Humanae*, Article 2, paragraph 2.

DIGNITATIS HUMANAE AND SEVENTH-DAY ADVENTISTS

Seventh-day Adventists[476] and Roman Catholics held a series of ecumenical discussions between the years 2001 to 2003.[477] During the meeting of April 8-9, 2001, the theologians discussed the "27 Fundamental Beliefs of SDAs."[478] The following year, May 20-22, both groups examined the distinctions regarding the observance of Sabbath and Sunday. In 2003, from May 19-21, scholars from both groups considered *Principles of Biblical Interpretation*, leading to the conclusion that,

> Catholics interpret the scriptures within the living tradition of the whole church, while Adventists do this only by reference to other scripture passages, following the principle of biblical intertextuality. This difference in interpretation leads to divergent understandings regarding matters such as purgatory, the veneration and efficacious intercession of the saints, indulgences and Mariology.[479]

---

[476] I use the terms "Seventh-day Adventist," "Adventist," and "SDA" interchangeably to refer to Seventh-day Adventists and to the SDA Church.

[477] Edward Idris Cardinal Cassidy, *Ecumenism and Interreligious Dialogue: Unitatis Redintegratio, Nostra Aetate* (Mahwah, NJ: Paulist Press, 2005), 75.

[478] There are now 28 Fundamental Beliefs, since the new doctrine of emphasis upon personal conversion was adopted by the General Conference of SDAs during its world session in 2005.

[479] Cassidy, 75.

Although these meetings resulted in a much greater understanding of the theological beliefs held by each group, these meetings never broached the topic of distinctions and similarities between Catholics and SDAs regarding *Dignitatis Humanae* (religious freedom). This chapter will address such issues, first by explaining a Seventh-day Adventist understanding of religious freedom. Statements made by a leading SDA pioneer, Ellen White,[480] will be used to explain the uniqueness of an SDA concept of religious freedom. The next section will analyze similarities and differences between both SDA and Roman Catholic positions. The chapter concludes by offering a Seventh-day Adventist understanding of Bible prophecy as it relates to religious freedom.

A Seventh-day Adventist Understanding of Religious Freedom

For Seventh-day Adventists, religious freedom is central to their identity for two reasons: they believe themselves to be the inheritors of the Protestant Reformation, and they identify themselves as the fulfillment of Bible prophecy predicting the existence of a unique religious movement in the end of time (Revelation 14:6-12). As heirs of the Protestant Reformation, one of their leading pioneers, Ellen White, wrote:

> The banner of truth and religious liberty which these Reformers [at the Diet of Spires [sic], 1529] held aloft has in this last conflict been committed to us. The responsibility for this great gift rests with those whom God has blessed with a knowledge of His word. We are to receive God's word as supreme authority. We must accept its truths for ourselves.[481]

As a characteristic of Adventism, not only is reference made to the religious liberty principles of the Reformers, but also another Reformation principle, *sola Scriptura*. Through close searching of the Scriptures, early Adventists concluded that their movement was a fulfillment of Bible prophecy. In Revelation 14:6-12, the Bible records:

---

[480] Although SDAs regard Ellen G. White as manifesting the prophetic gift, and thus refer to her writings as inspired counsel to guide the SDA Church, I refer to her writings in this chapter solely as a recognized leading authority within the Adventist Church and her writings as statements that define the Church's position on religious liberty.

[481] Ellen G. White, *Testimonies for the Church*, 9 vols., 6:402 in *The Ellen G. White Writings: Comprehensive Research Edition*, CD, 2008.

> And I saw another angel fly in the midst of heaven, having the everlasting gospel to preach unto them that dwell on the earth, and to every nation, and kindred, and tongue, and people. Saying with a loud voice, Fear God and give glory to Him; for the hour of his judgment is come: and worship Him that made heaven, and earth, and the sea, and the fountains of waters.

Adventists interpret Revelation 14:6-12 as referring to an end-time movement initiated by God to proclaim the Three Angels' messages to the whole world prior to Christ's return to the earth. They also identify themselves as the fulfillment of this movement and therefore advocate, promote, and defend religious freedom around the world in order that all people, regardless of their religious affiliation, can hear these messages and respond voluntarily. To facilitate this work, Adventists contend that all people need to enjoy complete religious freedom to hear, study, and arrive at their own conclusions regarding the message proclaimed by the Seventh-day Adventist Church.

In fact, the proclamation of the Seventh-day Adventist message and religious freedom are such synonymous terms that a leading pioneer of Adventism wrote:

> The peculiar work of the third angel has not been seen in its importance... When the National Reformers began to urge measures to restrict religious liberty, our leading men should have been alive to the situation and should have labored earnestly to counteract these efforts. It is not in the order of God that light has been kept from our people—the very present truth which they needed for this time . . . The National Reform movement has been regarded by some as of so little importance that they have not thought it necessary to give much attention to it and have even felt that in so doing they would be giving time to questions distinct from the third angel's message. May the Lord forgive our brethren for thus interpreting the very message for this time.[482]

The above message was given to arouse Seventh-day Adventist laborers to action in defense of religious liberty at a time when other organizations

---

[482] White, *Testimonies for the Church*, 9 vols., 5:715 in *The Ellen G. White Writings: Comprehensive Research Edition*, CD, 2008.

were advocating national legislative measures that would have greatly hindered religious freedom in America. The National Reform movement was a Christian coalition trying to pass legislation that, in their view, would ameliorate the deteriorating morality in society. However, their proposals, if adopted, would have hindered the religious practices of minority religious groups. Seventh-day Adventists commissioned Alonzo T. Jones, a minister, to debate the issue before the Senate Committee considering the proposal, resulting in its defeat.

Moved to action by this nearly-enacted legislation, Seventh-day Adventists chartered the International Religious Liberty Association in 1893. It is the longest-existing association of its type. Several of the more pertinent characteristics of this association, taken from their website,[483] are listed below:

> The IRLA has one of the best international networks among NGOs. It has national associations in 80 countries—including Kazakhstan, Azerbaijan, and Russia. Thirteen regional chapters cover the whole surface of the globe with correspondents in 200 countries.
>
> In 2003, the IRLA was recognized by the United Nations Economic and Social Council and given the status of United Nations Non-Governmental Organization Category II. We are represented in New York and Geneva and we take part in the Human Rights Council meetings every year.
>
> A primary aspect of the IRLA's work is to ensure that religious freedom has the highest possible visibility on the world scene. To that end, we hold congresses, regional conferences, national symposiums, and local meetings—all aimed at making sure issues of religious freedom remain high on society's agenda. For despite the importance of international covenants and national legislation, without public support for religious freedom, any gains remain at the level of theory rather than practice.

Some of the more recent congresses held by IRLA include the Religious Freedom Festivals, celebrated on June 22, 2006, at the Iberapuera

---

[483] International Religious Liberty Association, http://www.irla.org/about-us.htm (accessed May 29, 2012).

Gymnasium in Sao Paulo, Brazil (32,000 attendees);[484] on June 28, 2008, at a sports stadium in Luanda, Angola (45,000 attendees);[485] and on June 13, 2009, at the National Stadium in Lima, Peru (40,000 attendees).[486]

Principles of God's Government

In addition to advocating religious freedom for the sake of proclaiming the Gospel, Seventh-day Adventists believe that the principles of God's heavenly government should guide all human relationships. Beginning with the biblical description of God's very nature in the Old Testament, "The LORD, The LORD God, merciful and gracious, longsuffering, and abundant in goodness and truth, keeping mercy for thousands, forgiving iniquity and transgression and sin,"[487] as well as that in the New Testament, "God is love,"[488] Seventh-day Adventists believe that "The exercise of force is contrary to the principles of God's government; He desires only the service of love; and love cannot be commanded; it cannot be won by force or authority. Only by love is love awakened."[489]

Through love, God created man in His likeness and image,[490] bestowing

---

[484] Adventist News Network, "Brazil religious liberty event draws 32000 live, hundreds of thousands online," June 22, 2006, http://news.adventist.org/archive/articles/2006/06/22/brazil-religious-liberty-event-draws-32000-live-hundreds-of-thousands-onlin (accessed May 29, 2012).

[485] Adventist News Network, "Angola: rebuilding country promotes freedom of belief," July 8, 2008, http://news.adventist.org/archive/articles/2008/07/08/angola-rebuilding-country-promotes-freedom-of-belief (accessed May 29, 2012).

[486] Adventist News Network, "Religious freedom festival in Peru receives national endorsement," June 15, 2009, http://news.adventist.org/en/archive/articles/2009/06/15/religious-freedom-festival-in-peru-receives-national-endorsement (accessed May 20, 2012).

[487] Exodus 34:6, 7.

[488] 1 John 4:8.

[489] Ellen G. White, *The Desire of Ages*, 22 in *The Ellen G. White Writings: Comprehensive Research Edition*, CD, 2008.

[490] Genesis 1:27.

him with intelligence and free will.⁴⁹¹ "To deprive man of the freedom of choice would be to rob him of his prerogative as an intelligent being, and make him a mere automaton. It is not God's purpose to coerce the will. Man was created a free moral agent."⁴⁹²

Especially should Christian organizations reveal the characteristics of the One in whom they profess to believe. Just as Christ invited all to believe upon Him and follow Him as Savior and Lord,⁴⁹³ and yet forced none against their will,⁴⁹⁴ His followers should do likewise.⁴⁹⁵ "The Lord Jesus came to our world full of mercy, life, and light, ready to save those who should come unto Him. But He can save no one against his will. God does not force the conscience; He does not torture the body that He may compel men to compliance with His law. All this work is after the order of Satan. . ."⁴⁹⁶

Before Civil and Religious Authorities

In harmony with apostolic injunctions, "Submit yourselves to every ordinance of man for the Lord's sake: whether it be to the king, as supreme; or unto governors, as unto them that are sent by him for the punishment of evildoers, and for the praise of them that do well. . . Love the brotherhood.

---

⁴⁹¹ "And the LORD God commanded the man, saying, Of every tree of the garden *thou mayest freely eat*: but of the tree of the knowledge of good and evil, thou shall not eat of it: for in the day that thou eatest thereof thou shalt surely die." Genesis 2:16, 17.

⁴⁹² Ellen G. White, *Patriarchs and Prophets*, 331, 332 in *The Ellen G. White Writings: Comprehensive Research Edition*, CD, 2008.

⁴⁹³ "Come unto me, all ye that labor and are heavy laden, and I will give you rest. Take my yoke upon you, and learn of me, for I am meek and lowly in heart: and ye shall find rest unto your souls." Matt. 11:28, 29.

⁴⁹⁴ "No man can come to me, except the Father which hath sent me draw [attracts] him: and I will raise him up at the last day." John 6:44; "And whosoever will, let him take the water of life freely." Revelation 22:17.

⁴⁹⁵ "He that saith he abideth in him ought himself also so to walk, even as he walked." 1 John 2:6; "Preach the word; be instant in season, out of season; reprove, rebuke, exhort with all longsuffering and doctrine." 2 Tim. 4:2

⁴⁹⁶ Ellen G. White, *Youth's Instructor*, Aug. 17, 1893 in *The Ellen G. White Writings: Comprehensive Research Edition*, CD, 2008.

Fear God. Honor the king,"[497] Seventh-day Adventists believe in good citizenship and due respect to civil authorities. Ellen White echoed those sentiments when she counseled Seventh-day Adventists to follow biblical principles regarding the relation believers should sustain toward civil authority:

> Those who love God's commandments will conform to every good law of the land. . . We are to recognize human government as an ordinance of divine appointment and teach obedience to it as a sacred duty, within its legitimate sphere. . . We are not required to defy authorities. Our words, whether spoken or written, should be carefully considered. . . Teach the people to conform in all things to the laws of their state when they can do so without conflicting with the law of God.[498]

While Adventists are counseled to obey civil authorities as a sacred duty, they also bear in mind the limits of that duty stated by Jesus, "Render therefore unto Caesar the things which are Caesar's; and unto God the things that are God's."[499]

Ellen White underscored this counsel by reiterating with greater emphasis the believer's duty before God when the two authorities might conflict:

> I saw that it is our duty in every case to obey the laws of our land, unless they conflict with the higher law which God spoke with an audible voice from Sinai, and afterward engraved on stone with His own finger. "I will put My laws into their mind, and write them in their hearts: and I will be to them a God, and they shall be to Me a people." . . . God's people, taught by the inspiration of truth, and led by a good conscience to live by every word of God, will take His law, written in their hearts, as the only authority which they can acknowledge or consent to obey. . .[500]

---

[497] 1 Peter 2:13, 14, 17.

[498] Ellen G. White, *My Life Today*, 281 in *The Ellen G. White Writings: Comprehensive Research Edition*, CD, 2008.

[499] Matthew 22:21.

[500] Ellen G. White, *Testimonies for the Church*, 9 vols., 1:361 in *The Ellen G. White Writings: Comprehensive Research Edition*, CD, 2008.

This counsel is not based solely upon the hierarchy of authority, whereby God rules supremely over all earthly authority, but more specifically it is based on an Adventist eschatological view of earthly powers united in opposition to God's authority and His people.

Seventh-day Adventist Eschatology and Religious Freedom

Eschatology greatly influences a Seventh-day Adventist understanding of the need for religious freedom. In addition to their self-identity based on Revelation 14:6-12 as noted earlier, Seventh-day Adventists recognize another dimension of Bible prophecy that takes center stage in their eschatology. It is found in Revelation 13, which describes the persecuting activity of the Sea Beast (vv. 1-10) and the Land Beast (vv.11-17). Seventh-day Adventists have understood the time period referred to here as applicable to a short period of tribulation prior to the Second Advent of Christ. Thus, they anticipate a future time of persecution involving religious and political forces united in opposition to God's faithful saints. In the present "calm" before such a storm of persecution is when Adventists diligently promote religious freedom on a global scale in order to counteract those developments that will inevitably result in religious persecution.

Seventh-day Adventist and Roman Catholic Assertions

Although historically Seventh-day Adventists and Roman Catholics have maintained their distinct doctrinal differences,[501] there are similarities in assertions made by both groups in the area of religious freedom. The underlying principles in four areas allow for consonance. However, the practical application of those principles produces distinct areas of dissonance, which will also be noted in four areas.

Areas of Consonance

Regarding foundational *principles* that affect religious freedom – such as the source of civil authority, the relation between the transcendental and temporal orders, an objective moral order, and missiology – both the SDA Church and the Roman Catholic Church find common ground.

---

[501] Reinder Bruinsma, *Seventh-day Adventist Attitudes Toward Roman Catholicism: 1844-1965* (Berrien Springs, MI: Andrews University Press, 1994); P. Gerard Damsteegt, *Foundations of the Seventh-day Adventist Message and Mission* (Berrien Springs, MI: Andrews University Press, 1995, sixth printing), 46, 47.

The source of civil authority is divine. Seventh-day Adventists, appealing to Scripture, affirm that God is the author of civil authority:

> The power exercised by every ruler on the earth is Heaven-imparted; and upon his use of the power thus bestowed, his success depends. To each the word of the divine Watcher is, "I girded thee, though thou hast not known Me." Isaiah 45:5. And to each the words spoken to Nebuchadnezzar of old are the lesson of life: "Break off thy sins by righteousness, and thine iniquities by showing mercy to the poor: if it may be a lengthening of thy tranquility." Daniel 4:27.[502]

For this reason, Adventists affirm the biblical teaching that "promotion cometh neither from the east, nor from the west, nor from the south. But God is the judge: he putteth down one, and setteth up another."[503] And, "The king's heart is in the hand of the LORD, as the rivers of water: he turneth it whithersoever he will."[504]

Even those rulers who are wicked and abuse their God-given authority are still under His control:

> All earthly powers are under the control of the Infinite One. To the mightiest ruler, to the most cruel oppressor, He says, "Hitherto shalt thou come, but no further." Job 38:11. God's power is constantly exercised to counteract the agencies of evil; He is ever at work among men, not for their destruction, but for their correction and preservation.[505]

From such a belief, Seventh-day Adventists uphold civil authority and laws, provided they do not conflict with divine directives, as noted earlier. In cases of conflict, Adventists believe in following the apostle Peter's counsel found in Acts 5:29, "We ought to obey God rather than men."

---

[502] Ellen G. White, *Prophets and Kings*, 502 in *The Ellen G. White Writings: Comprehensive Research Edition*, CD, 2008.

[503] Psalm 75:6, 7.

[504] Proverbs 21:1.

[505] Ellen G. White, *Patriarchs and Prophets*, 694 in *The Ellen G. White Writings: Comprehensive Research Edition*, CD, 2008.

In similar fashion, Roman Catholic political philosophy, both pre-Vatican II and at Vatican II, emphasizes that the source of all authority, whether in civil society, among the priesthood, or that exercised by a father toward his children, derives from God:

> But now, a society can neither exist nor be conceived in which there is no one to govern the wills of individuals, in such a way as to make, as it were, one will out of many, and to impel them rightly and orderly to the common good; therefore God has willed that in a civil society there should be some to rule the multitude. And this also is a powerful argument, that those by whose authority the State is administered must be able so to compel the citizens to obedience that it is clearly a sin in the latter not to obey. *But no man has in himself or of himself the power of constraining the free will of others by fetters of authority of this kind. This power resides solely in God, the Creator and legislator of all things* . . . whatever there is of government and authority, its origin is derived from one and the same Creator and Lord of the world, Who is God."[506]

Agreeing that God originates civil authority, both Seventh-day Adventists and Catholics believe in showing due respect to all proper authority.

Transcendental principles are necessary in the temporal order. Since God originates civil authority, it naturally follows that the principles of God's government should be reflected in civil government as well. "Thy throne, O God, is for ever and ever: the scepter of thy kingdom is a right scepter. Thou lovest righteousness, and hatest wickedness."[507] "It is an abomination to kings to commit wickedness; for the throne is established by righteousness."[508] "A king that sitteth in the throne of judgment

---

[506] Pope Leo XIII, *Diuturnum Illud* (On Civil Government), issued June 29, 1881, in *Papal Thought on the State*, ed. Gerard F. Yates (New York: Appleton-Century-Crofts, Inc., 1958), 4 (italics in original). At Vatican II, the Council declared, "It is therefore obvious that the political community and public authority are based on human nature and hence belong to an order of things divinely foreordained. At the same time the choice of government and the method of selecting leaders are left to the free will of citizens." *Gaudium et spes* (Dec., 1965), Art. 74, par. 4, *Documents*, ed. Abbott, 284.

[507] Psalms 45:6, 7.

[508] Proverbs 16:12.

scattereth away all evil with his eyes."[509] Likewise, Ellen White wrote:

> In the law of the kingdom of God who rules the sinless inhabitants of heaven are to be found the principles that should lie at the foundation of the laws of earthly governments. The laws of these governments should be in harmony with the law of Jehovah, the standard by which all created beings are to be judged. No man should be forced to act in harmony with human laws that are in direct opposition to the law that God has given."[510]

Seventh-day Adventists, thus, believe a link exists between the transcendental sphere and the temporal sphere. God is not disinterested in the affairs of humanity.

Similarly, Roman Catholics believe and teach the transcendental sphere is associated with the temporal order. Pope Leo XIII, in the encyclical *Diuturnum Illud* (On Civil Government) wrote:

> Let princes take example from the Most High God, by whom authority is given to them; and placing before themselves his model in governing the State, let them rule over the people with equity and faithfulness, and let them add to that severity, which is necessary, a paternal charity. On this account they are warned in the oracles of the Sacred Scriptures, that they will have themselves some day to render an account to the King of kings and Lord of lords; if they shall fail in their duty, that it will not be possible for them in any way to escape the severity of God...[511]

Likewise, since one of the observations of the Second Vatican Council revolves around the premise of mankind living in an enlightened age, the Church admonishes the laity, not the State, to inscribe the divine law upon the temporal order. By shifting the focus to the citizen instead of the state,

---

[509] Proverbs 20:8.

[510] Ellen G. White, *Letter 187*, 1903, p. 5, as quoted in Ellen G. White Estate of the General Conference of Seventh-day Adventists, *Spirit of Prophecy Counsels Relating to Church-State Relationships* (Silver Spring, MD: Ellen G. White Estate, 1964; reprinted 2000), 8.

[511] Pope Leo XIII, *Diuturnum Illud* (On Civil Government), in Yates, 6.

Gaudium et spes reflects an adaptation to the modern democratic political order:

> Laymen should also know that it is generally the function of their well-formed Christian conscience to see that the divine law is inscribed in the life of the earthly city.[512]

Given that Seventh-day Adventists and Roman Catholics believe that transcendental principles should be reflected in civil authority, the logical corollary is that the subjects of civil authority must also have an objective moral order to which they are oriented by nature.

An objective moral order exists to which man is oriented by nature. Affirming through the act of creation that God has endowed mankind with a moral nature, Seventh-day Adventists believe and proclaim the principles of God's eternal kingdom to which man is amenable. "And God said, Let us make man in our image, after our likeness."[513] "And the LORD passed by before him [Moses] and proclaimed, 'The LORD, The LORD God, merciful and gracious, longsuffering, and abundant in goodness and truth, keeping mercy for thousands, forgiving iniquity and transgression and sin, and that will by no means clear the guilty."[514] Believing that a great part of redemption involves moral education, Ellen White wrote:

> To bring man back into harmony with God, so to elevate and ennoble his moral nature that he may again reflect the image of the Creator, is the great purpose of all the education and discipline of life. So important was this work that the Saviour left the courts of heaven and came in person to this earth, that He might teach men how to obtain a fitness for the higher life.[515]

Recognizing the importance of moral development in preparation for eternity, she wrote:

---

[512] *Gaudium et spes*, Art. 43, par. 5, in *The Documents of Vatican II*, ed. Abbot, 244.

[513] Genesis 1:26.

[514] Exodus 34:6, 7.

[515] Ellen G. White, *Counsels to Parents, Teachers, and Students*, 49 in *The Ellen G. White Writings: Comprehensive Research Edition*, CD, 2008.

Justice, honor, love, and truth are the attributes of God's throne. They are the principles of His government which is to be established on the earth, made pure by the fire of His retributive justice. These are the jewels to be sought after and cherished for time and for eternity. In view of these things, . . . build your character not after the worldly standard, but for eternity.[516]

Based on Scripture and the statements above, Seventh-day Adventists believe that an objective moral order exists with which man was originally in harmony and, despite the degradation caused by sin, to which man is still oriented.

Roman Catholics also believe and teach that an objective moral order exists to which man is obligated to follow. Part of this process involves the development of one's conscience in harmony with the eternal law of God and with natural law, as Pope Leo XIII explained in *Libertas Praestantissimum* (On Human Liberty):

Foremost in this office [of law to guide man's actions] comes the *natural law*, which is written and engraved in the mind of every man; and this is nothing but our reason, commanding us to do right and forbidding sin. . . It follows therefore [since man is not capable of being his own legislator], that the law of nature is the same thing as the *eternal law*, implanted in rational creatures, and inclining them *to their right action and end*; and can be nothing else but the eternal reason of God, the Creator and Ruler of all the world.[517]

At Vatican Council II, the same understanding was reiterated regarding man's nature and the divine law to which the Church must call his attention:

Therefore, by virtue of the gospel committed to her, the Church proclaims the rights of man. . . . Yet these [rights] movements must be penetrated by the spirit of the gospel

---

[516] Ellen G. White, *Letter 41*, December 7, 1877, written to F. E. Belden in Ellen G. White, *This Day with God*, 350 in *The Ellen G. White Writings: Comprehensive Research Edition*, CD, 2008.

[517] Pope Leo XIII, *Libertas Praestantissimum* (On Human Liberty), encyclical issued June 20, 1888 in Yates, 33, 34.

and protected against any kind of false autonomy. For we are tempted to think that our personal rights are fully ensured only when we are exempt from every requirement of divine law. . . .Christ . . . gave His Church no proper mission in the political, economic, or social order. The purpose which He set before her is a religious one. But out of this religious mission itself come a function, a light, and an energy which can serve to structure and consolidate the human community according to the divine law.[518]

Believing that an objective moral order exists to which man is oriented, Seventh-day Adventists and Roman Catholics proclaim their respective messages and educate people in order to elevate their moral nature.

The world is the mission field assigned by Christ to His Church. Initially, one may question how missiology relates to religious freedom. However, the command of Christ, "Go ye therefore and make disciples of all nations; baptizing them in the name of the Father, the Son, and the Holy Ghost; and teaching them to observe all things whatsoever I have commanded you,"[519] anticipates encounters with those of other religions, as well as efforts to proselytize. Seventh-day Adventist missiology, or a concept of missions, not only takes Christ's statement previously quoted in the most literal fashion, but also interprets Revelation 14:6-12 as a symbolic description of what the Lord's Church will do in the end of time: "And I saw another angel (messenger) flying in the midst of heaven, having the everlasting gospel to proclaim to those who dwell upon the earth, to every nation, tribe, tongue and people."[520] Thus, Seventh-day Adventists consider the world as their mission field. Some of their statistical information attests to how extensive is their mission work. They operate one of the largest Protestant educational system in the world with 7,806 schools and 1,668,754 students; a presence in 209 countries out of the 232 countries recognized by the United Nations, and a world membership of 17,214,683 as of June 30, 2011.[521]

---

[518] *Gaudium et spes* (Dogmatic Constitution of the Church), Articles 41, par. 7 and 42, par. 2, in *Documents*, ed. Abbott, 241.

[519] Matthew 28:19, 20.

[520] Revelation 12:6.

[521] General Conference of Seventh-day Adventists, "Seventh-day Adventist World Church Statistics, 2010." http://www.adventistarchives.org/docs/Stats/SDAWorldChurchStatistics2010.PDF (accessed May 31, 2012).

In similar fashion, the Roman Catholic Church describes herself as "the one, holy, catholic, and apostolic Church."[522] By "Catholic," she means "according to the totality," or "in keeping with the whole." Tracing herself in apostolic succession, she dates her beginnings from the day of Pentecost. Second, by "Catholic," she claims the mandate of Christ to reach all nations with the Gospel and believes that she was founded by divine order. In harmony with Vatican II's Decree on the Missionary Activity of the Church (*Ad Gentes*), "the Church has been sent to all nations that she might be "the universal sacrament of salvation."[523] Based on her divine foundation, she fulfills her mission relying upon the *libertas ecclesiastica* (freedom of the Church) and enters into negotiations with countries around the world, both at a diplomatic and spiritual level. Due to Vatican II, *Ad Gentes* focuses the work of mission upon the whole Church, the People of God, and includes pastoral work, "new evangelization," ecumenical activity, and theological dialogue regarding missiology.[524] With a world membership of 1.66 billion, the Church operates 135,549 total schools with a student population of 48.278 million as of 2008.[525]

Areas of Dissonance

While the Seventh-day Adventist Church and the Roman Catholic Church share four basic principles relative to religious freedom, they apply them so differently in practice that there are sharp and distinct differences between both groups.

Church and state relations. Although both SDAs and Roman Catholics believe civil authority originates with God, each develops this principle in distinctly different ways. Seventh-day Adventists believe that civil authority is given by God to restrain evil and to establish societal order: "the powers

---

[522] *Catechism of the Catholic Church*, Part One, Section Two, Chapter Three, Article Nine, Paragraph 3, "The Church is One, Holy, Catholic, and Apostolic," http://www.vatican.va/archive/ENG0015/__P29.HTM (accessed June 6, 2012).

[523] *Ad Gentes*, Art. 1, par. 1, in *Documents*, ed. Abbot, 584.

[524] Cassidy, *Ecumenism and Interreligious Dialogue*, 90-93.

[525] CARA Research Center, Georgetown University. http://cara.georgetown.edu/CARAServices/ requestedchurchstats.html (accessed May 31, 2012).

that be are ordained of God."[526] Seventh-day Adventists do not associate any spiritual, or religious, connotations with the office of civil servants. Paul uses the term λειτουργοί in Romans 13:6, which typically carries a cultic meaning, "For this cause pay ye tribute also: for they are God's *ministers*, attending continually upon this very thing." However, he twice uses the term διάκονός in verse 4, "For he is the *minister* of God to thee for good. But if thou do that which is evil, be afraid; for he beareth not the sword in vain: for he is the *minister* of God, a revenger to execute wrath upon him that doeth evil," which denotes a servant (deacons), without any cultic significance, as demonstrated by the distinction the apostles made between deacons chosen to serve the needs of the widows so that the apostles could attend unto the preaching of the Word in Acts 6:1-4. Paul's singular usage of λειτουργοί is in reference to paying tribute, or taxes, which seems to indicate that the believers in Rome, some of whom were converts from Judaism, may have had a tendency to resist Roman rule. This perspective harmonizes with the historical record[527] and would justify Paul's usage of a term that conveyed the sacred duty of not only obeying such civil servants, but also of paying tribute, as if it were a sacred, or cultic, act before God. Interestingly, this is the understanding implied by EllenWhite when she wrote:

> Those who love God's commandments will conform to every good law of the land. . . *We are to recognize human government as an ordinance of divine appointment and teach obedience to it as a sacred duty, within its legitimate sphere.* . . We are not required to defy authorities. Our words, whether spoken or written, should be carefully considered. . . Teach the people to conform in all things to the laws of their state when they can do so without conflicting with the law of God.[528]

Thus, Seventh-day Adventists do not ascribe to any civil authority the right, or power, to assume a religious role over its citizenry.

Slightly different from this position, the Roman Catholic Church

---

[526] Romans 13:1.

[527] Edwin Cook, "Parousia or Politics?" see section, The Relationship Between Jews and Christians, in *Liberty*, Jan/Feb 2005 at http://www.libertymagazine.org/index.php?id=1377 (accessed May 31, 2012).

[528] Ellen G. White, *My Life Today*, 281 in *The Ellen G. White Writings: Comprehensive Research Edition*, 2008 (italics mine).

ascribes more of a religious role to civil authorities, "As a consequence, the State, constituted as it is, is clearly bound to act up to the manifold and weighty duties linking it to God by the public profession of religion."[529] This statement of Pope Leo XIII is not much different from that adopted at Vatican II,

> Government is also to help create conditions favorable to the fostering of religious life, in order that the people may be truly enabled to exercise their religious rights and to fulfill their religious duties, and also in order that society itself may profit by the moral qualities of justice and peace which have their origin in men's faithfulness to God and to His holy will.[530]

Bearing in mind the historical context of Vatican II and of current times offers a broader understanding of how the Church considers civil authority. Since civil authority originates with God, and in the context of Vatican II, the Church confronted communist totalitarian states that were intent on eradicating religion from public life. In the modern context, the Church faces the dilemma of secular-minded states that are content with no religious overtones in society. In both contexts, the Church confronts the state to leave religion unmolested and unhindered, especially the Church in fulfilling her mission. Further, she has adopted the posture of promoting a unique form of religious freedom and fostering conditions favorable to religious life. Although this is generic language that resonates with current democratic governance regarding religious pluralism, it is worth noting that *Dignitatis Humanae* does make specific reference to the Catholic Church as the one true faith and that the Church attempts to receive legal recognition in nations where it has a presence. This and related points will be addressed more fully in Chapter Five, "Dignitatis Humanae's *Impact in Spain*," and Chapter Six, "Dignitatis Humanae's *Impact in Mexico*."

Limits of state authority. While both Adventists and Catholics believe that civil government should reflect principles of the transcendental order, Seventh-day Adventists recognize the limits of civil authority in religious matters in harmony with the biblical exegesis regarding conscience and religious freedom as found in this book in chapter three and as stated by Ellen G. White:

---

[529] Pope Leo XIII, *Immortale Dei* (The Christian Constitution of States), encyclical issued November 1, 1885 in Yates, 14.

[530] *Dignitatis Humanae*, Article 6, par. 4.

> To protect liberty of conscience is the duty of the state, and this is the limit of its authority in matters of religion. Every secular government that attempts to regulate or enforce religious observances by civil authority is sacrificing the very principle for which the evangelical Christian so nobly struggled.[531]

Furthermore, Seventh-day Adventists believe that when civil authority recognizes the individual's liberty of conscience in religious matters, it is reflecting one aspect of God's own character since He gives to man freedom to believe or disbelieve:

> God never forces the will or the conscience; but Satan's constant resort—to gain control of those whom he cannot otherwise seduce—is compulsion by cruelty. Through fear or force he endeavors to rule the conscience, and to secure homage to himself. To accomplish this, he works through both religious and secular authorities, moving them to the enforcement of human laws in defiance of the law of God.[532]

Upholding this principle of freedom of conscience, Seventh-day Adventists take their stand with a long line of Protestant Reformers, with American statesmen from the Founding Era,[533] and with American institutions today that vigilantly defend the civil liberties enshrined in the Bill of Rights.

Roman Catholicism adopts a different approach to the role of civil authority in a constitutional democracy with respect to the role of religion. As set forth in this book in chapters two and three, *Dignitatis Humanae* shifts

---

[531] Ellen G. White, *The Great Controversy*, 201 in *The Ellen G. White Writings: Comprehensive Research Edition*, CD, 2008.

[532] Ibid., 591.

[533] Ellen White states, "The framers of the Constitution recognized the eternal principle that man's relation to his God is above human legislation, and his right of conscience inalienable. Reasoning was not necessary to establish this truth; we are conscious of it in our own bosom. It is this consciousness, which, in defiance of human laws, has sustained so many martyrs in tortures and flames. They felt that their duty to God was superior to human enactments, and that man could exercise no authority over their consciences. It is an inborn principle which nothing can eradicate." Ellen G. White, *The Great Controversy*, 1888 edition, 295, in *The Ellen G. White Writings: Comprehensive Research Edition*, CD, 2008.

the role of moral authority to the populace, which in turn is to enact moral policies in harmony with the teaching of the Magisterium through the elected civil servants. In time, the result is a Christianization of society and, eventually, those who become a minority are granted a "civil right to religious freedom" defined as "an immunity from coercion" while in the pursuit of truth, recognizing that Catholicism is the "one true faith." Grave concerns to civil liberties under such a societal construct have already been delineated in chapter three. Under such conditions, if the constitutional construct is at odds philosophically with Roman Catholic moral and political philosophy, then civil servants are placed in the dilemma of whether to uphold the constitutional order, or to yield to the demands of democratic Catholicism.[534] This dilemma will be explored in greater detail in Chapter Seven, "Dignitatis Humanae *and the Future of Religious Freedom*."

Defining the objective moral order. Although both SDAs and Roman Catholics believe in an objective moral order, there are distinct differences regarding how to define it. For SDAs, the Law of God is the foundation for all good and just laws:

> I saw that it is our duty in every case to obey the laws of our land, unless they conflict with the higher law which God spoke with an audible voice from Sinai, and afterward engraved on stone with His own finger. "I will put My laws into their mind, and write them in their hearts: and I will be to them a God, and they shall be to Me a people."
> . . . The ten precepts of Jehovah are the foundation of all righteous and good laws. Those who love God's commandments will conform to every good law of the land. But if the requirements of the rulers are such as conflict with the laws of God, the only question to be settled is: Shall we obey God, or man?[535]

Based on this counsel, Seventh-day Adventists promote obedience to civil authority insofar as it does not conflict with the Ten Commandments, and even uphold societal laws in harmony *with the last six precepts of the Decalogue* (balanced with reason, of course; for example, if the tenth commandment,

---

[534] Díaz-Salazar speaks of a "regulated democracy" in Spain. Rafael Díaz-Salazar, *El Factor Católico en la Política Española* (Madrid: PPC Editorial, 2006), 278-303; cf., chapter six, this book.

[535] Ellen G. White, *Testimonies for the Church*, 9 vols., 1:361, 362 in *The Ellen G. White Writings: Comprehensive Research Edition*, CD, 2008.

"thou shalt not covet," were enacted into law, how could it be enforced?). However, government has no authority to promote, regulate, or coerce obedience to the first four commandments.

Seventh-day Adventists believe, as Roger Williams and other American advocates of religious freedom, that the first four commandments regulate man's relationship with God, *viz.*, specific acts of worship and reverence,[536] and that the last six commandments order man's relationship with his fellow man, *viz.*, civil society.[537] Jesus also drew this distinction when a lawyer asked Him, "Master, which is the great commandment in the law? Jesus said unto him, Thou shalt love the Lord thy God with all thy heart, and with all thy soul, and with all thy mind. This is the first and great commandment. And the second is like unto it, Thou shalt love thy neighbor as thyself. On these two commandments hang all the law and the prophets."[538] Thus, Adventists rely upon Scriptural principles for ordering society, a point that differs some from Catholicism.

Roman Catholic social teaching since Vatican II has shifted from a neo-scholastic approach that relied heavily upon philosophical arguments, to more of a focus upon Scripture and an appeal to the conscientiousness of man in the modern age of enlightened intellectual ability.[539] A standard natural law framework still prevails: there is an inner law to which man is compelled to obey; humanity is obligated to obey an objective standard of morality; and, human conduct strives for conformity with human nature. Vatican II also gave natural law teaching a Christological dimension, upholding Christ's example of meeting humanity's needs. Even though a modern Catholic approach to defining the moral order includes Scripture, Adventists differ from Catholics because of the Church's appeal to previous social teachings and natural law arguments.

Since Catholicism believes that transcendental principles should govern the temporal order, it argues that just human laws designed for ordering

---

[536] The first four commandments, paraphrased, are: Have no other gods before the LORD; Do not make or worship idols; Do not take the LORD's name in vain; and, worship the LORD on the Sabbath. Exodus 20:1-11.

[537] The last six commandments, paraphrased, are: Honor your father and mother; Do not kill; Do not commit adultery; Do not steal; Do not bear false witness; Do not covet anything of your neighbors. Exodus 20:12-17.

[538] Matthew 22:36-40.

[539] Stephen J. Pope, "Natural Law in Catholic Social Teachings," in Kenneth R. Himes, ed., *Modern Catholic Social Teaching* (Washington, D.C.: Georgetown University Press, 2005), 54-55.

society derive from natural and eternal law.[540] Believing that civil authority has a moral obligation to promote religion,[541] Catholicism believes part of its mission is to engage society through reasoned debate regarding the common good of society. Through the Christianization of society, the citizenry develop a "well-formed" conscience and attempt to "inscribe the divine law upon the earthly city,"[542] – i.e., through laws favoring Christian moral values. In modern times, such a posture has resulted in a violation of the religious freedom rights of minority groups in some countries. A more detailed discussion of this issue is found in the last section of this chapter, "Seventh-day Adventist and Roman Catholic Relations."

Missiology: diplomacy versus concordats. Since Seventh-day Adventists and Roman Catholics consider the world as their mission field, they naturally become competitors. Two areas of dissonance are most notable between both groups: 1) diplomatic relations with the countries where they have adherents, and, 2) proselytism.

Since Seventh-day Adventists proclaim religious freedom for every person, they do not seek diplomatic favors that would grant them a legal advantage over other religious groups. When necessary, they do engage the governments where they have converts for the sake of encouraging those governments to uphold the principle of religious freedom for all of their citizens, which benefits Seventh-day Adventists living there as well.[543]

Roman Catholicism adopts a different approach toward the governments where they have adherents. A Concordat "designates a diplomatic agreement signed between the Holy See and a state and is

---

[540] Pope Leo XIII, *Libertas Praestantissimum*, in Yates, 35.

[541] *Dignitatis Humanae*, Article 6, par. 4.

[542] *Gaudium et spes*, Art. 43, par. 5 in *The Documents of Vatican II*, ed. Abbot, 244.

[543] "Indeed, Adventists are called to be a voice for liberty of conscience to this world. Integral to this mission is the development of relationships with temporal rulers. In order to do this, the Seventh-day Adventist Church appoints representatives to governments and international bodies that have influence over the protection of religious liberty. This work must be viewed as essential to our gospel mission and should be accorded the resources necessary to ensure our representation is of the highest order." Declaration of the Seventh-day Adventist Church on Church-State Relations, under section titled "Representation to Governments and International Bodies," in *Statements, Guidelines & Other Documents*, compiled by the Communication Department of the General Conference Association of Seventh-day Adventists, (Review and Herald Publishing Assoc., 2010), 186-193.

intended to regulate matters of religious interest concerning them both."[544] Concordats have a long history within the Church. Prior to Vatican II, they historically were the standard mode the Church used to ensure the care of its members wherever they resided. After Vatican II, some groups believed concordats would fall into disuse since they could be viewed as contradictory to the Church's stance on religious freedom (*Dignitatis Humanae*), which was far from the case. By 1979, the Vatican had entered into formal relations with the Spanish government through a concordat.[545] A more detailed discussion of this topic is found in Chapters Five and Six, which cover religious freedom in Spain and Mexico, respectively.

Another area of dissonance between Seventh-day Adventists and Catholicism is proselytism. Evangelistic efforts mark the life of Adventists and contribute to continual growth. When trying to evangelize Roman Catholics, Seventh-day Adventists have observed that Church leaders do not allow their members to freely follow their conscience. Daniel Basterra Montserrat, a Seventh-day Adventist lawyer in Spain, analyzed portions of *Dignitatis Humanae* for his doctoral dissertation and concluded that the greatest objection to *Dignitatis Humanae* is not allowing "the possibility of changing religion, or of not having any [religion]."[546] Basterra reached his conclusions from a civil lawyer's perspective.

Similarly, John Graz, Secretary-General for the International Religious Liberty Association, raises the question of how much liberty of conscience is actually promoted by the Catholic Church in light of certain actions taken by it in conjunction with the World Council of Churches in 2006 regarding proselytism.[547] The joint document focuses on the evangelical evangelistic campaigns conducted in India and Sri Lanka. Both organizations have taken measures to restrict conversion of their members to other faith groups without considering this to be a violation of liberty of conscience. Graz argues that such action does not reflect true liberty of conscience. He further contends that such majority religious groups have not clearly

---

[544] Francesco Margiotta Broglio, "Concordat" in *The Papacy: An Encyclopedia*, 3 vols., ed. Philippe Levillain (New York: NY: Routledge, 2002), 396.

[545] Ibid., 397.

[546] Daniel Basterra Montserrat, doctoral dissertation, *La Libertad Religiosa en España y su tutela jurídica* (Universidad Complutense de Madrid, Facultad de Derecho, Departamento de Derecho Político, 1983), 26.

[547] John Graz, *El Adventista y . . .* (The Adventist and. . .) (Doral, FL: Asociacion Publicadora Interamericana, 2010), 109.

defined "aggressive proselytism,"[548] nor have they considered the aggressive dominance exercised by majority religious groups over minority religions which have been discriminated against.[549]

The Catholic Church in Latin America poses another example of the conflict between religious liberty and proselytism. Facing the "threat" and "challenge" of rapid growth among Protestant churches and sects, the Church has implemented strategies for retaining its members, and regaining former ones. However, it also adopts the following position toward other religious groups:

> This perspective, assumed by some theologians and by various Episcopal documents, is positive and recognizes the right of each religious group to offer their own message. However, it also deplores publicly the methods employed by some sects and religious movements at the time of presenting their saving message, but in no case does it consider Latin America as the exclusive monopoly of the Catholic Church.[550]

In fairness to the discussion regarding proselytism, there are some Catholic leaders who do not agree with the more passive attitude mentioned above. The Mexican Conference of Catholic Bishops requested that Father Flaviano Amatulli Valente should be in charge of the Department of the Faith Facing Sectarian Proselytism.[551] His responsibilities were to inform the Conference of all advances made by the sects. He went beyond this

---

[548] John Graz, *El Adventista y . . .* (The Adventist and. . .) (Doral, FL: Asociacion Publicadora Interamericana, 2010), 110.

[549] Ibid., 111.

[550] "Esta perspectiva, asumida por algunos teólogos y por diferentes documentos del Episcopado, es positiva y reconoce el derecho de cada grupo religioso a ofrecer su propio mensaje. Sin embargo, también deplora públicamente, los métodos empleados por algunas sectas y movimientos religiosos a la hora de presentar su mensaje salvífico, pero en ningún caso considera América Latina como monopolio exclusivo de la Iglesia Católica." P. Ignacio Garro, S. J., "Sects in Latin America" Series, part 3, "Catholic Response to Sects," under Section B: Protestant Sects and New Religious Movements as a "Challenge," http://formacionpastoralparalaicos.blogspot.com/2009/09/respuesta-catolica-sectas.html (accessed January 30, 2012).

[551] Flaviano Amatulli Valente, *Religious Proselytism: The Dominant Note in Latin America*, http://es.scribd.com/doc/24761588/EL-PROSELITISMO-RELIGIOSO (accessed January 30, 2012).

directive and produced a document, "Religious Proselytism: The Dominant Note in Latin America," in which he decries the Catholic hierarchy for a lack of organized and aggressive efforts to check the sectarian advances that are daily removing on average 400 Catholics from the fold of the Church. In this document, he outlines parish strategies – emphasizing primarily priestly visitation to adherents and thorough catechismal instruction – by which priests can retain members. He is not alone in such efforts. Father Ignacio Garro, S.J., has posted numerous articles on the phenomena of proselytism and how to resist its advances at his website, Pastoral Formation for Laity.[552]

Having analyzed areas of consonance and dissonance between Seventh-day Adventist and Roman Catholic concepts of religious freedom, the following section focuses more specifically on historical and current issues affecting relations between both groups, as well as offers an Adventist prophetic understanding of the current stance of the Catholic Church toward religious freedom.

Seventh-day Adventist and Roman Catholic Relations

In addition to competing assertions between Seventh-day Adventism and Roman Catholicism, there are several doctrines that set them at odds,[553] only one of which will be mentioned at the beginning of this section since it is the most historically contentious issue between both groups and because it highlights the conflict over one of the practical dimensions of religious freedom: Sabbath (Saturday) observance versus Sunday. Additionally, this information is listed here to note the historic position of the Catholic Church toward the Sabbath and why Seventh-day Adventist adherence to it puts the two groups at variance. It also addresses in more detail the third point mentioned previously under *Areas of Dissonance*, namely, *How to define the objective moral order*. Both Seventh-day Adventists and Roman Catholics believe the Law of God (for the former), or the eternal law (for the latter),

---

[552] Garro, S. J., http://formacionpastoralparalaicos (May 7, 2012).

[553] Seventh-day Adventists believe in: salvation by grace through faith alone (one of the foundational principles of the Protestant Reformation, which also set many Reformation groups at odds with Rome) and thus reject the whole sacramental system with its associated merits; baptism by immersion as a result of the believer's faith in Christ's vicarious Atonement at Calvary, and thus reject infant baptism; the non-immortality of the soul and thus reject any concept of limbo, or sacraments for the dead; celebration of the Lord's Supper (Communion) believing that the elements (bread and grape juice) are merely emblems that contain no inherent merit, and thus reject Transubstantiation; and several other doctrines.

should be the basis of just laws. Seventh-day Adventists, however, do not believe that civil authority has any jurisdiction to legislate the first four commandments that deal with man's relation to God. The Roman Catholic Church, however, has a history of enacting civil legislation to promote Sunday worship, as will be noted in what follows.

Unrest over the issue of Rest[554]

On May 31, 1998, Pope John Paul II promulgated the Apostolic Letter, *Dies Domini* (On keeping the Lord's Day holy), in which he discusses the Catholic Church's rationale for keeping Sunday holy as a day of worship. From a religious freedom perspective, the practical application of the Letter catches one's attention. In article 67, paragraph 2, Pope John Paul II admonished,

> *"Therefore, also in the particular circumstances of our own time, Christians will naturally strive to ensure that civil legislation respects their duty to keep Sunday holy.* In any case, they are obliged in conscience to arrange their Sunday rest in a way which allows them to take part in the Eucharist, refraining from work and activities which are incompatible with the sanctification of the Lord's Day, with its characteristic joy and necessary rest for spirit and body.[555]

Within a decade, this Letter has begun to produce results in the civil sphere in Europe despite the dominant threat of secularism.

Sunday laws in Europe. Since its promulgation, bishops and priests alike have obediently heeded the admonitions contained therein. In Croatia, a

---

[554] The following material on the history of Sunday laws first appeared in Edwin Cook, "Europe and the Issue of Rest," *Liberty*, Jan/Feb 2011, http://www.libertymagazine.org/index.php?id=1699 (accessed May 31, 2012).

[555] One may legitimately ask, how does such a position differ from the right of SDAs to try to influence civil legislation to respect their right to observe the Sabbath? The difference between both positions is twofold: 1) SDAs never seek to influence civil legislation to mandate rest on the seventh day. This would be to impose their beliefs upon the rest of society, which is contrary to their understanding of freedom of religion and conscience and which would be a religious establishment; 2) When SDAs have conflict with observing the Sabbath, they ask for religious accommodations for the individual rather than asking for a generally applicable law legislating the observance of the seventh-day.

country comprised of a pre-dominant Catholic populace (90%), efforts to pass a national Sunday law found fruition on January 1, 2009, after the cabinet had spent four years in preparing the legislation.[556] The law, making exceptions for bakeries, flower shops, newsstands, and stores located in bus, train, and metro stations, requires all businesses to remain closed on Sundays.[557] Despite the lack of support from the populace, the highly influential national leadership of the Church pressured Parliament to pass the law, without consideration of the effects upon minority religious groups who hold as sacred a day other than Sunday.

During the same year, debate on Sunday legislation escalated as Berlin had passed legislation allowing stores to be open for 10 Sundays a year, per contra the national law. Catholic and Lutheran churches had opposed Berlin's law and the case made its way to Germany's Constitutional Court, which ruled against Berlin's law of leniency.[558] The Court's ruling went into effect on January 1, 2010. Germany's protection for Sundays is found in Article 139 of Germany's Basic Law, a holdover from the Weimar Constitution of 1919.

While these steps were being taken in Croatia and Germany, the Commission of Bishops for the European Community (COMECE) had given hearty approval and support to the proposal brought by five ministers of state to the European Parliament, arguing in favor of a Sunday law for all of Europe since Sunday served as a proper "cultural patrimony and social model" for European society.[559] They argued for recognition of Sunday as a day of rest for the well-being of society. They reasoned that, in light of the current economic crisis, economies continued to function, indicating that the common seven-day work week is not as essential as believed. They concluded that amidst the hectic demands of modern, fast-paced society, families needed time together. Adeptly side-stepping any religious

---

[556] Mohit Joshi, "Croatian retailers sack workers as 'never on Sunday law' kicks in," January 8, 2009, TopNews.in, http://www.topnews.in/croatian-retailers-sack-workers-never-sunday-law-kicks-2106643 (accessed on 5/11/2010).

[557] Associated Press, "Sunday shopping banned in Croatia," July 15, 2008, http://abcnews.go.com/ International/wireStory?id=5378375 (accessed on 8/27/2008). Original article in author's files.

[558] "High Court reaffirms ban on Sunday shopping," *Deutsche Welle* , February 12, 2009, http://www.dw-world.de/dw/article/0,4953600,00.html (accessed on 5/11/2010).

[559] "Obispos europeos apoyan proyecto de ley sobre descanso dominical en UE," ACIPRENSA, Febrero 14, 2009, http://www.aciprensa.com/noticia.php?n=24334 (accessed on 5/11/2010).

connotations to their appeal, they focused their arguments on the detriment to society's moral tone due to parents who had no time for their children, or for their own health.

Other supporters have included pro-labor and pro-family organizations, from numerous European countries, such as Germany, Austria, Denmark, Croatia, Spain, France, and Italy. Most recently, debate on the topic was aired on the British Broadcasting Corporation's program, *The Big Questions*, which pitted Dr. Michael Schluter, director of the organization *Keep Sunday Special*, Alex Goldberg, head of the London Jewish Forum, Jenni Trent Hughes, work-life relations expert, and Cristina Odone, writer and broadcaster, against Richard Haddock, farmer and entrepreneur, and other UK citizens who are against Sunday legislation.[560]

Throughout the course of Sunday legislation developments in Croatia, Germany, and possibly for all of Europe, due to the European Union's legislative decision, the central issue revolves around the motivation behind Sunday rest: Is it solely to rest from labor, thus allowing time for families? Or, does it have another facet related to religious overtures? Sunday-rest advocates answer affirmatively the former question, and negatively the latter. The Commission of Bishops for the European Community recognize that Europe is comprised of a variety of religious groups that do not all share the sanctity for Sunday as the Catholic Church does.[561] Respecting those differences, the bishops concede that any day could be set aside as a day of rest from labor, *but the customary practice in European society is that public institutions and schools are closed on Sundays*. Thus, to facilitate family time, a work-free Sunday law should be enacted for all of Europe that contains not a hint of religious terminology or connotations.

As fair-minded as this argument sounds, however, its central weakness is that it does not answer the question, *upon what foundation – religious, or merely social – does the customary practice exist of closing public institutions and schools on Sundays?* When presented in this light, one avoids defending a practice just because it may have the advantage of ages of existence. Therefore, the issue demands further investigation, especially in light of the historic argument. As the eminent historian, A. H. Lewis, D. D., stated, "History is

---

[560] "The Big Questions: Keep Sunday Special?" Aired on March 24, 2010, www.bbc.co.uk/ thebigquestions; "Part 1: Dr. Michael Schluter CBE, Keep Sunday Special," http://www.youtube.comwatch?v=tN6KjM67vrk&feature= relmfu; "Part 2: Dr. Michael Schluter CBE, Keep Sunday Special," http://www.youtube.com/watch?v=Rred0PZQrdA (accessed May 9, 2010).

[561] Blanca de Ugarte, "Prohibido trabajar en domingo?" *El Imparcial*, 3 de Marzo, 2009, http://www.elimparcial.es/contenido/35248.html (accessed on 5/11/2010).

an organic whole, a series of reciprocal causes and effects. No period can be separated from that which has gone before, nor be kept distinct from that which follows after. . . . Every effort to remodel existing Sunday legislation, or to forecast its future, must be made in the light of the past."[562] Thus, it is necessary to examine both the theological and historic rationale surrounding the current Sabbath debate.

Saturday worship and Sabbatarians. Sabbatarians are believers who observe Saturday as the biblical Sabbath. They find in Scripture support for this practice. Because the biblical Sabbath is typically associated with Judaism, Sabbatarians are often mistakenly identified as Jewish believers, or "Judaizers." However, Sabbatarians understand the perpetuity of God's Ten Commandment law,[563] and recognize the fourth commandment at the heart of it. They believe that the Sabbath is a memorial both of Creation and Redemption.

God created the world in six literal days and rested on the seventh, thus completing His work of Creation.[564] Jesus Christ taught that the Sabbath was for mankind, by-passing any reference to the Jewish nature of the Sabbath, when He referred to the Creation week: "The Sabbath was made for man, and not man for the Sabbath. Therefore, the Son of Man is Lord also of the Sabbath."[565] The apostle Paul, many decades after Christ's crucifixion, continued this Creation-theme emphasis when he referred to the Sabbath of Creation and its enduring blessings to all who observe it: "For he spake in a certain place of the seventh day on this wise, 'And God did rest the seventh day from all His works. . . . There remaineth therefore a rest (Greek, *sabbaton*) to the people of God."[566]

---

[562] A. H. Lewis, *Critical History of Sunday Legislation from 321 to 1888 A.D.* (New York: D. Appleton and Company, 1888), v, vi.

[563] Several laws are mentioned in Scripture: 1) the Ten Commandment law (Exodus 20:1-17), 2) the "law [of sacrifices]," (Hebrews 10:1), 3) the "law of sin and death," (Romans 8:2) and, 4) the "law of faith" (Romans 3:27). Recognizing the multiple laws mentioned in Scripture requires close scrutiny to determine which ones were abolished by Christ's death at Calvary (the law of sacrifices and, partially, the law of sin and death, at least with respect to mankind's condemnation) and which ones were upheld (the Ten Commandment law as identifying sin, the law of sin and death as requiring the death of the sinner, in this case, Christ who bore our sins, and the law of faith, by which we gain access to God's grace).

[564] Genesis 2:1-3.

[565] Mark 2:27, 28.

[566] Hebrews 4:4, 9.

Sabbatarians also believe the Sabbath serves as a memorial of redemption. During the Passion Week, Jesus was crucified on Friday, rested in the tomb on Sabbath, and was resurrected on the first day of the week, Sunday.[567] On the Friday of His crucifixion, Christ declared, "It is finished!" as He breathed His last breath, indicating that His supreme sacrifice for mankind was a completed act.[568] During the Sabbath, Christ rested from His completed work of salvation, symbolic of the spiritual "rest" into which His followers enter by observing the Sabbath.[569] Thus, those who observe the Sabbath as a sign of their salvation in Jesus Christ cannot be accused of trying to "work their way to heaven" out of good merit, since they "have ceased from their own works, as God did from his" and trust fully upon the merits of a crucified and risen Savior.[570] Sabbatarians also believe that, although Sunday was the day of Christ's resurrection, He gave no specific command supporting the observance of it as a day of worship.[571]

In contrast to Sabbatarians, numerous Christians worship on Sunday. Those who observe Sunday as their sabbath have historically relied upon the tradition of the Church and their desire to dissociate themselves from any Jewish overtones that they believe are central to Sabbath (Saturday) observance. The historical record during the Christian era is replete with numerous periods of struggle between Sabbatarians and Sunday-observing Christians, which repeatedly resulted in legislatively enacted Sunday laws.

Sunday laws and the Catholic Church. The history of Sunday legislation indicates that it is integrally related to religious beliefs. History records that Sunday legislation traces as far back as the Roman Emperor Constantine,

---

[567] Luke 23:54-24:1.

[568] John 19:27.

[569] Hebrews 4:5, 9-11.

[570] Hebrews 4:10, "For he that is entered into his rest, he also hath ceased from his own works, as God did from his." Reference is here made to clarify that SDAs do not observe the Sabbath for the sake of meritorious gain, or from a legalistic perspective. No reference is intended to the Catholic theology of merit or the sacraments.

[571] There are only eight verses in the New Testament that refer to "the first day of the week" and none of them give the command to worship on that day as the fourth commandment orders the observance of Saturday: Matthew 28:1; Mark 16:2, 9; Luke 24:1; John 20:1, 19; Acts 20: 7; 1 Corinthians 16:1-4.

who on March 7, 321 A.D. enacted into law a decree to honor the "venerable day of the sun," by which citizens were to abstain from work on Sunday, a day dedicated to the worship of the sun god and to the observance of "its venerable rites."[572] As one Catholic historian transparently acknowledged regarding Constantine's efforts on behalf of the Church, "He invested the judicial decisions of the bishop with civil authority. He modified the Roman Law in the direction of Christian values.[573] Sunday, the day when Christians assembled, was made a day of rest. . . Under Constantine, the Church was firmly set on the road to union with the state."[574]

Several decades later, in 364 A. D., the Council of Laodicea was convened.[575] One of its decisions related to a practice dating back to the middle of the second century, to roughly 150 A.D. At that time, the Church had begun to encourage Christians to observe Sunday instead of the biblical Sabbath in order to distinguish Christians from Jewish believers. By the time of the Council of Laodicea, Christians were observing both days of the week.[576] In order to make a complete break with the Sabbath, and

---

[572] Henry Bettenson, ed., *Documents of the Christian Church* (London: Oxford University Press, 1963), 18, 19.

[573] Some may argue that Constantine was merely protecting the rights of Christians through this legislation. However, one should considers that "Christianity's subsequent progress owed less to legal prohibition [i.e., banning pagan worship] than to a subtler compound, composed of legal privilege, the faith's intrinsic appeal and a continuing use of force." Thus, history shows that legal privileges did actually contribute to the eventual establishment of Christianity with much more severe restrictions upon non-Christians in later decades. Robin Lane Fox, *Pagans and Christians* (New York, NY: Alfred A. Knopf, Inc., 1989), 667.

[574] Thomas Bokenkotter, *A Concise History of the Catholic Church* (New York: Doubleday, 1990), 39.

[575] Even though it was not a provincial or ecumenical council, it still reflects the posture of the Church toward the Sabbath, as demonstrated through the rest of this section.

[576] "It would seem therefore that though the resurrection is frequently mentioned both in the New Testament and in the early patristic literature, no suggestion is given that primitive Christians commemorated the event by a weekly or yearly Sunday service. The very fact that Passover, which later became the annual commemoration of the resurrection held on Easter Sunday, initially celebrated primarily Christ's passion and was observed by the fixed date of Nisan 15 rather than on Sunday, makes it untenable to claim that Christ's resurrection determined the origin of Sunday worship during the lifetime of the Apostles."

substitute it with Sunday, the Council of Laodicea stated, in Canon 29, "Christians must not judaize by resting on the Sabbath [Saturday], but must work on that day, rather honouring the Lord's Day [Sunday]; and, if they can, resting then as Christians. But if any shall be found judaizers, let them be anathema from Christ."[577] This overtly antagonistic stance toward the biblical Sabbath paved the way for atrocious and grueling torture of "Judaizers" during the Inquisition many centuries later.

A short sixteen years after the Council of Laodicea, the Church had Christianized society enough that Emperors Gratian and Theodosius established it as the basis of the whole social order.[578] Thomas Bokenkotter, professor at Xavier University, wrote:

> This was the intent of the epoch-making decree promulgated by Theodosius from Thessalonica on February 27, 380 A.D., which began: "We desire that all peoples who fall beneath the sway of our imperial clemency should profess the faith which we believe has been communicated by the Apostle Peter to the Romans and maintained in its traditional form to the present day. . .

Samuele Bacchiocchi, *From Sabbath to Sunday: A Historical Investigation of the Rise of Sunday Observance in Early Christianity* (Rome, Italy: The Pontifical Gregorian Press, 1977), 74-84. Dr. Bacchiocchi's work was "Vidimus et approbamus ad normam Statutorum Universitatis." ("We view and approve by University Statutory norms.") Dr. Bacchiocchi states that "Epiphanius (ca. A.D. 315-403) suggests that until A.D. 135 Christians everywhere observed Passover on the Jewish date, namely, on Nisan 15, irrespective of the day of the week. If our informer is correct, this would mean that prior to that time, no necessity had been felt to institute a Sunday memorial (whether annual or weekly) to honor the resurrection." Ibid., 81; J. N. Andrews, *History of the Sabbath* (Payson, AZ: Leaves of Autumn, 1991); Allen Walker, *The Law and the Sabbath* (Nashville, TN: Southern Publishing, 1957); per contra: H. M. Riggle, *The Sabbath and the Lord's Day* (Glendale, AZ: Life Assurance Ministries, n.d.); D. A. Carson, *From Sabbath to Lord's Day* (Eugene, OR: Wipf and Stock Publishers, 1982).

[577] "The Council of Laodicea in Phrygia Pacatiana, 364 A. D." http://reluctant-messenger.com/ council-of-laodicea.htm (accessed on 5/9/2010).

[578] Some may argue that such legislation was enacted due to Roman law, which stipulated that the religion of the emperor had to be the religion of the empire. If these emperors were Christians themselves, then this actually underscores the point brought out here that the Church was successful enough in Christianizing society that not only the majority of the populace, but also rulers became Christians and consequently, a doctrine of the Church became established by law.

." Paganism was declared illegal, while privileges were granted to the Catholic clergy; they were accorded immunity from trial except in ecclesiastical courts. Roman law was revised in harmony with Christian principles: The Sunday observance laws of Constantine were revived and enlarged, with the banning of public or private secular activities.[579]

Through a Christianization of society, the Church influenced societal values enough so that they became established through law.

A little more than a thousand years after the time of Emperors Gratian and Theodosius, the Church again voiced its opposition against Sabbath-keeping believers at the Council of Florence (1438-1445). From the perspective of Sabbatarians,[580] Catholic theologians failed to see the distinction between the moral Sabbath (Saturday) of God's Ten Commandment law and the ceremonial Sabbaths, *which required animal sacrifices that symbolized the long-awaited Messiah*. The moral Sabbath of the Ten Commandments (Saturday) was to be observed on a weekly basis,[581] but the ceremonial Sabbaths sometimes occurred in the middle of the week, and sometimes on the Sabbath (Saturday) of the Ten Commandments.[582] Ceremonial Sabbaths were also associated with circumcision, animal sacrifices, and the Jewish covenant. Although the ceremonial Sabbaths were fulfilled by the death of Jesus at Calvary,[583] the moral Sabbath of the Ten Commandments (Saturday) remained in vigor as part of God's moral law for humanity,[584] just as the apostle Paul stated, "Circumcision is

---

[579] Bokenkotter, 57.

[580] The term Sabbatarian used here refers to those Christians who observed the Sabbath both at the time referred to in the text, as well as those of the modern times since Sabbath observance among Christians dates to the time of Christ.

[581] Exodus 20:8-11; Deuteronomy 5:12-15.

[582] For example, the observance of the Day of Atonement occurred on the tenth day of the seventh month and was considered as "a sabbath of rest," even though it did not fall on the weekly Sabbath (Saturday) in some given years (Leviticus 23:27-38). Nonetheless, God made a clear distinction between it and the weekly, moral Sabbath when He commanded the observance of these feasts of Atonement (v. 37) "beside [or, in addition to] the sabbaths of the Lord" (v. 38).

[583] Daniel 9:27; Colossians 2:14-17.

[584] Romans 3:31.

nothing, and uncircumcision is nothing, but the keeping of the commandments of God."[585] Misunderstanding these fine theological nuances, Catholic theologians conflated ceremonial Sabbath observance with moral Sabbath observance. Thus, at the Council of Florence, they declared that all who observe the Sabbath (Saturday) are "alien to the Christian faith and not in the least fit to participate in eternal salvation, unless someday they recover from these errors."[586]

Within a century later, the Protestant Reformation had occurred, and the Catholic Church was already organizing its forces for the Counter-Reformation. Seeking to counteract Protestant advances, the Church at the Council of Trent, ordered the preparation of the Catechism of the Council of Trent, in which leading theologians formulated responses to the perceived Protestant heresies.[587] One of the doctrines re-emphasized was the teaching regarding the sabbath (Sunday) commandment.[588] Here again, the Catholic Church acknowledged the (attempted) transference of the sanctity of the biblical Sabbath from Saturday to Sunday, claiming the Church's authority to alter the divine law of God: "But the Church of God has thought it well to transfer the celebration and observance of the Sabbath to Sunday." Of utmost concern to the discussion of Sunday-rest laws, the Council of Trent not only solemnly admonished all to abstain from work on Sunday, but also continued to expound upon the obligation of all to use the day in "worship of God, which is the great end of the Commandment." Such worship included attendance at church, confession to the priest, performance of the Sacrament of Penance, and participation in the "Holy Sacrifice of the Mass."[589]

With such ideas about the moral Law of God, the Catholic Church

---

[585] 1 Corinthians 7:19.

[586] *A Decree in Behalf of the Jacobites* from the Bull "Cantata Domino," February 4, Florentine style, 1441, modern, 1442 as cited in Henry Denzinger, *The Sources of Catholic Dogma*, trans. Roy J. Deferrari (Fitzwilliam, NH: Loreto Publications), 229 (paragraph 712).

[587] Originally convened December 13, 1545, it was not until February 26, 1562 when a commission was actually appointed to prepare the Catechism. Note by translators, John A. McHugh and Charles J. Callan in *The Catechism of the Council of Trent*, authorized by The Council of Trent by decree of Pope Saint Pius V and ed. Saint Charles Borromeo (Rockford, IL: Tan Books and Publishers, Inc., 1982), xxiii.

[588] Borromeo, 402-407.

[589] Ibid., 403.

justified itself in the torture and murder of numerous "Judaizers" during the Inquisition. Historical records confirm that not all who observed the biblical Sabbath (Saturday) were Jewish in faith, yet they were classified as "Judaizers" because, in the eyes of the Church, they maintained an affinity to the Sabbath of the Ten Commandments.[590] Not only was the Catholic Church a persecuting force to Sabbatarians, but also the Reformed faith in Transylvania persecuted and confiscated property of Sabbath keepers during the Great Persecution of 1638.[591] Thus, history records that both Catholics and Protestants united in their efforts to suppress other Christians who held convictions about the Sabbath that were contrary to their own.

Any emphasis upon Sunday-rest does not involve the mere abstinence from work, but naturally leads to the observance of religious rites. As recently in the modern era as 1864, the Church voiced its authority, declaring that the State does not have the authority to allow servile work on certain holy days and feasts, contrary to the teachings of the Church – such men "make the impious pronouncement . . . that the law should be repealed 'by which on some fixed days, because of the worship of God, servile works are prohibited [by the Church].'"[592] *In those countries where governments acquiesce to the demands for Sunday-rest legislation, they will acknowledge by default that the Church has the upper hand. This in turn provides the opportunity for the Church not only to obligate citizens to rest on Sunday, but to worship on it as well.*

Some may argue that such accounts refer to Roman Catholicism of the past and that Vatican II (1962-1965) introduced dramatic reforms within the Church that affected her internal functioning, as well as her relations externally.[593] While there is some veracity to such an argument, one must

---

[590] Haim Benart, ed., *Records of the Trials of the Spanish Inquisition in Ciudad Real* (Jerusalem: The Israel Academy of Arts and Sciences, 1985), vol. 4:409-525. This section, Biographical Notes, relates personal information about the 700 citizens of Ciudad Real who were tried, and many of whom were burned at the stake, for observing the Sabbath (Saturday).

[591] Daniel Liechty, *Sabbatarianism in the Sixteenth Century: A Page in the History of the Radical Reformation* (Berrien Springs, MI: Andrews University Press, 1993), 68-77.

[592] Pius IX, from the encyclical, *Quanta cura*, December 8, 1864, as cited in *The Sources of Catholic Dogma*, ed. Denzinger, 431 (paragraph 1693).

[593] Stephen B. Bevans and Jeffrey Gros, *Rediscovering Vatican II: Evangelization and Religious Freedom: Ad Gentes, Dignitatis Humanae* (New York, NY: Paulist Press, 2009); Edward Idris Cardinal Cassidy, *Rediscovering Vatican II: Ecumenism and Interreligious Dialogue: Unitatis Redintegratio, Nostra Aetate* (New York, NY: Paulist Press, 2005); George Weigel and Robert Royal, eds., *Building the Free*

not overlook the immutable position of the Church with respect to Sunday. In *Dies Domini*, article 3, paragraph 1, Pope John Paul II stated,

> The fundamental importance of Sunday has been recognized through two thousand years of history and was emphatically restated by the Second Vatican Council: "Every seven days, the Church celebrates the Easter mystery. This is a tradition going back to the Apostles, taking its origin from the actual day of Christ's Resurrection — a day thus appropriately designated 'the Lord's Day'." Paul VI emphasized this importance once more when he approved the new General Roman Calendar and the Universal Norms which regulate the ordering of the Liturgical Year.

Although John Paul II is here referring to the General liturgical calendar, which specified what feasts and ceremonial days were to be observed universally by all Catholics, he associates with this calendar the weekly day of worship almost as an obligatory observance. For devout Catholics, John Paul II's statement is within the jurisdiction of the Church toward her members. However, the net result is that those Catholics heeding the admonitions of *Dies Domini*, "*will naturally strive to ensure that civil legislation respects their duty to keep Sunday holy.*"[594] Such efforts result in religious conflicts for Sabbatarians.

Not only was the immutable position of the Church regarding Sunday worship evident at Vatican II, but Catholic theologians have written extensively to promote Sunday worship. For example, one of the leading Catholic scholars in the "nouvelle theologie" movement, Henri de Lubac, refers to the periods of world history, the sixth one having begun with the Incarnation of Jesus and the seventh one beginning with His resurrection. By using numerology, mystical symbolism, and Church tradition, de Lubac attempts to rationalize why Sunday should be considered as a true sabbath of rest in honor of the resurrection.[595] Calendars should reflect this teaching, hence, the substitution of the biblical Sabbath (Saturday) with the sabbath (Sunday) that the Church has commanded should be observed.

Society: Democracy, Capitalism, and Catholic Social Teaching (Grand Rapids, MI: Eerdman's, 1993).

[594] John Paul II, *Dies Domini*, Art. 67, par. 2

[595] Henri de Lubac, *Catholicism: Christ and the Common Destiny of Man* (San Francisco, CA: Ignatius Press, 1988), 150-155.

In light of the foregoing efforts of the Church to promote Sunday worship by civil enactments, and especially when one considers the examples of Sunday laws being passed in Croatia and Germany mentioned at the beginning of this section, there remains an immovable shadow of doubt upon the position of the Church as a champion of religious freedom for those of other faiths, or at least for Sabbatarians such as Seventh-day Baptists, Jews who observe the Sabbath, Seventh-day Adventists, members of the Worldwide Church of God (Seventh-day), the Church of God of Prophecy, and various other Pentecostal Christians. This historic record highlights the hegemonic nature of the Catholic Church and also serves to explain in part why Seventh-day Adventists have historically identified the Catholic Church as fulfilling the characteristics of the Little Horn and the Beast powers described in the prophetic books of Daniel and Revelation.

The Little Horn and the Beast

The Little Horn of Daniel 7:7, 8, 15-23 and the Beast of Revelation 13:1-10 figure into any Christian discussion of religious freedom since both of these powers are described as persecuting God's people. The Little Horn made "war with the saints and prevailed against them. . . and shall wear out the saints of the most High."[596] Likewise, the Beast was given power "to make war with the saints, and to overcome them."[597]

Another characteristic describing both coercive entities is in reference to the term "times." Both prophetic books, Daniel and Revelation, use the term in reference to the Little Horn and the Beast, respectively. In Daniel 7:25, Scripture records that "they [the saints of the most High] shall be given into his [the Little Horn's] hand until *a time and times and the dividing of time.*" Adventists see a parallel description given in Revelation 12:14 where the woman (symbolic of the church, or God's people) flees from the persecution of the serpent (also referred to as "the great dragon. . . called the Devil, and Satan" in verse 9), "And to the woman were given two wings of a great eagle, that she might fly into the wilderness, into her place, where she is nourished for *a time, and times, and half a time,* from the face of the serpent." Interpreting these two passages in a parallel fashion, Adventists believe they refer to a time in Christian history when God's people faced persecution through an agency that unwittingly was used by Satan, or that reflected satanic characteristics of persecution and coercion.

In order to interpret the "times" referred to in these verses, Adventists

---

[596] Daniel 7:21, 25.

[597] Revelation 13:7.

rely upon "a year-to-day principle"[598] that they believe is supported by Scripture in a prophecy given to the prophet Ezekiel in which God symbolically portrayed the siege of Jerusalem. Ezekiel 4:6 states "And when thou hast accomplished them, lie again on thy right side, and thou shalt bear the iniquity of the house of Judah forty days: I have appointed thee each day for a year." Based upon this formulation, Adventists interpret "prophetic time" to calculate the literal time which is predicted to occur. Thus, one day in "prophetic time" equals one year in literal time.

Understanding the prophecy of the Little Horn in Daniel 7 to be a parallel description to the Dragon power in Revelation 12, as well as the Beast power in Revelation 13, Adventists interpret the sum of the "time, times, and dividing of time" in Daniel 7:25 as equivalent to the "thousand two-hundred and sixty days" of Revelation 12:14 and to the "forty-two months" of Revelation 13:5. Based on this, Adventists interpret the same event to occur, but with only a different descriptive term given to the length of time being described: 1) the "time" of Daniel 7:25 must be understood as a "year" of prophetic time, since it is described in 2) Revelation 12:14, as a "thousand two-hundred and sixty days," (3 "years" of prophetic time x 360 days/year = 1,260 "days" of prophetic time), and in 3) Revelation 13:5, as "forty-two months" (42 "months" of prophetic time x 30 days/month = 1,260 "days" of prophetic time). Applying the "year-day" formula (one prophetic "day" = one literal year) to the "times" in Daniel 7 and chapters 12 and 13 of Revelation, Adventists calculate the literal time to be 1, 260 years (1, 260 prophetic "days" = 1, 260 literal years) during which God's people have been persecuted. Table 4.1 illustrates the application of the "year-day" principle to the "times" of Daniel 7 and Revelation 12 and 13.

---

[598] This principle did not originate with Adventists, since many Jewish expositors used it, dating as far back as Flavius Josephus (37 A.D.) and continuing through 1697. Most of them also interpreted the four beasts (kingdoms) of Daniel 7 as leading up to the Roman Empire. Their views on prophecy influenced reformation expositors, Luther not the least among them. LeRoy Edwin Froom, *Prophetic Faith of Our Fathers*, 4 vols. (Washington, D.C.: The Review and Herald Publishing Association, 1948), 2:184-202, 270-279.

Table 4.1. The "year-day" principle in Daniel 7, and Rev. chaps. 12, 13.

Daniel 7	Revelation 12	Revelation 13
Little Horn	Dragon/Serpent	Beast
"made war with the saints and prevailed against them" v. 21	"[the Dragon] persecuted the woman" v. 13	"to make war with the saints and to overcome them" v. 7
"and [the saints] shall be given into his hand until a time, and times, and the dividing of time" v. 25	"the woman . . . fled into the wilderness. . . for a time, and times, and half a time from the face of the serpent" v. 14	"power was given unto him to continue forty and two months" v. 5
"day-year" principle: one day in prophecy equals one literal year. Thus, 3 ½ "times" = 3 ½ years prophetic time = 3 ½ x 12 months/year = 42 months prophetic time = 1,260 yrs.	"day-year" principle: one day in prophecy equals one literal year. Thus, 3 ½ "times" = "a thousand two hundred and three score days" v. 6, or 1, 260 literal years	"day-year" principle: one day in prophecy equals one literal year. Thus, "forty two months" = 42 x 30 days/month = 1, 260 days prophetic time = 1, 260 literal years

In addition to viewing the 1, 260 years of persecution as an identifying characteristic of the Little Horn power, Seventh-day Adventists interpret the characteristics in Table 4.2, based on Daniel 7:15-25, as applying to the identity of the Little Horn power. The "horns" in these verses are symbolic of "kingdoms" (or powers, vv. 17, 23). The Little Horn has a "mouth speaking great things" (Dan. 7:8, 20), or "blasphemies" (Rev. 13:5), indicating a religious entity. It is also "diverse" ("different," Dan. 7:19, 24) from the other "horns," indicating an entity that combines its religious authority with political intrigues. Allowing Scripture to interpret itself, Adventists believe that there is only one religio-political power that has existed for over 1,000 years and that fulfills the characteristics given in

Daniel 7: the Roman Catholic Church.[599]

Table 4.2. Interpretation of Daniel 7, identifying the Little Horn power.

Daniel 7	Interpretation[600]
Verses 19, 20 – "Then I would know the truth of the fourth... and of the ten horns that were in his head, and of the other which came up, and before whom three fell;"	Verse 23 – "the fourth beast shall be the fourth kingdom," referring to Rome Verse 24 – "the ten horns are ten kings," being the Nordic tribes that sacked Rome Verse 24 – "and another shall rise after them; and he shall be diverse from the first, and he shall subdue three kings," referring to the diversity of the papacy, which became a religio-political power as opposed to only a political power like the ten horns; it also refers to the three Nordic tribes (Ostrogoths, Visigoths, and Heruli) that were exterminated through papal influence since they were judged heretical for holding Arian beliefs about Christ

---

[599] This interpretation is the same one held by a long line of reformation Christians dating back to the early 1100s and includes such groups as the Waldenses, the Albigenses, Wyclif of England, John Huss of Bohemia, Jerome of Prague, and Girolamo Savonarola. Froom, *The Prophetic Faith*, 2:102-123. Martin Luther also was influenced by Wyclif's views regarding the Catholic Church and took the position of identifying the Pope as the Antichrist. English Reformers such as William Tyndale, Hugh Latimer, and Thomas Cranmer upheld this view as well. Froom, 2:354, 373-394.

[600] William H. Shea, *Selected Studies on Prophetic Interpretation*, Daniel and Revelation Committee Series (Washington, D.C.: Review and Herald Publishing, 1982), 1:27-34; *Daniel 1- 7*, The Abundant Life Bible Amplifier Series (Boise, ID: Pacific Press Publishing, 1996), 131-184.

Verse 20 – the little horn had "eyes, and a mouth that spake very great things, whose look was more stout than his fellows"

Verse 21 – "I beheld, and the same horn made war with the saints, and prevailed against them;"

Verse 22 – "Until the Ancient of days came, and judgment was given to the saints" cf. vv. 10, 11, "the judgment was set, and the books were opened. I beheld then because of the voice of the great words which the horn spake:. . even till the beast was slain, and his body destroyed."

Verse 25 – "And he shall speak great words against the most High," referring to the blasphemous claims of the papacy:

1. To claim the place of God[601]
2. To claim power to forgive sins[602]

Verse 25 – "and shall wear out the saints of the most High," referring to the religious persecution performed by the papacy

Verse 25 – "[the little horn] shall think to change times and laws," for which it comes into judgment by God and, as Seventh-day Adventists understand this verse, it applies to the efforts of the Roman Catholic Church to alter the Ten Commandment Law of God

---

Dignitatis Humanae *and Progressive Seventh-day Adventists*

The posture of the Roman Catholic Church toward non-Catholic religions from the time of Vatican Council II until the present has been viewed by many as that of an organization which champions religious freedom. The Declaration on Religious Freedom, *Dignitatis Humanae*, has been highly instrumental in such an assessment. Even some progressive Seventh-day Adventists are convinced that the traditional Seventh-day

---

[601] Jesus, the Son of God, was falsely accused of blasphemy: "The Jews answered Him, saying, For a good work we stone thee not; but for blasphemy; and because that thou, being a man, makest thyself God." John 10:33

[602] Jesus was falsely accused of blasphemy for declaring He had authority to forgive men's sins: "And the scribes and Pharisees began to reason, saying, Who is this which speaketh blasphemies? Who can forgive sins but God alone?" Luke 5:21

Adventist prophetic interpretation of the Little Horn and the Beast powers are not based on a proper interpretation of Scripture; that such conclusions do not take into account current developments within Catholicism (i.e., emphasis upon religious freedom through *Dignitatis Humanae*); and, that such views are not in the spirit of Jesus Christ, nor a part of His teachings. This section analyzes the views of both groups, as well as offers a conclusion based on the results thus far gathered through this book.

Among those questioning the historic SDA position regarding the Catholic Church, three individuals are the most notable in recent years: Húgo Méndez and David Pendleton (both former SDAs), and Loren Seibold (currently an ordained SDA minister). Húgo Méndez, a former Seventh-day Adventist theology student preparing for ministry, shares his testimony about converting to Roman Catholicism, part of which involved his questions regarding the historic position of the Seventh-day Adventist Church toward the Roman Catholic Church on religious liberty issues.[603]

Also, former Representative David Pendleton of Hawaii, a former Seventh-day Adventist minister, shares how *Dignitatis Humanae* challenged his thinking and attracted him into the fold of Roman Catholicism by its philosophical appeal.[604] He critiques, as well as challenges, Marvin Moore's conclusions in the book *Challenge to the Remnant*. Moore, editor of *Signs of the Times* magazine, upholds the traditional SDA view of Catholicism, to which Pendleton remarks,

> This book provides an occasion for Adventists to wrestle with whether this classic perspective on Catholicism is essential to Adventism. Does the belief that the Catholic Church is the beast of prophecy serve as the mark of authentic Adventism? If so, why didn't Jesus preach a single sermon on the topic? . . . is this belief excluded from the 28 Fundamental Beliefs precisely because it is not fundamental to Adventism? How should conscientious

---

[603] Húgo Méndez, originally available from the following sites: http://www.diesdomini.com/Papers/Q_ReligiousLiberty_EGW.pdf; http://www.diesdomini.com/Papers/Q_ReligiousLiberty_Source.pdf; http://www.diesdomini.com/Papers/Q_ReligiousLiberty_apol.pdf; http://www.diesdomini.com/Papers/Q_EGW_anticatholic.pdf, but now they are no longer available. Accessed on August 23, 2009, I have these pdf documents in my electronic archives.

[604] Story by Anna Weaver, "This Is Where My Faith Has Led Me" in *Hawaii Catholic Herald*, archived April 18, 2008 (accessed May 21, 2008).

Adventists interpret this intentional silence?"[605]

Pendleton's critique fails to take into consideration a statement recorded on April 15, 1997, by the General Conference of Seventh-day Adventists Administrative Committee (ADCOM) and released by the Office of the (then) president, Robert S. Folkenberg, part of which states:

> If, in expounding on what the Bible teaches, Seventh-day Adventists fail to express love to those addressed, we do not exhibit authentic Christianity.
> Adventists seek to be fair in dealing with others. Thus, while we remain aware of the historical record [of Catholic persecution during the medieval period] and continue to hold our views regarding end-time events [in which Roman Catholicism will play a key role], we recognize some positive changes in recent Catholicism, and stress the conviction that many Roman Catholics are brothers and sisters in Christ.[606]

This statement harmonizes with what Ellen G. White wrote in 1888:

> It is true that there are real Christians in the Roman Catholic communion. Thousands in that church are serving God according to the best light they have. . . [God] will reveal to them the truth, as it is in Jesus, and many will yet take their position with his people.[607]

Thus, a more balanced perspective of SDA views toward Catholicism is not anti-Catholic. Rather, Adventists regard historical actions of the Church as

---

[605] David A. Pendleton, "A Review of Marvin Moore's *Challenge to the Remnant*," http://www.spectrummagazine.org/reviews/book_reviews/2008/09/19/ review_marvin_moore%E2%80%99s_challenges_remnant, paragraphs 18-20 (accessed September 20, 2009).

[606] Seventh-day Adventist Administrative Committee (ADCOM), "How Seventh-day Adventists View Roman Catholicism," recorded April 15, 1997 in *Seventh-day Adventist Church: Statements, Guidelines & other documents*, compiled by the Communication Department of the General Conference Association of Seventh-day Adventists (Review and Herald Publishing Association, 2010), 96.

[607] Ellen G. White, *The Great Controversy*, 565 in *The Ellen G. White Writings: Comprehensive Research Edition*, 2008, CD.

fulfillment of Bible prophecy. At the same time, Adventists recognize sincere Christians in all denominations, even though they may hold beliefs considered by Adventists as erroneous.

Regarding the next question in Pendleton's critique, whether Jesus made reference to the Beast power, is to overlook the nature of biblical inspiration. Although one may argue that Jesus never preached a sermon on the topic as recorded in the Gospels, nevertheless, the Holy Spirit inspired later biblical authors to write apocalyptic messages, such as John who wrote the Revelation, which by the way begins as "The revelation *of Jesus Christ*, which God gave unto Him, to show unto His servants things which must shortly come to pass."[608] The last portion of Pendleton's critique questions why no specific doctrinal statement is made about the Catholic Church as the Beast power in the Fundamental Beliefs of SDAs. This concern is best addressed by the statement recorded by the SDA ADCOM and referenced earlier, another portion of which states:

> To blame past violations of Christian principles on one specific denomination is not an accurate representation of either history or the concerns of Bible prophecy. We recognize that at times Protestants, including Seventh-day Adventists, have manifested prejudice and even bigotry. If, in expounding on what the Bible teaches, Seventh-day Adventists fail to express love to those addressed, we do not exhibit authentic Christianity.[609]

To summarize a balanced SDA position, then, is to "speak the truth in love."[610] While SDAs believe the Roman Catholic Church (among other religious and political powers) will fulfill a central role in Bible prophecy, yet this is not the entire, nor central, message which the Adventist church believes it is called to proclaim. "Seventh-day Adventists seek to take a positive approach to other faiths. Our primary task is to preach the gospel of Jesus Christ in the context of Christ's soon return, not to point out flaws in other denominations."[611]

---

[608] Revelation 1:1.

[609] Seventh-day Adventist Administrative Committee (ADCOM), "How Seventh-day Adventists View Roman Catholicism," recorded April 15, 1997 in *Seventh-day Adventist Church: Statements, Guidelines & Other Documents*, Comm. Dept., 95-96.

[610] Ephesians 4:15.

[611] SDA ADCOM, 95.

Pastor Loren Seibold, although still an active member of the Seventh-day Adventist Church and practicing as an ordained minister, questions the historic interpretation of the Seventh-day Adventist Church regarding the Catholic Church as the fulfillment of the Beast of Revelation 13.[612] In an article titled, "Letting Catholics Off the Hook," he presents seven arguments to support his contention. His seven arguments follow, but have been rearranged by category, since some of his points overlap. First, he appeals to "conditional prophecy" to argue that "more than one-hundred years have passed since our prophet (Ellen White) approved these prophetic applications." He uses the conditional prophecies of the Old Testament in regard to Israel as the basis for arguing that the prophecies in Revelation may have a conditional element. If so, the Catholic Church at one time may have been the subject of reference regarding the religio-political entity that persecutes in the end of time, but now is no longer so due to a change in their stance on religious freedom. Or, stated otherwise, how can the traditional SDA eschatological scenario apply to the Roman Catholic Church since it is no longer an entity that persecutes? How can the non-persecuting stance of the Church be explained by Bible prophecy if the Church is still the power being referred to? A more detailed response to these questions is given in the next section of this chapter.

A second area, which encompasses Seibold's arguments 3, 4, 5, and 7, specifically addresses issues with Roman Catholicism. Seibold argues (his point #3) that "Ellen White fingered Roman Catholicism in a very different world," referring to the anti-Catholic sentiments prevalent in America that originated (in Seibold's view) more from anti-immigrant nativist reactions than specific religious issues. He refers to how America has had a "liberty loving" Roman Catholic president (Kennedy) and how we are now experiencing a young work force of Hispanic immigrants in America as reasons to drop the specific reference to the Catholic Church in SDA Bible prophecy discourses. While it is true that anti-immigrant nativist reactions fueled much of the anti-Catholic sentiments during the 1880s and 1890s, it is equally true that since the Founding Era (1780s and 1790s) in American history, leading statesmen voiced concern regarding Roman Catholic hegemony,[613] a point that is still active in American society today as

---

[612] Loren Seibold, "Letting Roman Catholics Off the Hook," http://69.89.30.254/letting-roman-catholics-hook (accessed January 11, 2010).

[613] During the debates in the States on the federal Constitution, Mr. Henry Abbot of North Carolina, on Wednesday, July 30, 1788, expressed the following concern about the last clause of Article VI: "Some are afraid, Mr. Chairman, that, should the Constitution be received, they would be deprived of the privilege of worshipping God according to their consciences, which would be taking from them a benefit they enjoy under the present constitution. They wish to know if

Catholic Bishops square-off with the Obama administration regarding what they consider to be a violation of their religious freedom rights under the First Amendment (this point will be more fully developed in Chapter Seven, "Dignitatis Humanae *and the Future of Religious Freedom*"). Seibold's reference to President Kennedy also overlooks the fact that Kennedy's position of church-state separation has not been approved by the Bishops to this day,[614] a point that actually argues strongly against Seibold's view and in favor of the traditional SDA view regarding the Catholic hierarchy.

He next argues (#4) that "the Roman Catholic Church of today is a much different institution than it was during Ellen White's time," appealing specifically to Vatican Council II and the reforms initiated by the Church. Most notably, Seibold refers to how the Church "affirmed religious liberty." This book has demonstrated thus far the fallacy of making such a broad claim as Seibold does here regarding the religious freedom advocated by the Catholic Church in *Dignitatis Humanae*.

In his point #5, Seibold contends that "by focusing on Roman Catholicism, we may miss more dangerous anti-Christian opponents." There is some truth to what Seibold argues, especially in light of the persecution of Christians that is occurring in various countries around the

---

their religious and civil liberties be secured under this system, or whether the general government may not make laws infringing their religious liberties. The worthy member from Edenton mentioned sundry political reasons why treaties should be the supreme law of the land. It is feared, by some people, that, by the power of [p.192] making treaties, they might make a treaty engaging with foreign powers to adopt the Roman Catholic religion in the United States, which would prevent the people from worshipping God according to their own consciences. The worthy member from Halifax has in some measure satisfied my mind on this subject. But others may be dissatisfied. . ." *Eliot's Debates*, vol. 4:191-192. Additionally, John Adams penned the following statement to Thomas Jefferson on July 19, 1821, "Can any free government possibly exist with the Roman Catholic religion?" Also, Alexis de Tocqueville, wrote the following, "If Catholicism could at length *withdraw itself from the political animosities to which it has given rise*, I have hardly any doubt but that *the same spirit of the age, which appears to be so opposed to it*, would become so favorable as to admit of its great and sudden advancement." (Tocqueville, "Of the progress of Roman Catholicism in the U.S.," in *Democracy in America*, vol. 2, Book 1, ch. 6; italics mine.).

[614] "[Kennedy's Houston speech] was sincere, compelling, articulate – and wrong. Not wrong about the patriotism of Catholics, but wrong about American history and very wrong about the role of religious faith in our nation´s life." Archbishop Chaput, "John F. Kennedy's View of the Role of Catholic Faith in Public Service Was Wrong," speech given at Houston Baptist University, March 2, 2010, Houston, TX, http://www.catholic.org/politics/story.php?id=35640 (accessed May 28, 2012).

world. However, Seibold fails to recognize that the characteristics given in Bible prophecy include more than just persecution. Such characteristics as "plucking up three horns [kingdoms],"[615] "speaking great words against the Most High[616] [or, "blasphemies"[617]]," "thinking to change times and laws,"[618] and having power to rule for "time, times, and the dividing of time[619] [or, "forty-two months"[620]]," all serve to narrow down the identity of the Little Horn, or Beast power to a specific entity, as noted in the previous section and in Table 4.2.

Seibold's point #7 posits that "religious liberty has arguably improved in countries where Catholicism has influence." Although this is true to some extent, it certainly does not present the whole picture. In many Latin American countries, such as Paraguay, Peru, Bolivia, and Mexico, church leadership changed its proselytism strategies, showing greater respect and latitude for indigenous religious practices, in accord with the Church's position taken at Vatican II.[621] However, there are other examples, such as Croatia and Germany referred to earlier in this chapter, which demonstrate a clearly opposite stance of the Church toward other religious groups. Further analysis and implications will be presented in Chapter Seven.

Seibold further contends that the Catholic Church cannot possibly be a fulfillment of the Beast of Revelation 13 based on current world events that indicate otherwise. In his point #2, he states "principles might be more diagnostic than players," referring to how the principle of defending religious liberty is far better to diagnose what power is violating it, rather than focusing on one player, the Catholic Church, that has violated it in the past. There certainly is merit in this contention, since an SDA eschatological view actually understands that the Catholic Church will be *one among other powers* that unite to persecute God's people in the end of time:

---

[615] Daniel 7:8, 20, 24.

[616] Daniel 7:8, 20, 25.

[617] Revelation 13:1, 5, 6.

[618] Daniel 7:25.

[619] Daniel 7:25; cf. Revelation 12:14, 6.

[620] Revelation 13:5; cf. 12:14, 6.

[621] Edward L. Cleary and Timothy J. Stegenga, *Resurgent Voices in Latin America: Indigenous Peoples, Political Mobilization, and Religious Change* (New Jersey: Rutgers, 2004), 9, 19, 45, 68, et al.

Seventh-day Adventists are convinced of the validity of our prophetic views, according to which humanity now lives close to the end of time. Adventists believe, on the basis of biblical predictions, that just prior to the second coming of Christ this earth will experience a period of unprecedented turmoil, with the seventh-day Sabbath as a focal point. In that context, we expect that world religions – including the major Christian bodies as key players – will align themselves with the forces in opposition to God and to the Sabbath. Once again the union of church and state will result in widespread religious oppression.[622]

From such an understanding of eschatology, SDAs certainly emphasize the need for vigilant defense of religious freedom.

From a global perspective, Seibold argues (point #6) that "God has given us [SDAs] time to become a world church, and that changes the cast of characters in our eschatology." On this point, Seibold misunderstands traditional SDA eschatology, which takes in a global perspective, as the reference in the previous paragraph indicates. Seibold portrays SDA eschatology as if it were limited only to the United States with a focus solely upon Sabbath-Sunday debate and persecution. Without entering into a detailed discussion of SDA eschatology, a simple observation is that from such a misperception as Seibold's, it is no wonder that he arrives at a conclusion contrary to a traditional SDA interpretation.

Although this section has demonstrated the weaknesses in several critiques of the traditional Adventist view of the Catholic Church as the Beast power in Revelation, there still remains the challenge of how to reconcile the current activity of the Church as an advocate of religious freedom, at least on some occasions, with the idea of the Beast power being a coercive, persecuting entity. The following section examines the possibility of *Dignitatis Humanae* being a document formulated for the current historical moment that could change under different circumstances.

The "Times" of Dignitatis Humanae

The "times" of *Dignitatis Humanae* refers to several concepts related to religious freedom. First, it describes the variety of time periods, or epochs, alluded to in the Document. Second, it alludes to the Document being

---

[622] Seventh-day Adventist Administrative Committee (ADCOM), "How Seventh-day Adventists View Roman Catholicism," recorded April 15, 1997 in *Seventh-day Adventist Church: Statements, Guidelines & other documents*, Comm. Dept., 95.

written only to address the current political system of constitutional democracy. If correct, this implies that the Document is not philosophically and politically broad enough to apply to future societal constructs that differ from the present one. Several Catholic authors seem to support this idea, as will be noted in the following pages.

At the end of chapter three, the possibility of a Catholic-dominated society was posited in relation to *Dignitatis Humanae* and if the Document would allow for a Catholic confessional state similar to the paternalistic model that preceded Vatican II. John Courtney Murray answered "No" to such a possibility. However, part of his response reveals that there is an aspect of the Church that continually seeks to adapt to the societal and political developments of each changing circumstance. Murray argued that an "affirmative answer [to the possibility of a Catholic confessional state]. . . would somehow imply a denial or neglect of that 'vital law of continual adaptation' which is the law of the Church's thought and action."[623]

Murray's answer implies that not only does the Church adapt to changing societal situations, but that *Dignitatis Humanae* would also need to adapt, at least in some minor ways, to conform to the changing demands of society. This conclusion is supported by another Catholic scholar, William Reiser, S. J., who states, "Yet although conciliar teaching [of Vatican II] is authoritative, it would be misleading to think of it as incapable of further development. The way the Catholic Church understands and then presents its message, its mission, and even its identity is necessarily affected by the historical and cultural settings in which it finds itself."[624]

Pietro Pavan, a Catholic theologian who worked with Murray in drafting *Dignitatis Humanae* implies that it contains principles of religious freedom that are evolving through the emphasis given by the then-recent popes (i.e., prior to the 1960s):

> The Council text, however, does not regard this teaching as having been defined by a Pope in its final form once and for all, but sees it as gradually developing through new papal contributions, especially in our own century. This doctrine develops, as it were, like a seed, which first germinates and then becomes an ever more vigorous plant. As is emphasized in the text, under the influence of the

---

[623] Murray, ms. 1949b, 229.

[624] William Reiser, S. J., "Roman Catholic Understanding of Religious Tolerance in Modern Times," in *Religious Tolerance in World Religions*, eds. Jacob Neusner and Bruce Chilton (West Conshohocken, PA: Templeton Foundation Press, 2008), 154.

evolving historical situation the Popes have increasingly emphasized the dignity of the human person and pronounced this to possess inviolable rights in the economic, social, political, cultural, moral and religious spheres.[625]

Pavan seems to indicate that religious freedom in *Dignitatis Humanae* evolves according to the historical situation. He further corroborates this understanding when he writes, "The summing up [in the third draft of *Dignitatis Humanae*] resumes and develops a motif of the two preceding drafts: *in our present pluralistic society* religious freedom is essential for preserving the peace both within the individual political communities and in the whole world."[626] Due to the evolving nature of religious freedom contained in *Dignitatis Humanae*, there has been more recent discussion of how to rightly interpret the Document.

Russell Hittinger, an erudite Catholic scholar, discusses the possibility of *Dignitatis Humanae* in a society that has been successfully Christianized:

> In a certain respect, this theological reflection has just begun. One can see why, in 1965, it would have been precipitous to force *Dignitatis Humanae* to attempt to resolve the issue of how religious liberty and confession of religious truth on the part of civil society might be synthesized in a distinctly contemporary mode – one in which democratic institutions prevail, the civil liberties of all are duly honored, and Christianization or rechristianization has progressed to the point that the essence of the Gospel has worked its way into a fully public manifestation. *Dignitatis Humanae* does not rule it out, but by the same token it does not bring it into view as a pressing problem. Just as *Dignitatis Humanae* does not revisit all of the past problems, it refuses to project its teaching, by way of hypothesis, into the distant future.[627]

---

[625] Pietro Pavan, Commentary on the Declaration of Religious Freedom, in *Commentary on the Documents of Vatican II*, 4 vols., ed. Herbert Vorgrimler (New York: The Crossroads Publishing Company, 1989), 4:64.

[626] Pavan, Introduction in *Commentary on the Documents*, 4:53 (italics mine).

[627] Russell Hittinger, "The Declaration on Religious Liberty," in *Vatican II: Renewal within Tradition*, eds. Matthew L. Lamb and Matthew Levering (New York: Oxford University Press, 2008), 366.

Hittinger's comment is enlightening on three levels: 1) it reveals that there is current Catholic discussion of the possibility of a successfully Christianized culture; 2) it declares that *Dignitatis Humanae* "does not rule out" this possibility; and 3) it implies that if such a future societal structure should develop, *Dignitatis Humanae* does not adequately address how such a society should be configured. The idea of the configuration of a Christianized society will be addressed in further detail in Chapter Seven, "Dignitatis Humanae *and the Future of Religious Freedom.*"

Interestingly, not only Catholic scholars have viewed *Dignitatis Humanae* through the lenses of the "times." Thomas Heilke offers a Radical Reformation perspective of *Dignitatis Humanae*,[628] arguing that the "times", or "epochs" alluded to within the document cover a vast period of Christian history, which include contradictory actions by the Church. He refers to the pre- and post-Constantinian periods, as well as the times of Church doctrine and Church tradition. He posits that such a variety of time periods allows the Church to choose which political model to adopt based on the changing times of society. Heilke cogently argues that *Dignitatis Humanae* is not a document providing a fixed principle of religious freedom, but instead one that changes with the fluctuating political winds.

There is an interesting parallel between Heilke's perspective of the "times" in *Dignitatis Humanae* and a Seventh-day Adventist interpretation of Bible prophecy. Both the Little Horn of Daniel 7 and the Beast of Revelation 13 are described as having some characteristics in common. Seventh-day Adventists have interpreted both passages as referring to the same religio-political power, the Papacy, as noted in a previous section of this chapter. The "times, time and the dividing of time" during which the Little Horn/Beast power exercised its authority by persecuting "the saints of the Most High" corresponds with the "times" of Heilke's interpretation of *Dignitatis Humanae*. This insight helps to possibly answer the question raised previously: how can one explain a biblical interpretation of the Beast power referring to the Catholic Church if the Church is not persecuting other religions, but instead promoting a form of religious freedom?

The Woman Who Rides the Beast

The Bible describes a woman who rides a beast in Revelation 17. The woman symbolizes the Church and the beast, the political power which

---

[628] Thomas Heilke, "The Promised Time of Dignitatis Humanae: A Radical Protestant Perspective," in *Catholicism and Religious Freedom: Contemporary Reflections on Vatican II's Declaration on Religious Liberty*, eds. Kenneth L. Grasso and Robert P. Hunt (NY: Rowman and Littlefield Publishers, 2006), 87-113.

sustains her.[629] According to this passage of Scripture, the woman's *nature of persecution* does not change – she is described as "drunken with the blood of the saints, and with the blood of the martyrs of Jesus"[630] – but the political power upon which she is founded does pass through phases of past-existence, non-existence, and re-existence ("the beast that was, and is not, and yet is"[631]). If one should interpret the phases of the woman/beast as persecuting, non-persecuting, and persecuting again, then an echo of Heilke's "times" becomes discernible, as well as that of a SDA theologian,[632] an evangelical Protestant,[633] and a Roman Catholic philosopher.[634] Thus, from an SDA perspective, the "times" of *variable* emphasis upon religious freedom alluded to in *Dignitatis Humanae* resonate with the "times" of past persecution, current non-persecution *and could also allude to a future time of persecution* described in Scripture with respect to the woman/beast power.[635] Figure 4.1 outlines the parallels between Heilke's "times" and the "times" of biblical prophecy regarding the woman/beast.

---

[629] Louis F. Were, *The Woman and the Beast in the Book of Revelation* (Berrien Springs, MI: LaRondelle, 1989), 164-171.

[630] Revelation 17:6

[631] Revelation 17:8

[632] Were, cited above; cf., "Babylon of," Ch. XI, *Seventh-day Adventist Bible Commentary*, 12 vols. (Logos Bible Software), 7:124.

[633] Dave Hunt, *A Woman Rides the Beast* (Eugene, OR: Harvest House Publishers, 1994), 204-207.

[634] Jacques Maritain, *Man and the State*, 180, fn. 30 (full text below in fn. 638 of this chapter).

[635] Incidentally, this conclusion contributes to the dialogue among SDA and Catholic scholars, such as SDA Pastor Loren Seibold, former SDA minister David Pendleton, and (former SDA) Húgo Méndez (now Catholic), who question the traditional position of SDAs regarding the Catholic Church, given that the Catholic Church is *currently* a promoter of global religious freedom.

Heilke notes "times" of pre- and post-Constantinian Church models, as well as "times" of persecution from the Inquisition referred to in *Dignitatis Humanae*	Heilke notes the current "time" of non-persecution, or religious freedom by the Church	Heilke is dubious regarding the permanency of religious freedom under *Dignitatis Humanae*
"five (kingdoms) have fallen" – Babylon, Medo-Persia, Greece, Pagan Rome, Persecuting Papal Rome (608 B.C. to 1798 A.D.)	"one is" – Non-persecuting Papal Rome (1798 to the present)	"the other has not yet come" (7th) – Persecuting Papal Rome (future time period) "the Beast which thou sawest even he is the eighth and is of the seven and goeth to perdition"
The Sea Beast that rules for 42 months = 3 ½ "times" = 1,260 "days" (years); Persecuting Papal Rome, 538 – 1798 A.D.	The Land Beast exercises all the authority of the Sea Beast, indicating a union with it. Neither persecute until the next "phase." Rev. 13:11-14	The Land Beast says "to them that dwell on the earth, that they should make an image to the Beast. . . And he had power to give life unto the image of the Beast. . . and as many as would not worship the image of the Beast should be killed." Rev. 13:14, 15

Figure 4.1. A diagrammatic outline based on Louis F. Were's interpretation of the "times" referring to the Woman, or Beast power of Revelation chapters 17:10 and Revelation 13:1-15.

The central argument upon which such an interpretation stands or falls is in relation to the metaphysical (coercive) authority claimed by the Church.[636] Does she retain such authority, but not exercise it only because of a change in the historical situation of modernity? Jacques Maritain argues in the affirmative:

> As concerns my attempt to outline a future type of Christian political society, whatever one may think of its particular features, what matters essentially to me is the fact that the same general principles are immutable; and that the ways of applying or realizing them are analogical, and change according to the variety of historical climates. So the principles which were applied in a given way by the sacral civilization of the Middle Ages always hold true, but they are to be applied in another way in modern secular civilization.[637]

In the footnote to this statement,[638] Maritain argues that the Church still

---

[636] Metaphysical, or dealing with abstract thought regarding truth, or concerned with first principles and ultimate grounds; translated here as the Church believing in Absolute Truth, Catholicism, and thus claiming authority as God's appointed agency in the temporal order to establish it.

[637] Maritain, *Man and the State*, 179-180; Cf. *Collected Works of Jacques Maritain: Integral Humanism, Freedom in the Modern World, and A Letter on Independence*, Otto Bird, ed., Otto Bird, Joseph Evans, and Richard O'Sullivan, trans. (Notre Dame, IN: University of Notre Dame, 1996), 240-243.

[638] Maritain, *Man and the State*, 180, footnote 30: "To express the same point otherwise, we might make use of the distinction, which I stressed in a previous chapter, between the possession of a right and its exercise. I can possess a right, for instance, to personal freedom, and be prevented in justice from claiming its actual exercise if my country is waging a just war and assigns me to be drafted. [New par.] The Church does not lose any of the essential rights she has claimed or exercised in the past. Nevertheless, she can renounce the exercise of certain of them, not because she is forced to do so, but voluntarily and by virtue of the consideration of the common good, the historical context having changed. She exercised in the past the right of making null and void a civil law which severely impaired the spiritual welfare of the people. She always possesses this right in its roots. If she made it emerge in actual exercise in the historical climate of today, this very exercise would harm the common good both of the church and of civil society. So by reason of justice (justice toward the common good both of civilization and of the Kingdom of God) does the Church give up the exercise of such a right." Cf. *True Humanism*, 172, "St. Albert the Great and St. Thomas

retains the right, but only chooses not to exercise it due to changed historical circumstances and for "the justice of the common good of civilization and the Kingdom of God." This leaves open the question as to whether the Church, retaining the right, would not use it to enforce her doctrines at some future time if the historical circumstances changed to allow it?

If one should think that constitutional guarantees regarding freedom of religion would disallow such a situation, it is important to remember the current Catholic discussion regarding the Christianization of society considers *Dignitatis Humanae* to be inadequate to postulate of how such a society should be ordered. Additionally, Etienne Gilson also refers to the circumstances under which the Church tolerates a separation of Church and State as demanded by the times, but not as an unchanging principle:

> It may be that, under certain circumstances, such as the exceptional good will of the political powers, the Church deems it preferable to acquiesce to a factual separation of Church and State, but in no case will she ever admit that Church and State should be kept separate. Their separation remains an evil even while, for reasons of expediency, it is being tolerated.[639]

Although his remark appeared in print in 1954, just over a decade before *Dignitatis Humanae* was promulgated, history and current events remind one that when President Kennedy affirmed the American concept of separationism (1960), the American Bishops have denounced his view from then until the present. Furthermore, this book has shown in chapter two the incompatibility between the religious freedoms espoused in *Dignitatis Humanae* and the religious freedom guarantees of the First Amendment.

Roman Catholic Hegemony and Seventh-day Adventists

Without doubt, *Dignitatis Humanae* has produced increased dialogue between Roman Catholics and Seventh-day Adventists. Although being historically at odds, both groups have had opportunity to reassess the other

---

explain by the diversity of states or ages of the church the fact that in the time of the apostles and the martyrs it was not appropriate to make use of forcible means *and that subsequently it became so*. That in yet another age it will again be appropriate to make no use of them is explicable in the same way." (italics mine)

[639] Etienne Gilson, *The Church Speaks to the Modern World: The Social Teachings of Leo XIII* (Garden City, NY: Image Books, 1954), 17.

in light of changed historical circumstances. To the credit of Catholics, the hierarchy has made some semblance of recognition for egregious wrongs committed during the Inquisition as well as demonstrating a practical application of religious freedom toward non-Catholic religions in those countries that have been predominantly Catholic. Additionally, Catholic leaders have met with Seventh-day Adventist leaders to discuss theological viewpoints.

When analyzing religious freedom concepts, Roman Catholics and Seventh-day Adventists share common principles that each believes governs the secular as well as the transcendental spheres in their respective worldviews. However, in practical application of those principles, there exist profound and apparently irreconcilable differences.

Most notably, the apparent root of difference lies in how each conceives of the transcendental order. For Roman Catholics, it consists of moral concepts regarding truth and error (metaphysics). Translated into the secular sphere, this produces obligations upon the secular power to uphold truth and suppress error. This was the stance definitely taken by the Church prior to Vatican II. Maritain argued that the Church always retains the right to coercion, even when she does not use it. On this question *Dignitatis Humanae* argues for immunity from coercion, but not a denial of the right to coerce. In other areas, however, *Dignitatis Humanae* offers solutions to the perennial conundrum of how Catholicism can be compatible with democratic concepts of religious pluralism. By creating an "immunity from coercion" that is to be guaranteed as a civil right, the Church attempted to skirt the more complex issues of religious freedom that suggest incompatibility between a Catholic moral order and the modern moral order based upon freedom of conscience. Thus, Catholicism can be seen across a spectrum of fluctuation between faithfully adhering to respect for the rights of indigenous non-Catholic religious groups and crossing the line of respect for religious pluralism by enacting laws that greatly restrict the religious freedom rights of other non-Catholics, especially with regards to Sunday legislation. The latter position demonstrates overt tendencies to Catholic hegemony.

Seventh-day Adventists conceive of God's moral order based upon His character. As a Just Sovereign, a Compassionate Judge, a Benevolent Creator, He rules the transcendental sphere based upon love and righteousness. He can only accept that homage that springs forth from love. With such high respect for the free will and conscience of the beings He has created, Seventh-day Adventists believe that secular governments must also respect the freedom of conscience of each person. No earthly government is competent to legislate in the realm of determining absolute religious values, much less to dictate the conscientious beliefs of its citizens.

From such a conception of God's transcendental order, and in light of what they believe to be their God-given mission, Seventh-day Adventists proclaim and defend the religious freedom rights of every human being – without recourse to metaphysical arguments or nebulous terminology. Neither do they solicit ratification of special treaties (concordats) that would grant them a favored position above other religious groups. Rather than relying upon force or legislative enactments, Seventh-day Adventists depend upon biblical arguments and the persuasive power of the Holy Spirit to accompany the preaching of the message they share with the world. Considering such distinct differences between Catholic metaphysics and Seventh-day Adventist's transcendental concepts, both groups ultimately remain at odds regarding their respective views of religious freedom.

Seventh-day Adventists have contributed greatly to the advancement of religious freedom around the world. They also have particular views of Bible prophecy that offer other perspectives related to religious freedom. In particular, their understanding of the prophetic books of Daniel and Revelation suggest a distinct view of the "times" of *Dignitatis Humanae* and one which may correspond to the "times" of religious persecution, non-persecution, and future persecution awaiting the people of God. If correct, and viewed in this light, the "time" of "immunity from coercion" specified in *Dignitatis Humanae* would precede a "time" when such immunity would no longer exist. From a Seventh-day Adventist perspective, such a distinct view would demonstrate a definitive form of Roman Catholic hegemony.

Through the International Religious Liberty Association (IRLA), Seventh-day Adventists conduct seminars and religious liberty festivals to promote the God-given freedom that all must cherish in the search for truth. Such actions have born fruit in those countries where Adventists have suffered persecution. Through sharing their understanding of religious freedom, they have been able to gain legal protections respecting their rights of conscience without imposing their faith upon others and without denying the rights of other religious groups. The next chapter explores some of their history in Spain, in "Dignitatis Humanae and Religious Freedom in Spain."

DIGNITATIS HUMANAE AND RELIGIOUS FREEDOM IN SPAIN

"The Pope (Benedict XVI) Sees Spain as the Battlefield Between Secularism and Faith," read the headline of one of Spain's most prominent newspapers, *El Mundo* (*The World*).[640] During this papal visit, Benedict referred to the "aggressive secularism" prevalent in Spain as on par with the climate "of strong and aggressive anti-clericalism that existed during the 1930s." His remarks caused much stir among the Spaniards since that era was a painful part of Spanish history. In the Editorial Opinion of the same edition, the editors expressed concern regarding Benedict's remarks because,

> Secularism, understood as separation between religious beliefs and the political organization of the state, is not the patrimony of the (political) right, or the left; or of Catholics, or agnostics. It is simply an attitude of respect toward the other that we should assume. And the first thing that needs to be respected is the freedom to choose religious convictions.[641]

The editorial board clarified as well that "the society in which we live now is very distinct from that of the 30s, during which they burned convents and

---

[640] Irene Hernandez Velasco, "El Papa ve España como el campo de batalla entre 'el laicismo y la fe,'" *El Mundo*, 7 de Noviembre, 2010.

[641] Grupo Unidad Editorial, "Un Papa profundo que ésta vez ha matizado muy poco, " *El Mundo*, 7 de Noviembre, 2010.

injured religious believers. Fortunately, today no one is persecuted, incarcerated, or even less, assassinated for their Catholic posture."

Pope Benedict's visit highlights the issues discussed in this chapter. Since *Dignitatis Humanae* is the Church's statement on religious freedom, this chapter focuses on how the Church's claims to promote religious freedom have developed in Spain. First, this discussion begins with a brief historical account of Spain's transition from Franco's dictatorship to democracy, including the highly influential role of the Church. Section two discusses some of the current issues related to religious freedom.

Historical Progress of Religious Freedom in Spain

The transition from an authoritarian regime to a democratic system in Spain may well be described as "a balanced transitionary period devoid of political extremism."[642] The single, most influential event that marked this transition period was the death of Generalissimo Ferdinand Franco in November, 1975.[643] Upon Franco's death, King Carlos, whom Franco had educated from his youth upward, took control of the government. Little did anyone suspect that he had cherished democratic principles that he would later implement in his political ambitions.[644] Franco also had appointed Carrero Blanco as his Head of Government, a title that Franco had held until then.[645] Blanco was strongly pro-Franco in his governmental outlook and certainly would have maintained an authoritarian regime.[646] Although a tragedy that shocked the nation, his assassination was

---

[642] Andrea Bonime-Blanc, *Spain's Transition to Democracy: The Politics of Constitution-making* (Boulder, CO: Westview Press, Inc., 1987), 25.

[643] Ibid., 20.

[644] Ibid., 20; Francisco Llorente notes that "on the opening day of the new parliament (July 22, 1977)," King Carlos "affirmed his 'recognition of the sovereignty of the Spanish people' and transferred the political power of the Crown to the parties responsible for organizing the new government [Francisco Rubio Llorente, "The Writing of the Constitution of Spain," in *Constitution Makers on Constitution Making: The Experience of Eight Nations*, eds. Robert A. Goldwin and Art Kaufman (Washington, D.C.: American Enterprise Institute for Public Policy Research, 1988), 248].

[645] Bonime-Blanc, 20.

[646] David Gilmour, *The Transformation of Spain: From Franco to the Constitutional Monarchy* (New York, NY: Quartet Books, 1985), 68.

recognized as another highly influential factor that allowed the progressive march toward democracy to occur.[647]

King Carlos had appointed Carlos Arias Navarro as his Prime Minister, who did not fulfill his duties sufficiently and was very weak in his reform policies.[648] King Carlos replaced him with Adolfo Suarez who – no one at the time would have guessed – would unite his influence with that of King Carlos to begin paving the pathway for democratic reform in Spain.[649]

Transition to Democracy

Although the factors leading up to democratic reform in Spain were numerous and varied, Bonime-Blanc outlines the necessary elements that provided a peaceful transition from an authoritarian regime to a democratic one. She first defines an authoritarian regime by quoting Juan J. Linz,

> Authoritarian regimes are political systems with limited, not responsible, political pluralism; without elaborate and guiding ideology (but with distinctive mentalities); without intensive or extensive political mobilization . . . and in which a leader (or occasionally a small group) exercises power within formally ill-defined limits but actually quite predictable ones.[650]

She further describes authoritarian regimes as "one with a minimal amount of liberalization (defined as political monopolization and non-contestation) and exclusiveness (defined as non-participation)."[651] Additionally, leaders of authoritarian regimes typically are a-constitutional (if there is a constitution), or at least abusive of constitutional limitations.[652]

> Democratic regimes, by contrast, are defined as ones with mostly unrestricted and responsible political pluralism;

---

[647] Bonime-Blanc, 22; Llorente, 242.

[648] Bonime-Blanc, 24.

[649] Ibid., 24.

[650] Ibid., 5.

[651] Ibid., 6.

[652] Ibid., 5-6.

with a variety of political ideologies and mentalities; with some political mobilization and participation possible through political parties; and whose leader(s) exercises power within formally well-defined limits (constitutional ones) that are normally quite predictable.[653]

Further characteristics include "a substantial amount of liberalization (defined as public contestation or political competition) and inclusiveness (defined as participation)."[654] Democratic executives "exercise well-defined powers that are limited by other constitutionally sanctioned powers (the judiciary and the legislative) and by constitutionally predictable limits (a specific term in office, electoral limitations, etc.)."[655]

Due to the vast differences in authoritarian and democratic systems, there are four points in the transition process from one to the other: "1) the pluralization and mobilization of society from below; 2) the liberalization of socioeconomic policies; 3) the constitutionalization of political activity; and 4) the liberalization and possible democratization of the bureaucracy."[656] The existence of each of these four elements has been credited with the successful transition to democracy in Spain. Bonime-Blanc emphasizes that long term pluralization is best for success in reaching the turning point for transition from an authoritarian regime to a democratic one.[657] Additionally, she notes that one of the most critical factors for which the Second Republic of Spain failed in the early 1930s after a short five years of existence was that its constitution-making process was dissensual and anti-clerical, overlooking the fact that the majority of Spain's citizenry were practicing Catholics.[658]

In contrast, the constitutional-making process in Spain in the 1970s was consensual,[659] seeking to embrace as much of the societal plurality in

---

[653] Bonime-Blanc, 6.

[654] Ibid., 6.

[655] Ibid., 6.

[656] Ibid., 6.

[657] Ibid., 7.

[658] Ibid., 14.

[659] Francisco Llorente observes, "It was a method designed to unite legality and power on the one hand, with democracy on the other" (Llorente, 251).

existence at the time of Franco's death.[660] Bonime-Blanc adds that Suarez's Reform Package was another essential key to a successful transition to democracy for Spain.[661] It included the Eighth Fundamental Law (the Political Reform Bill)[662], which maintained the structural form of government from Franco's regime and simultaneously introduced such democratic principles as "popular sovereignty, the supremacy of law, the inviolability of fundamental rights, universal suffrage and an implicit recognition of political pluralism."[663] Because both Francoist and democratic principles were present – the former to provide some form of governance during transition, and the latter to establish the seminal principles necessary for democracy to flourish – Spain experienced a balanced transitionary period.[664]

The structural elements from Franco's regime endured for roughly two years, until the elections held on June 15, 1977. By this time, several new, popular political groups had developed. They challenged the 40 year old, traditional political party, the Movimiento Nacional (MN),[665] which by 1977 had "little real or effective purpose."[666] The Unión del Centro Democrático (UCD), newly begun in 1977,[667] gained 35% of the popular vote, which garnered 165 seats in the Cortes (43.7% of all seats).[668] As a runner-up, the Partido Socialista Obrero Español (PSOE), which was a traditionally popular party dating to the 1930s,[669] received 29% of the popular vote, or

---

[660] Bonime-Blanc, 13; John F. Coverdale, *The Political Transformation of Spain after Franco* (New York: Praeger Publishers, 1979), 113.

[661] Bonime-Blanc, 24.

[662] Llorente, 244-245.

[663] Bonime-Blanc, 24-25.

[664] Ibid., 25.

[665] Gilmour uses the other commonly-known name for this group: the *Falange*. It was originally a Fascist party that Franco adopted and then transformed by uniting it in 1937 with the Juntas de Ofensiva Nacional Sindicalista (JONS). Thus, the MN actually became a party of Franco's own creation (Gilmour, 11-13).

[666] Bonime-Blanc, 27.

[667] Ibid., 27.

[668] Ibid., 31; Llorente, 247.

[669] Bonime-Blanc, 27.

116 seats (33.7% of all seats in the Cortes).[670] There were two extremist groups that fared more poorly, but nonetheless aided in reducing the number of votes available to the Movimiento Nacional party. The Alianza Popular (AP) was a right wing party founded in 1976,[671] which received only 8% of the popular vote, translating into 16 seats (4.6% of all seats)[672] during the elections. The other extremist group, the Partido Comunista Español (PCE) received 9% of the popular vote, or 20 seats (5.7% of all seats in the Cortes).[673] In the midst of all these political groups, the Roman Catholic Church did some political maneuvering of its own as it, too, was involved in the transition to Democracy.[674]

The Catholic Church Involved in the Transition to Democracy

Consideration of certain Constitutional guarantees must take into account the socio-governmental factor, which is the constitutionally defined relationship between the state and the individual. This factor broadly consists of certain rules, rights, and privileges that are guaranteed under normal societal conditions and that are also limited under times of national crisis.[675] During the initial phases of constitutional-making in Spain after Franco's death, the Roman Catholic Church "exercised extra-parliamentary involvement"[676] in deliberations about the socio-governmental factor. Although recognizing the need to adapt "to democratizing realities," the Church continued to express its concern publicly[677] about the potential loss

---

[670] Bonime-Blanc, 31; Llorente states, "118 seats," (247).

[671] Bonime-Blanc, 27.

[672] Ibid., 31.

[673] Ibid., 31; Llorente, 247.

[674] Interestingly, Gilmour notes that the Church in Spain was opposed to a Christian Democratic party (Gilmour, 168).

[675] Bonime-Blanc, 93.

[676] Ibid., 95.

[677] Llorente indicates that the Church "commented directly (in the declaration of the Episcopal Conference of November 26, 1977) or through its affiliated organizations (such as the Catholic Federation of Family Parents) concerning its points of view on divorce, abortion, and freedom of education" (Llorente, 258).

of the "moral fiber" in society if it was denied its previously privileged status with the state.[678]

During such discussions, debates were tense and confrontational.[679] Historically, the Roman Catholic Church had been so deeply woven in Spanish society that the terms could almost be used interchangeably. However, in spite of being so deeply rooted in Spanish society, the Church suffered during the Second Republic. The 1931 Constitution was definitively anti-clerical.[680] Not only did it declare that the Spanish State had no Official Religion, it also confiscated Church lands and property, making them the possession of the public.[681]

These deplorable conditions changed, however, when Franco won the civil war in 1939. He favored the Roman Catholic Church and through a concordat,[682] established a supportive relationship with it. In return, the Church gladly endorsed his regime, basking in the special status granted it. The privileges bestowed by Franco included: bishops sitting in the Cortes and the Council of the Realm, huge subsidies paid out of the state budget, and moral and educational issues becoming the preserve of the Church.[683] The Church controlled religious education in the schools, "divorce became illegal, adultery a crime, contraception was prohibited, and civil marriage was forbidden if either partner was a Catholic."[684] Additionally, through its favored legal status, the Church was allowed to hold meetings of more than twenty people. The only other group granted this privilege was the Movimiento Nacional.[685] The main area of concern for the Church, however, was that Franco insisted on appointing bishops instead of recognizing this spiritual role of the Church.[686]

---

[678] Bonime-Blanc, 45.

[679] Coverdale, 130.

[680] Bonime-Blanc, 102.

[681] Ibid., 115.

[682] Gilmour notes that the Concordat was signed in 1959, even though the Church had enjoyed many privileges during prior years (Gilmour, 54).

[683] Ibid., 54.

[684] Ibid., 54.

[685] Ibid., 27.

[686] Ibid., 54-55.

By the mid-1950s, and during the next decade, some liberalization began to occur in Spain. Illegal labor movements and political, student, and even some liberal Catholic groups began to place growing societal pressure upon Franco's regime.[687] During the 1960s, Franco responded by granting some piecemeal reforms.

Although supportive through most of Franco's regime, the Catholic clergy began to participate in the gradual pluralization of Spanish society during the decade preceding his death.[688] Through the influence of Vatican II,[689] the Spanish Catholic hierarchy was conforming to its directives.[690] Young, progressive-minded priests spontaneously made preparation for a transition to democracy.[691] It was not surprising, then, that the Church began to criticize publicly Franco's regime during the waning years of its existence.[692] Sensing the shifting political winds, the Church wished to avoid any potential backlash from a new regime.[693]

Such instincts proved accurate. At the time Franco's regime toppled in 1975, the progressive (liberal) movement decided that it must a-politicize certain institutional groups that had supported Franco's regime. Among these were the Roman Catholic Church, the Council of the Realm, "Sindicatos" (trade unions), and the military.[694] Catholic reactions to the liberal movement reflected a divided Church. Indicative of the Church's influence during Franco's regime, some of the hierarchy of the Roman Catholic Church wanted to continue with the authoritative regime after Franco's death. However, other Catholics wanted reform.[695]

---

[687] Bonime-Blanc, 18.

[688] Llorente, 240.

[689] Coverdale, 8. Gilmour notes the Vatican II stand on human rights, including "freedom of expression, freedom of association, and freedom to elect one's rulers" (Gilmour, 55).

[690] The Church used two of its freedoms granted under Franco – freedom to publish Church periodicals without State censorship and to associate – to foster the ideals of Vatican II (Gilmour, 55).

[691] Bonime-Blanc, 102; Coverdale, 8.

[692] Gilmour, 56.

[693] Coverdale, 8.

[694] Bonime-Blanc, 54.

[695] Ibid., 23

One of the first issues debated involved church-state relations. Historically, since the early 1800s, Spanish religious controversy has differed from that of other nations because it has not involved struggles between vying religious groups. Rather, it involved a struggle between primarily the Roman Catholic Church and secular groups. Hence, the conservative party, the PA, supported the continuation of a favored status for the Catholic Church that would allow it to receive state funding and to shape educational policy.[696] Most of the political parties – including the UCD, PCE, MC, and PNV – favored a middle position of compromise by which the state would be secularized and the Catholic Church would receive a subtly favored position among other religious groups.[697] The PSOE, however, steadfastly opposed this, pushing for a strict separationist position – to withdraw all funding from the Church and disallow its influence in educational policy.[698]

Eventually, the consensual position adopted granted recognition of religion as part of Spanish societal existence, with a subtle favored position for the Church.[699] Specifically, Article 16 delineates the guarantees of religious freedom. It does not establish any specific religious group, nor does it adopt an anti-clerical position. However, veiled tones of favoritism for Catholicism can be found in the last sentence, "The public authorities shall take the religious beliefs of Spanish society into account and shall in consequence maintain appropriate cooperation with the Catholic Church and the other confessions."[700] Thus, the Constitution adopts a secular position for Spanish society while also recognizing religious bodies, the predominant one being the Church.[701]

By such recognition, the Church had significant influence on other moral and societal issues. From the conservative perspective, the primary issues included the continuation of the death penalty in certain circumstances, rejection of divorce and abortion (since these were

---

[696] Bonime-Blanc, 103.

[697] Ibid., 103.

[698] Ibid., 103.

[699] The center and right of center political groups accepted separation of church and state, but determined to keep the Church involved in public affairs by article 16.3 (Llorente, 258); Gilmour, 198.

[700] Coverdale, 130.

[701] Bonime-Blanc, 104.

traditionally within the "jurisdiction" of the Church), and continued involvement of the Church in education.[702] The liberal and leftist camp, however, took exactly the opposite side on these issues, arguing for abolition of the death penalty, recognition by the state of abortion and divorce, and the strict separation of church and state, especially in the area of education.[703] In the initial stages of constitutional-making, the Church had more clout and thus, secured much of its conservative agenda.

The death penalty was revoked, except in extreme cases involving military law.[704] Abortion was de-railed through a clause stating that "all" have the right to life, instead of "all persons," which would have allowed for future constitutional debate on the issue.[705] Marriage, as traditionally governed by the Church, was sustained through a general clause referring to its governance by "law."[706]

Education, perhaps the most lengthy and complicated issue debated,[707] was somewhat of a compromised settlement between the Church and liberal groups.[708] The conservative UCD party acted contrary to the initial compromises made and now supported the Church's "continued official involvement in education."[709] Each side obtained certain clauses favoring their position, such as the Church maintaining influence through a clause guaranteeing the right of parents "to ensure that their children receive

---

[702] Bonime-Blanc, 95-96.

[703] Ibid., 96.

[704] Ibid., 98.

[705] Bonime-Blanc, 97-98; Gilmour contends this conclusion by arguing that "all" must be understood in its constitutional context, which means "all persons," i.e., to the exclusion of the fetus (see fn. 25, pp. 198-199).

[706] Bonime-Blanc, 98.

[707] Llorente identifies the "tensions and the difficult negotiations" regarding Article 27 on education as the cause of it being "exceptionally long" and "containing matters of dubious relevance" (Llorente, 261). Coverdale refers to government fostering pluralism as an argument used for state aid to parochial Catholic schools (131). Ironically, pluralism is designed to keep church and state separate, not unite them.

[708] Bonime-Blanc, 97; Gilmour, 198.

[709] Bonime-Blanc., 57.

religious and moral instruction."[710] For liberals, such clauses as the "right of everyone to education, through general planning,"[711] another clause allowing parents, students, and teachers to share in the control and management of educational centers sustained by public funds, and another that guaranteed "the autonomy of the Universities,"[712] seemed to vindicate their cause.

While the constitutional-making process may be described as consensual during most of its stages, some moral issues were definitely unilateral, such as divorce, abortion, and education, through the influence of the Catholic Church[713] and conservative political groups. Additionally, on such issues as military powers and church-state relations, ambiguity of language was the result of attempts at multi-lateral participation and agreement.[714] The PSOE had major problems with UCD's support of Articles 16, 28, 32, and 33, all of which deal with religious, education, and economic issues.[715]

During the next twenty years after the initial elections in 1977, the parliamentary political system in Spain has experienced much transition. The 1979 elections were very similar to the results in 1977 – the conservative UCD and other minor conservative groups maintained control of the government.[716] This gave the Catholic Church the opportunity to establish more formal relations with the government, as will be noted below. In 1982, the powerful UCD (Democratic Party) that was the conservative mainstay in 1977 fragmented due to erosion of its political

---

[710] Bonime-Blanc, 97.

[711] Ibid., 97.

[712] Ibid., 97; Gilmour, 198.

[713] Coverdale indicates that during the Constitutional Referendum, the Catholic Bishops Conference ratified a commission report that pointed out positive and negative aspects of the Constitution and did not "urge Catholics to vote one way or the other" (Coverdale, 118). He also notes that "the cardinal of Toledo made public a pastoral letter that stopped short of calling for a "no" vote, but emphasized the Constitution's shortcomings in the areas of education, family, etc." (Coverdale, 118, 119).

[714] Bonime-Blanc, 128-129.

[715] Ibid., 57.

[716] Kaare Strom, Wolfgang C. Muller, and Torbjorn Bergman, eds., *Delegation and Accountability in Parliamentary Democracies* (Oxford: Oxford University Press, 2003), 575.

platform, resulting in great gains for the PSOE.[717] The PSOE (Socialist party) had formed strong organizational links and was thus able to accomplish many energetic reforms.[718] By 1996, however, the PSOE party faced mounting challenges. Its leader, Felipe Gonzalez announced his retirement, and the party had been discredited by corruption.[719] Thus, the former AP (Alianza Popular) had re-organized under the new name, Partido Popular (PP), and won the election.[720]

Regarding the more recent (2006) political scene in Spain, perhaps one of the most insightful books published is *El Factor Católico en la Política Española* (The Catholic Factor in Spanish Politics). The author, Rafael Díaz-Salazar, is a professor among the faculty of Political Science and Sociology, Complutense University, Madrid. He argues that during Franco's regime, the Church served as the guarantor of social morals and in effect became more than just the religion of the nation – instead it became a form of nationalism, or an institutionalized religion. Now that democracy is gaining ground in Spain, Díaz-Salazar observes, the monolithic structure of the Church is beginning to crack. The socio-cultural transition caused by democratic principles penetrating society is outpacing the political dimension to such an extent that the Church is now becoming another actor among a society of actors, rather than holding its preeminent position. He predicts that the Church, if unable to adapt to this social reality, will become like most other social organizations that become specialized in order to compete among a group of other organizations in a pluralist society.[721] For this reason, he states, "the content of the encyclicals of John Paul II and the books of Ratzinger on ethics and politics defend *a regulation of democracy* toward Catholic truth."[722] He argues that the Church, following reforms initiated by John Paul II and now carried forward by Benedict XVI, is continuing down this path:

---

[717] Strom, Muller, Bergman., 575.

[718] Ibid., 575.

[719] Ibid., 576.

[720] Ibid., 576.

[721] Rafael Díaz-Salazar, *El Factor Católico en la Política Española* (Madrid: PPC Editorial, 2006), 278-303.

[722] Díaz-Salazar, 279 (italics mine).

To act as an ethical-political pressure group with religious inspirations in order to get governments to legislate according to objective Truth that is deposited in the Catholic institution and is interpreted correctly by its hierarchical authorities. To articulate culturally, socially, and politically to Catholics so that their relative majority in society may translate into a political majority, or into a conditional group with access to the power of one or the other [political] parties.[723]

He concludes by postulating that Benedict will maintain this course, unless some other major factors should lead him to re-route, in order to establish a new Catholic hegemony. From this political analysis of recent years, it is helpful to review some of the particular history of Spain regarding the development of religious freedom in order to postulate the type of religious freedom that could prevail in a future Catholic hegemony consisting of "regulated democracy."

Struggles at Implementation by the Bishops

Apart from the time of the Spanish Republic II (1934-1939), Spain has been so identified with the Catholic Church that a common refrain is that Spaniards are "más papista que el papa" ("more papal than the Pope"). Without doubt, then, the topic of religious liberty that was discussed at the Second Vatican Council caused no small stir among the Spanish populace. Various archbishops and bishops who attended Vatican II brought weekly reports to Spain regarding the progress of this proposal. Especially noteworthy are the weekly reports from *Ya* ("Now," or "Already") during the months of September through December 1964, just one year before *Dignitatis Humanae* was finally promulgated on December 7, 1965. These reports indicate that the Spanish hierarchy debated vociferously in the conciliar meetings upon the topic, more for the sake of clarification and to express their views, than to indicate opposition to the Document on Religious Liberty. A rumor had begun circulating that the Spanish hierarchy was "totally unfavorable to the text of the Declaration," but through an interview with Monsignor Muñoyerro, a periodical in Rome, *La Vanguardia Español*, dismissed it altogether.[724]

---

[723] Díaz-Salazar, 299.

[724] *La Vanguardia Español*, October 2, 1964. Archivo de la Fundación Fleidner, Madrid, España.

However, the practical application of *Dignitatis Humanae*, as outlined by the Spanish hierarchy, does not seem to distinguish it much from the then current law of toleration. In the weekly edition dated September 27, 1964, the archbishop of Madrid, Casimiro Morcillo, indicated that, "The legal project recognizes the right of non-Catholics to practice their worship, both privately and socially. We reiterate that up to the present, they have been able to do this in Spain within the limits of tolerance under which they have lived."[725] When asked if non-Catholic associations would be recognized legally, he responded,

> The religious associations of non-Catholics will also be recognized by law so that they may worship and perform their religious activities. Whenever there may be a non-Catholic religious community, they can open their church, their seminaries, and schools for non-Catholic children. They will also be able to publish their liturgical books and material on spiritual formation, whatever may be necessary.[726]

However, with respect to proselytism, he responded, "The proposed law, in harmony with the spirit of the Council and with the principles allowed through ecumenism, prohibits non-Catholics to proselytize and all forms of proselitistic propaganda, since they are dishonest means and recourses." Surprisingly, he went on to say, "In this form, the proposed law will square perfectly within the orientations that, without doubt, will emanate from the Council in the near future."[727]

Apparently, for the Spanish hierarchy, the manner in which they understood *Dignitatis Humanae* during the debates at Vatican II was that it allowed such restrictions,[728] or stated otherwise, it was religious liberty

---

[725] Luis de la Barga, seccion "La futura ley española se ajusta a las normas del concilio," bajo artículo titulado, "El arzobispo de Madrid explica a YA el contenido del proyecto de confesiones," en *Ya*, Domingo, 27 de Septiembre, 1964. Archivo de la Fundación Fleidner, Madrid, España.

[726] Ibid.

[727] Ibid.

[728] *Dignitatis Humanae*, article 6, par. 4, "If, in view of peculiar circumstances obtaining among peoples, special civil recognition is given to one religious community in the constitutional order of society," however, the Spanish hierarchy may have overlooked the rest of the paragraph, which states, "it is at the

within narrow limitations. This observation is much the same as that concluded by William J. Callahan, a professor from the University of Toronto, who writes, "Although the Spanish hierarchy was not in disagreement regarding the general lines of reforms that were suggested through Vatican Council II, a majority of the bishops considered that it was even possible to reconcile the privileges of the Church during Franco's regime, with the spirit of the Council."[729] Callahan offers an additional insight that supports part of the thesis of this book, namely that *Dignitatis Humanae* is not a document of universally-applicable principles of religious freedom, as much as it is a document with enough variability so that it may be applied in numerous settings according to the needs of the Catholic Church on a global scale. Callahan observed,

> The bishops, some not without certain reticence, accepted the Conciliar document, *Dignitatis Humanae*, that made a call to religious liberty based upon human dignity, liberty of conscience, and natural law, although they interpreted the text in the most restrictive manner possible, putting the accent in the fact that its promulgation should be subject to the specific circumstances of each country.[730]

There remains one other observable point from the position of the Catholic hierarchy in Spain that is also central to this book. The type of religious freedom derived from *Dignitatis Humanae* by the Spanish hierarchy – one defined within the narrow limitations of no proselytism – is no different than that put forth by the Church at the Diet of Speyer II (1529), and to which the Reformers refused to accept, knowing that it would stagnate the Reformation.[731] Such is the historical record regarding *Dignitatis Humanae*'s application in Spain. Years later, at the time of transition from Franco's rule to democracy, the Spanish Church hierarchy was again actively seeking to retain its hegemony.

Alfredo Grimaldos Feito is a well-published author who holds a degree in Information Sciences from Complutense University, Madrid. In one of

---

same time imperative that the right of all citizens and religious communities to religious freedom should be recognized and made effective in practice."

[729] William J. Callahan, *La Iglesia Católica en España* (Washington, D.C.: The Catholic University of America Press, 2000), 397.

[730] Ibid., 397.

[731] See section, "The Diet of Speyer II," in chapter three.

his books, *La Iglesia en España: 1977-2008* (The Church in Spain: 1977-2008), he refers to Spain as "the Crypto-Confessional State" because of the adept way in which the Church became the pre-eminent religious body legally recognized by the Spanish state.[732] He relates the Constitutional making process of 1978 and how the "Constitutional Fathers" had determined to make Spain a non-confessional state by disallowing any religion a favored position with the government. This roused the ecclesiastical indignation and ire immensely. Through subtle pressure, the stance of the Constitutional Fathers was changed like lightning. Thus, in the preliminary meetings on January 5, 1978, the statement regarding the non-confessional nature of the state was substituted with the expression "no confession will have state character." But this was not enough. The Catholic Church had to be expressly named in the place of relevance that the honor of God demanded.

Years later, one of the seven Constitutional Fathers, Gregorio Peces Barba, commented on this incident, saying,

> I believe we committed an error by accepting in the Constitution the express mention of the Catholic Church, but it was done because it appeared to us that it was so relevant. And we thought, furthermore, that the bishops had much better faith than they have had later. But we made a mistake. And they have used it to think that the State has to maintain a privileged relationship with the Catholic Church. But that is not so. . . .that was never our intention as legislators. I believe that will have to be placed in question at some time, asking again such topics as the Agreements with the Holy See, the teaching of religion, the juridical and economic responsibility regarding [maintaining] religious professors, or for example, religious symbols, that Catholics have solidified in public acts. These are things that have to disappear.[733]

From this astute legal move in 1978, the bishops laid the foundation so that the Holy See would be able to enter into four principal Agreements with the Spanish state in 1979.

---

[732] Alfredo Grimaldos Feito, *La Iglesia en España, 1977-2008* (Ediciones Península, 2008), 147, 148.

[733] Ibid., 149.

From Concordats to Agreements

During an International Theological Conference held from March 20-26, 1966, at the University of Notre Dame, John Courtney Murray entertained questions regarding the practical dimension of *Dignitatis Humanae*, and one of his interlocutors, only identified as "Gremillion," asked the following question, "What are the implications of the Declaration [on Religious Freedom] for the whole system of concordats and diplomatic relations and ambassadorial apparatus in the Catholic Church?" Murray responded, "That calls for prognosis. I don't know. I haven't really thought about it too profoundly, but my guess is that concordats don't have much of a future."[734]

What Murray was not able to foresee, however, was the interpretation given to *Dignitatis Humanae* by the Vatican. Pope John Paul II, on January 3, 1979, stipulated,

> Such concordats are an instrument of international rights, duly incorporated in the internal order, that have the objective of giving the Church security in its life and activity. . . Such concordats, also, recognize the just place of Catholicism in current Spanish society. . . nor is it strange that their end result is also better service regarding the common good of all Spaniards. . . the Holy See believes in the vitality and the validity of the concordats. They are offered, then, as an instrument of concord and not of privilege, because the recognition of religion and the Church, not only historically, but as they are currently in Spain, is recognition of a social reality of such great importance, without taking anything, in a pluralist society, from what may be due to the citizens of another religious faith or of distinct ideological convictions.[735]

From the perspective of John Paul II, *Dignitatis Humanae* apparently makes

---

[734] John Courtney Murray, "Session XIV Discussion," in John H. Miller, ed., *Vatican II: An Interfaith Appraisal* (London: University of Notre Dame Press, 1966), 583.

[735] John Paul II, cited by Maria Elena Olmos Ortega, "Los Acuerdos con la Santa Sede: Instrumentos Garantes de la Libertad Religiosa," in *Iglesia Católica y Relaciones Internacionales: Actas del III Simposio Internacional de Derecho Concordatorio*, eds. Maria del Mar Martin, Mercedes Salido, José Maria Vazquez Garcia-Penuela (Granada: Editorial Comares, 2008), 500-501.

allowance for the continued use of concordats (for the Church) and agreements, or bilateral treaties for other religious groups that enter into legal relations with governments. The distinction between concordats and agreements is based on the difference in nature between the Vatican, which is also recognized as a diplomatic entity, and other religious groups that do not have the same classification.

Understanding this distinction helps to explain why the Church in Spain retained a favored position even after *Dignitatis Humanae* was promulgated (1965). Rosa María Martínez de Codes, from the Complutense University, Madrid, explains,

> The impact of the principles contained in this Declaration [of Religious Freedom] on Spanish State Law was immense. Public powers were obligated to tailor their legislation to the authority of the Catholic Church. For both the government and the Spanish episcopacy this streamlining was delicate and complex. It meant the transfer over to the State's civil legal system of the notion of civil tolerance for religious freedom, [while] maintaining Catholicism as the key religion.[736]

Codes's statement gives a nuanced meaning to religious freedom as described in *Dignitatis Humanae,* which also suggests a type of Catholic hegemony, at least from a non-Catholic perspective since Catholicism still maintains its key role among the religions in Spain.

Another practical way that demonstrates the key role of the Church in Spanish society is with reference to the Organic Law of Religious Liberty (1980). Maria Elena Olmos Ortega indicates that the State enters into Agreements, or Compacts, with the religious confessions that are inscribed in the State Register, which can involve a lengthy time period. She adds, however, that the process of reaching these Agreements does not apply to the Catholic Church, "since it is a major Entity and does not need to be inscribed in the Register of Religious Entities; and besides, the concordats of the State with the Catholic Church, in whatever nation they occur, are formally entered into by the Holy See, which ostentatiously demonstrates an international juridical personality."[737]

---

[736] Rosa María Martínez de Codes, "The Spanish Answer to Religious Intolerance: From Institutional Intolerance to Institutional Tolerance," *Fides et Libertas* (2007), 104.

[737] Maria Elena Olmos Ortega, 493.

Victorino Mayoral Cortés, lawyer and Congressional deputy from Cáceres, analyzes the current (2006) condition of Spain as a secular state. He observes that "the confessional state went out the back door, but partially returned again through the window by using the scaffolding of the Concordats between the State and the Holy See, signed in Rome on January 3, 1979 barely one month after the Constitution had been approved."[738] He explains that "the Church wanted an aconfessional state, but not a secular one, which it continues to seek." In current church-state parlance, an aconfessional state is one which defines relations "between the State and religions" based on autonomy and cooperation, "admitting a prevailing or preeminent religion, with links and communication between both spheres."[739] The secular state, however, differs significantly from the aconfessional model, as José Camilo Cardoso defines the secular state as characterized by "total, strict and absolute separation between State and religions."[740]

Mayoral critiques the four Concordats of the Spanish government with the Vatican,[741] which are: 1) the Agreement on Juridical Affairs that establishes a single statutory administration that no other religious confession has; 2) the Agreement on Economic Affairs, which establishes a public financial system that supports the Church and that is not much different from the old worship and clergy endowment; 3) the Agreement on Educational and Cultural Affairs, which maintained the obligatory incorporation of the Catholic religion into the official study plans of the State, as well as the support of teachers of religion; and 4) the Agreement on Religious Presence at the Armed Forces events.

Instead of this scenario, Mayoral argues for separation of church and state so that "every person may be able to practice independently and unconditionally his or her freedom of conscience, or of religion, and that no church may be able to utilize directly or indirectly the power of the State in order to situate itself in a hegemonic position or in order to generalize its beliefs and opinions."[742] Having examined the more detailed aspects and

---

[738] Victorino Mayoral Cortés, *España: de la intolerancia al laicismo* (Spain: Ediciones del Laberinto, 2006), 86.

[739] José Camilo Cardoso, "The Progress of Religious Freedom in Latin America," in *Fides et Libertas* (2007), 52-53.

[740] Ibid., 52-53.

[741] Mayoral Cortés, 87, 88.

[742] Ibid., 88.

nuanced definitions of concordats,[743] agreements, and treaties, the next section deals more specifically with religious freedom issues facing non-Catholic Spaniards. It includes a report by the U. S. Department of State from 2007, as well as a section describing the Federation of Spanish Evangelical Religious Entities (FEREDE), of which Seventh-day Adventists are members. The final portion deals with laws against illicit proselytism.

Issues of Religious Freedom

In 2007, the U. S. Department of State returned a favorable review of the state of religious liberty in Spain.[744] The Center for Sociological Investigation for the year reported 44.7 million inhabitants. Of these, 79.1 percent identified themselves as Roman Catholic, but 54.7 percent of those indicated they do not attend Mass regularly. Religious freedom is allowed for other faith groups, which vary in size from operating one church (Mormons, and Unification Church; Jehovah's Witnesses have two) to operating 1,325 Protestant or evangelical entities, 443 Muslim entities, and 13 Orthodox entities. Several other groups make up minority religious entities.

Although the Constitution does not prescribe any state religion, and while it does allow for religious freedom, the Catholic Church enjoys a special status with the government, as noted previously. Religious leaders of other faith groups, such as Protestants, Jews, and Muslims, report that they continue to appeal to the Spanish government for comparable privileges to those of Catholics. They list as requests "public financing, expanded tax exemptions, improved media access, removal of Catholic symbols from some official military acts, and fewer restrictions on opening new places of worship." The government has attempted to address this issue of apparent lack of equality among religious groups regarding governmental financing.

One of the challenges facing non-Catholic believers is being able to overcome religious prejudice at the local levels, meaning that the national government tries to promote fairness and religious equality, but local administrations and citizens can pose significant problems, especially to Muslim communities who have tried to build mosques. Protestant and Muslim leaders reported that the process to obtain permits for building new churches and mosques was "difficult and lengthy."

Protestant and Muslim leaders have also petitioned the government for

---

[743] See Appendix B for additional information regarding concordats and treaties in other European countries.

[744] U. S. State Dept. Report – 2007. http://www.state.gov/j/drl/rls/irf/2007/90201.htm (accessed June 8, 2012).

more equitable representation of their respective faiths in public religious education. Currently, a great disproportion exists between Catholic and non-Catholic religious instructors. While part of this disproportion may be attributable to the large percentage of professed Catholics, minority religions feel that they are still not allowed enough teachers in proportion to their adherents.

Federación de Entidades Religiosas Evangélicas de España (FEREDE)

The Commission for the Defense of Spanish Evangelicals was the beginning of what today has become the Federation of Religious Evangelical Entities of Spain.[745] "The Commission was first founded on May 14, 1956 to protect Spanish Evangelicals against religious intolerance and to aid in obtaining religious freedom."[746] It has passed through three periods in its history: 1) religious intolerance (1956-1967); 2) religious tolerance (1967-1980); and 3) religious freedom since the passage of the Organic Law of Religious Liberty.

Currently, the Spanish government recognizes FEREDE as the single most notable organization that has contributed to uniting Protestant groups together in working capacity to meet government guidelines for legal recognition.[747] In 1986, some of the evangelical groups that joined FEREDE included the Federation of Evangelical Pentecostal churches of Spain, the "Good News" Christian Churches, and the Brotherhood of Christian Churches and Organizations. It was also during this year that the Seventh-day Adventist Church approached FEREDE for membership, which required some extra time because Adventists had not been recognized as evangelical in Spain.[748] After some deliberation, a third clause was added to the charter of membership which made it possible for this union. Roughly ten years later, over one-hundred churches did not wish to join FEREDE because of the continued misunderstanding about Adventists. Leadership of FEREDE examined the complaints and concluded they were unfounded.[749] Seventh-day Adventists continue to be

---

[745] Antonio Albert Domínguez, *Defensa del Protestantismo* (España: FEREDE, 2007), 189, 190.

[746] Ibid., 189.

[747] Ibid., 190.

[748] Ibid., 192-193.

[749] Ibid., 418-422.

members of FEREDE and prejudices among other religious groups towards Adventists are gradually diminishing.

Seventh-day Adventists

As discussed in chapter four, Seventh-day Adventists are known for observance of the Sabbath, which can pose certain problems related to employment and education. Bert B. Beach, honorary Secretary General of IRLA in 2000, submitted a report on the conditions of minority religious groups.[750] He indicated that cases of conflict between Seventh-day Adventists and their employers regarding scheduled hours of work on the Sabbath had decreased. He attributes this in a large part to several international declarations, two of which he cites: 1) The Convention, no. 106 in 1957 about Weekly Rest, that stipulates in article six, "employers should, as far as possible, respect the traditions and customs of the minority religions;" 2) The Declaration of All Forms of Intolerance (1981), which states in article six, paragraph "h," "that every person has the right to observe the day of rest . . . according to the precepts of his religion." He especially noted that Italy, Spain, and Poland had shown greater respect toward the conscientious convictions of Adventists.

In more recent years, however, Adventist students in higher education have had difficulties regarding Sabbath observance and meeting requirements for classes that meet on the Sabbath. One young lady who desired to begin her nursing career at Osakidetza, one of the more prestigious nursing schools in Spain, explained that she could not take the entry exams on the Sabbath and petitioned for another day to take them. Although she appealed through the assistance of FEDERE, her petition was denied on the grounds that the school maintains a strict policy of equality among all candidates and could not give her the advantage of taking the exams before others, which would place an undue burden on her, nor allow her to take them after other candidates, which would give her additional days to prepare.[751]

In another case, Doctor Sara Francés Tarazona had applied to the University of Zaragoza, for the fall of 2005, but after several letters of correspondence finally received notice on November 2, that she was denied since she would not be able to take the qualifying exams prior to entry in

---

[750] Beverly B. Beach, "La Libertad Religiosa desde una perspectiva no católica con atención especial a los derechos y los problemas de las iglesias minoritarias," *Conciencia y Libertad*, No. 12, (2000), 36-49.

[751] Public Affairs and Religious Liberty Department (PARL), European Union, scanned document #2135.

the program. Since the University is operated by the government, which declares itself to be non-confessional, it could not make any exceptions.[752] To do so, University officials reasoned, would be to recognize through law the faith in question. Two other cases of a similar nature were denied their petitions.

However, several other cases were resolved favorably. In particular, Pérez Sainero petitioned Politechnic Institute to take exams on a day other than the Sabbath.[753] When he was asked to present documentation of his association with the Adventist Church and his educational record of the previous years, he affirmed he was a member of the SDA Church by a letter from his pastor, but his previous educational record in high school demonstrated that he had taken three exams on the Sabbath. Several other factors were considered, such as the burden it might place upon the Institute to acquire another room for him to take the exams on another day, etc. Surprisingly, he was granted permission to take his exams on another day of the week. These cases, both favorable and unfavorable, demonstrate the complexity of Sabbath conflicts facing Adventists and the multiplicity of factors that are taken into consideration in each case.

Laws Against Illicit Proselytism

John Graz, Secretary-General for the International Religious Liberty Association (IRLA), describes how "proselytism is frequently thought of as an unfriendly word."[754] He quotes from a study document entitled, *The Challenge of Proselytism and the Calling to Common Witness*, which states, "Serious concern about tensions and conflict [are] created by proselytism in nearly all parts of the world." This document views proselytism as taking "advantage of people's misfortunes (e.g., poverty, mass migration, absence of pastoral care) to encourage people by unfair means to become members of other churches."[755] Another concern of some religious bodies, like the Russian Orthodox Church, is that proselytism opens the door to "post-Christian humanism" from the West since missionaries bring their cultural identity

---

[752] PARL Department, European Union, scanned document #2136.

[753] PARL, European Union, scanned documents for Israel Pérez Sainero.

[754] John Graz, *Issues of Faith and Freedom: Defending the Right to Profess, Practice, and Promote One's Beliefs* (Silver Spring, MD: Public Affairs and Religious Liberty Department, 2008), 78.

[755] Ibid., 79, quoting from The World Council of Churches, joint working group, *The Challenge of Proselytism and the Calling to Common Witness*, issued September 25, 1996.

with them. To avoid building a culture that privatizes religion, they would rather close the door to proselytism.[756]

While acknowledging these valid concerns, Graz also raises penetrating questions regarding freedom of religion, such as: Is it proper for government to restrict the rights of its own citizens in the pursuit of religious truth? If some religions are so associated with culture and tradition, is it proper to impose tradition by state mandate? Could not this be seen as imposing religion?[757] Similar issues confront Spanish society as well, only with the dominant religion being Roman Catholicism.[758]

Law professor Agustín Motilla, of the University of Carlos III, Madrid, Spain, describes the complexity of religions whose faith includes a communal element:

> The majority of religious confessions, especially those religious communities which base their relation with God upon integration within a community, tend to conceive of belonging to that community not as a voluntary act, but as a logical consequence of the social context in which the believer is born. Consequently, the spontaneous departure by the believer is not admitted.[759]

He further recounts the long history of Spain as a Roman Catholic country, even to the point of Catholicism becoming identified with national sentiment.

For this reason, prior to 1967, "all action of extreme manifestation of the beliefs of non-Catholic churches or communities was considered illicit

---

[756] Graz, 80.

[757] Ibid., 82.

[758] The Vatican Council II drafters of *Dignitatis Humanae* exercised far-reaching vision when formulating Article 6, par. 4, which addresses these questions: "If, in view of peculiar circumstances obtaining among peoples, special civil recognition is given to one religious community in the constitutional order of society, it is at the same time imperative that the right of all citizens and religious communities to religious freedom should be recognized and made effective in practice." Thus, *Dignitatis Humanae* allows previously established religious communities to maintain a preferred position in society, while granting some religious freedom to other groups, albeit not on par with the dominant religion.

[759] Agustín Motilla, "Proselitismo y Libertad Religiosa en el Derecho Espanol," in *Conciencia y Libertad* No. 12, (2000): 50-61.

proselytism and sanctioned." Beginning in 1967, the Law of Religious Liberty was passed that allowed sharing of religious beliefs within the limited parameters of not attacking Catholic dogma or morals. Within this Law, illicit proselytism was defined for the first time in Article 2.2 as, "considering those acts which are especially harmful to the rights recognized in this Law as those which suppose physical or moral coercion, threats, gifts or promises, deceitful capture, disturbance of family unity, and whatever other illegitimate form of persuasion with the purpose of gaining followers for a determined belief or confession or deviating them from another."[760] Motilla describes how the prevalence of new religious movements and sects that tend to use manipulative techniques to gain adherents has resulted in the most recent law of 1995, which has added the language referring to "violent groups, or those who alter the personality of individual(s)."[761]

Motilla describes the details of these laws to underscore that "these qualifying phrases, which are not applied to the traditional churches even in similar circumstances, constitute a prejudicial attempt to evaluate beliefs or doctrines by an organ of a lay state, which has the labor of judging and prohibiting based on an innate impartiality."[762] He argues that there are already general laws in the area of criminal jurisprudence that use the same language and which are designed for the protection of the citizens. Thus, to maintain a law against illicit proselytism endangers the rights of the citizens because: 1) the current law uses such ambiguous terminology which allows courts to give it their own interpretation – how can one distinguish between a legitimate apostolic (religious) leader, who is insistent about his message, and someone who uses psychological coercion?, 2) the courts can easily be influenced by public opinion toward marginalized religious groups and thereby deny them the justice of impartial law.[763]

Secularism in Spanish Society

Perhaps the greatest threat facing Spanish society currently is secularism. In November, 2011, Pope Benedict XVI visited several large cities in Spain and the primary topic of his addresses dealt with the inroads and dangers of secularism to a once vibrant, Spanish Catholicism. Not fearing to appear

---

[760] Motilla, 54.

[761] Ibid., 56.

[762] Ibid., 59.

[763] Ibid., 60, 61.

out of touch with the times, Benedict appealed to the Spanish populace for economic and social means so that "women can find their fullest realization in the home and in their work."[764] Believing that lack of sufficient economic support leads many women to abortion so that they can obtain jobs, Benedict stressed the need for solid, traditional families – implicit in his message was the Church's stance against homosexual unions. Speaking with firm tones against abortion and euthanasia, he emphasized that "the indissoluble love between a man and a woman is the successful mark and foundation of human life."

He then went on to call the attention of Spaniards to their roots, mentioning that Spain was the birthplace of Christian faith through the lives of such notable Christians as Ignatius Loyola, Mother Theresa of Avila, and San Juan de la Cruz. He also warned his hearers that in Spain "a laicite was born, an anticlericalism, a strong and aggressive secularism as in the 1930s (referring to the Spanish Republic II) and that dispute, or encounter, between faith and modernity, very alive and real, is taking place again in Spain."[765]

Some statistical information, provided by Alfredo Grimaldos Feito, drives home the point of Benedict's message regarding the lack religiosity of Spaniards, which is quite alarming:[766]

> The Episcopal Conference assures that ninety percent of Spaniards are Catholic. In 2007, the Center for Sociological Investigations (CIS) lowered that figure to seventy-six percent. Math and religion never have gone hand in hand in Spain. But if the citizens of this country are asked if they are religious, only forty-one percent so affirm, from which one can deduce that many Spaniards – some thirty-five percent – consider themselves as Catholics because they were baptized without being asked, and in reality they do not consider themselves religious. In the CIS survey, only twenty-six percent declared themselves practicing Catholics and less than half go to Mass regularly, only about twelve percent. In 1974, the statistic for practicing Catholics was seventy-nine percent.
> Among young people, the statistics are especially hard

---

[764] *El País*, 8 de Noviembre, 2010.

[765] *El Mundo*, 7 de Noviembre, 2010.

[766] Feito, *La Iglesia en España: 1977-2008*, 223, 224.

for the Episcopal Conference. According to the Santa Maria Foundation, only forty-nine percent of them declare themselves to be Catholic. Practicing [Catholics], less than ten percent, and that attend the Mass weekly, the stats do not even reach four percent. Spain is becoming less Catholic.

With such statistics, Benedict's concerns are not unfounded. From Benedict's perspective, laicite, or separation of religion and government lies at the heart of Spain's troubles.

However, two authors do not see the issues in this way. Javier Otaola defines laicite as a concept birthed in France during the Revolution which is more than anything a political and constitutional formula for designing a secular government.[767] Such a government is one that is not influenced by the particular religious convictions of legislators, nor by any particular ideology, or hegemony of any particular race or class in society. Rather, laicite offers the ideals for peaceful living together: Liberty, Equality, and Fraternity.

Another author, Victorino Mayoral Cortés, takes a more balanced approach when he describes laicite, or a secular state.[768] He describes it as one in which civil servants should fulfill their responsibilities from the perspective of serving their citizens and without recourse to their own ideologies, religious convictions, or preferences. Under such a construct, he believes that Spain would continue on the path of democracy that was begun in 1978. He also describes a type of civil religion that would exclude the Catholic Church from the affairs of State, that would disallow any civil servant to promote any particular religion, and that would establish a sense of unity among the Spaniards through mutual respect based on the common goal of building a democratic Spain. With ideas such as these becoming more of the popular sentiment, it is no wonder that Benedict has spoken out against what he perceives as the threat of laicite in Spain.

Catholic Hegemony and Religious Freedom in Spain

Spain under General Franco's rule experienced the dominance of the Catholic Church through government establishment. After Vatican II, the

---

[767] Javier Otoala, *Laicidad: Una estrategia para la libertad* (España: Ediciones Bellaterra, 1996), 9-10.

[768] Victorino Mayoral Cortés, *España: de la intolerancia al laicismo* (España: Ediciones Laberinto, 2006), 185-191.

practical implementation of *Dignitatis Humanae* fostered the transition to democracy that occurred in 1976, one year after General Franco's death. It was also instrumental in Spain's transition from a confessional state to a semi-confessional one,[769] which now includes a variety of non-Catholic religious groups. In this semi-confessional state, the Catholic hierarchy has entered into Agreements with the Spanish government that allow the Church more legal recognition and a more favored status than other religious groups. While religious freedom is guaranteed in writing and by law, it is notably lacking in practical application. Seventh-day Adventists, as well as other religious groups, still suffer governmental discrimination.

Church-State relations in Spain are one example of the Catholic hegemony thesis, which argues that the Church applies *Dignitatis Humanae* in a variety of ways to establish, or maintain its hegemony according to the given political and religious context. The Spanish Catholic hierarchy implemented *Dignitatis Humanae* according to what would best help the Church retain its privileged status. The religious freedom begun in Spain after the Second Vatican Council II was tailored to the Spanish context, which included no right for Protestants to proselytize, and other restrictions designed to maintain the status quo. Such actions by the Catholic hierarchy in Spain parallel the struggle between Catholics and Protestants at the Diet of Speyer II. Viewed in this light, the Spanish Roman Catholic hierarchy demonstrated overt hegemonic actions in fulfillment of the thesis argued in this book.

Another part of the Catholic hegemony thesis involves the compatibility of the Church within a constitutional democracy. In such a context of religious pluralism, the Catholic hegemony thesis argues that the Church will seek a position of preeminence among other religious groups, even doing so through constitutional means. When one rehearses Spanish history from the 1960s onward, one discovers that the Church, which had been so favored by Franco and which had supported his regime, began publicly to denounce it in preparation for the shifting of political winds toward democratic governance. During the Constitutional period in 1978, the Church asserted her *libertas ecclesiastica* (freedom of the Church) and astutely obtained specific legal recognition in the national constitution. Such action laid the way for formal agreements between the Spanish government and the Vatican, occurring in 1979. In light of other religious groups in Spain demanding equal rights, the Church has been willing to share some of the public space and funds, thus demonstrating the Catholic hegemony thesis in action.

---

[769] I use here the term "semi-confessional" because I believe the facts warrant this nomenclature. If Spain were truly a lay state, it would not have concordatory agreements with the Vatican.

Other factors that affect Catholic hegemony in Spain include a growing tide of secularism. While some may argue that this is the result of democratic reforms begun in 1978, one should also consider the disillusionment of Spaniards toward the Church due to its political support of Franco's regime, as well as its concerted efforts to assure itself of a place of preeminence under the democratic period. With respect to Catholic hegemony, time is needed to determine if Benedict's plans to "regulate democracy" in Spain will bear fruit by routing secularism's advances. The next chapter continues analyzing Catholic hegemony by evaluating "Dignitatis Humanae *and Religious Freedom in Mexico.*"

DIGNITATIS HUMANAE AND RELIGIOUS FREEDOM IN MEXICO

Beneath the towering statue of Christ, known as "Cristo Rey" (Christ the King), in Siloa, Mexico, a multitude of Catholic faithful made their pilgrimage to the site renowned in Mexican history during the Cristero crisis. The "Cristo Rey" statue symbolizes the perseverance of committed Catholics who, during the late-1920s, remained committed to their faith against repressive measures. Some would even say the site and the statue symbolize the victory gained by the Church through that period of conflict. On March 25, 2012, Pope Benedict XVI celebrated mass for 300,000 Catholics in the park where the statue overlooks any park visitors.[770]

While the "Cristo Rey" symbolizes the struggles of the faithful, it also highlights the intense struggles of those Mexicans committed to a national vision founded upon democracy, pluralism, and freedom. In short, the statue remains as a monument to one of the historic moments in Mexican history when citizens of the same country battled for the truths to which they were committed. This chapter gives a brief historical overview of those struggles between the Mexican government and the Church. Such a historical review will centralize the issues of conflict, some of which continue to the present. The next section analyzes the modern context of church-state relations, with a special focus upon the impact of *Dignitatis Humanae* in Mexican jurisprudence.

---

[770] David Agren, "Pope's Mexico trip a chance to explore church-state conflict," in *USAToday*, March 20, 2012, http://www.usatoday.com/news/religion/story/2012-03-19/pope-mexico-church-state/53657084/1, (accessed June 11, 2012).

Historical Review of Church-State Relations

James Breedlove best expresses the close link between Spain, Mexico, and the Roman Catholic Church, "As a result [of union between "altar and throne"], the relationship between church and state has been a major issue in the political and social history of all the former Spanish colonies of Latin America, especially in Mexico."[771] The involvement of the Roman Catholic Church in Mexico began after the discovery of the New World by Christopher Columbus (1492). Pope Alexander VI was the mediator between Spain and Portugal, determining which geographical portions of the new continent belonged to each.[772] For roughly three hundred years,[773] the native inhabitants were subject to dominance by the Church, primarily through clerical preaching about obedience to the king.[774] Typically, during this time period, the lay priests would tend to side with the native inhabitants against many of the measures and policies adopted by the Catholic hierarchy.[775] By the early 1800s, with Spanish imperial power

---

[771] James M. Breedlove, "Effect of the Cortes, 1810-1822, on Church Reform in Spain and Mexico," in *Mexico and the Spanish Cortes, 1810-1822*, ed. Nettie Lee Benson (Austin: University of Texas Press, 1966), 113.

[772] Derek Davis, ed., *Church-State Relations and Religious Liberty in Mexico: Historical and Contemporary Perspectives* (Waco, TX: J. M. Dawson Institute of Church-State Studies, Baylor University, 2002), 3-4; William Butler, *Mexico in Transition: From the Power of Political Romanism to Civil and Religious Liberty* (New York: Hunt and Eaton, 1892), 4-6;

[773] Butler provides the atrocious details of how Hernando Cortez subjugated the Aztec race, primarily out of lust for gold, and how the Church's coffers were enriched by his conquests. He marks the time of Mexican subjection from 1535 to 1821 (Butler, 9-15, 64). Enrique Krauze also refers to this period as the "Conquest" during which the priests used forced conversion techniques, along with accommodation of Indian cultic practices, that resulted in a syncretistic religion [Enrique Krauze, *Mexico, Biography of Power: A History of Modern Mexico, 1810-1996* (New York: Harper Collins, 1997), 33-34, 70-73.]

[774] Davis, 5-6; Alfonso Toro also mentions how the Inquisition was introduced in Mexico and how it was used to maintain the Church's power and influence [Alfonso Toro, *La Iglesia y el Estado en Mexico: Estudio sobre los conflictos entre el clero catolico y los gobiernos mexicanos desde la independencia hasta nuestros dias* (Mexico, 1927), 36-38, 48].

[775] Davis, 5. Especially was this so regarding abuses committed by the Catholic hierarchy against native inhabitants –"secular clergy" defended Indians against the "regular clergy" [Guillermo F. Margadant S., *An Introduction to the History of Mexican Law* (Dobbs Ferry, NY: Oceana Publications, Inc., 1983), 155-156;

weakening through Napolean's conquest of Spain,[776] the native inhabitants revolted under the leadership of Miguel Hidalgo, a parish priest.[777] Hidalgo was captured and put to death in July, 1811.

During the following decade, there was much confusion and instability of power in Spain.[778] King Ferdinand VII was restored to the throne in 1814 and overturned much of the work of the juntas (formal assemblies), even to the point of rejecting the Constitution of 1812.[779] In 1821, in Mexico, General Iturbide took advantage of the instability in Spain and led a rebellion to overthrow Spanish rule.[780] One of the major contributing factors that led Mexican priests to support Iturbide in the cause of independence from Spain was "the decrees concerning the Jesuits,[781] the *desafuero*, and monastic reform" that the Spanish *Cortes* enacted.[782] James Breedlove describes the response of Manuel de la Barcena, the Archdeacon of the cathedral of Valladolid de Michoacán,

Barcena argued that he had sworn to uphold the

---

hereafter *History*]. Toro also describes how the regular clergy ("alto clero," high clergy) received honors, great recognition, high salaries, and maintained a caste distinction between themselves, as Spaniards, and the secular clergy ("bajo clero," lower clergy), as Indians or mestizos (mixed breed), which all contributed to the revolution [Toro, 52-55].

[776] Butler, 65.

[777] Davis, 6; Butler, 55, 67-71. Guillermo F. Margadant offers a slightly different rendering regarding Hidalgo. He states that Hidalgo and other indigent priests led their rebellions because they did not have the higher clerical posts given by the Church predominantly to Spaniards. He also states that Hidalgo and Morelos were condemned by the Inquisition as "heretics" [Guillermo F. Margadant, *La Iglesia Mexicana y El Derecho* (Av. Republica Argentina, Mexico: Editorial Porrua, S.A., 1984), 135-136; hereafter, *Iglesia Mexicana*].

[778] Butler, 26.

[779] Davis, 6; Butler, 66. This is the same Constitution of Cadiz that New Spain's (Mexico's) clergy, either high or low, had no hesitation in taking the oath to uphold the document" (Breedlove, 122).

[780] Davis, 7; Butler, 76.

[781] The Jesuits were expelled in 1767 from all territories ruled by the Spanish Crown (Krauze, 80).

[782] Breedlove, 130; Krauze, 80-2.

Constitution and laws of Spain, but not to support the rule of tyrants, by whom he evidently meant the *Cortes*. He wrote that the extinction of monasteries and the *desafuero*[783] of the clergy had scandalized the people and were the impelling causes of the movement for independence.[784]

After an initial success, Iturbide was captured and put to death in July, 1824.[785] After his death, both the liberal and conservative (Catholic) groups balanced one another through the Mexican Constitution in 1824.[786] It allowed for each state to retain its sovereignty and to elect its own governor, legislature, and judiciary.[787] The Catholic Church became the national religion,[788] a favored position that it retained for nearly a decade.[789]

From the 1820s to the mid-1850s, a power struggle occurred between the liberal, secular group and the Catholic Church. Krauze describes how some *caudillo* leaders during these decades looked "toward the future, eager for a state that would be republican, secular, democratic, and constitutional.

---

[783] *Desafuero* here refers to the denial of the *fuero*, the favored status of the clergy that exempted them from the jurisdiction of the Spanish (civil) Cortes and allowed them to set up their own tribunals (Krauze, 74).

[784] Breedlove, 130-132.

[785] Butler, 80.

[786] Davis, 7; Butler, 81. Timothy E. Anna further describes how the competing political views of centralism (State's rights) and federalism (national sovereignty) were adopted by the Scottish Rite Masons and the Yorkshire Order of Masons, respectively [Timothy E. Anna, *Forging Mexico: 1821-1835* (Lincoln, NE: University of Nebraska Press, 1998), 167-168, 204-207; Margadant, *Iglesia Mexicana*, 140-141].

[787] Krauze, 129.

[788] Jaime O. Rodriguez, ed., *The Evolution of the Mexican Political System* (Wilmington, DE: Scholarly Resources, Inc., 1993), 2. Here, Rodriguez is citing Luis Villoro who refers to the Catholic Church as one of the founders of the First Federal Republic in 1824 (Luis Villoro, *El proceso ideologico de la revolucion de la independencia*, 2d. ed. (Mexico: UNAM, 1977), 2:356); Krauze, 129; Margadant, *Iglesia Mexicana*, 137.

[789] Davis, 7; Krauze, 137; For a variety of plans circulated during this time that favored the Church, see Thomas B. Davis and Amado Ricon Virulegio, *The Political Plans of Mexico* (Lanham, MD: University Press of America, Inc., 1987), 74-80.

.. The nascent Liberal state had no alternative but a fight to the death with this parallel state [the Catholic Church]."[790] In 1833, Vice-President Valentin Gomez Farias initiated the Reform that separated the church and state and that provided for secular education.[791] Shortly thereafter, President Santa Anna was advised to turn from military pursuits to correct this situation.[792] During the next twenty years, liberal forces continued working to disestablish the Catholic Church, which they succeeded in doing through the Constitution of 1857.[793] Under the leadership of Benito Juarez,[794] recognized as the "George Washington" of Mexico, all church property holdings (including church buildings) were nationalized,[795] "marriage became a civil union, cemeteries were secularized, monastic orders were abolished and strict separation of church and state was arduously enforced."[796] The Church reacted with total rejection of the Constitution and "priests poured out anathemas and excommunications."[797]

---

[790] Krauze, 88.

[791] Davis, 7; Ibid., 137.

[792] Davis, 7; Krauze, 137.

[793] Davis, 7; Butler, 119; Krauze interestingly describes how an intellectually brilliant and liberal minded priest, Melchor Ocampo, actually started raising questions about church-state relations that were unfavorable to the Church. Ocampo adopted the view of freedom of conscience for all men based on Kant's teachings (Krauze, 152-156).

[794] Krauze aptly describes Juarez as an Indian whose personal path to transformation included throwing off the societal yoke of Spanish customs and arbitrary chains of the Catholic Church. Juarez remarked that through the Church's doctrines of blind obedience, the result was [for the Indians] "Our poverty, our brutalization, our degradation and our enslavement for three hundred years." (Krauze, 162).

[795] Butler, 134. Krauze describes the influence of Ocampo on Juarez that aided the latter in understanding principles of anti-clericalism that matured with Juarez into separation of church and state (Krauze, 167).

[796] Davis, 7; Although initiated through Juarez, these practices continued in effect even until 1864 when Maximilian, the Austrian archduke who usurped power as "Emperor" of Mexico for three years, was continuing to rule. Butler includes a letter from Pope Pius IX in which he denounces these practices that were legalized under "The Law of Reform" and the repeal of which he admonished Maximilian to do (Butler, 179-181).

[797] Krauze, 169.

Enrique Krauze succinctly states, "Mexico had freed itself from the Crown in 1821, but had to wait until 1861 to free itself from the Church."[798]

During the ensuing fifteen years, power shifts and struggles for dominance continued between liberal forces and the Church. Benito Juarez and his republican forces fought without quarter, forcing a temporary retreat of Catholic priests from politics.[799] Under the presidency of Juarez (1867-1872) and Sebastian Lerdo de Tejada (1872-1876), attempts were made to rehabilitate the nation under a democratic system.[800] By 1876, General Porfirio Diaz took control of the government with the aid of the Church[801] and reached a church-state compromise.[802] This allowed for a *de juro* anti-clerical law (to satisfy the liberal forces) while also providing for a *de facto* liberty for the Church by not enforcing the anti-clerical law.[803] Diaz maintained peaceful rule until the Mexican Civil War in 1910.[804]

By 1917, the Mexican Constitution then adopted included the anti-clerical elements of the 1857 Constitution.[805] The "modus vivendi" of

---

[798] Ibid., 228.

[799] E. V. Niemeyer, Jr., Revolution *at Queretaro: The Mexican Constitutional Convention of 1916-1917* (Austin, TX: The University of Texas Press, 1974), 6; Toro, 350-351.

[800] Niemeyer, 6.

[801] Niemeyer states, "Under such an arrangement, the Church recouped much of its wealth while regaining power and prestige. Once more priests put business before religion, openly displayed their contempt for the laws regulating public religious acts, and entered the educational system with renewed vigor. In a real sense, the Church became a bulwark of the dictatorship: its prelates and clerics believed that their own best interest depended on the continuance of Porfirian rule" (Niemeyer, 10).

[802] Davis, 8; Butler states that under Diaz' rule "all forms of worship have been protected" (Butler, 287).

[803] Davis, 8; Krauze, 230.

[804] Niemeyer identifies the causes of the Mexican Civil War as the iniquities of the *porfiriato* (1876-1911): an inequitable land system that favored the upper and middle classes (8), the plight of rural and urban labor (9), the recovery of the Church (10), and the total destruction of democracy (10-11).

[805] Davis, 8. Guillermo Floris Margadant S. identifies the architectural framework of the 1917 Constitution as deriving directly from the 1857 Constitution (Margadant, *History*, 287).

striking a balance between state and church that was adopted by Diaz continued to govern these relations. In 1927, President Plutarco Elias Calles began to enforce the anti-clerical provisions of the Constitution, resulting in persecution of priests.[806] Under his rule, no foreign born priests were allowed to preside over churches, church lands were confiscated, and priests could not become involved in political issues.[807] The Church reacted violently by suspending all religious services and giving tacit approval to a rebellion group called Cristeros.[808] This rebellion ended three years later when the government, under President Gil, reverted to the "modus vivendi" of previous years.[809]

In 1934, Article 3 of the 1917 Constitution was amended to prescribe "socialist education,"[810] which was ill-received by faithful Catholics. President Manuel Avila Camacho, elected in 1940, sought national unity as a primary objective during his presidency. To achieve this, he began healing the wound between the Church and the state,[811] which traced back to the turbulent religious war of 1857-1861, and which was reflected in the 1917 Constitution. In response, political left and "solitary democratic and liberal voices" feared the re-entry of the Church into the political life of Mexico.[812] Nonetheless, Camacho's government amended Article 3, late in his regime (December, 1945).[813] The PAN (Partido Accion Nacional, National Action Party), initiated in 1939 by Manuel Gomez Morin, was closely identified

---

[806] Davis, 8; Krauze states that Calles was "jubilantly atheist" (405). Nonetheless, as governor of Sonora, he instituted tremendous moral reforms, such as outlawing all intoxicating beverages and gambling, as well as reforming the judicial system (409-411).

[807] As president of Mexico, he vigorously sought to enforce articles 3 and 130 of the 1917 Constitution, which were anti-clerical (Krauze, 420-421).

[808] Davis, 9. The resulting war that lasted three years (1927-30) is referred to as "Cristiada" and was fought by Cristeros against federal troops (Krauze, 422, 423).

[809] Davis, 9; Krauze indicates that Gil signed the agreement with Rome (430).

[810] Krauze, 506.

[811] Krauze, 506.

[812] Ibid., 506-507.

[813] Ibid., 507.

with the Catholic Church hierarchy, and was known for its opposition to the anti-clerical articles of the 1917 Constitution.[814] Thus, ideas and activities of the PAN played a significant role in the emendation. Its final version eradicated "socialist education" by placing emphasis upon "democratic and national" education.[815]

During the 1950s, the Mexican government granted minor concessions to the Church, such as allowing it to conduct some public worship services.[816] Through the politics of reconciliation begun by Camacho, the Church worked "to reconstitute its ancient wealth (though on a lesser scale and through the use of intermediaries) and especially to support, without serious restrictions, its specific areas of interest: pastoral activities and education."[817] In spite of this, throughout this decade and the ones following, the Church faced the growing challenge of pluralism as other religions sought the benefits of religious freedom.[818] Although there was a semblance of religious tolerance, the Church wielded tremendous power over public opinion, and there were incidents "where Protestants were attacked and beaten and their houses burned."[819]

The following period, roughly from the 1960s to the early 1980s may be termed "recovery of social space," as the efforts of the Church focused on: "social justice, moralization of customs and habits, and religious freedom."[820] Roberto Blancarte, Academic Director at the Mexiquense College and holding a Ph.D. in Social Sciences, mentions a point in this period of "recovery of social space" by the Church leadership that supports the thesis of this book, namely, that

[T]his demand for religious freedom [by the Mexican

---

[814] Ibid., 507, 517, 518.

[815] Ibid., 507.

[816] Davis, 9.

[817] Krauze, 582.

[818] Davis, 9.

[819] Krauze, 583.

[820] Roberto J. Blancarte, "Recent Changes in Church-State Relations in Mexico: An Historic Approach," in *Church-State Relations & Religious Liberty in Mexico: Historical and Contemporary Perspectives*, ed. Derek Davis (Waco, TX: J. M. Dawson Institute of Church-State Studies, 2002), 70.

bishops] would be linked slowly but surely to a demand for democracy in the political system, particularly the electoral system.

His observation substantiates the argument of the Catholic Hegemony thesis which posits that the Church's leadership applies *Dignitatis Humanae* (religious freedom) in the context of a constitutional democracy to establish or maintain its hegemony, or, as in this case, to regain it through the recovery of social space. A similar incident will be repeated later in Mexican history and noted several paragraphs below.

During the 1960s, the Church continued utilizing the reconciliation begun under Camacho to re-gain its strength and influence. It also used the Document on Religious Freedom from Vatican II in an effort to solidify its position:

> Regarding the right of the Church to exercise its prophetic voice concerning the socio-political trends of modern societies, the position of the Catholic Church has been strengthened, mostly the result of conciliar debates and especially some of their conclusions, such as the Councilor [sic] Declaration on Religious Freedom or *Dignitatis Humanae*, dated 7 December 1965.[821]

The Church successfully showed its power through an anti-Communist campaign carried on throughout the nation.[822] By this decade, the Church had become "the leading proprietor of private education in the country."[823] Other factors contributing to the growth of Catholic educational efforts in the 60s dated back to the enforcement by Calles in 1927 of the 1917 Constitution. The Church responded by training Mexican priests for service at seminaries outside of Mexico – primarily at Montezuma College in the United States and the Pio Latino Seminary in Rome.[824] Additionally, through the influence of Vatican II upon the Church's social doctrine, young priests began to take up the cause of the poor, eventually leading to the development of Liberation Theology.[825]

---

[821] Blancarte, 71.

[822] Krauze., 662.

[823] Ibid., 662.

[824] Krauze, 662.

[825] Ibid., 662-663.

The political elections in Chiapas in 1986 are significant to better understanding the intricacies of how Mexican Church leadership sought to restore their influence. In June of that year, the State Electoral Commission declared the Institutional Revolutionary Party (PRI) the winner of most of the civil positions. However, there was clear evidence of corruption in the process. The archbishop communicated to the bishops throughout the state, and they staged a mass closing of all the churches on the following Sunday, the same action taken during the Cristeros crisis and exactly sixty years after the same event (1926). Their obvious message was to recall the vote. Dr. Blancarte offers his analysis,

> of Mexican church-state relationships [which] shows that the participation of the Catholic Church in political affairs has been significant in the last decade. . . [and] is the revival of an "integral" position defining a social project, within which the democratization of political life is essential for the recovery of ecclesiastical rights.[826]

Again, Dr. Blancarte associates democratic involvement by the Church with a recovery of ecclesiastical rights.

The status of "modus vivendi" (i.e., the priests lived with what they could not change) prevailed until Carlos Salinas de Gortari was elected as President (1988-1994). Although raised a Catholic, he had only a nominal association with the Church. Electoral history indicates that some dishonesty had been associated with his campaign to win the presidency. Additionally, Raúl González Schmal (M.A. in Law), describes how Gortari's actions at his inauguration foreshadowed the direction his term would take when he "invited a group of dignitaries from the Catholic Church to join him [for the inauguration]."[827] Shortly into his term, his intents to restore relations with the Catholic Church had leaked to the public, causing strong reactions among the liberal political party, the PRI (Partido Revolucionario Institucional, Revolutionary Institutional Party), which decried Salinas' actions as un-constitutional. It regarded his actions as a violation of the principle of separation of church and state as implied in the historical background to the constitutions of 1857 and 1917.

President Gortari's favor toward the Church can be traced back to the

---

[826] Blancarte, 73.

[827] Raúl González Schmal, "La libertad religiosa como principio regulador de las relaciones Estado-Iglesia," in Secretaría de Gobernación, *Relaciones Estado-Iglesia: Encuentros y Desencuentros* (México: Secretaría de Gobernación, 2001), 271.

late 70s and early 80s, when he had already begun dialogue with the Catholic hierarchy regarding a "modern concept" of church-state relations which would eliminate much of the anti-clerical elements in the Constitution.[828] Krauze notes that the changes implemented, by abolishing Article 130, which was strongly anti-clerical, resulted in giving to the Church juridical personality and full internal autonomy; by removing all restrictions on religious rites; and by permitting priests to give their public opinions and to vote.[829] In response to his critics, Salinas' rationale is "to co-opt, or at least neutralize, in a political sense, the Catholic Church"[830] by such concessions.

Additionally, as if in harmony with the Church's emphasis upon the poor, Salinas' government changed Article 27 of the Constitution to allow the peasant to set his own terms for his own land: "he could retain communal membership in the *ejido* (farming cooperative) or convert his land into private property."[831] Salinas enacted a program, Solidarity, by which "funds and projects" were offered directly to the peasants.[832]

The second most favorable act toward the Church that President Gortari performed was "the designation of a personal representative before the Holy See in February, 1990."[833] Thus, through a gradual process of biding its time, influencing the political systems, and eventually leading various presidential administrations to amend certain anti-clerical articles of the Constitution, the Church had been re-gaining its power and prestige. Due to the close relations between President Gortari and Catholic leaders, Carlos Martínez Assad, a professor who teaches Sociology and History at the Institute of Sociological Studies, Universidad Nacional Autonómica de México, observed,

> In 1992, the articles in the Constitution that regulated relations between the Church and the State were changed in order to establish a new norm. Although the Law of Religious Associations and Public Worship was the rule of

---

[828] Krauze, 776.

[829] Ibid., 776.

[830] Roderic Ai Camp, "Political Modernization in Mexico," in *The Evolution of the Mexican Political System*, ed. Jaime O. Rodriguez, 257.

[831] Krauze, 775.

[832] Ibid., 775.

[833] Schmal, 271.

the constitutional reforms and used to that end, it is the Catholic Church and not other churches that was converted into the principal interlocutor of the government.[834]

Professor Assad's observation is the same as that of Roberto J. Blancarte, who commented on Gortari's term in office:

> The goal of the Mexican government was not to develop new policies concerning religions in Mexico, but to improve links with the Catholic Church, positively with the Church's hierarchy. The decision to address the needs of the other religions of Mexico was a mere byproduct of an overall strategy centered on improving relations with the Catholic Church.[835]

It seems that Drs. Assad's and Blancarte's observation may be accurate when one studies the changes made to the 1917 Constitution, as noted in the following section.

The Law of Religious Associations and Public Worship, 1992

The historic context prior to the constitutional change reveals that the Constitution of 1917 was "reformed on hundreds of occasions, but not even a comma was changed in the statements regulating religious matters,"[836] for seventy-five years. Raul González Schmal explains that this was due primarily to successive governments and certain sectors of society that considered these articles as "true foundational norms, untouchable and without substitute, even though they did not resonate with the fifth part of our historical patrimony,"[837] referring to the short seventy-five years of anti-clericalism as opposed to several centuries of Church dominance in Mexican society. From a lawyer's perspective who has studied international law, he further explains the fundamental difference in principle between the

---

[834] Carlos Martínez Assad, "La iglesia católica entre el pasado y el presente," in Secretaría de Gobernación, *Relaciones Estado-Iglesia: Encuentros y Desencuentros* (México: Secretaría de Gobernación, 2001), 265.

[835] Blancarte, "Recent Changes," 56.

[836] Schmal, 271.

[837] Ibid., 271.

former version of the Constitution and the new changes made to the religion articles, which is the difference between separationism and religious freedom. He indicates that the concept of religious freedom is becoming more of "the needle around which laws regulating religious entities now rotate."[838]

As he defines religious freedom, he refers to a common axiom, "Let there be as much freedom as possible, and only as much restraint as necessary."[839] He also appeals to language that is common to *Dignitatis Humanae* without actually citing it:

> The human right to religious freedom, as it is understood in the modern doctrine of human rights, is an immunity from coercion of a person before other people, groups and public powers, which consists in no one being obligated in religious matters to act against their conscience, nor can anyone be impeded from acting according to their conscience.[840]

As noted in the historical section, the Mexican Church hierarchy clamored for religious freedom under the oppressive restrictions of the 1917 Constitution. And, as Schmal describes the religious freedom desired, it parallels that mentioned in *Dignitatis Humanae*. However, as the rest of this section demonstrates, the Law of Religious Associations and Public Worship did grant a level of religious freedom that had not been allowed in Mexico during the previous seventy-five years, but it also had the effect of restraining the Church from its hegemonic tendencies. What follows is a brief contrast of each of the articles that were changed from the 1917 Constitution and after that a brief explanation of how the hegemony of the Church was restrained.

Article 3

Article three contains four paragraphs which read the same in both the 1917 and reformed 1917 Constitutions, except for the following: paragraph one clearly states that school education will be "guaranteed by Article 24 on freedom of belief, such education will be lay (secular)." Paragraph four

---

[838] Schmal, 276.

[839] Ibid., 277.

[840] Ibid., 275; cf., compare to *Dignitatis Humanae*, Article 2 regarding "immunity from coercion as a civil right."

used to read "religious corporations, ministers of worship, societies associated with any type of religious creed, will not enter in educational institutes of primary, secondary, or normal (high school) level, nor to workers or field laborers."[841] It now simply specifies that educational institutes should conduct educational efforts in harmony with the lay (secular) aim as stated in paragraph one.

Article 5

Article five in the reformed Constitution removes anti-clerical sentiments from the older version, which included "whether it be for reasons of work, for education, or for religious vote. The law, in consequence, does not allow the establishment of monastic orders, whatever the denomination from which they come."[842] Thus, it is not overtly anti-Catholic.

Article 24

Freedom of religious belief is guaranteed under Article 24, and those words left out were restrictions regarding the location of where worship services could be conducted, "in the churches or in one's particular residence."[843] As they are left out of the new version, there is more freedom for conducting religious services in different locations, but "always so as to not constitute a crime or fault punished by law."[844] As applied, all religious services outside of churches or one's residence must be under the supervision of local authorities.

Article 27

The only two primary changes to this article are in terminology from "churches" to "associations," and from a prohibition of owning property to allowing religious associations to own property, instead of it becoming the property of the State. Restrictions are placed upon how much religious

---

[841] Armando Méndez Gutiérrez, *Una ley para la libertad religiosa* (México: Editorial Diana, 1992), 313-314.

[842] Ibid., 315.

[843] Ibid., 315.

[844] Gutiérrez, 315.

organizations can acquire – "no more than needed for their objective."[845] This adjustment was made to prevent religious groups from following the example of the Catholic Church that had accumulated sizeable amounts of money during its history in Mexico.

Article 130

Primarily, this article grants more autonomy to religious associations and grants more rights to ministers, such as being able to vote. However, ministers cannot run for civil offices (unless they leave their ministry) or preach in their churches about any political issues, or endorse candidates.[846] This explains, in part, why the involvement by Catholic priests in the politics of 1986 drew such heavy criticism from many parts of Mexico. The principles in this article, favoring a separation between church and state, are also what caused the major political party, PRI, to complain about President Gortari's overtures toward the Church's hierarchy.

From a short review of the Constitutional changes made in 1992, one can state that there is definitely less anti-clerical sentiment in the new articles. However, there are two areas that were specifically targeted, and to which the Catholic hierarchy agreed to uphold: ministers of worship (or clergy) could not become involved in politics, and they could not accumulate material goods (hoarding of wealth).[847] Through the negotiations that President Gortari initiated, the Church now had a role in Mexican society. Ironically, though the Church hierarchy hegemonically tried to regain their social sphere through an emphasis upon religious liberty, they not only received a limited type, but also their efforts opened the way for Protestant contenders to enter the religious field of competition, as will be noted in a later section. Additionally, Catholic hegemony was restricted in regards to concordats and the Church's jurisdiction.

Concordats and Catholic Jurisdiction

José Luis Lamadrid Sauza, licensed in law from the University of Guadalajara, offers several insightful reasons as to why the Mexican government refused to enter into concordatory relations, or even

---

[845] Gutiérrez, 315, 316.

[846] Ibid., 317-318.

[847] Sauza, 34.

diplomatic agreements with the Vatican, even when other countries, including the Unites States (1984) had done so.[848] First, he explains that to do so is to acknowledge the juridical character of the Church. As a part of jurisprudence, any entity granted "legal personality" is entitled to its corresponding rights, duties, etc. As such, when the Church enters into concordatory relations with a state, it is implicit that the state recognizes the "legal personality" of the Church. Since the Church argues that its existence predates the state, it therefore argues that its norms supersede those of the state. Since the Church is recognized as an international entity by all states entering into concordatory relations with it, the Church has further grounds to argue for its rights. In essence, the Church gains the upper hand against the state in the juridical order. Lamadrid Sauza states,

> Such a conception [of having members in most every country], from which also derives its classification as a subject of international rights, implies the primacy of the juridical order of the Church, as a universal organization, over the juridical orders of the partial (non-universal) communities (i.e., states). Thus, to the extent that the Church pretends to postulate the absolute and permanent truth of its moral order, necessarily grants it primacy over the positive juridical orders, which by definition are relative and mutable.[849]

In essence, Lamadrid Sauza means that through concordats, the state acknowledges the Church as a superior entity, whose norms surpass its own.

He further explains that precisely to avoid such a situation, the Mexican government, from 1917 to 1992, had used "religious associations" as the means to give legal recognition to churches. These associations do not confer any type of juridical authority presumed by the entities themselves, but only recognize their internal authority, viz., over their own members. In addition, this classification grants to churches the ability to own and dispose of property, as well as to enter into courts regarding legal disputes. More than anything else, the classification obligates all churches who file for it to remain subject to all laws of the provinces wherein they reside, as well as to state laws. No church is granted legal recognition without filing with the state under the status of "religious association." Lamadrid Sauza

---

[848] Sauza, 35-38.

[849] Ibid., 37.

concludes by stating that through this system, "the historic principle of separation between church and state, as well as equality among all churches, is maintained. . . . Thus, the law ensures juridical equality of all religious associations and avoids the privileges and discriminations that are implied by [concordatory] recognition of the juridical personality of the Catholic Church."[850]

This explanation serves as the basis from which the Law of Religious Associations was designed to require all religious groups to register with the Government Secretary for Religious Associations. It also is the means by which the government places the Catholic Church on the same level as all other religious organizations, thereby curtailing its hegemony and denying recognition of its claims as an international entity with rights superior to those of the state. The corollary effect of the restriction of the Church's hegemony by placing it on a par with other religious groups is that those groups actually enjoy the benefits of religious freedom.

Evangelical Religious Groups

In recent years, according to Alberto Hernández, Ph.D. in Sociology, the number of evangelical groups has exploded in Mexico.[851] As of 2001, they represented 5% (3.5 million) of the total population, and in some states like Chiapas, they averaged 10%. Prior to the Revolutionary War (1812), there were only about twelve religious organizations in Mexico, but now they number slightly over 120 different groups. The most important period of Evangelical history was when they became "naturalized," which occurred due to two events: 1) Mexican citizens were trained to care for their own churches, and 2) the separation from their home base, usually located in the United States, during times when Mexico desired more independence from American influence. This period indicated a turning point for those groups because they now were formally accepted into Mexican society.

Dr. Hernández explains that the Law of Religious Associations had a variety of results upon Evangelical churches, some of which were negative and some positive.[852] For smaller churches, they had to unite with larger, national churches in order to meet the minimum required number of members. For all churches, they are now required to pay social security tax

---

[850] Sauza, 38.

[851] Alberto Hernández, "Las iglesias evangélicas y la ley de las asociaciones religiosas y de culto público," in Secretaría de Gobernación, *Relaciones Estado-Iglesia: Encuentros y Desencuentros* (México: Secretaría de Gobernación, 2001),237-248.

[852] Hernández, 244.

and other taxes to their employees. The benefit for all churches is that they now meet the conditions to obtain some financial benefits from the government. Another benefit is that they are allowed to conduct services outdoors, but only under the supervision of local civil officials, and provided they do not disturb the public order.

Regarding the use of mass communication, Dr. Hernández reports that this restrictive law affects Evangelicals as well as Catholics. It prohibits the use of such things as loudspeakers and microphones with speakers when religious groups meet outdoors. Regarding television, the only hours allowed for religious programming are during non-commercial hours (i.e., late night and early morning). On the rare occasion of a slot being open during commercial hours, the cost is exorbitant. Additionally, churches who can buy a slot of time must also have a sponsor. To avoid these restrictions, some churches have been able to enter into contracts with local radio stations, but usually this requires a close, personal friendship with station owners.[853]

Catholic Hegemony and Mexican Independence

A study of the history of church-state relations in Mexico reveals numerous factors that have contributed to that dynamic. Two, dominant, contending forces – those faithful to the Church and those seeking to construct a democratic society – have been the primary figures that have led the nation. After decades of tumultuous upheavals in government as each of the two forces has vied for control of state affairs, by the 1930s, the nation settled into a routine democratic electoral process, thereby bringing stability to the nation. A part of that stability may be credited to the religion articles in the 1917 Constitution that kept the Church out of the affairs of politics. However, through President Gortari's unprecedented reforms of those religion articles, the issue of church-state conflict had the potential of manifesting itself again.

The foundational principle differentiating the pre-1992 Constitutional changes and the post-1992 changes centers on separationism versus religious freedom. The former term is designed to keep religion out of the affairs of state, whereas the latter is broad enough as to allow a variety of definitions and applications. In particular, religious freedom as demonstrated in the Mexican context reveals parallels to that espoused in *Dignitatis Humanae*, that is to say, a religious freedom that recognizes the *libertas ecclesia* (the freedom of the Church). It was for that concept of freedom that the Mexican Catholic hierarchy struggled during the "modus vivendi" period in efforts to regain their social space. It is also this

---

[853] Ibid., 247-248.

historical account that lends credence to the Catholic hegemony thesis by which the Church uses *Dignitatis Humanae* to establish or maintain its hegemony in a variety of different religious and political contexts.

Through the influence of President Gortari, reforms were started in 1992, some of which benefitted the Church and others that curtailed the Church's hegemony. In particular, the Church's hegemony is limited in three ways: 1) through constitutional reforms that do not authorize religious associations to participate in politics; 2) through designating all religious associations as equal before the law and requiring them to register with the Secretary of Religious Associations; and, 3) by fighting and obtaining religious freedom for herself, the Church has opened the way by default for non-Catholic competitors to enter the field of competition. Although attempting to re-establish her hegemony, the Church has faced formidable democratic bulwarks that have kept her efforts from becoming fully manifest. In light of the Church's hegemonic nature, the next chapter explores "*Dignitatis Humanae* and the Future of Religious Freedom."

DIGNITATIS HUMANAE AND THE FUTURE OF RELIGIOUS FREEDOM

December 2005 marked the 40th anniversary of *Dignitatis Humanae*, and three American dignitaries traveled to the Centro di Studi Americani (Center for American Studies) in Rome to celebrate the event. "U.S. Ambassador to the Holy See, Francis Rooney welcomed Cardinal Theodore McCarrick of the Archdiocese of Washington, D.C.; Mr. Jim Towey, Director of the White House Office for Faith-based and Community Initiatives; and Dr. Scott Appleby, the John M. Regan, Jr. Director of the Joan B. Kroc Institute for International Peace Studies [at the University of Notre Dame]." Each one presented a particular perspective of "the Vatican document and its influence on religious freedom throughout the world."[854]

Indeed, *Dignitatis Humanae* has had a world-wide impact in religious freedom and public policy debates. This chapter explores such an impact and offers plausible scenarios for the future of religious freedom based on the analysis of the Document in this book and in light of current events.

Implementation of Dignitatis Humanae

Dignitatis Humanae has been promoted ever since 1965 by all levels of the Roman Catholic Church wherever the Church has had a presence. Analysis for this book has focused specifically on the theoretical claims of the Document (chapters one through four). Also, its practical application has been examined in Spain, Mexico and America. The next two sections offer

---

[854] *"Dignitatis Humanae* – 40 Year Anniversary Conference", Centro di Studi Americani, Rome, January 18, 2006, http://vatican.usembassy.it/events/2006/dignitatis/default.asp (accessed Nov. 3, 2007).

a comparative evaluation of this information. The last two sections summarize the elements of *Dignitatis Humanae* that may pose threats to religious freedom and postulates on the future of religious freedom.

The Dignitatis Humanae Institute

The Dignitatis Humanae Institute was founded in 2009 by (Catholic) Benjamin Harnwell for the purpose of being "a platform through which Christian politicians can better present coherent, moderate, and mainstream responses to the growing opposition to Christian values in public life."[855] Originally founded in Britain, it now has a Rome-based think-tank to address social issues.[856]

On November 30, 2011, the Dignitatis Humanae Institute invited the head of the United States Commission on International Religious Freedom (USCIRF), Leonard Leo, to speak to UK lawmakers about increasing persecution of Christians worldwide.[857] On the following month, Nirj Deva, MP in Britain and also the Director of the Institute, publicly expressed his approval that the USCIRF had received Senate backing to continue operating at least until 2018.[858] The Institute has also given support to the United States Conference of Catholic Bishops (USCCB) as they face the Obama administration regarding health care. Cardinal Renato Raffaele Martino, Honorary President of the Institute, commended Cardinal Raymond Burke for taking a stand on this issue and seeking to rally the faithful in America in support of religious freedom.[859]

---

[855] Edward Pentin, "A Platform for Christian Politicians," in Dignitatis Humanae Institute website, http://www.catholicworldreport.com/Item/1002/A_Platform_for_Christian_Politicians.aspx, (accessed December 4, 2011).

[856] Edward Pentin, "Promoting Human Dignity," *National Catholic Register*, October 17, 2011, http://www.ncregister.com/site/article/promoting-human-dignity/ (accessed October 18, 2011).

[857] Eurasia News, "US Religious Freedom TSAR tells UKMPs: Christians Facing Increasing Persecution Worldwide," http://www.eurasiareview.com/01122011-us-religious-freedom-tsar-tells-uk-mps-christians-face-increasing-persecution-worldwide/ (accessed December 4, 2011).

[858] Eurasia Review, "US Senate Backs Down, Religious Freedom Watchdog to Stay," http://www.eurasiareview.com/20122011-us-senate-backs-down-religious-freedom-watchdog-to-stay/ (accessed January 26, 2012).

[859] Eurasia Review, "Vatican Cardinal: US Healthcare Mandate is 'Contrary to the very Foundation of Our Nation,'" April 11, 2012, http://www.eurasiareview.com/11042012-vatican-cardinal-us-healthcare-mandate-is-contrary-

Dignitatis Humanae *in America*

Given that John Courtney Murray, the principal author of *Dignitatis Humanae* was an American, it is of no surprise that the Document would have an impact in the same country. In chapter two, a section was dedicated to exploring how some have viewed Murray's concept of religious freedom on a par with the First Amendment religion clauses and how this book does not affirm that view. Two other areas which have been impacted by *Dignitatis Humanae* are worth exploring briefly, namely, American foreign policy and domestic public policy.

In foreign policy. Thomas F. Farr, formerly the first Director of the Office of International Religious Freedom, U.S. Department of State, observes, "Additional research shows that until religious liberty is established in culture and law, democratic governments will not stabilize."[860] From this point, he argues "how a broad and vigorous understanding of religious freedom is essential to U. S. foreign policy objectives, particularly the democratization of the Muslim countries of the Greater Middle East." He believes that "principles articulated in *Dignitatis Humanae* can provide an important corrective to America's faltering efforts to foster Islamic democracy."[861] In essence, Farr critiques current U.S. foreign policy as advocating a purely secular concept of church-state relations that is really a form of strict separationism. He contends that for Islamic countries to develop into stable democracies, they need a concept of religious freedom that not only permits religious expression in the public square, but one in which government also fosters it. In this way, he posits, Muslims will not feel that democracy is anti-Islamic. Farr proposes two principles from *Dignitatis Humanae* that are applicable in democracies: man is by nature a religious being, and government should recognize this by granting protections for the development of a person's beliefs, such as freedom to dialogue with others in the pursuit of truth; and, the principles applicable to the human being are also applicable to the faith community of which he is a part. Farr concludes by recommending that leaders within the U. S. Foreign Policy establishment consider opening new positions for government employees who are skilled at the interplay between democracy

---

to-the-very-foundation-of-our-nation/ (accessed May 13, 2012).

[860] Janneke Pieters, "Secular Stampede? Religious Liberty Getting Battered," in *National Catholic Register* online, January 10, 2010, http://www.ncregister.com/site/article%20/secular_stampede/ (accessed January 15, 2010).

[861] Thomas F. Farr, "Religious Realism in Foreign Policy: Lessons from Vatican II", in *The Review of Faith and International Affairs*, winter 2005-2006, 25-34.

and religion.

John L. Allen, Jr., a senior correspondent for the National Catholic Register, offers another perspective regarding the application of principles from *Dignitatis Humanae* to the Arab Spring.[862] He criticizes those Christian religious leaders from the Middle East who support oppressive regimes merely for the sake of staying in their favor and to avoid retaliation that could harm their congregations. He states, "In effect, Catholicism in the Middle East is the twenty-first century's most passionate heir to *Dignitatis Humanae*..." From *Dignitatis Humanae*, he offers three suggestions for U.S. Foreign Policy in the Middle East: 1) make it clear that protection of religious minorities, including Christians, is the *sine qua non* of diplomatic recognition and material assistance, 2) Muslim proponents of the Arab Spring should make the defense of Christian minorities a far more explicit element of their program, and 3) Christians of the West need to focus a far more intense spotlight on the fate of their co-religionists in the Middle East.

In essence, both Farr and Allen see in *Dignitatis Humanae* a religious freedom that is a robust promotion of religion, and one that does not seek to silence its voice in society, or require its members to privatize their faith. Fortunately, both Farr and Allen see these principles as *generally applicable*, even to Muslim communities, which is a fair application. However, other Catholic scholars view *Dignitatis Humanae* in relation to Islam in a different way.

During an interview with the editors of *Zenit* news, Richard John Neuhaus noted what he perceived to be differences between religious freedom concepts in *Dignitatis Humanae* and Islam:

> Q: What is the significance of the document [*Dignitatis Humanae*] in view of the terrorist attacks of Sept. 11, 2001?
>
> Father Neuhaus: That is a painful but inescapable question, forcing us to face honestly the question of Islam and religious freedom, and, more generally, Islam and human rights. Could there be anything like an Islamic "declaration on religious freedom"?
>
> Some scholars want to answer that in the affirmative, and we must pray that they are right, but I'm afraid the evidence at present is overwhelmingly on the other side. The declaration makes a clear distinction between religious

---

[862] John L. Allen, "Liberating the Christian Voice in the Arab Spring," *National Catholic Reporter*, August 12, 2011, http://ncronline.org/blogs/all-things-catholic/liberating-christian-voice-arab-spring (accessed August 14, 2011).

freedom grounded in reason and the natural order -- see Chapter 1 -- and religious freedom grounded in revelation -- see Chapter 2. That distinction is alien to Islam. Islam is radically monistic.[863]

Neuhaus states that Islam is "radically monistic," implying that *Dignitatis Humanae* is pluralistic, allowing for other religious groups besides Catholicism to exist and flourish.

It has been demonstrated that Catholicism utilizes *Dignitatis Humanae* to advocate a form of religious freedom in which Catholicism is (or becomes) pre-eminent among a plurality of religious groups. So, when Neuhaus argues for the application of the document in Islamic countries, it seems to imply a strategy of weakening Islamic hegemony in order to allow Catholic (and other religious groups) to exist there. From a juridical perspective, one would expect Neuhaus to argue against government establishment of Islam, which is exactly what he does:

> The Catholic Church is crucial in eliciting from the Islamic world whatever capacities it has for embracing religious freedom and democratic values more generally. It is very worrying, however, that even under U.S. supervision in Afghanistan and Iraq it appears that the new constitutions will establish Islam as the official religion and Shariah as the supreme law.[864]

Neuhaus's concern is to avoid an Islamic confessional state, and perhaps he is suggesting a model similar to that implemented under *Dignitatis Humanae* in several Latin American countries (Argentina, Paraguay, and Peru). They were once confessional states, but now operate under a "system of cooperative or autonomous recognition," which means that "relationships between the State and religions are based on autonomy and cooperation, admitting a prevailing or preeminent religion, with links and communication between both spheres."[865] In those countries, the Catholic Church is the preeminent religious group that functions with other religious

---

[863] Editors of zenit.org news, "Richard Neuhaus on the Declaration on Religious Freedom," New York, Nov. 20, 2003, http://www.zenit.org/article-8747?l=english (accessed on November 4, 2007).

[864] Editors of zenit.org news, "Richard Neuhaus on the Declaration on Religious Freedom," 3.

[865] Jose Camilo Cardoso, "Progress on Religious Freedom in Latin America," in *Fides et Libertas* (2007), 52.

groups. If this model were implemented, it would not only recognize Islam as the preeminent religion, but it would also allow other religious groups to enjoy religious freedom, as described by another Catholic scholar.

John Borelli of Georgetown University was instrumental in organizing the three official regional Catholic-Muslim dialogues in the United States. He said, "'a whole variety of issues come into play' in assessing the current state of Catholic-Muslim relations and the challenges for the future.' On the diplomatic and political level, Borelli cited a need to address concerns of religious freedom and pastoral care for Christian minorities in some Islamic countries that deny religious rights to non-Muslims."[866]

Borelli noted some positive aspects in this dialogue, but also raised concerns, which "will be how to deal with 'the negative realities' of lack of religious freedom for non-Muslims in some Islamic countries. 'If you're looking at Shariah (Islamic religious law incorporated into civil law), for Christians this is a very difficult issue,' he said."[867]

Pope Benedict XVI, in 2005, urged great caution regarding the entry of Turkey into the European Union, arguing that such cultural differences existed to prove it unwise at the current time.[868] "Yet in his first address as Pope, Benedict XVI said that he wished to work with all religions for the 'common good of humanity'. He was careful not to claim that all were equal. To do so would be unthinkable for him and offensive to other religions."[869]

In summary, the Catholic Church believes the concept of religious freedom found in *Dignitatis Humanae* offers viable options for aiding the Islamic community to transition to democracy. Several Catholic scholars from America believe that the implementation of those concepts will aid not only Islamic states to make this transition, but also to allow freedom of religious practice for non-Muslims. From the perspective of this book, such actions could be beneficial. However, further investigation into the autonomous model that operates in Argentina, Paraguay, and Peru should be done first to determine if the dominant religion there, i.e., Catholicism, does truly allow full religious freedom rights to the non-Catholics residing there, or if the national Catholic leadership narrowly applies *Dignitatis*

---

[866] Mary Ann Walsh, ed., *From Pope John Paul II to Benedict XVI* (New York: Rowman and Littlefield, 2005), 182.

[867] Ibid., 183-184.

[868] Michael Collins, *Pope Benedict XVI: Successor to Peter* (New York: Paulist Press, 2005), 80.

[869] Ibid., 80.

Humanae as the Spanish Catholic leadership did for nearly thirty years to restrict the growth of Protestant and other religions in Spain. If the latter case should prove correct, then one could suspect that Catholic promotion of *Dignitatis Humanae* for the Middle East would serve the longer range purpose of allowing the Church to proselytize and advance its hegemony.

In domestic public policy. In the fall of 2011, the U. S. Conference of Catholic Bishops (USCCB) formed the Ad Hoc Committee on Religious Freedom, headed by Bishop William Lori. He appeared before the U. S. Senate on October 26 to address the concerns of the Roman Catholic Church regarding the *libertas ecclesia* (freedom of the Church, as an institution) against perceived threats from groups advocating abortion and contraceptive rights.[870] On November 8, 2011, he told Catholic News Agency (CNA), the first goal of the ad hoc committee was "to lift up the whole area of religious freedom, beginning with the teachings of the Church in *Dignitatis Humanae* – the Second Vatican Council's declaration on religious freedom" and also to recoup "the vision of our Founding Fathers of the United States" regarding religious freedom.[871] He alleges that religious freedom, one of the chief cornerstones of American society, is being violated through restrictions on the free exercise of religion in the public square by some liberal groups.

Determined to bring these issues to the forefront of debate in America, the USCCB developed a website, "Fortnight for Freedom,"[872] where one can find several Church documents related to religious freedom (including a study guide on *Dignitatis Humanae*), information on how to become involved in this effort, etc. The USCCB is planning to begin their "fortnight" on June 21, 2012 and conclude on July 4, symbolizing that their efforts resonate with America's Independence Day ethos. They are encouraging laity to organize small study groups in their respective dioceses, and to

---

[870] Michael Shawn Winters, "Bishops Lori's Testimony on Religious Freedom," *National Catholic Reporter* online, October 27, 2011, http://ncronline.org/blogs/distinctly-catholic/bishop-loris-testimony-religious-liberty (accessed Oct. 30, 2011).

[871] David Kerr, "Bishop Lori reveals details of Religious Liberty Committee," *Catholic News Agency*, November 10, 2011, http://www.catholicnewsagency.com/news/bishop-lori-reveals-details-of-religious-liberty-committee/ (accessed Nov. 24, 2011).

[872] USCCB, "Fortnight for Freedom," http://www.usccb.org/issues-and-action/religious-liberty/fortnight-for-freedom/index.cfm (accessed June 4, 2012).

conduct religious liberty rallies, "Stand Up for Religious Freedom."[873] Thus far, they have held two nation-wide rallies, one on March 23, 2012 and the other on June 8, 2012. The latter of the two drew roughly 49,000 people in various states. With such efforts put forth on this issue, what are the underlying concerns of the USCCB that leads them to argue that their religious freedom rights have been violated?

Attempting to argue that pro-choice abortion legislation and other societal moral issues, such as contraceptive services required as part of health care insurance, euthanasia, and same-sex marriages – when legalized – become a denial of Catholics' free exercise of religion rights, assumes that society is founded upon Roman Catholic moral values. Current statistics do not support the implied contention that America is a Roman Catholic nation.[874] Even among those Catholics living in America, the majority of them do not agree with the moral teachings of the Magisterium on the issue of birth control.[875] Contrary to ideas of Catholic dominance, America is a republic founded upon a constitutional democracy. Democracy, by definition, is government of those governed – *demos*, meaning "people" in Greek, and *krateo*, meaning "to rule, to govern," thus, a "government of the people, by the people, and for the people."

The USCCB, by means of its Ad Hoc Committee on Religious Freedom, attempts to portray the Catholic Church and Catholics as being denied their religious freedom guaranteed under the First Amendment.[876] Recent legislation requiring all institutions, whether private or public, to provide contraceptive options to their employees and clients is *demos*

---

[873] Eric Scheidler, "Stand Up for Freedom Rallies," http://standupforreligiousfreedom.com/ (accessed June 6, 2012).

[874] Based on the most recent census information, Roman Catholics only make up 24.5% of the current U. S. population. Adherents.com, http://www.adherents.com/adh_dem.html, (accessed Feb. 15, 2012).

[875] According to Newsmax, a group supporting expanded access to birth control indicated that 57% of American Catholic women support the Obama health care law that includes making contraceptive services available to those insured. Newsmax, "U.S. Bishops: Rescind the Obama Health Care Rule," Feb. 12, 2012, http://www.newsmax.com/Newsfront/obama-birth-control-shift/2012/02/10/id/429117?s=al&promo_code=E27F1-1, (accessed Feb. 13, 2012).

[876] Joan Frawley Desmond, "Bishop Lori: Religious Liberty: The Pre-eminent Social Justice Issue of Our Time," National Catholic Register, Nov. 30, 2011, http://www.ncregister.com/daily-news/bishop-lori-religious-liberty-the-preeminent-social-justice-issue-of-our-ti/, (accessed January 27, 2012).

benefit-focused, rather than *anti-Catholic*-focused. Such legislation is not arbitrary action by the Obama administration. Just as the federally mandated minimum wage law was passed for the benefit of all American citizens, so also a national, federally mandated, health insurance coverage law has been enacted for the benefit of all American citizens.

Furthermore, the claims of the USCCB are unfounded in light of our current administration's response to their inquietudes. The Obama administration has made an exemption for religious institutions that, according to the dictates of their conscience, cannot offer such services. By requiring health insurance companies to nonetheless offer such services, removes the responsibility from those religious institutions while it also grants freedom of conscience and choice to the individual. Such a position is in harmony with the free exercise of religion clause of the First Amendment, which not only guarantees the free *religious* exercise of the individual, but also, guarantees the free *irreligious* (not based on religious convictions) exercise of the individual citizen. This means that government is obligated to protect the conscientious convictions of the individual citizen, apart from religious foundations (the choice to use contraceptives), while also prohibiting the establishment of a religion, or its teachings, in society (in this case, Catholic moral theology).

The nearly three-hundred Catholic bishops in America are trying to present this issue in terms of a violation of the free exercise of religion, but one of the leading American Catholic media sources does not view it in that light. The *National Catholic Register* (NCR) describes the religious freedom of the Church advocated at Vatican Council II and how it applies to issues of euthanasia and contraception:

> The principle of religious liberty that the Catholic church observes, and that the church must ask the polity to observe as well, is not the insistence that the deprivation of artificial nutrition and hydration be punishable under civil law, but that to the extent one's freely chosen faith belief requires such forced feeding that the law not make it impossible for the believer to pursue that care. If the law allows for religious beliefs to be observed or unobserved as the authoritative family member may decide, the church really should not complain about the president if its own believer makes the wrong choice in terms of Catholic doctrine. In such circumstance, the church's focus should be upon the education and conversion of heart of its own

believer, not whether the law permits a contrary belief.[877]

Mr. Kmiec, the author of this article, goes on to state, "This same principle explains the limits of the law with respect to all manner of subjects, from abortion to artificial contraception." He argues that just because a law *allows* (not forces) for certain practices contrary to Catholic doctrine, does not mean it is a violation of religious freedom. Instead, such allowance gives the individual, whether believer or not, the freedom to choose, which is a foundational principle in a democracy. Kmiec concludes by stating, "Had the HHS regulation gone farther and demanded a religious employer to affirmatively endorse or require the use of artificial contraception or any other choice contrary to its own teaching or face a penalty, that would violate the principle of religious liberty."[878]

As Mr. Kmiec aptly observes, it is the responsibility of the Church to see that its own members are adequately educated and converted to its doctrine, not to try and legislate a moral position under the false claim of a violation of religious freedom. If Catholics (or any other faith group) are properly instructed and converted to the doctrines they profess, then it matters not if any law is passed *allowing them* (not forcing them) to act contrary to those teachings, because they will uphold the principles enshrined in their hearts. So the real issue rests with the Church (and all religions regarding their respective beliefs), not with the government or its enacted laws.

Another Catholic, Paul Moses, in a *Commonweal Magazine* article entitled, "The bishops, religious liberty, and conscience," raises the question regarding the inconsistencies of religious freedom practiced within the Church by its leadership trying to control the consciences of its members on issues that are not mortal sin, while also claiming religious liberty for the Church to impose those same moral theological values upon non-Catholic citizenry in America by influencing Catholic voters through its Faithful Citizenship guidelines. If true religious freedom were practiced within the Catholic Church, Mr. Moses states:

> In the public arena, certain bishops would cease trying to limit the freedom of individual Catholics to make decisions in conscience when it comes to voting. A comment newly added to the Faithful Citizenship guidelines for voting

---

[877] David W. Kmiec, "Obama cannot be at war with Catholics if he is at peace with religious freedom," National Catholic Register, Nov. 22, 2011, http://ncronline.org/news/politics/obama-cannot-be-war-catholics-if-he-peace-religious-freedom, (accessed Nov. 24, 2011).

[878] Ibid.

reflects the influence of this rather large number of bishops. It says the document "applies Catholic moral principles to a range of important issues and warns against misguided appeals to 'conscience' to ignore fundamental moral claims."[879]

All American citizens can be grateful to those American Catholics who truly cherish and practice the American spirit of charity toward a fellow citizen, enough to recognize and respect his conscientious religious (or not) convictions, even when they differ from one's own.

Another dimension of the First Amendment religion clauses comes into focus, namely, "direct" and "corollary" effects. A "direct" effect, under the Establishment Clause, would be disallowed by the Supreme Court, but a "corollary" effect seems to be permissible in some instances, such as school vouchers. Under this argument, government cannot give money directly to private, religious schools in violation of the Establishment Clause,[880] but it can give that money indirectly ("corollary") in the form of vouchers to the parents of those children who opt to send them to parochial schools, provided that religious schools are one among many educational options.[881]

Regarding contraceptive services as part of the health care insurance law, the USCCB vociferously argues against what it terms "corollary effects" – i.e., *the individual choosing* contraceptive services *violates the conscience of the Church*. Even though this law grants an exemption to religious institutions (out of respect for their conscientious convictions), but still requires the insurance company to offer contraceptives in order to give free choice to the individual, the USCCB considers this to be a "corollary" malfeasant and thus a violation of the Catholic Church's religious free exercise rights. It becomes evident, then, that the Catholic Church desires to receive public funding for its schools through vouchers, which has the indirect effect ("corollary") of promoting Catholic religious teachings, but also desires to restrict the conscientious, free choice of its employees, some of whom may not even be Catholic – even though this has only an indirect effect upon

---

[879] Paul Moses, "The bishops, religious liberty, and conscience," *Commonweal Magazine*, Nov. 16, 2011, http://www.commonwealmagazine.org/blog/?p=15944, (accessed Nov. 24, 2011).

[880] *Lemon v. Kurtzman* (1971); *Committee for Public Education and Religious Liberty v. Nyquist* (1973); *Levitt v. Committee for Public Education and Religious Liberty* (1973); *Meek v. Pittenger* (1975); *Wolman v. Walter* (1977); et al. Cf. Ronald B. Flowers, *That Godless Court: Supreme Court Decisions on Church-State Relationships* (Louisville, KY: John Knox Press, 2005), 69-98.

[881] *Zelman v. Simmons-Harris*, 2002.

Catholic institutions ("corollary"). In the former case of school vouchers, "corollary" effects are a boon, and thus allowed, because they aid the Church, but in the latter case of contraceptive services covered by health insurance, "corollary" effects are a bane because they run contrary to Catholic moral theology, and thus are condemned.

Not only are religious freedom guarantees at play in this debate, but also economic considerations. Stated otherwise, if an institution purporting to exist for the benefit of our nation's citizens seeks federal funding to operate, then it should be willing to accommodate the *demos* from all backgrounds and be willing to offer them all available services. Thus, the *demos* is given freedom of conscience to choose what service options are best in his or her case, rather than a religious institution trying to dictate the conscientious choices of its clients. Since the *demos* is required by law to pay taxes, should not the institutions offering services to the *demos* also be subject to laws that affect the availability of such services to the *demos*?

Reactionary responses to such statements include those conscientious believers who work at private, religious institutions, but who are placed under legal obligation to offer services that they in good conscience cannot perform. Thus, it becomes a *demos*-conscience versus a *religio*-conscience. Whose conscience is guaranteed protection under the First amendment? Both.

The *demos* is the spirit behind the Constitution and the Bill of Rights. While some *demos*-consciences may not be religious in orientation, they nonetheless are protected by the First Amendment religion guarantees because Congress is prohibited from establishing any religion, whether Catholic or Christian (or other), and because the Enlightenment influence behind the "free exercise" of religion also includes unbelief, that is to say, no religious orientation.

The *religio*-conscience also finds protection under the First Amendment, through the "free exercise" clause. The essential difference between both types of conscience, however, is the issue of federal funding. The *demos*-conscience is obligated by law to pay taxes, some of which under current church-state rubric, is given to private, religious institutions. Should not the *demos*-conscience be able to secure services where federal subsidies make services affordable? Debating this viewpoint, the *religio*-conscience will argue for his right to practice his faith – i.e., not being legally obligated to offer, or perform services contrary to his convictions – but will still argue for his right, or his institution's right, to receive federal funding. *Conscientious religious, or irreligious, convictions are guaranteed protection under the First Amendment religion clauses, but not the right to federal funding that derives from all tax-payers' dollars.* To argue in support of such an erroneous view is the same as telling someone he has the legal obligation to pay a travel agency for services rendered, but also stating that the travel agency has the right to choose and prepare his travel itinerary regardless of the client's wishes.

The alternative scenario is to encourage such religious groups to adhere to a more robust concept of church-state separationism, as originally espoused by Madison and Jefferson, by cutting their federal funding for non-compliance of federal guidelines. If such religious groups cannot find the fine line of balance between providing for clients' needs and at the same time respecting their conscience, then perhaps those groups should seek funding elsewhere. To fail to do so is to argue for a religious institution's right to conscientiously follow its doctrinal teachings, even by imposing them upon its employees and clientele, while at the same time receiving federal funding – in other words, a religious establishment, and thus, directly in violation of the First Amendment Establishment Clause, "Congress shall make no law respecting an establishment of religion."

In summary of this section, Catholic concepts of religious freedom as found in *Dignitatis Humanae* are being used in American public policy debates. *Some of the confusion in this debate centers on how Catholic scholars and some media sources have attempted to portray the religious freedom advocated in* Dignitatis Humanae *and the religious freedom guaranteed under the First Amendment, as if they were the same in principle.* However, the religious freedom concepts from both sources are distinctly different, as this book has addressed at the end of chapter two. Proponents of *Dignitatis Humanae* argue that the religious freedom rights of the Church are being violated without realizing that the concepts of *Dignitatis Humanae* do not harmonize with the religious freedom concepts foundational to American democracy. Once this distinction is made, the position of the USCCB becomes the right of the *libertas ecclesia* (freedom of the Church) to impose Catholic moral theology upon non-Catholics. The contrary position is to uphold the First Amendment religious freedom clauses by not allowing an establishment of religion upon American society. Another factor to consider is the moral dilemma that faces Catholics in public office as the USCCB continues to pursue their agenda. From the perspective of this book, whatever decision the Supreme Court may render,[882] the actions of the USCCB by appealing to *Dignitatis Humanae* demonstrate one of the claims of the Catholic Hegemony thesis of this book, namely, that *Dignitatis Humanae* is used in a variety of ways, depending on extant political or religious factors, to advance the hegemony of the Catholic Church.

---

[882] When the draft of this book was finished in June, 2012, the constitutionality of the Affordable Care Act had not come before the Supreme Court.

Elements of Dignitatis Humanae *that Threaten Religious Freedom*

Each chapter of this book has dealt with specific elements of *Dignitatis Humanae* that pose potential threats to religious freedom as understood from a biblical concept of conscience, as well as religious freedom declared through the First Amendment and the United Nations Declaration of Human Rights, Article 18. The information in this section is a concise summary of those elements.

The Latent Authority to Coerce

Chapter three dealt specifically with the issue of *Dignitatis Humanae* and coercive authority. The conclusion of that chapter argues that "immunity from coercion" actually implies coercive authority ascribed to a "merely human power." Several Catholic authors cited there indicate that the Church still retains its coercive authority, though it is not used. Thus, several questions may properly be asked, what power has authority to coerce – the Church or civil power? Was not *Dignitatis Humanae* promulgated in an era of Communist-dominated countries that posed a threat to religion through their totalitarian regimes? Is not this the type of coercive power which *Dignitatis Humanae* addresses?

William Harris Rule, a historian of the Medieval Era and the Inquisition, offers the following insight that can help answer these questions:

> Many canons were framed [at Lateran Council III, 1179]. Amongst others we find one that renewed the regulations of Tours in respect to heretics; named certain sects most obnoxious to the Roman Church, and determined that all who bestowed even the least kindness on sectarians should undergo equal punishment with the sectarians themselves; that persons *relaxed*, that is to say, informed against as being guilty of heresy, should be outlawed. The word *relaxatos* should be noted, because it does not, in the peculiar vocabulary of the Holy Office mean what it would mean anywhere else. It does not mean released, but is repeated in the Spanish *relaxado*, that is to say, *delivered over* to the Inquisitors, and no more to be held under the protection of any power in the world.[883]

---

[883] William Harris Rule, *History of the Inquisition*, 2 vols. (New York, NY: Scribner, Welford & Co., 1874), 1:10.

The answer to the above questions is that *both* Church and civil authority have power to coerce: the Church within its spiritual sphere and the civil authority within its temporal sphere. Under the ideal arrangement, the Church was aligned with the transcendental sphere, then followed the civil authority aligned with the Church, *viz.*, it was favorable to religion and promoted it. The third factor to add to this equation was the human being, or citizen. When the citizen was aligned with the teachings of the Church, he enjoyed the protections offered by the civil authority. When declared a heretic, or *delivered over*, he no longer enjoyed civil protections and was thus subject to the coercive power of the Church through the Inquisition. If unrepentant, then he was *delivered over* to the civil authority, as a heretic without any rights, and thus subject to the coercive power of the civil authority. The civil authority, aligned with the Church, was obligated to mete out sentence against the heretic.

With the beginnings of the totalitarian state, however, this dynamic changed. The Church needs to restrict the oppressive power of such regimes, doing so through *Dignitatis Humanae*. However, the Church could not deny its own moral authority, thus the phrase "any merely human power" is used to obligate governments to grant an "immunity from coercion" to its citizens, thereby allowing them to seek religious truth. The key phrase is "any merely human power," which does not apply to the Church since it is considered as of divine origin in Catholic theology. So, in the modern context, the Church retains its moral authority in those things concerning man's ultimate end (God) and is thus obligated to restrict the state's coercive authority since it is not aligned with the mission of the Church. In the future, however, should the State once again align itself with the Church, the guarantee to "immunity from coercion" would need to be reformulated to reflect the Christianization of society.

The Moral Sphere and the "Erroneous Conscience"

Pietro Pavan stated, "Thus it is clear that the problems of the true or the erroneous conscience are not touched on at all in [*Dignitatis Humanae*]."[884] Yves Congar affirms this position when he states that the determination of an "erroneous" or "upright" conscience is left to the juridical conditions prevailing in a given constitutional context.[885] A more contemporary Catholic scholar, Christopher Cullen, S. J., also addresses the "erroneous conscience" that was not addressed by *Dignitatis Humanae* when he states,

---

[884] Pavan, Commentary, 66.

[885] Yves Congar, *La liberté religieuse* (Paris: Editions du Cerf, 1967), 85.

Nor can the argument be that the right to religious liberty is rooted in the sincere but erroneous conscience. This would still ground the right in error. The decree is clear that the basis for the right is man's dignity. A medieval Cathar might sincerely have acted from an objectively erroneous conscience that judged suicide a good act because this act liberates one from the body, but said Cathar cannot claim that such an erroneous judgment gives such a person a right to suicide. A bishop may sincerely act from an objectively erroneous conscience that judges suicide to be a justified act of protest against other unjust acts, but one cannot claim that this erroneous judgment gives the bishop a right to suicide.[886]

Cullen is here arguing that the right to religious freedom arguably can be affirmed only when defined by "human dignity," and not by an "erroneous conscience." The dilemma posed by this formulation is who defines both terms? One would expect that since this discussion is based on a document promulgated by the Church that it would naturally determine these definitions.

This is precisely the case as found in the *Catechism of the Catholic Church*, Part Three: Life in Christ, Section One: Man's Vocation Life in the Spirit, Chapter One: The Dignity of the Human Person, Article Six: Moral Conscience, Number 1780:

> The dignity of the human person implies and requires *uprightness of moral conscience*. Conscience includes the perception of the principles of morality (synderesis); their application in the given circumstances by practical discernment of reasons and goods; and finally judgment about concrete acts yet to be performed or already performed. The truth about the moral good, stated in the law of reason, is recognized practically and concretely by the *prudent judgment* of conscience. We call that man prudent who chooses in conformity with this judgment.[887]

---

[886] Christopher Cullen, "*Dignitatis Humanae* and a Catholic Society: The Confessional State as a Perennial Possibility," in *The Human Person and a Culture of Freedom*, eds. Peter A. Pagan Aguiar and Terese Auer (Washington, D.C.: Catholic University of America Press, 2009), 252.

[887] *Catechism of the Catholic Church*, http://www.vatican.va/archive/ccc_css/archive/catechismp3s1c1a6.htm, (accessed June 10, 2012).

Several paragraphs later, under the next section, "The Formation of Conscience," Numbers 1783, and 1785, the *Catechism* states,

> Conscience must be informed and moral judgment enlightened. A well-formed conscience is upright and truthful. It formulates its judgments according to reason, in conformity with the true good willed by the wisdom of the Creator. The education of conscience is indispensable for human beings who are subjected to negative influences and tempted by sin to prefer their own judgment and *to reject authoritative teachings*.
>
> In the formation of conscience the Word of God is the light for our path, we must assimilate it in faith and prayer and put it into practice. We must also examine our conscience before the Lord's Cross. We are assisted by the gifts of the Holy Spirit, aided by the witness or advice of others and *guided by the authoritative teaching of the Church*.[888]

Thus, the religious freedom guarantees in *Dignitatis Humanae* are conditioned upon the properly formed conscience, in harmony with the dignity of the human person, which is developed through Scripture and guided by the authoritative teachings of the Catholic Church. In fairness, and from the perspective of religious pluralism, one may say that this is admissible for *Roman Catholic members*, but not for the rest of humanity. To place these conditions upon religious freedom reveals a form of religious freedom that is distinctly Roman Catholic, as opposed to traditional, Enlightenment thought that forms the foundation of Western civilization.

This conclusion, then, returns to the "erroneous conscience," which is not addressed by *Dignitatis Humanae*, leading one to assume that "Religious freedom, in turn, which men demand as necessary to fulfill their duty to worship God, has to do with immunity from coercion in civil society. Therefore [religious freedom in *Dignitatis Humanae*] *leaves untouched traditional Catholic doctrine on the moral duty of men and societies toward the true religion and toward the one Church of Christ*."[889] Part of the traditional Catholic doctrine on the moral nature of men toward religion involves the ordering of the common good in society.

---

[888] *Catechism of the Catholic Church*, 1783, 1785 (italics mine).

[889] *Dignitatis Humanae*, Article 1, par. 4.

The Common Good

Dignitatis Humanae, Article seven, paragraph one, states,

> The right to religious freedom is exercised in human society: hence its exercise is subject to certain regulatory norms. In the use of all freedoms the moral principle of personal and social responsibility is to be observed. In the exercise of their rights, individual men and social groups are bound by the moral law to have respect both for the rights of others and for their own duties toward others and *for the common welfare of all*. Men are to deal with their fellows in justice and civility.[890]

Pietro Pavan indicates that in the discussion regarding what criteria should be used to limit the right to religious freedom in society, "the first criterion proposed by the fathers during the evolution of the document was the common good: The government can and may consider itself authorized to limit the exercise of the right to religious freedom if the common good demands it."[891] However, after further debate, the Council fathers felt this was too vague to use. Finally, Bishop Carol Wojtyla, the future Pope John Paul II, "made a crucial intervention when he asked that *Dignitatis Humanae*, article seven make clear that when the state limits liberty, it do so *ordini morali objectivo conformes* – "in conformity with the objective moral order." In Catholic parlance, this means in accordance with natural law."[892] In his footnote (number 27) to this statement, Hittinger refers to the *Catechism of the Catholic Church*, number 2109, to clarify that the right to religious freedom can only be limited after determining "each social situation by political prudence, according to the requirements of the common good."[893]

Developing further the idea of the common good as it relates to religious freedom, Christopher Cullen, S.J., writes, "In general, the *Catechism*

---

[890] *Dignitatis Humanae*, Article 7, par. 1.

[891] Pietro Pavan, "Commentary," in *Commentary on the Documents of Vatican II*, 5 vols., ed. Herbert Vorgrimler (New York, NY: Crossroad Publishing, 1989), 4:73, 74.

[892] F. Russell Hittinger, "The Declaration on Religious Liberty, *Dignitatis Humanae*," in *Vatican II: Renewal within Tradition*, eds. Matthew Lamb and Matthew Levering (New York, NY: Oxford University Press, 2008), 368.

[893] *Catechism of the Catholic Church*, no. 2109, as cited by Hittinger, 368, fn. 27.

of the Catholic Church presents a more tightly organized presentation of the same issues than are found in *Dignitatis Humanae*. The *Catechism* makes clear that the state's role is to ensure the common good. . . (citing *Catechism* 1898)."[894] Cullen goes on to explain:

> [The *Catechism*] ties the common good to the development of the human vocation. The distinctly human vocation is to union with God in Christ. This point is made clear in the first statement of the section of the *Catechism* on the 'Communal Character of the Human Vocation:' 'All men are called to the same end: God himself.' 'The vocation of humanity is to show forth the image of God and to be transformed into the image of the Father's only Son.'"[895]

By explaining that government may limit the right to religious freedom only when in harmony with the common good, as defined in relation to the objective moral order, *Dignitatis Humanae* recognizes that there may be cases "when the existing public order is the product of an erroneous ideology and is used by the State as a means for preserving and advancing this ideology"[896] (i.e., in such cases, the State has no authority to limit the religious freedom of its citizens, such as communist states). Thus, some conclusions that can be drawn from *Dignitatis Humanae* and the common good are: 1) *Dignitatis Humanae* implies a standard of criteria, the common good, that does distinguish between a proper public order and one based upon "an erroneous ideology;" 2) therefore, it alludes to the ability to distinguish between a proper religion and one that could be identified as "erroneous;" and 3) it proposes the proper public order is that which is based on the common good, as defined by the objective moral order, or, stated otherwise, it proposes the establishment of a Catholic society.

Establishes a Catholic Society

In view of *Dignitatis Humanae*'s influence in the United Nations and American public policy, it seems fair to raise the question, whether the language of the Document *allows* for a confessional state to develop that would also remain democratic and respect religious freedom guarantees?

---

[894] Cullen, 249.

[895] Ibid., 250.

[896] Pavan, Commentary, 74.

While Christopher Cullen, S. J., "is not advocating a confessional state," he does argue that *Dignitatis Humanae* does allow for one:

> The Church, of course, did not begin in 1965, and so I want to read *Dignitatis Humanae* mindful of the previous history and in the light of the *Catechism of the Catholic Church*, which is the most important doctrinal document on religious liberty since the Council. Hence, I am led to my current thesis: the decree of the Second Vatican Council on religious liberty, *Dignitatis Humanae*, does not preclude the possibility of a Catholic confessional state. There are two fundamental reasons why this is so. First, the document carefully avoids limiting the state to concern for mere public order. The council unambiguously affirmed that the state exists to insure the common good. The common good as understood in the Catholic tradition encompasses the virtuous life of the citizens, including the virtue of religion. Secondly, the document clearly teaches the obligatory nature of the truth. Those who have not found the truth are obliged in duty to seek it, and those who have found it are bound in duty to adhere to it. It is in this context, then, that the Council clearly presents religious liberty as a limited, not an absolute, right that must be set within due limits. Hence, the pursuit of, and adherence to, the truth allows the state in a Catholic society to defend and promote the truth of Jesus Christ and of the Catholic Church, while prescribing the right within appropriate limits. A confessional state in a predominantly Catholic society remains a perennial possibility.[897]

Relying upon the two arguments set forth above, Cullen develops his thesis by referring to certain conditional phrases used in *Dignitatis Humanae* that support a cogent defense of his thesis. If such a Catholic society should prevail as a result of a (re-) Christianization of society, what practical aspects could a citizen expect to find? Cullen is quite explicit in his delineation of characteristics of a Catholic society:

> A Catholic confessional state, without violating the religious freedom of its citizens, could re-introduce those

---

[897] Cullen, 243.

principles eliminated at the birth of the liberal state: the pursuit of virtue and the recognition of transcendence. A confessional state, therefore, could (1) recognize the truth of the Catholic faith in its state papers, i.e., in an official capacity, thereby attempting to shape civil society by orienting it to a transcendent meaning and purpose; (2) affirm the human vocation to live the virtuous life; (3) enact laws that are in accord with the natural law and that prudently inculcate the virtues, especially the virtue of religion, such as what the *Catechism* calls for, namely, the public and legal recognition of Sundays and feasts; (4) require that the head of government and/or head of state be Catholic; (5) respect and defend the freedom of the Church (*libertas ecclesiae*) which is so highly sought by *Dignitatis Humanae*; (6) actively support the works of the Church by various means, financial and otherwise (for example, a confessional state could support Catholic institutions that perform spiritual and corporal works of mercy, such as schools and hospitals); (7) shape the culture of such a society through education and censorship; and (8) secure and protect the borders from influences deemed detrimental to the common good. In short, the *cura ecclesiae* would fall within the competence of the state insofar as this affects civil society, that is, insofar as it affects the common good. The Church would work to sustain and foster the health of the body politic, without losing its own independence.[898]

Cullen's conclusions resonate with a long history of Catholic scholars who have advocated a religiously-oriented society as the basis of the common good. Referring to the historical context of the First Amendment religion clauses, Chester Antieau, Arthur Downey, and Edward Roberts attempt to argue that since Sunday laws, blasphemy laws, public funds to aid church schools, etc. were still practiced shortly after the ratification of the First Amendment, then those same practices should guide juridical deliberations regarding the application of the religion clauses in current American society.[899]

---

[898] Cullen, 253.

[899] Chester James Antieau, Arthur T. Downey, and Edward C. Roberts, "Chapter Eight: The Practices of the Times as Casting Light Upon the Meaning of the Establishment Clause of the First Amendment," in *Freedom from Federal*

The Political Nature of Dignitatis Humanae

With respect to the political nature of *Dignitatis Humanae*, there are three areas which demonstrate Catholic hegemony. Given that many areas of the world have developed democratic systems of governance, *Dignitatis Humanae* is suited to function in such a political climate. Its use of terms such as "constitutional order," "civil right to immunity," and "religious freedom" (albeit from a uniquely Catholic perspective) are appropriate terminology adapted to a constitutional democratic order. However, the danger of such terminology as contained within *Dignitatis Humanae* is that it blurs the distinction between modern documents on religious freedom founded upon Enlightenment thought, such as the UNDHR, Article 18, or the religion clauses of the First Amendment to the U. S. Constitution. These documents are not anchored to an objective Catholic moral order as that found in *Dignitatis Humanae*.

On the practical level, this danger becomes apparent when one observes the attempts by some Catholic scholars in America who try to equate the religious freedom guarantees of the First Amendment with the religious freedom propounded by *Dignitatis Humanae*. One example, previously noted, of the net effect of such confusion can be seen in the public debate regarding health care legislation under the Obama administration and how the USCCB has claimed it to be a violation of their freedom of conscience.

By declaring the right of the Church to carry forward its mission in the world without hindrance from government or any other organization, the Church unequivocally manifests her intent to dominate both social policy and religious arenas. From this perspective, *Dignitatis Humanae* has become a two-edged sword that the Church has wielded effectively to establish and protect its hegemony. The document has broad enough principles regarding religious freedom that it allows for a variety of applications based on the prevailing political and religious contexts within any given country. For example, one Catholic scholar observed,

> The Catholic Church is but one of a large number of religious groups competing for adherents and cooperating for common good in the United States, and there the

---

Establishment: Formation and Early History of the First Amendment Religion Clauses (Milwaukee, WI: The Bruce Publishing Company, 1964), 159-188; Christopher Cullen echoes these ideas when he quotes from the *Catechism of the Catholic Church*, no. 2188, "In respecting religious liberty and the common good of all, Christians should seek recognition of Sundays and the Church's holy days as legal holidays. They have to give everyone a public example of prayer, respect and joy and defend their traditions as a precious contribution to the spiritual life of society." Cullen, 252.

Church has often supported state policies to help religious minorities. In other countries, however, the Church has more of a monopoly power, and it has sought policies and laws to make it harder for religious minorities to proselytize.[900]

The analysis of *Dignitatis Humanae*'s impact in the countries of Spain and Mexico (chapters five and six) demonstrate the truth of this statement. In America, the USCCB cannot control freedom of the press, but in Spain, the Episcopal Committee of Spain (CEE) interpreted *Dignitatis Humanae* to broadly restrict Protestant (and other religions') proselytism activities. Another example of this statement is how R. Scott Appleby and John McGreevy, two professors from Notre Dame University (and the bishop of New York City) supported Muslims who were trying to build their mosque in New York City,[901] but in Spain, Muslims face unbending resistance from local and regional governments, as noted in Chapter Five.

A broad analysis of Catholic hegemony also includes consideration of "internal and external Church goals and politics," as Eric O. Hanson insightfully observes.[902] He further explains,

> Major conflicts between internal and external values occur when the Vatican and hierarchies face choices between the maintenance and strengthening of the ecclesiastical institution and the promotion of a consensus for Catholic values within society, such as advocacy of human rights in a totalitarian regime or denunciation of abortion. *Only in the defense of religious liberty do these values completely coincide*, though certain opportunities do appear for ecclesiastical actions that promote Catholic values and strengthen the church's organizational position in the society at the same time.[903]

---

[900] Paul Christopher Manuel, Lawrence C. Reardon, and Clyde Wilcox, eds., *The Catholic Church and the Nation-State* (Washington, DC: Georgetown University Press, 2006), 3.

[901] R. Scott Appleby and John T. McGreevy, "Catholics, Muslims and the Mosque Controversy," http://www.nybooks.com/blogs/nyrblog/2010/aug/27/catholics-muslims-mosque-controversy/ (accessed October 18, 2010).

[902] Eric O. Hanson, *The Catholic Church in World Politics* (Princeton, NJ: Princeton University Press, 1987), 13.

[903] Ibid., 13 (emphasis mine).

Hanson recognizes that the Church has at least two specific objectives regarding its hegemony: the ecclesiastical institution (or the Church's organizational position in society) and seeking to infuse society with Catholic values. Both of these objectives are achieved only through the promotion of religious liberty, since religious liberty aids the institutional nature of the Church by giving it recognition as an advocate for the religious rights of humanity and, in those countries where it lacks a significant, or no, presence, advocacy of religious liberty gives it entry into the society in consideration. On the level of disseminating Catholic social values until a consensus of the same is achieved within a given society, as Hanson points out, the advocacy of religious liberty facilitates this because it allows the Church to challenge non-Catholic social values, even within totalitarian regimes, under the argument of freedom of conscience as a part of religious freedom. Thus, *Dignitatis Humanae* achieves precisely this two-fold objective of promoting the public face of the Church as an advocate of the religious rights of all, and at the same time providing it with the very means of penetrating society with its social values. By this two-fold approach, the Church certainly achieves both political and religious hegemony.

The "Times" of Dignitatis Humanae

From conclusions reached in chapter four, the "times" of *Dignitatis Humanae* reveal that it is a document whose principles were written for a specific time, primarily one in which the Church needed to exercise its *libertas ecclesia* (freedom of the Church) to fulfill its mission. Many Catholic scholars – Congar, Hittinger, Cullen, *et al.* – indicate that it was not formulated for a future societal construct in which society may be successfully (re-) Christianized. This poses the concern of uncertainty regarding religious freedom guarantees in the future since a new document would need to be formulated. Additionally, the "times" of Church history alluded to within *Dignitatis Humanae* have been contradictory to one another. Reference is made to periods of time when the Church persecuted those differing with her beliefs, and now, under the prevailing concern for human rights, the Church produces this Document on Religious Freedom. Combining these two elements – no fixed principles for future religious freedom in a (Catholic) Christianized society and contradictory actions by the Church during her history – leave one dubious of the Church's intentions when the "times" should change to favor Christianity. From this viewpoint, it leaves open the possibility of coercive measures being used in a future "time" when political exigencies should change.

The Unchanging Nature of Catholic Hegemony

Regarding the Church and its relations with other Christian groups, C. F. Pauwels addressed the problem of ecumenical theology and conversions to the Catholic Church. He began by citing a statement from Karl Rahner, S. J., "'If this Catholic desire for converts is judged to be something unecumenical, non-Catholics have to understand that this 'will to proselytize' is founded in the claim of absoluteness of the Catholic Church.'"[904] Pauwels then explains in the next four pages several reasons why non-Catholic Christians reasonably could reject the Church's call to conversion (i.e., right to proselytize) and then concludes:

> But the main point is this: the Catholic Church is always the *Catholica*, and, even when showing not only wonderful signs of divine origin and nature, but also painful signs of her human weakness, is always recognizable as the *Catholica*. She is, therefore, always rightly claiming to be acknowledged as the *Catholica* and always rightly calling for conversion to her. The work of the Holy Spirit in the souls of non-Catholic Christians can always bring about real conversions and justified conversions, even when all the members of the World Council of Churches would call them the 'results of a bad proselytism.'[905]

Such statements by Rahner and Pauwels underscore the hegemonic nature of the Church, in spite of much ecumenical dialogue and reference to the religious freedom of all.

Hegemony calls into question the nature of the contending parties: the Catholic Church and all other religions. What are their origins and what claims do they sustain? Pietro Pavan, commenting on the reciprocal right to immunity from coercion for the individual as well as for the community of believers, stresses that this clause was added to *Dignitatis Humanae* in order to distinguish between all other religions as the product of man's social nature, whereas the Catholic Church "differs in origin from all other religious communities. . . . Nevertheless the Catholic Church is a divine

---

[904] Karl Rahner, "Einige Bemerkungen uber die Frage der Konversionen," *Catholica*, Vierteljahresschrift fur Kontrovers-Theologie, XVI (1962), I, pp. 1/19, as cited by C. F. Pauwels, "Ecumenical Theology and Conversions: Genesis of a Problem: Proselytism vs. Ecumenical Fellowship," in *Vatican II: The Theological Dimension*, ed. Anthony D. Lee (USA: The Thomist Press, 1963), 584.

[905] Pauwels, "Ecumenical Theology and Conversions," 588-589.

foundation: it was established by Christ and is the only true religion (cf. Article 13)."[906]

Areas for Future Research

Perhaps the most fascinating area for future research resulting from this book is the idea of hybrid church-state models. Historically, church-state models consist of theocratic, confessional state, separationist (or secular state), and the lay state (anti-clerical, or even anti-religious). Through the unique concepts found in *Dignitatis Humanae*, such as government advancing religion, the preeminent role of the Catholic Church, and religious freedom defined as "immunity from coercion," which is to become a civil right, hybrid church-state models are produced such as those examined in this book, viz., in Spain and in Mexico. In Spain, the state is not confessional, but neither is it a wholly secular state. Government aids, to some extent, all religions, but the Church retains a preeminent role that includes concordatory privileges. In Mexico, the Church has sought to obtain concordatory privileges, but due to the Law of Religious Associations, the Church is treated on an equal par with all other religions and is granted an Agreement. All religions have the benefit of more religious freedom than what existed under the 1917 Constitution, resulting in a fostering of religious pluralism. In other countries where the Church has a presence, examination of the intricacies of the church-state model prevailing, and viewed through the analysis provided by this book, can result in identifying a variety of other church-state models.

A second area for future research that could prove to be very enlightening is to do a comparative analysis of the application of *Dignitatis Humanae* made by the Bishops from differing countries in response to existing societal conditions. In some cases, it may be due to a religious factor, or lack thereof, that elicits a particular response. In other cases, it may be certain political factors that cause the Bishops to aid in the efforts to establish a democratic system of governance, as in Spain a decade before Franco's death. By comparing how *Dignitatis Humanae* is applied from country to country, research results can become an accurate tool to predict the long-term, global goals of the Church and how it is progressing toward achieving them. It can also serve as a template to predict the future outcome of situations particular to the countries being studied when compared with countries that have similar research results.

---

[906] Pietro Pavan, "Declaration on Religious Freedom," in *Commentary on the Documents of Vatican II*, ed. Herbert Vorgrimler, 5 vols. (New York: Crossroad Publishing Co., 1969), 4:70.

Conclusion

This book has analyzed the Document on Religious Freedom, *Dignitatis Humanae*, promulgated by the Roman Catholic Church at the Second Vatican Council, 1965, from the thesis of Catholic hegemony which states,

> the Catholic Church applies *Dignitatis Humanae* in different ways, depending upon extant political and religious conditions in a given country – in some cases to maintain its hegemony, and in others, to establish its hegemony over time. Hegemony, as used here, does not refer to singular dominance, as demonstrated by the Church during the medieval era. Rather, it refers to the Church seeking and maintaining a place of preeminence among other religious groups within a pluralistic society founded upon a constitutional democracy.

Based on the foregoing seven points, which are a summary evaluation of *Dignitatis Humanae* as analyzed in this book, the suggestion is posited that the thesis of Catholic hegemony is found to be an accurate evaluation.

Catholic Hegemony, Dignitatis Humanae, *and the Future of Religious Freedom*

The future of religious freedom under *Dignitatis Humanae* is quite complex. Since it is a political document adapted to constitutional democratic ideas, as democracy progresses so does the possibility of Catholic hegemony. The most uncertain political factor is whether the Church can instill a "regulated democracy" through means of public debate regarding social policies. If successful, the Christian (Catholic?) conscience of the laity will manifest itself through public laws.

In America, this has yet to be resolved to the satisfaction of the Vatican. American democracy is well enough established, and broadly formulated philosophically, that it tends to distill competing ideologies. Nonetheless, areas of concern arise in light of historic revisionism regarding such foundational concepts as religious liberty under the First Amendment clauses – whether the Founding Fathers espoused a "benevolent neutrality," with tendencies toward separationism, or whether they favored a robust promotion of religion in the public square that endorses accommodationism. Currently, the latter position seems to be making headway in America, despite the efforts of civil libertarians and constitutional theorists to the contrary. Through careful analysis, the morphing from a separationist model to an accommodationist model patterns a Catholic concept of religious freedom as presented in *Dignitatis Humanae*. "Non-preferentialism," whereby government pro-actively supports all religions, may not prove to be the most irenic solution to the ordering of civil society, especially if one, or more, religious groups has tendencies to hegemony.

In other countries, such as those examined herein, the establishment of democracy depends greatly upon its foundational character at the time it is implemented, much like the DNA of genes determine the body produced. As noted in Spain, the Catholic leadership there became part of the constitutional order with future consequences that are still being debated and hammered out today in public policy. In a constitutional democracy, the ethos of the people themselves becomes the greatest determining factor regarding the direction of the country. From this perspective, one can certainly expect the battlefield to focus upon Catholic efforts to re-evangelize[907] the country *from a societal perspective*. By means of public debate, facilitating more educational efforts, and attempting to reposition the Church as a benefactor to society, will all aid in the Church's efforts to reestablish itself in society. Initially, the Church may have to focus its efforts on regional gains, as opposed to nationwide ones. As demonstrated by the U.S. Department of State report, there is still much of a Catholic sentiment among the Spanish populace, most notably in rural areas where non-Catholic religions have not made as much inroads.

The future configuration of church-state relations under *Dignitatis Humanae*, in conjunction with counsel from *Gaudium et spes*, *Ad gentes*, and *Nostrae aetate*, anticipates the advancement of a Catholic notion of religious freedom whereby all religions are promoted in the public square, united upon a common social agenda, and thereby presenting a united front against secularism and any atheistic tendencies.[908] The net effect will be to produce a religious society with the Catholic Church *seeking* (but not always obtaining), not a dominant or monolithic position, but a preeminent role among the religious groups. The nuanced organizational structure of this formation will vary from country to country based upon several factors, such as: 1) the constitutional order – whether the Church is recognized in the constitution or not; whether the constitution maintains a separationist approach to church-state relations, how deeply embedded philosophical

---

[907] Documentation Information Catholiques Internationales, "Pope Benedict XVI encourages the new evangelization," October 15, 2011, http://www.dici.org/en/news/benedict-xvi-encourages-the-new-evangelization/, (accessed June 1, 2012).

[908] Daniel P. Payne and Jennifer M. Kent, ""An Alliance of the Sacred: Prospects for a Catholic-Orthodox Partnership against Secularism in Europe," *Journal of Ecumenical Studies* Wntr, 2011.

concepts of democracy have become in the body politic, etc., 2) the ethos of the people in a given country – whether they are more communal, or have tendencies toward individualism, and 3) the dominant religion that is part of the cultural history of the country, or region.

The final factor to consider regarding the future of religious freedom under *Dignitatis Humanae* is, how hegemonic is the Catholic Church? Does the Church have internal governance that tends to self-restraint, equality, and fairness toward other religions *even when political or societal factors would favor its hegemony*? The history of the Church's actions in Spain, by restricting proselytism of other religions; in Croatia, by passage of a Sunday law that burdens the religious freedom of Sabbatarians; in Mexico, by seeking political dominance; in America, by clamoring for government financial support of religious education and charitable relief work, not to mention seeking to guide public policy by Catholic moral theology; in the Philippines, by seeking to impose principles of *Humanae vitae* upon non-Catholics; and globally, by advancing a form of religious freedom through *Dignitatis Humanae* that in reality contains uniquely-tailored concepts of Catholic religious freedom which advance the Church's public image as well as its institutional policies, all seem to indicate the Church operates with tendencies to hegemony, rather than the contrary. The legacy of *Dignitatis Humanae*, as recorded in the pages of this book, and as analyzed by a non-Catholic relying primarily upon Catholic authors, provides guiding principles for those who are ever vigilant to maintain religious freedom and freedom of conscience.

APPENDIX A

DECLARATION ON RELIGIOUS FREEDOM[909]

Dignitatis Humanae

Promulgated By His Holiness, Pope Paul VI On December 7, 1965

1. A sense of the dignity of the human person has been impressing itself more and more deeply on the consciousness of contemporary man,[1] and the demand is increasingly made that men should act on their own judgment, enjoying and making use of a responsible freedom, not driven by coercion but motivated by a sense of duty. The demand is likewise made that constitutional limits should be set to the powers of government, in order that there may be no encroachment on the rightful freedom of the person and of associations. This demand for freedom in human society chiefly regards the quest for the values proper to the human spirit. It regards, in the first place, the free exercise of religion in society. This Vatican Council takes careful note of these desires in the minds of men. It proposes to declare them to be greatly in accord with truth and justice. To this end, it searches into the sacred tradition and doctrine of the Church--the treasury out of which the

---

[909] The entire text of *Dignitatis Humanae* comes from *The Declaration on Religious Freedom of Vatican Council II: The Text and Commentary* by Enda McDonagh (London: Darton, Longman & Todd, 1967), 13-32. One may access it online as well at http://www.vatican.va/archive/hist_councils/ii_vatican_council/documents/vat-ii_decl_19651207_dignitatis-humanae_en.html (accessed November 1, 2012).

Church continually brings forth new things that are in harmony with the things that are old.

First, the council professes its belief that God Himself has made known to mankind the way in which men are to serve Him, and thus be saved in Christ and come to blessedness. We believe that this one true religion subsists in the Catholic and Apostolic Church, to which the Lord Jesus committed the duty of spreading it abroad among all men. Thus He spoke to the Apostles: "Go, therefore, and make disciples of all nations, baptizing them in the name of the Father and of the Son and of the Holy Spirit, teaching them to observe all things whatsoever I have enjoined upon you" (Matt. 28: 19-20). On their part, all men are bound to seek the truth, especially in what concerns God and His Church, and to embrace the truth they come to know, and to hold fast to it.

This Vatican Council likewise professes its belief that it is upon the human conscience that these obligations fall and exert their binding force. The truth cannot impose itself except by virtue of its own truth, as it makes its entrance into the mind at once quietly and with power.

Religious freedom, in turn, which men demand as necessary to fulfill their duty to worship God, has to do with immunity from coercion in civil society. Therefore it leaves untouched traditional Catholic doctrine on the moral duty of men and societies toward the true religion and toward the one Church of Christ.

Over and above all this, the council intends to develop the doctrine of recent popes on the inviolable rights of the human person and the constitutional order of society.

2. This Vatican Council declares that the human person has a right to religious freedom. This freedom means that all men are to be immune from coercion on the part of individuals or of social groups and of any human power, in such wise that no one is to be forced to act in a manner contrary to his own beliefs, whether privately or publicly, whether alone or in association with others within due limits.

The council further declares that the right to religious freedom has its foundation in the very dignity of the human person as this dignity is known through the revealed word of God and by reason itself.[2] This right of the human person to religious freedom is to be recognized in the constitutional law whereby society is governed and thus it is to become a civil right.

It is in accordance with their dignity as persons--that is, beings endowed with reason and free will and therefore privileged to bear personal responsibility--that all men should be at once impelled by nature and also bound by a moral obligation to seek the truth, especially religious truth. They are also bound to adhere to the truth, once it is known, and to order their whole lives in accord with the demands of truth. However, men cannot discharge these obligations in a manner in keeping with their own nature unless they enjoy immunity from external coercion as well as psychological freedom. Therefore the right to religious freedom has its foundation not in the subjective disposition of the person, but in his very nature. In consequence, the right to this immunity continues to exist even in those who do not live up to their obligation of seeking the truth and adhering to it and the exercise of this right is not to be impeded, provided that just public order be observed.

3. Further light is shed on the subject if one considers that the highest norm of human life is the divine law--eternal, objective and universal--whereby God orders, directs and governs the entire universe and all the ways of the human community by a plan conceived in wisdom and love. Man has been made by God to participate in this law, with the result that, under the gentle disposition of divine Providence, he can come to perceive ever more fully the truth that is unchanging. Wherefore every man has the duty, and therefore the right, to seek the truth in matters religious in order that he may with prudence form for himself right and true judgments of conscience, under use of all suitable means.

Truth, however, is to be sought after in a manner proper to the dignity of the human person and his social nature. The inquiry is to be free, carried on with the aid of teaching or instruction, communication and dialogue, in the course of which men explain to one another the truth they have discovered, or think they have discovered, in order thus to assist one another in the quest for truth.

Moreover, as the truth is discovered, it is by a personal assent that men are to adhere to it.

On his part, man perceives and acknowledges the imperatives of the divine law through the mediation of conscience. In all his activity a man is bound to follow his conscience in order that he may come to God, the end and purpose of life. It follows that he is not to be forced to act in a manner contrary to his conscience. Nor, on the other hand, is he to be restrained from acting in accordance with his conscience, especially in matters religious. The reason is that the exercise of religion, of its very nature, consists before all else in those internal, voluntary and free acts whereby man sets the course of his life directly toward God. No merely human power can either command or prohibit acts of this kind.[3] The social nature of man, however, itself requires that he should give external expression to his internal acts of religion: that he should share with others in matters religious; that he should profess his religion in community. Injury therefore is done to the human person and to the very order established by God for human life, if the free exercise of religion is denied in society, provided just public order is observed.

There is a further consideration. The religious acts whereby men, in private and in public and out of a sense of personal conviction, direct their lives to God transcend by their very nature the order of terrestrial and temporal affairs. Government therefore ought indeed to take account of the religious life of the citizenry and show it favor, since the function of government is to make provision for the common welfare. However, it would clearly transgress the limits set to its power, were it to presume to command or inhibit acts that are religious.

4. The freedom or immunity from coercion in matters religious which is the endowment of persons as individuals is also to be recognized as their right when they act in community. Religious communities are a requirement of the social nature both of man and of religion itself.

Provided the just demands of public order are observed, religious communities rightfully claim freedom in order that they may govern themselves according to their own norms, honor the Supreme Being in public worship, assist their members in the practice of the religious life, strengthen them by instruction, and promote institutions in which they may join together for the purpose of ordering their own lives in accordance with their religious principles.

Religious communities also have the right not to be hindered, either by legal measures or by administrative action on the part of government, in the selection, training, appointment, and transferral of their own ministers, in communicating with religious authorities and communities abroad, in erecting buildings for religious purposes, and in the acquisition and use of suitable funds or properties.

Religious communities also have the right not to be hindered in their public teaching and witness to their faith, whether by the spoken or by the written word. However, in spreading religious faith and in introducing religious practices everyone ought at all times to refrain from any manner of action which might seem to carry a hint of coercion or of a kind of persuasion that would be dishonorable or unworthy, especially when dealing with poor or uneducated people. Such a manner of action would have to be considered an abuse of one's right and a violation of the right of others.

In addition, it comes within the meaning of religious freedom that religious communities should not be prohibited from freely undertaking to show the special value of their doctrine in what concerns the organization of society and the inspiration of the whole of human activity. Finally, the social nature of man and the very nature of religion afford the foundation of the right of men freely to hold meetings and to establish educational, cultural, charitable and social organizations, under the impulse of their own religious sense.

5. The family, since it is a society in its own original right, has the right freely to live its own domestic religious life under the guidance of parents. Parents, moreover, have the right to determine, in accordance with their own religious beliefs, the kind of religious education that their children are to receive. Government, in consequence, must acknowledge the right of parents to make a genuinely free choice of schools and of other means of education, and the use of this freedom of choice is not to be made a reason for imposing unjust burdens on parents, whether directly or indirectly. Besides, the right of parents are violated, if their children are forced to attend lessons or instructions which are not in agreement with their religious beliefs, or if a single system of education, from which all religious formation is excluded, is imposed upon all.

6. Since the common welfare of society consists in the entirety of those conditions of social life under which men enjoy the possibility of achieving their own perfection in a certain fullness of measure and also with some relative ease, it chiefly consists in the protection of the rights, and in the performance of the duties, of the human person.[4] Therefore the care of the right to religious freedom devolves upon the whole citizenry, upon social groups, upon government, and upon the

Church and other religious communities, in virtue of the duty of all toward the common welfare, and in the manner proper to each.

The protection and promotion of the inviolable rights of man ranks among the essential duties of government.[5] Therefore government is to assume the safeguard of the religious freedom of all its citizens, in an effective manner, by just laws and by other appropriate means.

Government is also to help create conditions favorable to the fostering of religious life, in order that the people may be truly enabled to exercise their religious rights and to fulfill their religious duties, and also in order that society itself may profit by the moral qualities of justice and peace which have their origin in men's faithfulness to God and to His holy will.[6]

If, in view of peculiar circumstances obtaining among peoples, special civil recognition is given to one religious community in the constitutional order of society, it is at the same time imperative that the right of all citizens and religious communities to religious freedom should be recognized and made effective in practice.

Finally, government is to see to it that equality of citizens before the law, which is itself an element of the common good, is never violated, whether openly or covertly, for religious reasons. Nor is there to be discrimination among citizens.

It follows that a wrong is done when government imposes upon its people, by force or fear or other means, the profession or repudiation of any religion, or when it hinders men from joining or leaving a religious community. All the more is it a violation of the will of God and of the sacred rights of the person and the family of nations when force is brought to bear in any way in order to destroy or repress religion, either in the whole of mankind or in a particular country or in a definite community.

7. The right to religious freedom is exercised in human society: hence its exercise is subject to certain regulatory norms. In the use of all freedoms the moral principle of personal and social responsibility is to be observed. In the exercise of their rights, individual men and social groups are bound by the moral law to have respect both for the rights of others and for their own duties toward others and for the common

welfare of all. Men are to deal with their fellows in justice and civility.

Furthermore, society has the right to defend itself against possible abuses committed on the pretext of freedom of religion. It is the special duty of government to provide this protection. However, government is not to act in an arbitrary fashion or in an unfair spirit of partisanship. Its action is to be controlled by juridical norms which are in conformity with the objective moral order. These norms arise out of the need for the effective safeguard of the rights of all citizens and for the peaceful settlement of conflicts of rights, also out of the need for an adequate care of genuine public peace, which comes about when men live together in good order and in true justice, and finally out of the need for a proper guardianship of public morality.

These matters constitute the basic component of the common welfare: they are what is meant by public order. For the rest, the usages of society are to be the usages of freedom in their full range: that is, the freedom of man is to be respected as far as possible and is not to be curtailed except when and insofar as necessary.

8. Many pressures are brought to bear upon the men of our day, to the point where the danger arises lest they lose the possibility of acting on their own judgment. On the other hand, not a few can be found who seem inclined to use the name of freedom as the pretext for refusing to submit to authority and for making light of the duty of obedience. Wherefore this Vatican Council urges everyone, especially those who are charged with the task of educating others, to do their utmost to form men who, on the one hand, will respect the moral order and be obedient to lawful authority, and, on the other hand, will be lovers of true freedom--men, in other words, who will come to decisions on their own judgment and in the light of truth, govern their activities with a sense of responsibility, and strive after what is true and right, willing always to join with others in cooperative effort.

Religious freedom therefore ought to have this further purpose and aim, namely, that men may come to act with greater responsibility in fulfilling their duties in community life.

9. The declaration of this Vatican Council on the right of man to religious freedom has its foundation in the dignity of the person, whose exigencies have come to be more fully known to human reason through centuries of experience. What is more, this doctrine of freedom has

roots in divine revelation, and for this reason Christians are bound to respect it all the more conscientiously. Revelation does not indeed affirm in so many words the right of man to immunity from external coercion in matters religious. It does, however, disclose the dignity of the human person in its full dimensions. It gives evidence of the respect which Christ showed toward the freedom with which man is to fulfill his duty of belief in the word of God and it gives us lessons in the spirit which disciples of such a Master ought to adopt and continually follow. Thus further light is cast upon the general principles upon which the doctrine of this declaration on religious freedom is based. In particular, religious freedom in society is entirely consonant with the freedom of the act of Christian faith.

10. It is one of the major tenets of Catholic doctrine that man's response to God in faith must be free: no one therefore is to be forced to embrace the Christian faith against his own will.[8] This doctrine is contained in the word of God and it was constantly proclaimed by the Fathers of the Church.[7] The act of faith is of its very nature a free act. Man, redeemed by Christ the Savior and through Christ Jesus called to be God's adopted son,[9] cannot give his adherence to God revealing Himself unless, under the drawing of the Father,[10] he offers to God the reasonable and free submission of faith. It is therefore completely in accord with the nature of faith that in matters religious every manner of coercion on the part of men should be excluded. In consequence, the principle of religious freedom makes no small contribution to the creation of an environment in which men can without hindrance be invited to the Christian faith, embrace it of their own free will, and profess it effectively in their whole manner of life.

11. God calls men to serve Him in spirit and in truth, hence they are bound in conscience but they stand under no compulsion. God has regard for the dignity of the human person whom He Himself created and man is to be guided by his own judgment and he is to enjoy freedom. This truth appears at its height in Christ Jesus, in whom God manifested Himself and His ways with men. Christ is at once our Master and our Lord[11] and also meek and humble of heart.[12] In attracting and inviting His disciples He used patience.[13] He wrought miracles to illuminate His teaching and to establish its truth, but His intention was to rouse faith in His hearers and to confirm them in faith, not to exert coercion upon them.[14] He did indeed denounce the unbelief of some who listened to Him, but He left vengeance to God in expectation of the day of judgment.[15] When He sent His Apostles

into the world, He said to them: "He who believes and is baptized will be saved. He who does not believe will be condemned" (Mark 16:16). But He Himself, noting that the cockle had been sown amid the wheat, gave orders that both should be allowed to grow until the harvest time, which will come at the end of the world.[16] He refused to be a political messiah, ruling by force:[17] He preferred to call Himself the Son of Man, who came "to serve and to give his life as a ransom for the many" (Mark 10:45). He showed Himself the perfect servant of God,[18] who "does not break the bruised reed nor extinguish the smoking flax" (Matt. 12:20).

He acknowledged the power of government and its rights, when He commanded that tribute be given to Caesar: but He gave clear warning that the higher rights of God are to be kept inviolate: "Render to Caesar the things that are Caesar's and to God the things that are God's" (Matt. 22:21). In the end, when He completed on the cross the work of redemption whereby He achieved salvation and true freedom for men,

He brought His revelation to completion. For He bore witness to the truth,[19] but He refused to impose the truth by force on those who spoke against it. Not by force of blows does His will assert its claims.[20] It is established by witnessing to the truth and by hearing the truth, and it extends its dominion by the love whereby Christ, lifted up on the cross, draws all men to Himself.[21]

Taught by the word and example of Christ, the Apostles followed the same way. From the very origins of the Church the disciples of Christ strove to convert men to faith in Christ as the Lord; not, however, by the use of coercion or of devices unworthy of the Gospel, but by the power, above all, of the word of God.[22] Steadfastly they proclaimed to all the plan of God our Savior, "who wills that all men should be saved and come to the acknowledgment of the truth" (1 Tim. 2:4). At the same time, however, they showed respect for those of weaker stuff, even though they were in error, and thus they made it plain that "each one of us is to render to God an account of himself" (Romans 14:12),[23] and for that reason is bound to obey his conscience. Like Christ Himself, the Apostles were unceasingly bent upon bearing witness to the truth of God, and they showed the fullest measure of boldness in "speaking the word with confidence" (Acts 4:31)[24] before the people and their rulers. With a firm faith they held that the Gospel is indeed the power of God unto salvation for all who believe.[25] Therefore they rejected all "carnal weapons"[26] they followed the example of the gentleness and respectfulness of Christ and they preached the word of God in the full confidence that there was resident in this word itself a divine power able to destroy all the forces arrayed against God[27] and bring men to faith in Christ and to His service.[28] As the Master, so too the Apostles recognized legitimate civil authority. "For there is no power except from God," the Apostle teaches, and thereafter commands: "Let everyone be subject to higher authorities.... He who resists authority resists God's ordinance" (Romans 13:1-5).[29] At the same time, however, they did not hesitate to speak out against governing powers which set themselves in opposition to the holy will of God: "It is necessary to obey God rather than men" (Acts 5:29).[30] This is the way along which the martyrs and other faithful have walked through all ages and over all the earth.

12. In faithfulness therefore to the truth of the Gospel, the Church is following the way of Christ and the apostles when she recognizes and gives support to the principle of religious freedom as befitting the dignity of man and as being in accord with divine revelation. Throughout the ages the Church has kept safe and handed on the doctrine received from the Master and from the apostles. In the life of the People of God, as it has made its pilgrim way through the vicissitudes of human history, there has at times appeared a way of acting that was hardly in accord with the spirit of the Gospel or even opposed to it. Nevertheless, the doctrine of the Church that no one is to be coerced into faith has always stood firm.

Thus the leaven of the Gospel has long been about its quiet work in the minds of men, and to it is due in great measure the fact that in the course of time men have come more widely to recognize their dignity as persons, and the conviction has grown stronger that the person in society is to be kept free from all manner of coercion in matters religious.

13. Among the things that concern the good of the Church and indeed the welfare of society here on earth-- things therefore that are always and everywhere to be kept secure and defended against all injury--this certainly is preeminent, namely, that the Church should enjoy that full measure of freedom which her care for the salvation of men requires.[31] This is a sacred freedom, because the only-begotten Son endowed with it the Church which He purchased with His blood. Indeed it is so much the property of the Church that to act against it is to act against the will of God. The freedom of the Church is the

fundamental principle in what concerns the relations between the Church and governments and the whole civil order.

In human society and in the face of government the Church claims freedom for herself in her character as a spiritual authority, established by Christ the Lord, upon which there rests, by divine mandate, the duty of going out into the whole world and preaching the Gospel to every creature.[32] The Church also claims freedom for herself in her character as a society of men who have the right to live in society in accordance with the precepts of Christian faith.[33]

In turn, where the principle of religious freedom is not only proclaimed in words or simply incorporated in law but also given sincere and practical application, there the Church succeeds in achieving a stable situation of right as well as of fact and the independence which is necessary for the fulfillment of her divine mission.

This independence is precisely what the authorities of the Church claim in society.[34] At the same time, the Christian faithful, in common with all other men, possess the civil right not to be hindered in leading their lives in accordance with their consciences. Therefore, a harmony exists between the freedom of the Church and the religious freedom which is to be recognized as the right of all men and communities and sanctioned by constitutional law.

14. In order to be faithful to the divine command, "teach all nations" (Matt. 28:19-20), the Catholic Church must work with all urgency and concern "that the word of God be spread abroad and glorified" (2 Thess. 3:1). Hence the Church earnestly begs of its children that, "first of all, supplications, prayers, petitions, acts of thanksgiving be made for all men.... For this is good and agreeable in the sight of God our Savior, who wills that all men be saved and come to the knowledge of the truth" (1 Tim. 2:1-4). In the formation of their consciences, the Christian faithful ought carefully to attend to the sacred and certain doctrine of the Church.[35] For the Church is, by the will of Christ, the teacher of the truth. It is her duty to give utterance to, and authoritatively to teach, that truth which is Christ Himself, and also to declare and confirm by her authority those principles of the moral order which have their origins in human nature itself. Furthermore, let Christians walk in wisdom in the face of those outside, "in the Holy Spirit, in unaffected love, in the word of truth" (2 Cor. 6:6-7), and let them be about their task of spreading the light of life with all

confidence [36] and apostolic courage, even to the shedding of their blood.

The disciple is bound by a grave obligation toward Christ, his Master, ever more fully to understand the truth received from Him, faithfully to proclaim it, and vigorously to defend it, never--be it understood--having recourse to means that are incompatible with the spirit of the Gospel. At the same time, the charity of Christ urges him to love and have prudence and patience in his dealings with those who are in error or in ignorance with regard to the faith.[37] All is to be taken into account-- the Christian duty to Christ, the life-giving word which must be proclaimed, the rights of the human person, and the measure of grace granted by God through Christ to men who are invited freely to accept and profess the faith.

15. The fact is that men of the present day want to be able freely to profess their religion in private and in public. Indeed, religious freedom has already been declared to be a civil right in most constitutions, and it is solemnly recognized in international documents.[38] The further fact is that forms of government still exist under which, even though freedom of religious worship receives constitutional recognition, the powers of government are engaged in the effort to deter citizens from the profession of religion and to make life very difficult and dangerous for religious communities.

This council greets with joy the first of these two facts as among the signs of the times. With sorrow, however, it denounces the other fact, as only to be deplored. The council exhorts Catholics, and it directs a plea to all men, most carefully to consider how greatly necessary religious freedom is, especially in the present condition of the human family. All nations are coming into even closer unity. Men of different cultures and religions are being brought together in closer relationships. There is a growing consciousness of the personal responsibility that every man has. All this is evident. Consequently, in order that relationships of peace and harmony be established and maintained within the whole of mankind, it is necessary that religious freedom be everywhere provided with an effective constitutional guarantee and that respect be shown for the high duty and right of man freely to lead his religious life in society.

May the God and Father of all grant that the human family, through careful observance of the principle of religious freedom in society, may be brought by the grace of Christ and the power of the Holy Spirit to the sublime and unending and "glorious freedom of the sons of God" (Rom. 8:21).

Each and every one of the things set forth in this Declaration has won the consent of the Fathers of this most sacred Council. We too, by the apostolic authority conferred on us by Christ, join with the Venerable Fathers in approving, decreeing, and establishing these things in the Holy Spirit, and we direct that what has thus been enacted in synod be published to God's glory.

Rome, at St. Peter's, 7 December 1965

I, Paul, Bishop of the Catholic Church

There follow the signatures of the Fathers.

ENDNOTES

1. Cf. John XXIII, encycl. "Pacem in Terris," April 11, 1963: AAS 55 (1963) p. 279; ibid., p. 265; Pius XII, radio message, Dec. 24, 1944: AAS 37 (1945),pg. 14.

2. Cf. John XXIII, encycl. "Pacem in Terris," April 11, 1963: AAS 55 (1963), pp. 260-261; Pius XII, radio message, Dec. 24, 1942: AAS 35 (1943) p. 19; Pius XI, encycl. "Mit Brennender Sorge," March 14, 193i: AAS 29 (1937), p. 160- Leo XIII, encycl. "Libertas Praestantissimum," June 20, 1888: Acts of Leo XIII 8 (1888), pp. 237-238.

3. Cf. John XXIII, encycl. "Pacem in Terris," April 11, 1963: AAS 55 (1963), p. 270- Paul VI, radio message, Dec. 22, 1964: AAS 57 (1965), Pp. 181-182.

4. Cf. John XXIII, encycl. "Mater et Magistra," May 15, 1961: AAS 53 (1961), p. 417; idem, encycl. "Pacem in Terris," April 11, 1963: AAS 55 (1963), p. 273.

5. Cf. John XXIII, encycl. "Pacem in Terris," April 11, 1963: AAS 55 (1963) pp. 273-274; Pius XII, radio message, June 1, 1941: AAS 33 (1941),pg. 200.

6. Cf. Leo XIII, encycl. "Immortale Dei," Nov. 1, 1885: AAS 18 (1885) n. 161.

7. Cf. Lactantius "Divinarum Institutionum," Book V, 19: CSEL 19, pp. 463464, 465: PL 6, 614 and 616 (ch. 20); St. Ambrose, "Epistola ad Valentianum Imp.," Letter 21: PL 16, 1005; St. Augustine, "Contra Litteras Petiliani," Book II, ch. 83: CSEL 52 p. 112: PL 43, 315; cf. C. 23, q. 5, c. 33, (ed. Friedberg, col. 939); idem, Letter 23: PL 33, 98; idem, Letter 34: PL 33, 132; idem, Letter 35: PL 33, 135; St. Gregory the Great, "Epistola ad Virgilium et Theodorum Episcopos Massiliae Galliarum," Register of Letters I, 45: MGH Ep. 1, p. 72: PL 77, 510-511 (Book I, ep. 47); idem, "Epistola ad Johannem Episcopum Constantinopolitanum," Register of Letters, III, 52: MGH Letter 1, p. 210: PL 77, 649 (Book III, Letter 53), cf. D. 45, c. 1 (ed. Friedberg, col. 160); Council of Toledo IV, c. 57: Mansi 10, 633; cf. D. 45, c. 5 (ed. Friedberg, col. 161-162); Clement III: X., V, 6, 9: ed. Friedberg, col. 774; Innocent III, "Epistola ad Arelatensem Archiepiscopum," X., III, 42, 3: Friedberg, col. 646.

8. Cf. CIC, c. 1351- Pius XII, allocution to prelate auditors and other officials and administrators of the tribune of the Holy Roman Rota, Oct. 6, 1946: AAS 38 (1946), p. 394; idem. Encycl. "Mystici Corporis," June 29, 1943: AAS (1943) p. 243.

9. Cf. Eph. 1:5.

10. Cf. John 6:44.

11. Cf. John 13:13.

12. Cf. Matt. 11:29.

13. Cf. Matt. 11:28-30; John 6:67-68.

14. Cf. Matt. 9:28-29; Mark 9:23-24; 6:5-6; Paul VI, encycl. "Ecclesiam Suam," Aug. 6, 1964: AAS 56 (1964), pp. 642-643.

15. Cf. Matt. 11:20-24; Rom. 12:19-20; 2 Thess. 1:8.

16. Cf. Matt. 13:30 and 40-42.

17. Cf. Matt. 4:8-10; John 6:15.

18. Cf. Is. 42:1-4.

19. Cf. John 18:37.

20. Cf. Matt. 26:51-53; John 18:36.

21. Cf. John 12:32.

22. Cf. 1 Cor. 2:3-5; 1 Thess. 2:3-5.

23. Cf. Rom. 14:1-23; 1 Cor. 8:9-13; 10:23-33.

24. Cf. Eph. 6:19-20.

25. Cf. Rom. 1:16.

26. Cf. 2 Cor. 10:4; 1 Thess. 5:8-9.

27. Cf. Eph. 6:11-17.

28. Cf. 2 Cor. 10:3-5.

29. Cf. 1 Pet. 2:13-17.

30. Cf. Acts 4:19-20.

31. Cf. Leo XIII, letter "Officio Sanctissimo," Dec. 22, 1887: AAS 20 (1887), p. 269; idem, letter "Ex Litteris," April 7, 1887: AAS 19 (1886), p. 465.

32. Cf. Mark 16:15; Matt. 28:18-20; Pius XII, encycl. "Summi Pontificatus," Oct. 20, 1939: AAS 31 (1939). pp. 445-446.

33. Cf. Pius XI, letter "Firmissiman Constantiam," March 28, 1937: AAS 29 (1937), p. 196.

34. Cf. Pius XII, allocution, "Ci Riesce," Dec. 6, 1953: AAS 45 (1953), p. 802.

35. Cf. Pius XII, radio message, March 23, 1952: AAS 44 (1952) pp. 270-278.

36. Cf. Acts 4:29.

37. Cf. John XXIII, encycl. "Pacem in Terris (1963), April 11, 1963:AAS 55pp. 299-300.

38. Cf. John XXIII, encycl. "Pacem in Terris," April 11, 1963: AAS 55 (1963) pp. 295-296.

APPENDIX B

This appendix examines briefly conditions prevailing in some other countries with a Catholic majority in order to perform a comparative analysis. Balázs Schanda, Senior Counselor at the Constitutional Court and Lecturer of the Pázmány Péter Catholic University, Republic of Hungary, describes church-state relations among the new member states of the European Union, which are the countries of Cyprus, the Czech Republic, Estonia, Hungary, Latvia, Lithuania, Malta, Poland (only one of the ten with a true Concordat), Slovakia, and Slovenia. He mentions that there are usually two objections to concordats (or, bilateral relations, known as treaties): 1) such settlements or agreements limit the sovereignty of the state, and 2) the privileges of the Catholic Church raises the danger of inequality between denominations.[910]

Schanda answers, "In my opinion, these objections do not hold." He explains why:

> First, international agreements do limit state sovereignty, but we have good reason to appreciate this, especially when human rights are in play. Practice disproves the second argument as well. A thorough survey of the content of recent agreements shows the Catholic Church does not seek exclusive rights in the agreements concluded with the states, especially not since the Second Vatican Council. Thus, concordats or other agreements with the Holy See may promote the issues of religious freedom for all.[911]

However, before one concludes that concordats, or even religious freedom as defined at Vatican II through *Dignitatis Humanae* promotes religious freedom equally, it is essential to enquire, what kind of conditions prevail

---

[910] Balázs Schanda, "Church and State in the New Member States of the European Union," *Fides et Libertas* (2004), 102, 103.

[911] Schanda, 102.

under that kind of religious freedom? Schanda goes on to describe the role of the Church in the nomination of its bishops, which one may concede in fairness is the proper arrangement to follow.

It is quite a different story in the area of education, however. Of these ten countries, Poland, Lithuania, and Slovakia are predominantly Catholic; Estonia has more Lutherans than Catholics; Hungary and Slovakia have Catholic majorities, with Calvinist and Lutheran minorities, respectively; and Latvia is divided between Lutherans and Catholics.[912] Bearing this in mind, what he reports regarding public education is quite astounding:

> Religious education *in public schools* is guaranteed by all the agreements. Primarily, the rights of the parents are recognized (in harmony with *Dignitatis Humanae*, art. 5, my insertion). *The program of teaching of Catholic religion* is conducted on the basis of a curriculum approved by the bishops' conference in agreement with the competent state authorities. In Poland, the ecclesiastical authority only has to let the competent civil authority know the program and the textbooks. . .
>
> Equal funding for church schools is granted in Hungary, Lithuania, and Slovakia; financial support is foreseen in Latvia, whereas in Poland the criteria of the subventions are to be determined by the civil laws.[913]

Schanda's report is quite revealing and presents several points that support the contention of this book, namely: 1) Catholic emphasis upon *Dignitatis Humanae* as an instrument to promote religious freedom is actually used to advance Catholicism where possible; 2) the extant situation among these countries regarding public education reflects exactly what is stipulated in *Dignitatis Humanae*, article five (regarding parents having the right to determine the education of their children and have the right not to be burdened to do so, i.e., the government should pay for it); and, 3) it reveals a very subtle form of Catholic hegemony, based on similar circumstances that prevailed at the time of the Diet of Speyer (1544), by which both Protestants and Catholics received public funds to support their education.[914]

---

[912] Schanda, 97.

[913] Ibid., 103 (italics mine).

[914] See under "Diet of Speyer II, 1529," in Chapter Three.

BIBLIOGRAPHY

Conscience in the New Testament

Aland, Kurt and others, eds. *The Greek New Testament.* Third corrected edition with Greek dictionary, Federal Republic of Germany: Biblia-Druck GmbH Stuttgart, 1983.

Austad, Torleiv. "Attitudes towards the state in Western theological thinking." *Themelios* 16, no. 1 (Oct/Nov 1990): 18-22.

Barton, Wayne. "The Christian Conscience in an Age of Crisis." *Southwestern Journal of Theology* 4, no. 2 (April, 1962): 93-111.

Bauer, Walter, William Arndt, Wilbur Gingrich. *A Greek-English Lexicon of the New Testament* 2nd ed. Chicago: Univ. of Chicago Press, 1979.

Berman, Harold J. "Conscience and Law: The Lutheran Reformation and the Western Legal Tradition." *The Journal of Law and Religion* 5, no. 1 (1987): 177-202.

Borghi, Ernesto. "La notion de conscience dans le Nouveau Testament." *Filologia Neotestamentaria* 10 (Mayo-Noviembre, 1997):85-98.

Boyer, Susan I. "Exegesis of Romans 13:1-7." *Brethren Life and Thought* 32, no. 4(Autumn 1987): 208-216.

Cook, Edwin. "Conscience in the New Testament." In *Journal of the Adventist Theological Society,* 15/1 (Spring 2004): 142–158. http://www.atsjats.org/publication_file.php?_id=12&journal=1&type=pdf.

———. "Parousia or Politics?" Section, "The Relationship Between Jews and Christians." In *Liberty*, Jan/Feb 2005. http://www.libertymagazine.org/index.php?id=1377 (accessed May 31, 2012).

Costigane, Helen. "A History of the Western Idea of Conscience." In *Conscience in World Religions*, ed. Jayne Hoose. Notre Dame, IN: University of Notre Dame Press, 1999.

Coulson, John. "The Authority of Conscience." *The Downside Review* 77, no. 248 (Spring, 1959): 141-158.

Dunn, James D. G. "Romans 13:1-7 – A Charter for Political Quietism?" *Ex Auditu* 2 (1986): 55-68.

Espy, John M. "Paul's 'Robust Conscience' Re-Examined." *New Testament Studies* 31(1985): 161-188.

Feinberg, Paul D. "The Christian and Civil Authorities." *The Master's Seminary Journal* 10, no.1 (Spring 1999): 87-99.

Fletcher, Joseph. "Concepts of Moral Responsibility." *The Journal of Pastoral Care* 6, no. 1 (Spring 1952): 39-45.

Gates, Larry. "Conscience as the Voice of God: A Jungian View." *Journal of Religion and Health* 31, no. 4 (Winter 1992): 281-286.

Glasser, John W. "Conscience and Superego: A Key Distinction." *Theological Studies* 32 (March 1971): 30-47.

Gooch, Paul W. "'Conscience' in 1 Corinthians 8 and 10." *New Testament Studies* 33, no. 2 (April 1987): 244-254.

Hallesby, O. *Conscience*. London: Inter-Varsity Fellowship, 1950.

Hodge, Charles. *Commentary on the Epistle to the Romans*. Revised edition, 1886; thirteenth printing, Grand Rapids: Eerdmans, 1977.

Kempson, J. Olbert. "Comments on Structure of the Conscience." *The Saint Luke's Journal of Theology* 4, no. 1 (Lent, 1961): 11-21.

Klauck, H. J. "Accuser, Judge, and Paraclete – On Conscience in Philo of Alexandria," *Skrif en Kerk* 20, no. 1 (1999): 107-118.

Knight, James A. "Conscience." *Union Seminary Quarterly Review*, 19 (Jan., 1964): 131-139.

Kodera, T. James. "Reshaping of Conscience: Religion, Education, and Multiculturalism." *Anglican Theological Review* 78, no. 3 (Summer 1996): 475-492.

Lee, Jeong Woo (James). "To every man's conscience in the sight of God." *Kerux: A Journal of Biblical-Theological Preaching* 15, no. 3 (Dec., 2000):10-18.

Lee, Page. "'Conscience' In Romans 13:5." *Faith and Mission* 8, no. 1 (Fall 1990): 85-93.

Marietta, Jr., Don E. "Conscience in Greek Stoicism." *Numen* 17 (Dec., 1970): 176-187.

May, William E. "The natural law, conscience, and developmental psychology." *Communio* (Spring, 1975): 3-31.

Mobbs, Frank. "Conscience and Christian Morality." *St. Mark's Review* 160 (Summer 1995): 32-33.

Nauss, Allen. "Freud's 'Superego' and the Bilical *Syneidesis*." *Concordia Theological Monthly* 33, no. 5 (May 1962):273-282.

Oates, Wayne E. "The Hindering and Helping Power of Religion." *Pastoral Psychology* 6, no. 54 (May, 1955): 43-49.

Peterson, Raymond E. "Jeremy Taylor on Conscience and Law." *Anglican Theological Review* 48 (July, 1966): 243-263.

Porter, Stanley E. "Romans 13:1-7 as Pauline Political Rhetoric." *Filologia Neotestamentaria* 3, no. 6 (Nov 1990): 115-137.

Redmond, Walter. "Conscience as Moral Judgment: The Probabilist Blending of the Logics of Knowledge and Responsibility." *Journal of Religious Ethics* 26, no. 2 (Fall 1998): 389-405.

Rodgers, V. A. "Συνειδησις and the Expression of Conscience." *Greek-Roman-and Byzantine-Studies* 10, no. 3 (Autumn, 1969): 241-254.

Selby, Gary S. "The Meaning and Function of Συνειδησις in Hebrews 9 and 10." *Restoration Quarterly* 28, no. 3 (3rd quarter, 1985/86): 145-154.

Sell, A. P. F. "'Conscience' in Recent Discussion." *Theology* 66, no. 522 (Dec., 1963): 498-504.

Spohn, William C. "Conscience and Moral Development." *Theological Studies* 61, no. 1 (March 2000): 122-138.

Stein, Robert H. "The Argument of Romans 13:1-7." *Novum Testamentum* 31, no. 4 (Oct 1989): 325-343.

Stepien, Jan. "Syneidesis: La Conscience dans L'Anthropologie de Saint Paul." *Revue D'Histoire et de Philosophie Religieuses* 60, no. 1 (Jan – Mar 1980): 1-20.

Straton, Douglas. "The Meaning of Moral Law." *Andover Newton Quarterly* (January, 1965): 31-39.

Strunk, Orlo, Jr. "Religion, the Id, and the Superego." *The Journal of Bible and Religion* 28, no. 3 (July, 1960): 317-322.

Verhey, Allen. "The Person as a Moral Agent." *Calvin Theological Journal* 13, no. 1 (April, 1978): 5-15.

Webster, John. "God and Conscience," *Calvin Theological Journal* 33, no. 1 (April, 1998): 104-124.

Whitchurch, I. G. "A Forum for Conscience." *Scottish Journal of Theology* 22 (March 1969): 60-77.

Zalba, Marcelino. "Papel de la conciencia en la calificación de los actos morales." *Gregorianum* 62, no. 1 (1981): 135-157.

Zuck, Roy B. "The Doctrine of Conscience." *Bibliotheca Sacra* 126, no. 504 (Oct- Dec, 1969): 329-340.

Dignitatis Humanae

Abejon, Gerardo del Pozo. *La Iglesia y la libertad religiosa*. Madrid: Biblioteca de Autores Cristianos, 2007.

Adherents.com. http://www.adherents.com/adh_dem.html, accessed Feb. 15, 2012.

Albornoz, A. E. Carrillo De. "The Ecumenical and World Significance of the Vatican Declaration on Religious Liberty." *The Ecumenical Review*, vol. xviii (1966).

Alfayate, Enrique Valcarce. *El Concilio y la ONU: En la libertad religiosa de los pueblos*. Madrid: Afrodisio Aguado, S.A., 1966.

Allen, John L. "Liberating the Christian Voice in the Arab Spring." *National Catholic Reporter*, August 12, 2011. http://ncronline.org/blogs/all-things-catholic/liberating-christian-voice-arab-spring (accessed August 14, 2011).

Antieau, Chester James, Arthur T. Downey, and Edward C. Roberts. "Chapter Eight: The Practices of the Times as Casting Light Upon the Meaning of the Establishment Clause of the First Amendment." In *Freedom from Federal Establishment: Formation and Early History of the First Amendment Religion Clauses*. Milwaukee, WI: The Bruce Publishing Company, 1964.

Appleby, R. Scott and John T. McGreevy. "Catholics, Muslims and the Mosque Controversy." http://www.nybooks.com/blogs/nyrblog/2010/aug/27/catholics-muslims-mosque-controversy/ (accessed October 18, 2010).

Asian Journal Press. "David Pendleton: Former Hawaii State Representative, Board Member, Hawaii Labor and Industrial Relations Appeals Board." *Asian Journal Press*, September 1, 2009. http://www.asianjournal.com/voice-of-fil-america/72-voice-of-fil-america/2786-david-pendleton-former-state-representative-of-hawaii-board-member-hawaii-labor-and-industrial-relations-appeals-board.html (accessed August 14, 2011).

Associated Press, The. "R.I. bishop asked Rep. Kennedy to avoid Communion." *USA Today*, November 22, 2009. http://www.usatoday.com/news/religion/2009-11-22-kennedy-communion_N.htm?obref=obinsite (accessed November 23, 2009).

Baierl, Joseph J. *The Catholic Church and the Modern State*. Rochester, NY: St. Bernard's Seminary, 1955.

Basile, Fr. *Le droit à la liberté religieuse dans la Tradition de l'Eglise: Un cas de développement doctrinal homogène par le magistère authentique*. Editions Sainte-Madeleine, 2005.

BBC News. "More Anglican priests to join Catholic Church." *BBC News UK*, January 11, 2011. http://www.bbc.co.uk/news/uk-12260569 (accessed August 10, 2011).

Bedoya, Juan G. "Report: From the Light of Trent to a Country of Mission[ary Need]." *El Pais*, October 31, 2010. http://www.elpais.com/articulo/reportajes/luz/Trento/ pais/mision/elpepusocdmg/20101031elpdmgrep_2/Tes. (accessed July 14, 2011).

Benedict XVI, Pope. *Christmas Message*, December 22, 2005. http://www.vatican.va/ holy_father/benedict_xvi/speeches/2005/december/documents/hf_ben_xvi_spe_20051222_roman-curia_en.html (accessed November 29, 2011).

Berger, Joseph. "Leading Archbishop Challenges Vatican on Silencing Dissent." *The New York Times*, September 24, 1986. http://www.nytimes.com/1986/09/24/us/leading-archbishop-challenges-vatican-on-silencing-dissent.html (accessed August 30, 2011).

Bernas, Joaquin G. "Religion and the RH Bills." *Philippine Daily Enquirer*, Oct. 25, 2010, under Religion and Belief, Family planning. http://opinion.inquirer.net/inquireropinion/columns/view/20101025-299587/Religion-and-the-RH-bills (accessed Nov. 2, 2010).

———. "A War of Religions." *Philippine Daily Enquirer*, May 2, 2011, under Religion and Belief, Family planning. http://opinion.inquirer.net/inquireropinion/columns/view/20110502-334122/A-war-of-religions (accessed May 3, 2011).

Bernstein, Carl. "The Holy Alliance: Ronald Reagan and John Paul II." *Time*, Feb. 24, 1992, page 9, under "The Secret Directive." http://www.time.com/time/magazine/ article/0,9171,97493,00.html#ixzzlTpmAeoJD (accessed August 1, 2011).

Bevans, Stephen B. and Jeffrey Gros. *Evangelization and Religious Freedom: Ad Gentes, Dignitatis Humanae*. New York: Paulist Press, 2009.

Bigongiari, Dino. *The Political Ideas of St. Thomas Aquinas*. New York: Haffner Press, 1953.

Bird, Otto, ed. *Collected Works of Jacques Maritain: Integral Humanism, Freedom in the Modern World, and A Letter on Independence*. Translated by Otto Bird, Joseph Evans, and Richard O'Sullivan. Notre Dame, IN: University of Notre Dame, 1996.

Bloch, Tamara. *Die Stellungnahmen der römisch-katholischen Amtskirche zur Frage der menschenrechte seit 1215*. Frankfurt am Main: Peter Lang, 2008.

Bosquet, Francois. *Pour Une Conscience Vive et Libre: "Dignitatis Humanae" – Une déclaration prophétique de Vatican II*. Editions Parole et Silence, 2006.

Broglio, Francesco Margiotta. "Concordat." In *The Papacy: An Encyclopedia*, 3 vols. Edited by Philippe Levillain, 1:396-400. New York: Routledge, 2002.

Brown, Robert McAfee. "Leonardo Boff: Theologian for all Christians." *Christian Century*, July 2-9, 1986, p. 615. http://www.religion-line.org/showarticle.asp?title=1045 (accessed August 30, 2011).

Cacciottolo, Mario. "Divorce in Malta: Referendum causes acrimonious split." BBC News, May 27, 2011 under "Europe." http://www.bbc.co.uk/news/world-europe-13559970 (accessed August 24, 2011).

Carrol, James. "The Americanist heresy: When should dogma bow to experience?" The Boston *Globe*, March 19, 2009. http://www.boston.com/bostonglobe/ideas/articles/2009/04/19/the_american_heresy/?page=1 (and 2 and 3), (accessed April 20, 2009).

Cassidy, Edward Idris Cardinal. *Ecumenism and Interreligious Dialogue*: Unitatis Redintegratio, Nostra Aetate. Mahwah, New Jersey: Paulist Press, 2005.

Castelli, Enrico, editeur. *L'Herméneutique de la Liberté Religieuse*. Paris: Aubier Editions Montaigne, 1968.

CARA Research Center, Georgetown University. http://cara.georgetown.edu/CARAServices/requestedchurchstats.html (accessed May 31, 2012).

Catechism of the Catholic Church. http://www.vatican.va/archive/ccc_css/archive/catechism/p3s1c1a6.htm, (accessed June 10, 2012).

Cavanaugh, William T. *Torture and the Eucharist*. Malden, MA: Blackwell Publishers, 1998.

Chaput, Archbishop. "John F. Kennedy's View of the Role of Catholic Faith in Public Service Was Wrong." Speech given at Houston Baptist University, March 2, 2010, Houston, TX. http://www.catholic.org/politics/story.php?id=35640 (accessed May 28, 2012).

CIA political analyst. Memorandum, "The Impact of a Polish Pope on the USSR," Central Intelligence Agency, National Foreign Assessment Center, 19 October, 1978, from folder entitled "Pope John Paul II and CIA Files." *The Paperless Archives*, The Library Collection, DVD-ROM Disc No. 7 (BACM Research: 1999-2007), W. R. Poage Legislative Library, Baylor University, Waco, TX.

Cloud, David W. *Evangelicals and Rome*. Port Huron, MI: Way of Life Literature, 1999.

Collins, Michael. *Pope Benedict XVI: Successor to Peter*. New York: Paulist Press, 2005.

Colson, Chuck and Richard John Neuhaus, eds. *Evangelicals and Catholics Toward a Common Mission Together*. Dallas, TX: Word Publishing, 1995.

Congar, Yves. *La liberté religieuse*. Paris: Les Editions du Cerf, 1967.

———. *Vaticano II: La libertad religiosa*. Madrid: Taurus Ediciones, S.A., 1969; first published 1966.

Conley, John. "Religious Freedom as Catholic Crisis." In *The Human Person and a Culture of Freedom*. Edited by Peter A. Pagan Aguiar and Terese Auer, 226-241. Washington, D.C.: The Catholic University of America Press, 2009.

Corral, Carlos, S.J., José M. Díaz-Alegría, S.J., José M. Fondevila, S.J., Matías García, S.J. *La Libertad Religiosa: Análisis de la Declaración 'Dignitatis Humanae'*. Madrid: Editorial Razon y Fe, S.A., 1966.

Davies, Michael. *The Second Vatican Council and Religious Liberty*. Long Prairie, MN: The Neumann Press, 1992.

Desmond, Joan Frawley. "Bishop Lori: Religious Liberty: The Pre-eminent Social Justice Issue of Our Time." *National Catholic Register*, November 30, 2011. http://www.ncregister.com/daily-news/bishop-lori-religious-liberty-the-preeminent-social-justice-issue-of-our-ti/, (accessed January 27, 2012).

"*Dignitatis Humanae* – 40 Year Anniversary Conference." Centro di Studi Americani, Rome, January 18, 2006. http://vatican.usembassy.it/events/2006/dignitatis/default.asp (accessed Nov. 3, 2007).

Dionisio, Eleanor R. "On the Sweet Insidiousness of Dialogue." *The Philippine Daily Inquirer*, July 11, 2011, under "Commentary." http://opinion.inquirer.net/7510/on-the-sweet-insidiousness-of-dialogue (accessed July 13, 2011).

Documentation Information Catholiques Internationales. "Pope Benedict XVI encourages the new evangelization." October 15, 2011. http://www.dici.org/en/news/benedict-xvi-encourages-the-new-evangelization/, (accessed June 1, 2012).

Dougherty, Jude P. *Jacques Maritain: An Intellectual Profile*. Washington, D.C.: Catholic University of America, 2003.

Duffy, Eamon. *Saints and Sinners*. U.S.A.: Yale University Press, 2006.

Economist, The. "The Institutional Pillars of Global Order: The Nation-State is Dead; Long Live the Nation-State." (Originally titled, "The Nation-State is Dead. Long live the Nation-State," in *The Economist*, Dec 23-Jan 5, 1996). In *The Global Agenda: Issues and Perspectives*, edited by Charles W. Kegley, Jr. and Eugene R. Wittkopf, 232-240. Boston, MA: McGraw-Hill, 1998.

Espinoza, Elias L. "Espinoza: Foul smell from septic waste." *The Sun Star Cebu*, May 19, 2011, under "Free Zone." http://www.sunstar.com.ph/cebu/opinion/2011/05/19/espinoza-foul-smell-septic-waste-156269 (accessed May 19, 2011).

Eurasia News. "US Religious Freedom TSAR tells UKMPs: Christians Facing Increasing Persecution Worldwide." http://www.eurasiareview.com/01122011-us-religious-freedom-tsar-tells-uk-mps-christians-face-increasing-persecution-worldwide/(accessed December 4, 2011).

———. "US Senate Backs Down, Religious Freedom Watchdog to Stay." http://www.eurasiareview.com/20122011-us-senate-backs-down-religious-freedom-watchdog-to-stay/ (accessed January 26, 2012).

———. "Vatican Cardinal: US Healtcare Mandate is 'Contrary to the very Foundation of Our Nation,'" April 11, 2012. http://www.eurasiareview.com/11042012-vatican-cardinal-us-healthcare-mandate-is-contrary-to-the-very-foundation-of-our-nation/(accessed May 13, 2012).

Farr, Thomas F. "Dignitatis Humanae and Religious Freedom in American Foreign Policy: A Practitioner's Perspective." In *After 40 Years: Vatican Council II's Diverse Legacy*. Edited by Kenneth D. Whitehead, 237-250. South Bend, IN: St. Augustine's Press, 2007.

———. "Religious Realism in Foreign Policy: Lessons from Vatican II." *The Review of Faith and International Affairs* Winter (2005-2006): 25-34.

Favier, Jean. "Theocracy, Papal, Middle Ages." In *The Papacy: An Encyclopedia*, 3 vols. Edited by Philippe Levillain, 3:1482-1486. New York: Routledge, 2002.

Ferrara, Christopher A. and Thomas E. Woods, Jr. *The Great Façade: Vatican II and the Regime of the Novelty in the Roman Catholic Church*. 2002.

Fletcher, Jeannine Hill. "Responding to Religious Difference: Conciliar Perspectives." In *From Trent to Vatican II: Historical and Theological Investigations*. Edited by Raymond F. Bulman and Frederick J. Parrella, 267-281. New York: Oxford University Press, 2006.

Ford, John T., ed. *Religious Liberty: Paul VI and "Dignitatis Humanae."* Brescia: Istituto Paulo VI, 1995.

Garro, P. Ignacio, S. J. "Sects in Latin America" Series, part 3, "Catholic Response to Sects," under Section B: Protestant Sects and New Religious Movements as a "Challenge." http://formacionpastoralparalaicos.blogspot.com/2009/09/respuesta-catolica-sectas.html (accessed January 30, 2012).

Gilbert, Kathleen. "Cardinal Arinze to pro-choice pols: law against murder a 'Divine law, not a tennis club regulation.'" July 11, 2011. http://www.lifesitenews.com/news/cardinal-arinze-to-pro-choice-pols-law-against-murder-is-divine-law-not-a-t/ (accessed August 6, 2011).

Gilson, Etienne. *The Church Speaks to the Modern World: The Social Teachings of Leo XIII*. Garden City, NY: Image Books, 1954.

Gonnet, Dominique. *La liberté religieuse à Vatican II: La contribution de John Courtney Murray*. Paris: Les editions du Cerf, 1994.

Graham, Robert A. *Vatican Diplomacy: A Study of Church and State on the International Plane*. Princeton, NJ: Princeton University Press, 1959.

———. "Introduction: Reflections on Vatican Diplomacy." In *Papal Diplomacy in the Modern Age*. Edited by Peter C. Kent and John F. Pollard, 1-9. Westport, CT: Praeger Publishing, 1994.

Grasso, Kenneth L. "A Special Kind of Liberty: *Dignitatis Humanae*." In *Building the Free Society: Democracy, Capitalism, and Catholic Social Teaching*. Edited by George Weigel and Robert Royal, 107-130. Grand Rapids: Eerdman's, 1993.

Grasso, Kenneth L. and Robert P. Hunt, eds. *Catholicism and Religious Freedom: Contemporary Reflections on Vatican II's Declaration on Religious Liberty*. New York: Rowman & Littlefield Publishers, 2006.

Gregory XVI, Pope. *Mirari vos*, August 15, 1832. http://www.papalencyclicals.net/Greg16/g16mirar.htm, (accessed December 15, 2011).

Gres-Gayer, Jaques. "Gallicanism." In *The Papacy: An Encyclopedia*, 3 vols., edited by Philippe Levillain, 2:615-618. New York, NY: Routledge, 2002.

Guimaraes, Atila Sinke. *In The Murky Waters of Vatican II*. 1997.

Hanson, Eric O. *The Catholic Church in World Politics*. Princeton, NJ: Princeton University Press, 1987.

Harrison, Brian W. "Marcel Lefebvre: Signatory to Dignitatis Humanae." *CatholicCulture.org* http://www.catholicculture.org/culture/library/view.cfm?id=857&CFID=80441610&CFTOKEN=56631028 (accessed May 10, 2011).

Hellin, Francisco Gil. *Declaratio de Libertate Religiosa – Dignitatis Humanae*. Roma: Pontificia Universitas Sanctae Crucis, 2008.

Hili, Carmel. "Launching of Kattolici: Iva Ghax Dritt – 14 May, 2011," under "Press Releases." http://www.ivadritt.org/launching-of-kattolici-iva-ghax-dritt-14th-may-2011/ (accessed May 24, 2011).

———. "Catholic Marriage – 18 May, 2011 (English)," under "Press Releases." http://www.ivadritt.org/catholic-marriage-18-may-2011/ (accessed on May 18, 2011).

Himes, Kenneth R., ed. *Modern Catholic Social Teaching: Commentaries and Interpretations*. Washington, D.C.: Georgetown University Press, 2005.

———. "Vatican II and Contemporary Politics." In *The Catholic Church and the Nation-State: Comparative Perspectives*. Edited by Paul Christopher Manuel, Lawrence C. Reardon, and Clyde Wilcox, 15-32. Washington, D.C.: Georgetown University Press, 2006.

Hittinger, F. Russell. "The Declaration on Religious Liberty, *Dignitatis Humanae*." In *Vatican II: Renewal within Tradition*. Edited by Matthew L. Lamb and Matthew Levering, 359-382. New York: Oxford University Press, 2008.

Hollenbach, David. *The Global Face of Public Faith*. Washington, D.C.: Georgetown University Press, 2003.

Hooper, J. Leon, ed. *Religious Liberty: Catholic Struggles with Pluralism*. Louisville, KY: Westminster/John Knox Press, 1993.

Hughes, Philip. *The Pope's New Order: A Systematic Summary of the Social Encyclicals and Addresses, from Leo XIII to Pius XII*. New York: The MacMillan Co., 1944.

John of Paris. *On Royal and Papal Power (De Potestate Regia et Papali)*. Translated by Arthur P. Monahan. New York: Columbia University Press, 1974.

John Paul II. *Centesimus Annus*, encyclical promulgated May 5, 1991. http://www.vatican.va/edocs/ENG0214/__P7.HTM (accessed June 4, 2012).

———. *Dies Domini*. http://www.vatican.va/holy_father/john_paul_ii/apost_letters/documents/hf_jp-ii_apl_05071998_dies-domini_en.html (accessed November 18, 2009).

———. *Veritatis Splendor*. http://www.vatican.va/holy_father/ john_paul_ii/encyclicals/documents/hf_jp-ii_enc_06081993_veritatis-spendor_en.html, (January 7, 2010).

Kent, Peter C. and John F. Pollard, eds. *Papal Diplomacy in the Modern Age*. Westport, CT: Praeger Publishing, 1994.

Kerr, David. "Bishop Lori reveals details of Religious Liberty Committee." *Catholic News Agency*, November 10, 2011. http://www.catholicnewsagency.com/news/bishop-lori-reveals-details-of-religious-liberty-committee/ (accessed Nov. 24, 2011).

———. "Vatican reveals European evangelization project." *Catholic News Agency*, July 12, 2011. http://www.catholicnewsagency.com/news/vatican-reveals-european-evangelization-project/ (accessed August 19, 2011).

Kerry, John. Political views, under section four, "Stance on Social Issues," sub-section 4.1, "Abortion." http://www.rtbot.net/John_Kerry_presidential_campaign,_2004#Abortion (accessed March 11, 2012).

Kmiec, David W. "Obama cannot be at war with Catholics if he is at peace with religious freedom." *National Catholic Register*, Nov. 22, 2011. http://ncronline.org/news/politics/obama-cannot-be-war-catholics-if-he-peace-religious-freedom (accessed Nov. 24, 2011).

Komonchak, Joseph A. "The Council of Trent at the Second Vatican Council." In *From Trent to Vatican II: Historical and Theological Investigations*. Edited by Raymond F. Bulman and Frederick J. Parrella, 61-80. New York: Oxford University Press, 2006.

Konig, Franz Cardinal. "The Right to Religious Freedom: The Significance of *Dignitatis Humanae*." In *Vatican II, by those who were there*. Edited by Alberic Stacpoole, 283-290. London: Geoffrey Chapman, 1986.

Landi, Aldo. "Conciliar Movement." In *The Papacy: An Encyclopedia*, 3 vols. Edited by Philippe Levillain, 1:389-392. New York: Routledge, 2002.

La liberté religieuse dans l'enseignement des Papes. Abbaye Saint-Pierre de Solesmes, 1989.

Lecler, Joseph. *Histoire de la Tolerance au Siecle de la Reforme.* Aubiers, Editions Montaigne, 1955.

———. *The Two Sovereignties: The Relationship between Church and State.* London: William Clowes and Sons Limited, 1952.

Lefebvre, Marcel. *Dubia sur la Déclaration Conciliaire sur la Liberté Religieuse.* Editions saint-remi, 1987.

Leo XIII, Pope. Apostolic letter *Testem benevolentiae nostrae*, January 22, 1899. http://www.papalencyclicals.net/Leo13/l13teste.htm (accessed December 14, 2011).

Linnan, John E. "Declaration on Religious Liberty: Dignitatis Humanae, 7 December, 1965." In *Vatican II and Its Documents: An American Reappraisal.* Edited by Timothy E. O'Connell, 167-179. Wilmington, DE: Michael Glazier, 1986.

Lombardi, Gabrio. *Persecuzioni Laicità, Libertà Religiosa: Dall'Editto di Milano alla "Dignitatis Humanae."* Roma: Edizioni Studium, 1991.

Love, Thomas T. *John Courtney Murray: Contemporary Church-State Theory.* Garden City, NY: Doubleday & Co., Inc., 1965.

McDonagh, Enda. *The Declaration on Religious Freedom of Vatican Council II: The Text and Commentary.* London: Darton, Longman, & Todd, 1967.

McDonald, Lee Cameron. *Western Political Theory: Part 1, Ancient and Medieval*, 3 parts. New York: Harcourt, Brace, Jovanovich, 1968.

McElroy, Msgr. Robert W. "Prudence and Eucharistic Sanctions." *America*, January 31, 2005. http://www.americamagazine.org/content/article.cfm?article_id=3982 (accessed December 8, 2010).

McGreevy, John T. *Catholicism and American Freedom.* New York: W.W. Norton & Company, Inc., 2003.

Manuel, Paul Christopher, Lawrence C. Reardon, and Clyde Wilcox, eds. *The Catholic Church and the Nation-State: Comparative Perspectives.* Washington, D.C.: Georgetown University Press, 2006.

Maritain, Jacques. *Christianisme et Démocratie.* New York: Editions de la Maison de Francaise, 1943.

———. *Collected Works of Jacques Maritain: Integral Humanism, Freedom in the Modern World, and A Letter on Independence*. Eidted by Otto Bird. Translated by Otto Bird, Joseph Evans, and Richard O'Sullivan. Notre Dame, IN: University of Notre Dame, 1996.

———. *Du Régime Temporel et de la Liberté*. Paris: Desclee de Brouwer & CIE, 1933.

———. *Man and the State*. Chicago: University of Chicago Press, 1951.

———. *Reflections on America*. New York: Charles Scribner's Sons, 1958.

———. *The Rights of Man and the Natural Law*. London: Geoffrey Bles, 1958.

———. *The Social and Political Philosophy of Jacques Maritain: Selected Readings*. Joseph W. Evans and Leo R. Ward, compilers. New York: Charles Scribner's Sons, 1955.

———. *The Things That Are Not Caesar's*. Translated by J. F. Scanlan. New York: Charles Scribner's Sons, 1931.

———. *True Humanism*. Translated by M. R. Adamson. London: Butler and Tanner, 1938.

Martens, Kurt. "*Dignitatis Humanae*: A Hermeneutic Perspective on Religious Freedom as Interpreted by the Roman Catholic Church." In *Hermeneutics, Scriptural Politics, and Human Rights: Between Text and Context*. Edited by Bas de Gaay Fortman, Kurt Martens, and M.A. Mohamed Salih, 143-161. New York: Palgrave MacMillan, 2009.

Méndez, Húgo. "The Catholic Church and Change." Jan. 5, 2010. http://sda2rc.blogspot.com/2010/01/catholic-church-church.html (accessed January 9, 2010).

Moses, Paul. "The bishops, religious liberty, and conscience." *Commonweal Magazine*, Nov. 16, 2011. http://www.commonwealmagazine.org/blog/?p=15944, (accessed Nov. 24, 2011).

Murray, John Courtney. Ms. 1949b. "Contemporary Orientations of Catholic Thought on Church and State in the Light of History." *Theological Studies*, 10 (June): 177-234. http://woodstock.georgetown.edu/library/Murray/1949b.htm (accessed May 20, 2012).

———. "The Declaration on Religious Freedom." *War, Poverty, Freedom: The Christian Response, Concilium*, XV. New York: Paulist Press, 1966.

———. "The Issue of Church and State at Vatican II." *Theological Studies* 27 (December 1966): 580-606.

———. "Religious Freedom" Introduction to *Dignitatis Humanae*. In *The Documents of Vatican II*. Edited by Walter M. Abbott, 672-696. New York: The Crossroad Publishing Company, 1989.

———. *Religious Liberty: an End and a Beginning*. New York: The Macmillan Co., 1966.

———. "Separation of Church and State." *America* 76 (December 7, 1946):261-263.

———. "Separation of Church and State: True and False Concepts." *America* 76 (February 15, 1947):541-545.

———. "Session XIV: The Declaration on Religious Freedom." In *Vatican II: An Interfaith Appraisal*. Edited by John H. Miller, 565-585. Notre Dame, IN: Univ. of Notre Dame Press, 1966.

Murray, John Courtney, E. Schillebeeckx, A. F. Carrillo de Albornoz, and P. A. Liégé. *La liberté religieuse: exigence spirituelle et problème politique*. Paris: Editions du Centurion, 1965.

Newsmax. "U.S. Bishops: Rescind the Obama Health Care Rule." February, 12, 2012. http://www.newsmax.com/Newsfront/obama-birth-control-shift/2012/02/10/id/429117?s=al&promo_code=E27F1-1, (accessed Feb. 13, 2012).

Nowak, Christopher. "The Vatican and the SSPX: the discussion begins." In *The Grand Rapids Catholic Examiner*, September 16, 20009. http://www.examiner.com/x-20920-Grand-Rapids-Catholic-Examiner~y2009m9d16-The-Vatican-and-the-SSPX-the-discussion-begins (accesed September 17, 2009).

O'Brien, Thomas W. *John Courntey Murray in a Cold War Context*. Dallas: University Press of America, 2004.

O'Malley, John W. *What Happened at Vatican II?* Cambridge, MA: Harvard University Press, 2008.

Papetti, Renato and Rodolfo Rossi, eds. *"Dignitatis Humanae": La Liberta Religiosa in Paolo VI*. Brescia: Istituto Paolo VI, 2004.

Parker, T. M. *Christianity & the State in the light of history*. London: Adam and Charles Black, 1955.

Pastoureau, Michel. "Keys." In *The Papacy: An Encyclopedia*, 3 vols. Edited by Philippe Levillain, 2:891. New York, NY: Routledge, 2002.

Paul VI, Pope. *United Nations General Assembly Address*, October 4, 1965, under section, "Disarmament Essential to Brotherhood." http://www.christusrex.org/www1/pope/UN-1965.html (accessed December 21, 2011).

Pauwels, C. F. "Ecumenical Theology and Conversions." In *Vatican II: The Theological Dimension*. Edited by Anthony D. Lee. USA: The Thomist Press, 1963.

Pavan, Pietro. "Declaration on Religious Freedom." In *Commentary on the Documents of Vatican II*, 4 vols. Edited by Herbert Vorgrimler, 4:49-86. New York: The Crossroads Publishing Company, 1989.

Pawlikowski, John T. "*Gaudium et spes* and *Dignitatis Humanae*: Are they in conflict: Reflections in light of the current controversy regarding Catholicism and politics." http://www.stthomas.edu/cathstudies/CST/conferences/gaudium/papers/Pawlikowski.pdf (accessed March 26, 2010).

Payne, Daniel P. and Jennifer M. Kent. "An Alliance of the Sacred: Prospects for a Catholic-Orthodox Partnership against Secularism in Europe." *Journal of Ecumenical Studies* Wntr, 2011.

Pelotte, Donald E. *John Courtney Murray: Theologian in Conflict*. New York, NY: Paulist Press, 1976.

Pentin, Edward. "A Platform for Christian Politicians." Dignitatis Humanae Institute website. http://www.catholicworldreport.com/Item/1002/A_Platform_for_Christian_Politicians.aspx, (accessed December 4, 2011).

———. "Promoting Human Dignity." *National Catholic Register*, October 17, 2011. http://www.ncregister.com/site/article/promoting-human-dignity/ (accessed October 18, 2011).

Perez-Llantada y Gutierrez, Jaime. *La Libertad Religiosa en España y el Vaticano II.* Madrid: Instituto de Estudios Politicos, 1974.

Pieters, Janneke. "Secular Stampede? Religious Liberty Getting Battered." In *National Catholic Register,* January 10, 2010. http://www.ncregister.com/site/article%20/secular_stampede/ (accessed January 15, 2010).

Pius X, Pope. *Vehementer nos,* Feb. 11, 1906. http://www.vatican.va/holy_father/pius_x/encyclicals/documents/hf_p-x_enc_11021906-_vehementer -nos_en.html (accessed December 14, 2011).

Pope, Stephen J. "Natural Law in Catholic Social Teachings." In *Modern Catholic Social Teaching.* Edited by Kenneth B. Himes, 41-71. Washington, D.C.: Georgetown University Press, 2004.

Prado, Joaquin López de. "Análisis Jurídico." In *La Libertad Religiosa: Análisis de la Declaración 'Dignitatis Humanae'.* Corral, Carlos, S.J., Jose M. Díaz-Alegría, S.J., José M. Fondevila, S.J., Matías García, S.J. Madrid: Editorial Razon y Fe, S.A., 1966.

Rico, Herminio. *John Paul II and the Legacy of "Dignitatis Humanae."* Washington, D.C.: Georgetown University Press, 2002.

Rommen, Heinrich. *The State in Catholic Thought: A Treatise in Political Philosophy.* St. Louis, MO: B. Herder Book, Co., 1945.

Ryan, John A. and Francis J. Boland. *Catholic Principles of Politics.* New York: The MacMillan Co., 1941.

Scatena, Silvia. *La Fatica della Libertà: L'elaborazione della dichiarazione "Dignitatis Humanae" sulla Libertà Religiosa del Vaticano II.* Bologna: Societa editrice il Mulino, 2003.

Schanda, Balázs. "Church and State in the New Member States of the European Union." *Fides et Libertas* (2004).

Scheidler, Eric. "Stand Up for Freedom Rallies." http://standupforreligiousfreedom.com/ (accessed June 6, 2012).

Schreck, Alan. *Vatican II: The Crisis and the Promise.* Cincinnati, OH: Servant Books, 2005.

Schuck, Michael J. "Early Modern Roman Catholic Social Thought, 1740-1890." In *Modern Catholic Social Teaching*. Edited by Kenneth B. Himes, 99-124. Washington, D.C.: Georgetown University Press, 2004.

Scicluna, Martin. "Divorce, the Church, and our conscience." *The Malta Independent Online*, posted April 27, 2011. http://www.independent.com.mt/news.asp?newsitemid= 124185 (accessed April 28, 2011).

———. "Strike a blow for justice, fairness, and your civil rights." *The Malta Independent Online*, posted May 25, 2011. http://www.independent.com.mt/news.asp?newsitemid=125929 (accessed May 27, 2011).

Sigmund, Paul E. "Catholicism, Roman." In *The Encyclopedia of Democracy*, 4 vols. Edited by Seymour Martin Lipset, 1:181-185. Washington, D.C.: Congressional Quarterly, 1995.

Stransky, Thomas F. *Declaration on Religious Freedom of Vatican Council II: Commentary by Thomas F. Stransky, C.S.P.* New York: Paulist Press, 1967.

Sungenis, Robert. "Was God Behind the Ambiguities of Vatican II? A Biblical Answer to an Intriguing Question." *Catholic Family News*, February, 2003.

Sweeney, James. "Catholicism and Freedom: *Dignitatis Humanae* – the Text and its Reception." In *Reading Religion in Context*. Edited by Elisabeth Arweck and Peter Collins, 17-33. Burlington, VT: Ashgate Publishing, 2006.

Ullmann, Walter. *A Short History of the Papacy in the Middle Ages*. London: Methuen and Co., 1972.

USCCB. "Fortnight for Freedom." http://www.usccb.org/issues-and-action/religious-liberty/fortnight-for-freedom/index.cfm (accessed June 4, 2012).

Valcarce, Enrique. *El Concilio y la ONU en la libertad religiosa de los pueblos*. Madrid, Spain: Talleres Afrodisio Aguado, 1966.

Valente, Flaviano Amatulli. *Religious Proselytism: The Dominant Note in Latin America*. http://es.scribd.com/doc/24761588/EL-PROSELITISMO-RELIGIOSO (accessed January 30, 2012).

Velasco, Irene Hernández. "El Papa ve España como el campo de batalla entre 'el laicismo y la fe.'" *El Mundo*, 7 de Noviembre, 2010.

Veliko, Lydia and Jeffrey Gros, eds. *Growing Consensus II: Church Dialogues in the United States, 1992-2004*. Washington, D.C.: United State Conference of Catholic Bishops, 2005.

Vischer, Lukas. "*Dignitatis Humanae*: Zur Notwendigkeit eines kirchlichen Menschenrechtsprogramms." In *Das Zweite Vatikanische Konzil und Die Zeichen der Zeit Heute*. Edited by Herausgegeben von Peter Hunermann, 439-442. Freiburg: Herder, 2006.

Walsh, Mary Ann, ed. *From Pope John Paul II to Benedict XVI*. New York: Rowman and Littlefield, 2005.

Weaver, Anna. "This is where my faith has led me." *Hawaii Catholic Herald*, posted March 21, 2008. http://www.hawaiicatholicherald.com/Home/tabid/256/newsid884/1259/Default.aspx (accessed April 10, 2008).

Weigel, George and Robert Royal, eds. *Building the Free Society: Democracy, Capitalism, and Catholic Social Teaching*. Grand Rapids, MI: Eerdman's, 1993.

Whitmore, Todd David. "Immunity or Empowerment?: John Courtney Murray and the Question of Religious Liberty." In *John Courtney Murray and the Growth of Tradition*. Edited by J. Leon Hooper and Todd David Whitmore. Kansas City, MO: Sheed & Ward, 1996.

Winters, Michael Shawn. "Bishops Lori's Testimony on Religious Freedom." *National Catholic Reporter*, October 27, 2011. http://ncronline.org/blogs/distinctly- catholic/bishop-loris-testimony-religious-liberty (accessed Oct. 30, 2011).

———. "MSW replies to Fr. Komonchak." *National Catholic Reporter*, September 21, 2011. http://ncronline.org/blogs/distinctly-catholic/msw-replies-fr-komonchak (accessed November 12, 2011).

Yates, Gerard F. *Papal Thought on the State: Excerpts from Encyclicals and Other Writings of Recent Popes*. New York: Appleton-Century-Crofts, Inc., 1958.

Zenit.org news, editors. "Vatican-Pius X Society Talks Set for October." *Zenit news*, September 15, 2009. http://www.zenit.org/article-26878?l=english (accessed July 19, 2011).

Inquisition

Aquinas, Thomas. *Summa Theologica*, Book II-II, Question 10, "Of Unbelief in General," Article Eleven, "Ought the Rites of Unbelievers to be Tolerated?" In *Saint Thomas Aquinas: On Law, Morality, and Politics*. Edited by William P. Baumgarth and Richard J. Regan, 254-255. Indianapolis, IN: Hackett Publishing Co., 1988.

Benart, Haim, ed. *Records of the Trials of the Spanish Inquisition in Ciudad Real*, vol. 4:409-525. Jerusalem: The Israel Academy of Arts and Sciences, 1985.

Benrath, K. "The Inquisition, I. In the Older Church." *The New Schaff-Herzog Encyclopedia of Religious Knowledge*. Vol. 6:1-4. Grand Rapids, MI: Baker Book House, 1977. http://www.ccel.org/ccel/schaff/encyc06/Page_1.html, (accessed March 30, 2012).

Carroll, Rory. "Pope says sorry for sins of Church." *The Guardian*, March 13, 2000. http://www.guardian.co.uk/world/2000/mar/13/catholicism.religion (accessed February 28, 2012).

Evans, G. R. *The Roots of the Reformation: Tradition, Emergence, and Rupture*. Downer's Grove, IL: InterVarsity Press, 2012.

Froude, James Anthony. *Lectures on the Council of Trent*. New York: Charles Scribner's Sons, 1896.

Kidd, B. J. *The Counter-Reformation: 1550-1600*. London: SPCK, 1963.

Lea, Henry Charles. *A History of the Inquisition of the Middle Ages*, 3 vols. New York: Russel & Russel, 1958; orig. pub. 1887.

Limborch, Philip A. *The History of the Inquisition*, 2 vols. Translated by Samuel Chandler. London: J. Gray, 1731; reproduced by Eighteenth Century Collections Online Print Editions.

Medina, José Toribio. *Historia del Tribunal del Santo Oficio de la Inquisición en Chile*, 2 vols. Santiago, Chile: Fondo Histórico y BibliográficoMedina, 1952.

———. *Historia del Tribunal del Santo Oficio de la Inquisición de Lima*, 2 vols. Santiago: Gutenburg Press, 1887; reprinted by Nabu Public Domain Reprints, n.d.

———. *Historia del Tribunal del Santo Oficio de la Inquisición en México.* México: Miguel Angel Porrua, Grupo Editorial, 1998.

O'Brien, Miles and Jim Bittermann. "Pope John Paul II Makes Unprecedented Apology for Sins of Catholic Church." Sunday Morning News, aired March 12, 2000. http:// transcripts.cnn.com/ TRANSCRIPTS/0003/12/sm.06.html (accessed February 28, 2012).

Orti y Lara, Juan Manuel. *La Inquisición.* Madrid: Imprenta de la Viuda e Hijo de Aguado, 1877; reprinted by Nabu Public Domain Reprints.

Pink, Thomas. "What is the Catholic doctrine of religious liberty?" http:// kcl.academia. edu/ThomasPink/Papers/647475/What_is_the_ Catholic_ doctrine_of_religious_liberty (accessed November 23, 2011).

Priolkar, A. K. *The Terrible Tribunal for the East: The Goa Inquisition.* New Delhi, India: Voice of India, second reprint, 1998.

Reiser, William. "Roman Catholic Understanding of Religious Tolerance in Modern Times." In *Religious Tolerance in World Religions.* Edited by Jacob Neusner and Bruce Chilton, 153-173. West Conshohocken, PA: Templeton Foundation, 2008.

Rule, William Harris. *History of the Inquisition*, 2 vols. New York, NY: Scribner, Welford & Co., 1874.

San Francisco State University. *Ad Extirpanda.* http://userwww.sfsu.edu/ ~draker/history/Ad_ Extirpanda.html, (accessed February 21, 2012).

Tanon, Celestin Louis. *Histoire des Tribunaux de L'Inquisition en France.* Paris, France: Larose & Forcel, 1893; reprinted by Nabu Public Domain Reprints, n.d.

Mexico

Acevedo, Carlos Alvear. *La iglesia en la historia de México.* México, D.F.: Editorial Jus, 1995.

Agren, David. "Pope's Mexico trip a chance to explore church-state conflict." In *USAToday,* March 20, 2012. http://www.usatoday.com/news/religion/story/2012-03-19/pope-mexico-church-state/53657084/1, (accessed June 11, 2012).

Alcala, Rodolfo Vidal Gomez. *La ley como limite de los derechos fundamentales.* México: Editorial Porrua, 1997.

Anna, Timothy E. *Forging Mexico, 1821-1835.* Lincoln, NE: University of Nebraska Press, 1998.

Assad, Carlos Martínez. "La iglesia católica entre el pasado y el presente." In *Relaciones Estado-Iglesia: Encuentros y Desencuentros.* Editado por Secretaria de Gobernación, México: Secretaria de Gobernación, 2001.

Austin, Flannery. *Vatican Council II: The Documents.* Grand Rapids, MI: Erdmans, 1975.

Blancarte, Roberto J. *Para entender el estado laico.* México, D.F.: Nostra Ediciones, 2008.

———. "Recent Changes in Church-State Relations in Mexico: An Historic Approach." In *Church-State Relations & Religious Liberty in Mexico: Historical and Contemporary Perspectives.* Edited by Derek Davis. Waco, TX: J. M. Dawson Institute of Church-State Studies, 2002.

———. *Sexo, religión y democracia.* Mexico, D.F.: Editorial Planeta Mexicana, 2008.

———., ed. *Los retos de la laicidad y la secularización en el mundo contemporáneo.* México, D.F.: Colegio de México, 2008.

Breedlove, James M. "Effect of the Cortes, 1810-1822, on Church Reform in Spain and Mexico." In *Mexico and the Spanish Cortes, 1810-1822.* Edited by Nettie Lee Benson. Austin: University of Texas Press, 1966.

Butler, William. *Mexico in Transition from the Power of Political Romanism to Civil and Religious Liberty.* New York, NY: Hunt and Eaton, 1892.

Camp, Roderic Ai. "Political Modernization in Mexico." In *The Evolution of the Mexican Political System.* Edited by Jaime O. Rodriguez. Wilmington, DE: Scholarly Resources, 1993.

Cantor, Ernesto Rey. *Control de Convencionalidad de las Leyes y Derechos Humanos*. México, D.F.: Editorial Porrua, 2008.

Carrillo de Albornoz, A. F. *Roman Catholicism and Religious Freedom*. Geneva: World Council of Churches, 1959.

Codes, Rosa Maria Martinez de. *Los bienes nacionales de origen religioso en México (1833-2004): Estudio historic-jurídico*. México, D.F.: Universidad Nacional Autonoma de México, 2007.

Davis, Derek, ed. *Church-State Relations & Religious Liberty in Mexico: Historical and Contemporary Perspectives*. Waco, TX: J. M. Dawson Institute of Church-State Studies, Baylor University, 2002.

Davis, Thomas B. and Amado Ricon Virulegio. *The Political Plans of Mexico*. Lanham, MD: University Press of America, Inc., 1987.

Ferrari, Silvio. *El espíritu de los derechos religiosos: Judaísmo cristianismo e islam*. Translated by Gilberto Canal Marcos. Barcelona: Herder Editorial, 2004.

Galeana, Patricia, ed. *Relaciones Estado-Iglesia: Encuentros y Desencuentros*. México, D.F.: Secretaria de Gobernación, 2001.

Galindo, Jorge Lee. *Ley de Asociaciones Religiosas y Culto Público, Comentada*. México, D.F.: Editorial SISTA, 2009.

Garizabal, Mario Madrid Malo. *Aproximación a los Concordatos*. Bogota: CEPLA Editores, 1977.

Goddard, Jorge Adame. *Estudios sobre Política y Religión*. Mexico, D.F.: Universidad Nacional Autonoma de México, 2008.

Goddard, Jorge Adame, Jean-Pierre Bastian, Roberto J. Blancarte. *Derecho Fundamental de Libertad Religiosa* en *Cuadernos del Instituto de Investigaciones Jurídicas*, Serie L, Derechos Humanos, Numero 1. Distrito Federal, México: Universidad Nacional Autonoma de México, 1994.

Goddijn, H. y W. *Sociologia de la religión y de la Iglesia* . Buenos Aires, Argentina: Ediciones Carlos Lohle, 1973.

Gutierrez, Armando Mendez. *Una Ley para La Libertad Religiosa*. México, D.F.: Editorial Diana, 1992.

Hernández, Alberto. "Las iglesias evangélicas y la ley de las asociaciones religiosas y de culto público." In *Relaciones Estado-Iglesia: Encuentros y Desencuentros*. Editado por Secretaria de Gobernación. México: Secretaria de Gobernación, 2001.

Ibañez, Yolanda Mariel de. *El tribunal de la inquisición en méxico*. México: Editorial Porrua, 1984.

Krauze, Enrique. *Mexico, Biography of Power: A History of Modern Mexico, 1810-1996*. New York, NY: Harper Collins, 1997.

Kung, Hans. *Libertad del Cristiano*. Barcelona: Editorial Herder, 1975.

Margadant S., Guillermo F. *An Introduction to the History of Mexican Law*. Dobbs Ferry, NY: Oceana Publications, Inc., 1983.

———. *La Iglesia Mexicana y El Derecho*. México: Editorial Porrua, S.A., 1984.

Martinez-Torron, Javier, Mariano Palacios Alcocer, Alberto Pacheko Escobedo, et al. *Estudios jurídicos en torno a la Ley de Asociaciones Religiosas y Culto Público*. México, D.F.: Universidad Nacional Autonoma de México, 1994.

Maza, Enrique. *La libertad de expresión en la iglesia*. México, D.F.: Editorial Oceano de México, 2006.

Medal, Ramon Sanchez. *La Nueva Legislación sobre Libertad Religiosa*. México, D.F.: Editorial Porrua, 1997.

Medina, José Toribio. *Historia de tribunal de santa oficio*. México, D.F.: Miguel Angel Porrua, 1998.

Monsivais, Carlos. *El estado laico y sus malquerientes*. México, D.F.: Universidad Nacional Autonoma de México, 2008.

Niemeyer, Jr., E. V. *Revolution at Queretaro: The Mexican Constitutional Convention of 1916-1917*. Austin, TX: The University of Texas Press, 1974.

Pavan, Pietro. *La Libertad Religiosa y los Poderes Publicos*. Barcelona: Talleres Raiclan, 1966.

Rahner, Karl. *Tolerancia, Libertad, Manipulación*. Barcelona: Editorial Herder, 1978.

Ratzinger, Cardinal Joseph. *Iglesia, ecumenismo y política*. Madrid: Biblioteca de Autores Cristianos, 2005.

Ricoeur, Paul, Julia Kristeva, Fracoise Heritier, et al. *La Intolerancia*. México, D.F.: Granica, 2002.

Roche, Jean. *Iglesia y Libertad Religiosa*. Barcelona: Editorial Herder, 1969.

Rodriguez, Jaime O., ed. *The Evolution of the Mexican Political System*. Wilmington, DE: Scholarly Resources, 1993.

Saldana, Javier, ed. *Diez años de vigencia de la Ley de Asociaciones Religiosas y Culto Público en México (1992-2002)*. México, D.F.: Secretaria de Gobernación, 2003.

Sauza, José Luis Lamadrid. *La larga marcha a la modernidad en materia religiosa*. México, D.F.: Fondo de Cultura Económica, 1994.

Schmal, Raúl González. "La libertad religiosa como principio regulador de las relaciones Estado-Iglesia." In Secretaria de Gobernación, *Relaciones Estado-Iglesia: Encuentros y Desencuentros*. México: Secretaria de Gobernación, 2001.

Setien, José Maria. *Laicidad del Estado e Iglesia*. México, D. F.: Asociación Mexicana de Promoción y Cultura Social, 2007.

Teso, Leonor and William Merrill. *Los Negocios Eclesiásticos de la Independencia a la Reforma: Guía documental del Minsterio de Justicia y Negocios Eclesiásticos del Archivo General de la Nación*. México, D.F.: Secretaria de Gobernación, 1998.

Toro, Alfonso. *La Iglesia y el Estado en México: Estudio sobre los conflictos entre el clero catolico y los gobiernos mexicanos desde la independencia hasta nuestros dias*. México, 1927.

Valades, Patricia Galeana de. *Las relaciones iglesia-estado durante el Segundo imperio*. México, D.F.: Universidad Nacional Autonoma de Mexico, 1991.

Villoro, Luis. *El proceso ideológico de la revolución de la independencia*, 2d. ed. México: UNAM, 1977.

Zuniga, Cristina Gutierrez. "Los nuevos movimientos religiosos, nuevos movimientos sociales?" *Religiones y Sociedad*, Año 4, número 8 (enero-abril, 2000), 75-90. México, D.F.: Secretaria de Gobernación, 2000.

Protestant Reformation and Theology

Armstrong, John. *The Catholic Mystery*. Eugene, OR: Harvest House Publishers, 1999.

⸻. *Roman Catholicism: Evangelical Protestants Analyze What Divides and Unites Us*. Chicago: Moody Press, 1984.

D'Aubigne, J. H.Merle. *The History of the Reformation of the Sixteenth Century*. Rapidan, VA: Hartland Publications, n.d.; reprinted from 1846 ed., London.

Bainton, Roland. *Here I Stand: A Life of Martin Luther*. New York, NY: The New American Library, Inc., 1950.

Cathcart, William. *The Papal System*. Watertown, WI: Baptist Heritage Press, 1989; originally published in Philadelphia by Ferguson and Woodburn, 1872.

Durant, Will. *The Reformation*. New York: Simon and Schuster, 1957.

Hillerbrand, Hans J. *The Division of Christendom: Christianity in the Sixteenth Century*. Louisville, KY: Westminster John Knox Press, 2007.

⸻., ed. and trans. *The Reformation in its own Words*. London: SCM Prestt, Ltd., 1964.

Immenkotter, Herbert. "Augsburg, Peace of." Translated by Hans J. Hillerbrand. In *The Oxford Encyclopedia of the Reformation*, 4 vols. Edited by Hans J. Hillerbrand, 1:91-93. New York: Oxford University Press, 1996.

Jedin, Hubert. *A History of the Council of Trent*. Translated by Dom Ernest Graf, O.S.B., 2 vols. St. Louis, MO: B. Herder Book Co., English version, 1957.

McCarthy, James G. *The Gospel According to Rome*. Eugene, OR: Harvest House Publishers, 1995.

Olson, Roger E. *The Story of Christian Theology: Twenty Centuries of Tradition and Reform*. Downer's Grove, IL: InterVarsity Press, 1999.

Ozment, Steven. *Protestants: The Birth of a Revolution*. New York: Doubleday, 1991.

Tonkin, John. *The Church and the Secular Order in Reformation Thought*. New York: Columbia University Press, 1971.

Wallace, Peter G. *The Long European Reformation*. New York, NY: Palgrave Macmillan, 2004.

White, James R. *The Roman Catholic Controversy*. Minneapolis, MN: Bethany House Publishers, 1996.

Wolgast, Eike. "Speyer, Protestation of," Translated by Susan M. Sisler. In *The Oxford Encyclopedia of the Reformation*, 4 vols. Edited by Hans J. Hillerbrand, 4:103-105. New York: Oxford University Press, 1996.

Wylie, J. A. *The History of Protestantism*, 2 vols. Carginagh, Kilkeel, Co. Down, N. Ireland: Mourne Missionary Trust, 1985.

———. *Papacy*. London: Hamilton, Adam, and Co., 1867.

Zins, Robert M. *On the Edge of Apostasy: Evangelical Romance with Rome*. Huntsville, AL: White Horse Publications, 1998.

Roman Catholic History, Politics and Social Philosophy

Allitt, Patrick. *Catholic Intellectuals and Conservative Politics in America, 1950-1985*. Ithaca, NY: Cornell University Press, 1995.

Bettenson, Henry, ed. *Documents of the Christian Church*. London: Oxford University Press, 1963.

Bokenkotter, Thomas. *A Concise History of the Catholic Church*. New York: Doubleday, 1990.

Borromeo, Saint Charles, ed. *The Catechism of the Council of Trent.* Authorized by The Council of Trent by decree of Pope Saint Pius V. Translated by John A. McHugh and Charles J. Callan. Rockford, IL: Tan Books and Publishers, Inc., 1982.

Buchanan, Tom and Martin Conway, eds. *Political Catholicism in Europe, 1918-1965.* New York: Oxford University Press, 1996.

Byrnes, Timothy A. *Catholic Bishops in American Politics.* Princeton, N.J.: Princeton University Press, 1991.

Coleman, John, ed. *Christian Political Ethics.* Princeton, NJ: Princeton University Press, 2008.

———., ed. *One Hundred Years of Catholic Social Thought.* Maryknoll, NY: Orbis Books, 1991.

Coleman, John and William Ryan, eds. *Globalization and Catholic Social Thought: present crisis, future hope.* Maryknoll, NY: Orbis Books, 2005.

Conway, Martin. *Catholic Politics in Europe, 1918-1945.* New York, NY: Routledge, 1997.

Corrin, Jay P. *Catholic Intellectuals and the Challenge of Democracy.* Notre Dame, IN: University of Notre Dame Press, 2002.

"The Council of Laodicea in Phrygia Pacatiana, 364 A. D." http://reluctant-messenger.com/council-of-laodicea.htm (accessed on May 9, 2010).

A Decree in Behalf of the Jacobites from the Bull "Cantata Domino," February 4, Florentine style, 1441, modern, 1442. Cited in Henry Denzinger, *The Sources of Catholic Dogma*, 229 (paragraph 712). Translated by Roy J. Deferrari. Fitzwilliam, NH: Loreto Publications.

Fox, Robin Lane. *Pagans and Christians.* New York, NY: Alfred A. Knopf, Inc., 1989.

Grasso, Kenneth, Gerard V. Bradley, and Robert P. Hunt, eds. *Catholicism, Liberalism, and Communitarianism.* Lanham, MD: Rowman & Littlefield, 1995.

Hoare, F. R. *The Papacy and the Modern State*. London: Burns, Oates, Washbourne, Ltd., 1940.

Kaiser, Wolfram and Helmut Wohnout, eds. *Political Catholicism in Europe, 1918-1945*. New York, NY: Routledge, 2004.

Lader, Lawrence. *Politics, Power and the Church: The Catholic Crisis and Its Challenge to American Pluralism*. New York, NY: MacMillan, 1987.

Laski, Harold J. *Studies in the Problem of Sovereignty*. New Haven, NJ: Yale University Press, 1917.

Lubac, Henri de. *Catholicism: Christ and the Common Destiny of Man*. San Francisco, CA: Ignatius Press, 1988.

Maldonado, Carlos Eduardo. *Derechos humanos, solidaridad y subsidiariedad*. Santa Fe de Bogota: Editorial Temis, S.A., 2000.

Murphy, Cornelius F. *Theories of World Governance: A Study on the History of Ideas*. Washington, D.C.: The Catholic University of America Press, 1999.

Neuhaus, Richard John. *Appointment in Rome*. New York, NY: Crossroads, 1999.

———. *The Naked Public Square*. Grand Rapids, MI: Erdmans, 1984.

Nichols, Aidan. *The Thought of Pope Benedict XVI*. London: Burns & Oates, 2007.

Nichols, Peter. *The Politics of the Vatican*. New York, NY: Praeger, 1968.

Novak, Michael. *The Catholic Ethic and the Spirit of Capitalism*. New York, NY: Maxwell Macmillan International, 1993.

Riccards, Michael. *Vicars of Christ: Popes, Power, and Politics in the Modern World*. New York, NY: Crossroads, 1998.

Sheppard, Vincent F. *Religion and the Concept of Democracy: A Thomistic Study in Social Philosophy*. Washington, D.C.: The Catholic University of America Press, 1949.

Viaene, Vincent, ed. *The Papacy and the New World Order: Vatican diplomacy, catholic opinion and international politics in the time of Leo XIII*. Leuven, Belgium: Leuven University Press, 2005.

Wethersfield Institute, The. *When Conscience and Politics Meet: A Catholic View*. San Francisco, CA: Ignatius Press, 1993.

Witte, John, and Frank S. Alexander, eds. *The Teachings of Modern Roman Catholicism on Law, Politics and Human Nature*. New York, NY: Columbia University Press, 2007.

Yamane, David. *The Catholic Church in State Politics: Negotiating Prophetic Demands and Political Realities*. Lanham, MD: Sheed & Ward, 2005.

Zavodnyik, Peter. *The Age of Strict Construction: A History of the Growth of Federal Power, 1789-1861*. Washington, D.C.: The Catholic University of America Press, 2007.

Seventh-day Adventists and Religious Liberty

Adventist News Network. "Angola: rebuilding country promotes freedom of belief," July 8, 2008. http://news.adventist.org/archive/articles/2008/07/08/angola-rebuilding-country-promotes-freedom-of-belief (accessed May 29, 2012).

———. "Brazil: religious liberty event draws 32000 live, hundreds of thousands online," June 22, 2006. http://news.adventist.org/archive/articles/2006/06/22/brazil-religious-liberty-event-draws-32000-live-hundreds-of-thousands-onlin (accessed May 29, 2012).

———. "Religious freedom festival in Peru receives national endorsement," June 15, 2009, http://news.adventist.org/en/archive/articles/2009/06/15/religious-freedom-festival-in-peru-receives-national-endorsement (accessed May 20, 2012).

Andrews, J. N. *History of the Sabbath*. Payson, AZ: Leaves of Autumn, 1991.

Associated Press. "Sunday shopping banned in Croatia," July 15, 2008. http://abcnews.go.com/International/wireStory?id=5378375 (accessed on 8/27/2008).

Bacchiocchi, Samuele. *From Sabbath to Sunday: A Historical Investigation of the Rise of Sunday Observance in Early Christianity*. Rome, Italy: The Pontifical Gregorian Press, 1977.

Beach, Bert B. *Bright Candle of Courage*. Boise, ID: Pacific Press, 1989.

"The Big Questions: Keep Sunday Special?" Aired on March 24, 2010, www.bbc.co.uk/thebigquestions; "Part 1: Dr. Michael Schluter CBE, Keep Sunday Special," http:// www.youtube.com/watch?v= tN6KjM67vrk&feature=relmfu; "Part 2: Dr. Michael Schluter CBE, Keep Sunday Special," http://www.youtube.com/watch?v= Rred0PZQrdA (accessed May 9, 2010).

Bruinsma, Reinder. *Seventh-day Adventist Attitudes Toward Roman Catholicism: 1844-1965*. Berrien Springs, MI: Andrews University Press, 1994.

Carson, D. A. *From Sabbath to Lord's Day*. Eugene, OR: Wipf and Stock Publishers, 1982.

Cleary, Edward L. and Timothy J. Stegenga. *Resurgent Voices in Latin America: Indigenous Peoples, Political Mobilization, and Religious Change*. New Jersey: Rutgers, 2004.

Cook, Edwin. "Europe and the Issue of Rest," *Liberty*, Jan/Feb 2011. http://www.libertymagazine.org/index.php?id=1699 (accessed May 31, 2012).

Damsteegt, P. Gerard. *Foundations of the Seventh-day Adventist Message and Mission*. Berrien Springs, MI: Andrews University Press, 1995.

Daniel 1- 7. In The Abundant Life Bible Amplifier Series. Boise, ID: Pacific Press Publishing, 1996.

Declaration of the Seventh-day Adventist Church on Church-State Relations, under section titled "Representation to Governments and International Bodies," in *Statements, Guidelines & Other Documents*, compiled by the Communication Department of the General Conference Association of Seventh-day Adventists, 186-193. Review and Herald Publishing Assoc., 2010.

Froom, LeRoy Edwin. *The Prophetic Faith of Our Fathers*, 4 vols. Washington, D.C.: Review and Herald Publishing Association, 1948.

General Conference Association of Seventh-day Adventists. *Seventh-day Adventists Believe: A Biblical exposition of 27 fundamental doctrines.* Washington, D.C: Ministerial Association, General Conference of Seventh-day Adventists, 1988.

———. "Seventh-day Adventist World Church Statistics, 2010." http://www.adventistarchives.org/docs/Stats/SDAWorldChurch Statistics2010.PDF (accessed May 31, 2012).

Goldstein, Clifford. *El Gran Compromiso.* Miami, FL: Asociacion Publicadora Internacional, 2003.

Gratz, John. *El Adventista y . . . el ecumenismo, la política, la libertad religiosa, los católicos, la discriminación, el proseletismo, y los derechos humanos.* Doral, FL: Asociacion Publicadora Interamericana, 2010.

———. *Issues of Faith and Freedom: Defending the Right to Profess, Practice, and Promote One's Beliefs.* Silver Spring, MD: Public Affairs and Religious Liberty Department, 2008.

Heilke, Thomas. "The Promised Time of Dignitatis Humanae: A Radical Protestant Perspective." In *Catholicism and Religious Freedom: Contemporary Reflections on Vatican II's Declaration on Religious Liberty.* Edited by Kenneth L. Grasso and Robert P. Hunt, 87-113. NY: Rowman and Littlefield Publishers, 2006.

"High Court reaffirms ban on Sunday shopping." *Deutsche Welle,* February 12, 2009. http://www.dw-world.de/dw/article/0,,4953600,00.html (accessed on 5/11/2010).

Hunt, Dave. *A Woman Rides the Beast.* Eugene, OR: Harvest House Publishers, 1994.

Joshi, Mohit. "Croatian retailers sack workers as 'never on Sunday law' kicks in," January 8, 2009, TopNews.in. http://www.topnews.in/croatian-retailers-sack-workers-never-sunday-law-kicks-2106643 (accessed on 5/11/2010).

Liechty, Daniel. *Sabbatarianism in the Sixteenth Century: A Page in the History of the Radical Reformation.* Berrien Springs, MI: Andrews University Press, 1993.

Lewis, A. H. *Critical History of Sunday Legislation from 321 to 1888 A.D.* New York: D. Appleton and Company, 1888.

Loewen, M. E. *Religious Liberty and the Seventh-day Adventist.* Nashville, TN: Southern Publishing, 1964.

Miller, Peter W. "Differing from Other Councils...", *Seattle Catholic*, Jan. 3, 2003. http://www.seattlecatholic.com/article_20030103_ Differing_from_Other_ Councils.html, (accessed March 18, 2007).

Montserrat, Daniel Basterra. *La Libertad Religiosa en España y su tutela jurídica.* Universidad Complutense de Madrid, Facultad de Derecho, Departamento de Derecho Politico, 1983.

Moore, Marvin. *Challenges to the Remnant.* Nampa, ID: Pacific Press, 2008.

———. *Could It Really Happen? Revelation 13 in the light of history and current events.* Nampa, ID: Pacific Press, 2007.

Morgan, Douglas. *Adventism and the American Republic: The Public Involvement of a Major Apocalyptic Movement.* Knoxville, TN: University of Tennessee Press, 2001.

"Obispos europeos apoyan proyecto de ley sobre descanso dominical en UE." ACIPRENSA, Febrero 14, 2009. http://www.aciprensa.com/ noticia.php?n=24334 (accessed on 5/11/2010).

Olsen, V. Norskov. *Papal Supremacy and American Democracy.* Loma Linda, CA: Loma Linda University, 1987.

———. *Supremacía Papal y Libertad Religiosa.* Miami, FL: Asociación Publicadora Interamericana, 1992.

Pendleton, David A. "A Review of Marvin Moore's *Challenge to the Remnant*," *Spectrum*, September 19, 2009. http://www. spectrummagazine.org/reviews/book_ reviews/2008/09/19/review _marvin_moore%E2%80%99s_challenges_remnant, paragraphs 18-20 (accessed September 20, 2009).

Reinach, Christa and Alan J. Reinach, eds. *Politics and Prophecy.* Nampa, ID: Pacific Press, 2007.

Riggle, H. M. *The Sabbath and the Lord's Day.* Glendale, AZ: Life Assurance Ministries, n.d.

Scarone, Daniel. *El Nuevo Orden Mundial.* Miami, FL: Asociacion Publicadora Internacional, 2000.

Seventh-day Adventist Bible Commentary, vol. 7. Logos Bible Software.

Shea, William H. *Selected Studies on Prophetic Interpretation*, ed. Daniel and Revelation Committee Series. Washington, D.C.: Review and Herald Publishing, 1982.

Ugarte, Blanca de. "Prohibido trabajar en domingo?" *El Imparcial*, 3 de Marzo, 2009, http://www.elimparcial.es/contenido/35248.html (accessed on 5/11/2010).

Walker, Allen. *The Law and the Sabbath.* Nashville, TN: Southern Publishing, 1957.

Were, Louis F. *The Woman and the Beast in the Book of Revelation.* Berrien Springs, MI: LaRondelle, 1989.

White, Ellen G. *The Great Controversy.* Nampa, ID: Pacific Press Publishing, 2005.

———. *The Ellen G. White Writings: Comprehensive Research Edition*, CD. Silver Spring, MD: The Ellen G. White Estate, 2008.

———. *Spirit of Prophecy Counsels Relating to Church-State Relationships.* Compiled by The Ellen G. White Estate of the General Conference of Seventh-day Adventists. Silver Spring, MD: Ellen G. White Estate, 1964; reprinted 2000.

———. *Testimonies for the Church*, 9 vols. In *The Ellen G. White Writings: Comprehensive Research Edition*, CD, 2008.

World Council of Churches, The. *The Challenge of Proselytism and the Calling to Common Witness*, issued September 25, 1996.

Spain

Barga, Luis de la. "La futura ley española se ajusta a las normas del concilio," bajo artículo titulado, "El arzobispo de Madrid explica a YA el contenido del proyecto de confesiones." En *Ya*, Domingo, 27 de Septiembre, 1964. Archivo de la Fundación Fleidner, Madrid, España.

Beach, Beverly B. "La libertad religiosa desde una perspectiva no católica con atención especial a los derechos y los problemas de las iglesias minoritarias" in *Conciencia y libertad*, no. 12 (2000): 36-49.

Beldarrain, Javier Larena. *La Libertad Religiosa y su Protección en el Derecho Español*. Sevilla: Publicaciones Digitales, S.A., 2002.

Berenguer, Remigio Beneyto. *Fundaciones Sociales de la Iglesia Católica: Conflicto Iglesia-Estado*. Valencia: EDICEP C.B., 1996.

Blanco, María. *La Libertad Religiosa en España: Precedentes de dos organismos estatales para su protección*. Pamplona: Ediciones Universidad de Navarra, S.A., 2001.

———. *Libertad religiosa, laicidad, y cooperación en el derecho eclesiástico*. Granada: Editorial Comares, 2008.

———. *La primera ley español de libertad religiosa: génesis de la ley de 1967*. Pamplona: Ediciones Universidad de Navarra, S.A., 1999.

Bonime-Blanc, Andrea. *Spain's Transition to Democracy: The Politics of Constitution-making*. Boulder, CO: Westview Press, Inc., 1987.

Callahan, William J. *La Iglesia Católica en España (1875-2002)*. Barcelona: Critica, S.L., 2003.

Cardona, José. "El Derecho a la libertad religiosa y su actual regulación jurídica en España" in *Llamados a ser lo que somos como discípulos de Cristo en la España de hoy*. Madrid: Iglesias Evangélicas de España, 1967.

Cardona, José and Ignacio Mendoza. "Iglesia y Estado" in *Evangelio, norma y compromiso: Temas de la Conferencia de Iglesias y Ministros Evangélicos de España*. Madrid: Iglesias Evangélicas de España, 1979.

Cardoso, José Camilo. "The Progress of Religious Freedom in Latin America." In *Fides et Libertas* (2007).

Carvajal, José G. M. de. *Iglesia y Estado en España: Regimen Jurídico de sus relaciones*. Madrid: Ediciones Rioduero,1980.

Cenzano, José Carlos de Bartolome. *Derechos fundamentales y libertades públicas*. Valencia: Tirant lo blanch, 2003.

Champin, Amadeo de Fuenmayor y. *Derecho eclesiástico del estado Español*. Granada: Editorial Comares, 2007.

Ciaurriz, María José. *El derecho de proselitismo en el marco de la libertad religiosa*. Madrid: Diseno Grafico Gallego y Asociados, 2001.

Codes, Rosa María Martínez de. "The Spanish Answer to Religious Intolerance: From Institutional Intolerance to Institutional Tolerance." *Fides et Libertas* (2007).

Codes, Rosa María Martínez de, and Jaime Rossell. *Religious Freedom, Tolerance and Non-Discrimination in Education*. Caceres, Spain: Universidad de Extremadura, Servicio de Publicaciones, 2001.

Cologne, Rafael. "El nuevo mapa religioso de España: enfoque historico y sociológico." En *Conciencia y libertad*, no. 19 (2009): 45-51.

Coornhert, D.V. *Synod on the Freedom of Conscience*. Gerrit Voogt, trans. and ed. Amsterdam: Amsterdam University Press, 2008.

Corral Salvador, Carlos. *La Libertad Religiosa en la Comunidad Europea: Estudio Comparado*. Madrid: Instituto de Estudios Políticos, 1973.

Cortés, Victorino Mayoral. *España: De la intolerancia al laicismo*. Madrid: Graficas Fernandez Ciudad, 2006.

Coverdale, John F. *The Political Transformation of Spain after Franco*. New York: Praeger Publishers, 1979.

De Carli, Romina. *El derecho a la libertad religiosa en la transición democrática de España (1963-1978)*. Madrid: Graficas, S.A., 2009.

Díaz-Salazar, Rafael. *El Factor Católico en la Política Española: Del Nacionalcatólicismo al laicismo*. Madrid: PPC Editorial, 2006.

Dominguez, Antonio Alberto. *Defensa del Protestantismo: 50 Aniversario de la Comisión de Defensa Evangélica Española – FEREDE*. Madrid: Federación de Entidades Religiosas Evangélicas De Espana, 2007.

Estruch, Juan. *Los Protestantes Españoles*. Barcelona: Editorial Nova Terra, 1967.

Feito, Alfredo Grimaldos. *La Iglesia en España, 1977-2008*. Barcelona: Ediciones Peninsula, 2008.

Galende, Helena Villarejo. *Regimen jurídico de los horarios comerciales*. Granada: Editorial Comares, 1999.

Garcia, Pablo. *La Iglesia Evangélica Española: Iglesia Protestante, 125 Anos de Vida y Testimonio*. Barcelona: Departamento de Publicaciones de la IEE, 1994.

Garzon, Jacobo Israel, Alejandro Baer, Alberto Benasuly. *Los judios en la España contemporánea: Apuntes historicos y jurídicos*. Madrid: Publidisa, 2008.

Gilmour, David. *The Transformation of Spain: From Franco to the Constitutional Monarchy*. New York, NY: Quartet Books, 1985.

Gómez-Quintero, Álex Seglers, ed. *Las dimensiones jurídico-públicas de la Dignitatis Humanae*. Granada: Editorial Comares, 2007.

———. *Libertad Religiosa y Estado Autonómico*. Granada: Editorial Comares, 2005.

Gonzalez Rivas, Juan Jose, ed. *Pluralismo Religioso y Estado de Derecho*. Madrid: Cuaderno de Derechos Judiciales, 2004.

Gonzalez, Casimiro Morcillo. *Concilio Vaticano II: Constituciones, Decretos, Declaraciones con Documentos pontificios complementarios*. Madrid: Biblioteca de Autores Cristianos, 1965.

Gregori, José Cardona. *La Jerarquía eclesiástica Española y la libertad religiosa*. Madrid: Asamblea de los Hermanos, 1967.

Hera, Alberto de la. *Pluralismo y La Libertad Religiosa y*. Sevilla: Anales de la Universidad Hispalense, 1971.

Hera, Alberto de la, Agustín Motilla, Joaquin Mantecon Sancho. *La Libertad Religiosa a los veinte años de su ley orgánica*. Madrid: Ministerio de Justicia, Secretaría General Técnica, 1999.

Hera, Alberto de la, Agustín Motilla, and Rafael Palomino. *El Ejercicio de la Libertad Religiosa en España: Cuestiones Disputadas*. Madrid: Ministerio de Justicia, Secretaría General Técnica, 2003.

Hera, Alberto de la and Daniel Irastorza, eds. *La Financiación de la Libertad Religiosa*. Madrid: Ministerio de Justicia, Secretaría General Técnica, 2002.

Hera, Alberto de la and Rosa María Martínez de Codes, eds. *Encuentro de las tres confesiones religiosas: Cristianismo, Judaísmo, Islam*. Madrid: Ministerio de Justicia, Secretaría General Técnica, 2002.

———., eds. *Encuentro sobre Dignidad Humana y Libertad Religiosa*. Madrid: Ministerio de Justicia, Secretaría General Técnica, 2000.

———., eds. *Foro Iberoamericano sobre Libertad Religiosa*. Madrid: Ministerio de Justicia, Secretaría General Técnica, 2001.

———., eds. *La Libertad Religiosa en la educación escolar*. Madrid: Ministerio de Justicia, Secretaría General Técnica, 2002.

———., eds. *Proyección Nacional e Internacional de la Libertad Religiosa*. Madrid: Ministerio de Justicia, Secretaría General Técnica, 2001.

———., eds. *Spanish Legislation on Religious Affairs*. Madrid: Ministerio de Justicia, Centro de Publicaciones, 1998.

Iglesias, Juan. *Estudios: Historia de Roma, Derecho Romano, Derecho Moderno*. Madrid: Universidad Complutense de Madrid, 1975.

Llorente, Francisco Rubio. "The Writing of the Constitution of Spain." In *Constitution Makers on Constitution Making: The Experience of Eight Nations*. Edited by Robert A. Goldwin and Art Kaufman (Washington, D.C.: American Enterprise Institute for Public Policy Research, 1988.

Lopez, Fernando Santaolalla. *Ley Orgánica Libertad Religiosa: Trabajos Parliamentarios*. Madrid: Publicaciones de las Cortes Generales, 1981.

Mantecon, Joaquin and Rosa María Martínez de Codes. *Guía de Entidades Religiosas de España*. Madrid: Ministerio de Justicia, Secretaría General Técnica, 1998.

Martin, María del Mar, Mercedes Salido, and José María Vazquez Garcia-Peñuela, eds. *Iglesia Católica y Relaciones Internacionales*. Granada: Editorial Comares, 2008.

Martínez, Isidoro Martin. *Iglesia y Comunidad Política en la Enseñanza del Episcopado Mundial Despues del Vaticano II*. Madrid: Fundación Universitaria Español, 1976.

Martínez, José M. *La España evangélica ayer y hoy: Esbozo de una historia para una reflexión*. Barcelona: Editorial CLIE, 1994.

Martínez-Torron, Javier, ed. *La libertad religiosa y de conciencia ante la justicia constitucional*. Granada: Editorial Comares, 1998.

———. *Religión, derecho y sociedad: Antiguos y nuevos planteamientos en el derecho eclesiástico del estado*. Granada: Editorial Comares, 1999.

Monroy, Juan A. "La España evangélica hacia el siglo XXI" in *Una fe, un pueblo, un proposito*. Barcelona: Editorial CLIE, 1998.

Montero y Gutierrez, Eloy. *El Nuevo Concordato Español*. Madrid: Edición del autor, 1954.

Motilla, Agustín. "Proselitismo y Libertad Religiosa en el Derecho Español." In *Conciencia y Libertad* No. 12, (2000): 50-61.

Murgoitio, José Manuel. *Igualdad religiosa y diversidad de trato de la Iglesia Católica*. Pamplona: Ediciones Universidad de Navarra, S.A., 2008.

Navarro-Valls, Rafael and Rafael Palomino. *Estado y Religion: Textos para una reflexión critica*. Barcelona: Editorial Ariel, S.A., 2003.

Ojea, Gonzalo Puente. *Ateismo y religión: Debate moderno*. Barcelona, 2010.

Ortega, Abraham Barrero. *La libertad religiosa en España*. Madrid: Taravilla, 2006.

Ortega, Maria Elena Olmos. "Los Acuerdos con la Santa Sede: Instrumentos Garantes de la Libertad Religiosa." In *Iglesia Católica y Relaciones Internacionales: Actas del III Simposio Internacional de Derecho Concordatorio*. Edited by Maria del Mar Martin, Mercedes Salido, Jose Maria Vazquez Garcia-Peñuela. Granada: Editorial Comares, 2008.

Otaola, Javier. *Laicidad: una estrategia para libertad*. Barcelona: Ediciones Bellaterra, 1999.

Perez-Agote, Alfonso and Jose Santiago. *La Nueva Pluralidad Religiosa*. Madrid: V.A. Impresores, S.A., 2009.

Prieto, Paulino Cesar Pardo. *Laicidad y acuerdos del estado con confesiones religiosas*. Valencia: Torant lo Blanch, 2008.

Prisco, Jose San Jose and Myriam M. Cortes Dieguez, eds. *Derecho Canónico II: El derecho en la misión de la Iglesia*. Madrid: Biblioteca de Autores Cristianos, 2006.

Public Affairs and Religious Liberty Department (PARL), European Union. Scanned document #2135.

———. Scanned document #2136.

———. Scanned documents for Israel Pérez Sainero.

Quadro-Salcedo, Tomas de la, Gustavo Suarez Pertierra, Carlos Amigo Vallego. *La nueva realidad religiosa Española: 25 años de la Ley Orgánica de Libertad Religiosa*. Madrid: EGRAF, S.A., 2006.

Ripoll, Emilio Castelar y. *Discurso sobre la libertad religiosa*. Barcelona: Linkgua ediciones S.L., 2007.

Rivas, Juan Jose Gonzalez, ed. *Pluralismo religioso y Estado de derecho*. Madrid: Consejo General del Poder Judicial, 2004.

Reyes, Roman. *Europa, Siglo XXI: Secularización y Estados Laicos*. Madrid: Artes Graficas Cofas, S.A., 2006.

Robbers, Gerhard. "La religión en la Constitución para Europa." In *Conciencia y libertad*, no. 15 (2003-2004): 26-31.

Rodriguez, Manuel Lopez. *La España Protestante: Crónica de una minoria marginada (1937-1975)*. Madrid: SEDMAY Ediciones, S.A., 1976.

Rossell, Jaime. "Las leyes de libertad religiosa Española y portuguesa: un análisis comparativo." En *Conciencia y libertad*, no. 16 (2005): 100-130.

Rubio, Santiago Catala. *El derecho a la personalidad jurídica de las entidades religiosas*. Cuenca: Ediciones de la Universidad de la Castilla-La Mancha, 2004.

Ruiz, Maximo Garcia. *Libertad religiosa en España: Un largo camino*. Madrid: Grafitec, 2006.

Salvador, Carlos Corral. *Libertad religiosa hoy en España*. Madrid: Ediciones Graficas Ortega, 1992.

———. *La relación entre la Iglesia y la comunidad política*. Madrid: Biblioteca de Autores Cristianos, 2003.

Sanchez, Isidoro Martin. *Curso de derecho eclesiástico del estado*. Valencia: Tirant lo blanch, 1997.

Sancho, Joaquin Mantecon. "El Reconocimiento de las Confesiones Minoritarias en España." En *Libertad Religiosa: Actas del Congreso Latinoamericano de Libertad Religiosa*. Lima: Fondo Editorial de la Pontificia Universidad Católica del Peru, 2001.

Soria, Salvador Tarodo and Irina Alejandra Junieles Acosta. *Derechos humanos, minorias culturales y religiosas en Colombia y España*. Zarautz: Itxaropena, 2006.

Strom, Kaare, Wolfgang C. Muller, and Torbjorn Bergman, eds. *Delegation and Accountability in Parliamentary Democracies*. Oxford: Oxford University Press, 2003.

U. S. State Dept. Report – 2007. http://www.state.gov/j/drl/rls/irf/2007/90201.htm (accessed June 8, 2012).

Vanguardia Español, La. October 2, 1964. Archivo de la Fundación Fleidner, Madrid.

Vazquez, Paloma Lorenzo. *Libertad religiosa y enseñanza en la Constitución*. Madrid: Imprenta Nacional del Boletin Oficial del Estado, 2003.

Vera Urbano, Francisco de Paula. *Derecho Eclesiástico I: Cuestiones fundamentales de Derecho Canónico, Relaciones Estado-Iglesias, y Derecho Eclesiástico del Estado.* Madrid: Ediciones Tecnos, 1990.

———. *La Libertad Religiosa como Derecho de la Persona: Estudio Filosófico-Jurídico.* Madrid: Instituto de Politica, 1971.

Vilar, Juan Bautista. *La Cuestión Social en la Iglesia Española Contemporánea.* Madrid: El Escorial, 1981.

Vilar, Juan B. *Intolerancia y libertad en la españa contemporanea: Los Origines del Protestantismo Español Actual.* Madrid: Graficas Lavel, S.A., 1994.

The U. S. Constitution, The First Amendment, and UNDHR 18

Abbot, Henry of North Carolina, July 30, 1788. In *Eliot's Debates*, vol. 4:191-192. *The American Reference Library* CD. The Western Standard Publishing Company and World Book Encyclopedia, Inc., 2000.

Alley, Robert S., ed. *The Constitution and Religion.* Amherst, NY: Prometheus Books, 1999.

Brenner, Lenni, ed. *Jefferson and Madison on Separation of Church and State: Writings on Religion and Secularism.* Fort Lee, NJ: Barricade Books Inc., 2004.

Cassirer, Ernst. *The Philosophy of the Enlightenment.* Boston, MA: Beacon Press, 1962.

Clough, Wilson Ober. *Intellectual Origins of American National Thought: Pages from the Books Our Founding Fathers Read.* New York, NY: Corinth Books, 1961.

Conkle, Daniel O. "Free Exercise Clause." In *Encyclopedia of Religious Freedom.* Edited by Catharine Cookson, 136-139. New York: Routledge, 2003.

Dawson, Joseph Martin. *America's Way in Church, State, and Society.* New York: Macmillan, 1953.

Denenfeld, Philip S. "The Conciliar Declaration and the American Declaration." In *Religious Liberty: an End and a Beginning*. Edited by John Courtney Murray, 120-132. New York: Macmillan, 1966.

Flowers, Ronald B. *That Godless Court? Supreme Court decisions on Church-State Relationships*. Louisville, KY: Westminster John Knox Press, 2005.

Gaustad, Edwin S. *Sworn on the Altar of God*. Grand Rapids, MI: Eerdmans, 1996.

Kaminski, John P. and Richard Leffler. *Creating the Constitution*. Action, MA: Copley Publishing Group, 1999.

Green, Evarts B. *Religion and the State: The Making and Testing of an American Tradition*. New York: New York University Press, 1941.

Koch, Adrienne. *Jefferson & Madison: The Great Collaboration*. London: Oxford University Press, 1976.

Lawler, Peter Augustine. "Murray's Natural-Law Articulation of the American Proposition." In *John Courtney Murray and the American Civil Conversation*. Edited by Robert P. Hunt and Kenneth L. Grasso, 116-134. Grand Rapids, MI: Eerdman's, 1992.

Laycock, Douglas. "Religion and the State: Article: The Origins of the Religion Clauses of the Constitution: 'Non-preferential' aid to religion: A False Claim about Original Intent." *William and Mary Law Review*, 27 (Summer, 1986): 875.

McConnell, Michael W., John H. Garvey, and Thomas C. Berg. *Religion and the Constitution*. New York: Aspen Publishers, 2002.

Mclaren, John and Harold Coward, eds. *Religious Conscience, the State, and the Law: Historical Contexts and Contemporary Significance*. New York, NY: State University of New York Press, 1999.

Marshall, Paul. "Religious Freedom and the United Nations' Universal Declaration of Human Rights." In *Fifty Years After the Declaration: The United Nations' Record on Human Rights*. Edited by Teresa Wagner and Leslie Carbone. Lanham, MD: University Press of America, 2001.

Mason, David T. "Animadversions on John Courtney Murray's Political Ontology." In *John Courtney Murray and the American Civil Conversation*. Edited by Robert P. Hunt and Kenneth L. Grasso, 135-163. Grand Rapids, MI: Eerdman's, 1992.

Miller, Robert T. and Ronald B. Flowers. *Toward Benevolent Neutrality: Church, State, and the Supreme Court*, 5th ed. 2 vols. Waco, TX: Baylor University Press, 1996.

Morsink, Johannes. *The Universal Declaration of Human Rights: Origins, Drafting, and Intent*. Philadelphia, PA: University of Pennsylvania Press, 1999.

Mueller, William A. *Church and State in Luther and Calvin*. Nashville, TN: Broadman Press, 1952.

Perry, Richard L., ed. *Sources of Our Liberties: Documentary Origins of Individual Liberties in the United States Constitution and Bill of Rights*. Chicago: American Bar Foundation, 1978.

Pfeffer, Leo. "Religious Liberty." In *The First Amendment: Selections from the Encyclopedia of the American Constitution*. Edited by Leonard W. Levy, Kenneth L. Karst, and Dennis J. Mahoney, 439-451. New York: MacMillan, 1990.

Smith, Elwyn A. *Religious Liberty in the United States*. Philadelphia, PA: Fortress Press, 1972.

Stokes, Anson Phelps. *Church and State in the United States*, 3 vols. New York: Harper & Bros., 1950.

Sullivan, Kathleen M. and Gerald Gunther. *First Amendment Law*. New York: Foundation Press, 1999.

Tahzib, Bahiyyih G. *Freedom of Religion or Belief: Ensuring Effective International Legal Protection*. The Hague, Netherlands: Martinus Nijhoff Publishers, 1996.

Tocqueville, Alexis de. "Of the progress of Roman Catholicism in the U.S." In *Democracy in America*, vol. 2, Book 1, ch. 6. *The American Reference Library* CD. The Western Standard Publishing Company and World Book Encyclopedia, Inc., 2000.

Whelan, Ruth. "Bayle, Pierre." In *Encyclopedia of the Enlightenment*, 4 vols. Edited by Alan Charles Kors, 1:121-125. New York: Oxford University Press, 2003.

Internet Sources

Cornell University Law School, Legal Information Institute. http://www.law.cornell.edu/supct/.

International Religious Liberty Association, http://www.irla.org/354.htm.

Murray, John Courtney. On-line library, http://woodstock.georgetown.edu/library/Murray/0_murraybib.html.

Vatican Archives, Code of Cannon Law. http://www.vatican.va/archive/ENG1104/_ INDEX.HTM.

INDEX

(*DH* = *Dignitatis Humanae*; numbers after "footnote" refer to **page** number)

A

Abortion, as common social issues with Protestants, 33; as a moral issue challenged by the laity, 33, 34; Cardinal Arinze to U.S. legislators, 35, 36; some progressive Catholics see *DH* as allowing, 63; John Kerry and, 101; Catholic political leaders who support, 101; religious freedom of *DH* and, 167; debate of during transition to democracy in Spain, 238-240; Benedict XVI regarding, in Spain, 254-255; and Obama Health Care Law, 284-287; as a societal goal, 300. In footnotes, 101, 235.

Absolutism, religious, 52, 60.

Accidental power, defined, 71; in relation to the papacy, 84; overlooked by Murray r.e. papal power, 99.

Accomodationism, 304. See also non-preferentialism in footnote, 7.

Aconfessional state, 248.

Ad extirpanda, as part of the Inquisition, 127; jurisdictional authority of, 128; means by which the Church gained secular support, 161.

Ad gentes, 188, 305. In footnotes, 188, 208, 311.

Ad Hoc Committee on Religious Freedom, 284, 285.

Albornoz, A. F. Carillo de, in footnote, 141.

Amendment, First, 4, 227, 288-289, (different from *DH*) 94, 290, 291, 298-299, 304; Catholic Church claims equal to *DH*, 280; Catholic Church claims denial of in America, 285-286. In footnotes, 4-7, 43, 85, 88, 89, 90, 94, 161, 298.

Americanism, defined, 57, 85; Murray's, 68, 69; Political, 70; Ecclesial, 70.

Anabaptists, 168.

Anglican, and ecumenism, 31, 32; and Jefferson, 87.

Aquinas, Thomas, adapted the political thought of Aristotle, 21; contrary to Scripture, 149-150; on conditional toleration, 147, 154; on death of heretics, 148; summary of application, 151. In footnotes, 21, 22, 122, 148-151, 154.

Auto de fe, 133.

B

Bainton, Roland, 133.

Baptist(s), and James Madison, 87; Seventh-day, 209.

Bayle, Pierre, 87, 88.

Beach, Bert, 251.

Beast of Revelation Chapter 13, 209, 217, 219, 223.

Benedict XVI, and secularism in Europe, 27; and Roman Catholicism in Spain, 27, 28; and the nature of man, 43; and interpretation of *DH*, 75-76; and the Church regarding religious freedom, 98, 230-231; celebration of the Mass in honor of the Cristeros, 259; and regulation of democracy in Spain, 242, 242, 258; and the threat of laicism in Spain, 254-256; and the common good of humanity, 283; caution regarding Turkey joining the European Union, 283.

Bishop(s), ecumenical efforts of in America, 31, 101; in Philippines r.e. Reproductive Health Bill, 34-35; Archb. Tobin and Rep. Patrick Kennedy, 35; in Malta, 38; Archb. Weakland challenged Vatican silencing, 39-40; papal appointment of vs. laity appointment, 57-58; and Americanism, 69-70; responsibilities of local, during Inquisition, 128; and proselytism in Mexico, 196; and Sunday advocacy in Europe, 198-200; and Constantine, 126, 203; American, and J. F. Kennedy on separationism, 218, 227; and Franco, 236; in Spain, accept *DH* with reticence, 242-244; in Spain, influenced the Constitutional foundation to grant the Church favor, 245; in Mexico, as organizing political activism, 267-268; and Obama Health Care Law as a violation of religious freedom, 279, 284-286; and restriction of Catholics' conscience in America, 287-288; used hypothetically r.e. conscience, 293; Carol Wojtyla (John Paul II) and *DH*, 295; in New York City mosque controversy, 300; efforts to establish democracy in Spain, 303; conferences and state governments in European Union states, 323.

Boff, Leonardo, 34, 39.

Boniface VIII, 71, 74.

Brethren, separated; religious freedom as part of the ecumenical effort to regain, 30-33, 45; Protestants defined as, with common social goals, 173; Catholic Jurisdictional Authority helps define, 146.

Bruinsma, Reinder, in footnote, 181.

C

Catholic, areas of consonance with SDAs, 181-188; areas of dissonance with SDAs, 188-197; defined, 188; statistics of, 188; Church still retains coercive authority, 291-292; *Catechism of the Church* and the "erroneous conscience," 292-294; scholars who advocate the "common good" based on a religious society founded upon the Church's teachings, 294-298; scholars in America who distort the First Amendment with *DH*, 299; *DH* allows the Church to challenge non- social values, 299-301; uncertainty of the future of religious freedom under *DH* based on scholars of the Church, 301; uniqueness of the *Catholica*, 302; the Church and *DH* produce hybrid church-state models, 303; the Church applies *DH* in different ways to establish or maintain its hegemony, 304; hegemony thesis is accurate, 304; hegemony and "regulated democracy," 304; accommodationism patterns the Church's model of religious freedom from *DH*, 304-305; the Church's re-evangelization of Spain, 305; the Church seeks a preeminent role among religious groups, 305; the Church's hegemony, 306; *DH* contains uniquely tailored concepts of the Church's religious freedom, 306; the one true faith subsists in the and Apostolic Church, 308; *DH* leaves untouched the traditional doctrine of the moral duty of all men to the true religion and the one Church of Christ, 308; doctrine that man's response to God must be free, 314; objections to concordats, 322; does not seek exclusive rights in the agreements with the States, 322; at the Diet of Speyer (1544), and Protestants received funds to support their educational efforts, 324; *et alli*.

Christianization, of society and *DH*, 163; religious freedom in, 227; future prospects of, 192, 222, 297; during 4th and 5th centuries, 205; practical implications for minority religions, 194.

Civic duties, in relation to toleration, 156.

Civil right, as immunity from coercion, 41, 299, 303; of *DH* different from Enlightenment, 42; of *DH* as portrayed by media, 45; as part of "Political Americanism," 70; distinct from Catholic confessional state, 80; narrow in application, 92; why needed, 94; of the Church to coerce, 101, 102; compared to Diet of Speyer II, 142; not a guarantee against coercion, 145; not as empowerment, 151; not as commonly understood, 156; to curtail the State in religious matters, 158; legal recourse decreed by the Church to which one appeals, 160-161; to seek the truth, 172; as distinguished from the moral sphere, 172; granted to minority religions in a Catholic dominated society, 192; not as freedom of conscience, 228.

Coercion, immunity from by any human power, 14, 15, 158-159; in the history of Malta, 36; immunity from versus toleration, 43, 147, 153, 154, 156-158; Murray based immunity from upon misreading of the First Amendment, 94; immunity from implies power to, 94, 157, 168; Jesus condemned all forms of, 117; church discipline to members is not, 124; the Inquisition and the Church's use of, 125-130; historical comparison, 140, 142; will is still free whether under subtle or direct, 144-145; act of faith free from all, 145; Church retains power to, but does not exert it, 147, 228; immunity from is similar to the Church's position at the Diet of Speyer (1526), 147; Murray's rationale for immunity from, 151-152; immunity from in *DH* is revocable or a permanent principle, 155; if immunity is removed, 160-161; modern state is at the disposition of the Church to grant immunity from, 161; Church claims to support immunity from, 163; freedom from for the community and the individual, 165; freedom of the will by nature even if under, 171; Satanic character, 210; by "immunity from" Catholicism avoids the issue of freedom of conscience, 228; SDA interpretation of *DH*'s "immunity from", 229; difficult for Spanish courts to determine who uses psychological, 254; both the Church and civil authority have power to, 291-292.

Coercitio, defined, 160; as used by Roman magistrates, 160; of modern states, 161.

Communism, as threat to society, 21; threat to the Church, 23; fall of in Europe, 25; fall of, attests to political power of *DH*, 44-45; aggressive hegemony counteracts, 45; contributed to UNDHR 18, 94.

Concordats, as a form of Catholic hegemony, 18; as part of Catholic missiology, 194; history of, 195; not used by Seventh-day Adventists, 229; substituted by Agreements, 245-249; in Mexico, disallowed, 274; claimed to promote religious freedom for all, 322-323.

Condorcet, Marie Jean de (Fr. *philosophe*), 87.

Confessional state, functions best under monarchy, 30; SSPX uphold classical view of, 48; as distinct from Murray's apolitical Catholicism, 80; Traditionalist Catholics want all to be, 98; as an exception to the rule, 164; Murray argued against, 221; Church in Spain as Crypto-, 245, 247, 248; Spain from, to semi-, 257; former, now under autonomous recognition, 282; Neuhaus on Islamic, 282; as a future possibility, 296-298; as classical model of church-state relations, 303.

Congar, Yves, S. J., 156, 171, 292, 301.

Congregation for the Doctrine of the Faith, and silencing, 39; and investigating Boff and Curran, 39.

Congregation for the Evangelization of the Peoples, 28, 305.

Congress, office is a secular one, 87; Madison formulated restraints of, from *Memorial and Remonstrance*, 89; no power to coerce, 92-94; Jefferson's concerns of a corrupt, 93; liberty, held by IRLA, 177; prohibition of, in First Amendment, 289, 290.

Conley, John, S.J., argues that *DH* allows for a Catholic confessional state, 79-80.

Conscience, Vatican II promoted human rights and freedom of, 12; Pope Leo XIII opposed freedom of, 12; Protestant Reformers and the Peace of Augsburg, battle for freedom of, 17; Progressive Catholics seek complete freedom of, 34; Catholic hierarchy do not apply *DH* to give complete freedom of, 36; some Maltese Catholics respect the freedom of non-Catholics, 37, 38; contradictions between "silencing" and freedom of, 39; and immunity from coercion, 42, 43; in *DH* apparent respect for freedom of, 45; freedom of condemned, 53, 54; Progressive Catholics and freedom of, 63; freedom of must be understood in historical context, 68, 69; to avoid extreme freedom of, such as atheism and religious indifference, 85; Bayle on freedom of, 87-88; *DH* does not allow for freedom of apart from a religious mooring, 90, 91; freedom of in First Amendment and UNDHR 18 contrasted with *DH*, 92-96; *DH* offers a narrow interpretation of freedom of, 99; the Church persuades the moral, 100; the New Testament teaching r.e., 102-115; summary of New Testament teaching r.e., 123-125; Luther and the struggle for freedom of, 130; Luther's defense of individual freedom of, 135; protest of the princes and Protestant princes, 138; unfolding of the Protestant struggles for, 139; for Murray, liberty of, but not religious indifference, 152, 153; Congar and the erroneous, 156; freedom of subject to the authority of the Church, 162; societal and Christianization, 163; Murray's *sacerdotium* and *civis idem Christianum* subject to Church authority, 166; Catholic hegemony, coercion, and, 170-173; God does not force the, 179, 191; when in conflict with civil authority r.e. moral principles, follow the Word of God and, 180; Catholic laymen who follow, should see that the divine law is inscribed in the life of the earthly city, 185; development of in harmony with the eternal law and natural law, 186; freedom of, the duty of the state to uphold, 191; proselytism and freedom of, 195-196; obliged in to arrange Sunday rest, 198; the Church skips the complex issue of freedom of through *DH*, 228; secular governments should respect freedom of, 228; *DH* and freedom of, 244; separation and freedom of, 248; modern legal definition of freedom of, 271; Affordable Care Act offers freedom of to both religious institutions and the individual, 286, 289; Catholic Bishops try to control, 287, 288; the moral sphere and the erroneous, 292-294; religious freedom guarantees of *DH* conditional upon a properly formed, 294; the Church uses *DH* to confront totalitarian regimes by arguing for freedom of, 301; the Christian, or Catholic, manifest through public laws, 304; this book offers guiding principles to those seeking to preserve freedom of, 306; in *DH*, 308, 309, 314, 315, 317.

Constantine, theocratic notions from, until 16th century, 74; assumed jurisdiction in ecclesial affairs, 84; letter *Aeterna et religiosa* to the bishops in Arles, 126; and union of church with state, 203; and Sunday laws, 203, 205.

Constitutional, as part of Catholic Hegemony Thesis, 1; *DH* is adapted to democratic ideas, so the progress of democracy includes the possibility of Catholic hegemony, 31, 44, 304; *DH* places limits upon the power of government r.e. religious freedom, 44; limitations of pope's powers, 54; Murray's "political Americanism" includes principles, 69; model of religious freedom founded upon challenges a theocratic model, 74; guaranteed freedom of conscience, 88; hypothetical order in which religious freedom is curtailed, 164; if order differs from Catholic moral and political philosophy, then Catholic civil servants face the dilemma of which to uphold, 192; *DH* written to address the current political system of, 221; guarantees of to preserve religious freedom not always secure, 227; definition of limitations for a healthy government, 232-233; making of in Spain, the Church gained its conservative agenda, 239-240; in Spain, comments of Constitutional Fathers, 245; during period in 1978 in Spain, the Church asserted its *libertas ecclesiastica* to gain preeminence, 257; President Gortari's favor to the Church in Mexico was un-, 269; reforms in Mexico aided the Catholic Church, 270; in 1992, changes to Mexican, 273; reforms that limit religious associations from political activity, 277; *DH* uses language adapted to, 299, 304; order can give special civil recognition to one religion, 312; religious freedom as guarantee in *Dignitatis Humanae*, 312, 317, 318;

Contraception, in *Humanae Vitae*, 21, 35; challenge of the Church, 33; in Philippines, 34; and Progressive Catholics, 63; in Spain during Franco, 236; applying *DH* to, 286; in the U.S., 287.

Corpus Christianum, 15, 127, 128.

Cristeros, 265, 268.

Croatia, and national Sunday law, 199, 200, 209, 219, 306.

Cuius regio, eius religio, 18. In footnotes, 52.

Curran, Charles, 34, 39, 64.

D

Damsteegt, Gerard, in footnotes, 9, 181.

Daniel, Book of, indicating God's control over earthly rulers, 182; "times" of Daniel 7 and Rev. 12-13, 209-210; identity of the Little Horn, 211; interpretation of Daniel 7, 212; Daniel 7 and Rev. 13 parallel, 223; and the "times" of *DH*, 229.

Davies, Michael, a Catholic Traditionalist, 50; calls for a repeal of *DH*, 60; no reference to "doctrinal error" in *DH*, 60-61; no Catholic State and no "true religion" in *DH*, 61; on "public order" in *DH*, 62; no tolerance in *DH*, 62.

De Civitate Dei, 74.

Deist(ic), Jefferson was, 87; concepts and Madison r.e. First Amendment, 91; framers of UNDHR distanced from notions, 96; concepts leading to UNDHR 18, 98; notions in contrast to *DH*, 98.

Democratic Catholicism, 192, 241, 242, 258.

Demos, defined, 285; role of moral authority in society, 173; health care benefits to, are not anti-Catholic, 286; required to pay taxes, 289; some not religiously oriented, 289; spirit behind the Constitution, 289; versus religio-conscience, 289; and private health care institutions, 289; freedom of conscience to choose best health care, 289; obligations of health care institutions r.e., 289.

Dies Domini, 198, 208.

Diet of Speyer (1526), 16, 17, 135, 136, 137, 143, 147.

Diet of Speyer II (1529), 17, 136, 137, 141, 142, 172, 244, 257.

Diet of Speyer (1544), 324; also in footnote, 139.

Diet of Worms, 16, 133, 134, 135, 136, 137.

Dignitatis Humanae, concepts from Catholic position at Diet of Speyer II (1526) similar to, 140, 142; applied in Spain, 242-245, 257; and Concordats, 245-249; applied in Mexico, 266-268; Implementation of, 278, 279; Institute, 279; in U.S. foreign policy, 280-284; in U.S. domestic policy, 284-290; does not harmonize with American religious freedom concepts, 290; and latent authority to coerce, 291-292; and the Moral Sphere, 292-294; and the Common Good, 294-296; and the establishment of a Catholic society, 296-298; the political nature of, 298-301; interpreted and applied differently in America and Spain, 300; contradictory periods of Church history within, 301; and future research, 303; Catholic Hegemony Thesis, 304; Catholic hegemony and the future of religious freedom under, 304-306; advances the Church's public image and institutional policies, 301, 306; document itself in Appendix A, 307-321; *et alli*.

Dignitatis Humanae Institute, 279.

Disfellowship, 171.

E

Eck, Johann, 151.

Ecumenical (-ism), *Dignitatis Humanae* adopted to promote relations, 30; Catholic Church relinquishes overt hegemony to foster relations, 30; dialogue among

Orthodox, historical Protestant, and Anglicans, 31; Bishop's Committee on, and Interreligious Affairs, 31; Catholic pursuit of, with Protestants, 32; consensus r.e. ethical and theological need for religious freedom, 158; meetings with Seventh-day Adventists, 174; as part of the new evangelization, 188; theology of, and conversion to Catholic Church, 302; and Catholic hegemony, 302.

Encyclical, most significant on church-state relations, 55; debate between Progressive and Traditional Catholics r.e., 57-58; modern laid foundation for religious freedom, 65; no definitive position on religious freedom in, 67; Murray predominantly appeals to Pope Leo XIII's, 68; proper way to interpret, 77, 80.

Enlightenment, modern religious freedom based on, 42; rebuked by Pope Leo XIII, 54; concept of the state, 54; emphasis upon the individual led Vatican II to focus on Christian anthropology, 79; corollary ideas of, 85; First Amendment founded upon and political practicalities, 89; no synthesis with Catholic objective moral order, 94; thought and UNDHR 18 best define "conscience", 94-95; offers appealing structure to societal governance based on general religion and morality yet less dogmatic than formal religion, 95; common reference to deity in, 95; Locke was a thinker of the, 88, 95;incompatibility between the First Amendment religion clauses and *DH* because of, 96; UNDHR 18 surpasses deistic notions of, 96, 98; philosophical foundation of *DH* contrary to, 98-99; Catholic scholars acknowledge that *DH* not founded upon, 99; freedom of conscience and non-belief inherent to, 99; influence upon "free exercise" includes non-belief, 289; modern religious freedom documents contrasted with *DH*, 299.

En re religiosa (in religious matters), 158, 160.

Excommunicate, of Luther, 16, 132; warning of against Sen. Kerry, 101; of heretics, 149.

Exsurge domine, Bull condemning Luther's views,131-132, 161.

F

Farr, Thomas, believes *DH* should guide U.S. foreign policy, 280-281.

Folkenberg, Robert S., 215.

Foreign policy (U.S.), 280-281.

Foro interno, sacredness of inner sanctuary, 114.

Fortnight for Freedom, 284.

France, Gallicanism in, 54; as a lay state, Pope Leo XIII condemned, 58, 69; Philip

IV of, vs. Pope Boniface VIII, 71; Philip of, resisted the papacy, 83; Jefferson living in, at ratification of U.S. Constitution, 93; Inquisition in, 129; Sunday rest laws in, 200; laicite birthed in, 256.

Franco, Generalissimo Francisco, death of in 1975, 231; structural elements of government endured after his death, 234; Catholic Church exercised extra-parliamentary involvement after his death, 235; privileges for the Church bestowed by, 236; appointed bishops rather than allowing the Church to do so, 236; granted reforms to liberal groups in 1960s, 237; Church and other institutions that supported, 237; after death of, some Church hierarchy wanted authoritative regime, others wanted reform, 237; Church became nationalized under, 241; in transition from, to democracy, Church retained hegemony, 244; some Church hierarchy attempted to reconcile privileges under, with Vatican II, 244; Church supported and denounced, 256-258.

G

Gaudium et spe, practical application, 19, 64, 66, 185; Pope Benedict XVI issued minimalist interpretation, 75; basis of the Public Church Model, 100; in conjunction with *Dignitatis Humanae*, *Ad gentes*, *Nostra aetate* to define religious freedom, 305.

Gelasius I, 71, 74.

Germany, opposed the Papacy, 54; the Inquisition in, 129; *Exsurge domine* spread throughout, 131; in 1484, Inquisition established in north, 134; Diet of Speyer II in, 135-137; Papacy feared all of, would become Protestant, 143; Sunday rest law in, 200, 209, 219.

Gilson, Etienne, influenced by Jacques Maritain and contributed to Vatican II documents, 27; hermeneutics of r.e. papal teachings, 77; Murray may not follow hermeneutics of, 78; Church tolerates a temporary separation of Church and State, 227.

Gortari, Carlos Salinas de, invited Catholic dignitaries to his Presidential Inauguration, 268; dialogue with Catholic Church r.e. modern concept of Church-State relations, 269; appointed personal representative to the Holy See, 269; political efforts favored Catholic Church, 270, 273; Church regained societal influence through, 271; reforms favoring the Church have potential to renew Church-State conflicts, 276-277; ecclesiastical reforms, 277.

Graham, Robert A., S.J., describes the religious and political nature of the Papacy, 46.

Graz, John, questions the religious liberty of conscience promoted by the Catholic

Church, 195-196; describes negativity r.e. proselytism, 252; questions state establishment of religion, 253.

Great Controversy, The, in footnotes, 9, 191, 215.

H

Harrison, Fr. Bryan, 64.

Health Care, 285, 288, 299.

Hegemony, Catholic thesis defined, 1, 15; subtle form of Catholic by Murray, 6; struggle for religious between Catholics and Protestants, 16; religious still a factor today, 17; issues that define Catholic, 18; shift from paternalistic to public church role, 19; why the Church relinquished outright, overt, 29; pre-Vatican II overt relinquished to foster ecumenical relations, 30; *DH* contains unchanging concepts that aid the Church in its quest for, 40; semi-overt form of, 44; includes societal influence by the Church, 45; liberty of the Church does not require, or deny political, 45; *DH* allows for both aggressive and passive forms of, 45; dual nature of the Church impacts, 45-46; exchange of religious and political, 46; by advancing religious freedom, the Church obtains, 46; the Church retained through the majority of its citizens, 52; outright Catholic denied in many countries by *DH*, 98; variety of factors reveal, 98-99; overt form of through Murray's misapplication of John of Paris's model, 99; Traditional and Progressive Catholics r.e., 99; overt Catholic becomes evident in *DH* by historical analysis and comparison, 140, 141; versus individual conscience, 172; Sunday laws demonstrate overt tendencies of Catholic, 217, 228; in Spain, the Church retains, 244, 247; in Spain, a demonstration of the Catholic thesis, 257; in Spain, recovery of depends upon regulation of democracy, 242, 257-258; in Mexico, the Church uses *DH* to recover, 267; restriction of by denial of Concordat, 274; reverse effect of in Mexico, 275; in Mexico, the Church faces a variety of bulwarks to establish, 277; weakening of Islamic to allow Catholic and other religions in the Middle East, 282-284; *DH* used to advance the Church's, 290; political dimension of *DH* reveals three areas of, 299; the Church uses *DH* as a two-edged sword, 299; the Church's two-fold strategy to obtain, 301; questions the nature of contending parties, 302; the Catholic thesis is defined and accurate, 304; through *DH* the spread of democracy includes Catholic, 304; non-preferentialism not ideal with religious groups, 305; the Catholic Church has tendencies toward, 306.

Heilke, Thomas, views of *DH*, 223-224.

Hittinger, F. Russel, Catholic scholar and a Thomist, 45; identifies Church's modern teaching on religious freedom as beginning in the 1940s, 65; contrasts Madison's *Memorial and Remonstrance* with *DH*, 89-90; fails to point out that *DH* pro-actively supports religion with a special regard for Roman Catholicism, 90; argues that religious freedom would remain in effect for everyone in a Christianized society, 163; teachings of *DH* are conditional upon time and circumstances, 164; differs from Murray r.e. perpetuity of *DH*, 164; defends *DH* as a document through which the Church defends religious freedom, 167; indicates that *DH* focuses upon the right of the Church to Christianize society, 167; indicates that *DH* denies to any entity, including the Church, the right to coerce, 164, 171; explains *DH* in view of a Christianized society, 222-223; *DH* not formulated for a future, Christianized, societal construct, 163, 301.

Hobbes, Thomas, 81.

Humanae vitae, explains the Church's stance on contraception, 21; not violate the conscience of any, 35; *DH* and, in apparent contradiction, 34-35; imposed upon non-Catholics, 34, 306.

I

Immortale Dei, defined, 55; used by Pope Pius X, 57; Progressive and Traditionalist Catholics debate over, 58.

Immunity, language of *DH* to define religious freedom, 12; *DH* guarantees the right of the Church to fulfill its mission and the right of the individual to, 41; limits the constitutional power of government, creating a sacred space of, 44; Murray assumed that government had authority to coerce in religious matters and thus required, 94; contrasted with the biblical concept of toleration, 102; relation between the Church and state in medieval period gives insights r.e., 127; at Diet of Speyer II as a suspension of force, 140, 142; in *DH* refers more to the Church retaining coercive authority and not using it, 147; reflects different reference points and different subjects upon whom obligations rest, 147; distinction between right as empowerment, 151-152; from coercion harmonizes with the Church's belief that the act of faith must be free, 152; for Murray, based on consciousness of humanity r.e. its own dignity to search for truth, 152; contrasted with religious freedom, 155; contrasted with toleration, 156-157, 4243; does not reflect the Lockean concept of inalienable rights, 160; if withdrawn, coercive authority remains, 161; *DH* presupposes the modern state to be at the Church's disposition to grant from coercion, 161; from coercion by a government pro-actively supporting Christianity, 165; under Constantine, priests enjoyed from regular courts, 205; from coercion used by the Church to skirt larger issue of religious freedom based on freedom of conscience, 228; SDA view of *DH*, "times" precede future when no longer have, 229; from coercion equated with modern doctrine of human rights, 271; from coercion implies coercive authority ascribed to, 157, 168, 291; language of *DH* obligates states to grant from coercion, 292; from coercion in civic society related to worship of God, 294; language of *DH* adapted to a constitutional, democratic order, 299; from coercion for individual and community of believers, 302; from coercion of *DH* produces hybrid church-state models, 303; in Articles 1, 2, 4, 9 of *DH*, 308, 309, 310, 313.

Indifferentism, religious condemned in *Mirari vos*, 53; under a Catholic confessional state, religious not allowed, 60; *DH* does not allow for religious, 151-152; as part of a definition of toleration, 154-155.

Indulgences, 16, 174.

Intolerance, when Catholics are in the majority, 29; in Israel, 118; periods of in the history of FEREDE in Spain, 250; the Declaration of All Forms of (1981), 251.

Inquisition, different from biblical teaching, 121-122; papal apology for, 125; foundations of, 126; organization of, 127; extent of, 128, 133; in Germany by 1484, 134; development of toleration from to the 20th century, 151; role of the state toward the Church not the same as during, 161; state support of Church dogma during, 161; restrictions of religious freedom during, 171; "Judaizers" during, 204; torture and murder during, 207; modern Catholic hierarchy and, 227-228; heretics delivered over to civil authority by, 291-292.

IRLA (International Religious Liberty Association), described, 177; promotes religious freedom, 229; minority religious report in Spain, 251; describes how proselytism is viewed negatively, 252.

Islam, moral principles of, 110; *DH* aids Middle Eastern states to transition to democracy and religious freedom, 280-283.

J

Jefferson, Thomas, French philosophers who influenced, 87; influenced by Locke, 88; influence upon Madison, 88; properly functioning Congress has no power to coerce, 93-94; First Amendment and Deism, 98; concepts of religion and government interaction, 111; separationism means no public funding of religious institutions, 290.

Jesuit(s), John Courtney Murray, 23 35; Leonardo Boff, 39; Frederico Lombardi, 48; John Conley, 79; Ignacio Garro, 197; William Reiser, 221; in 1767, expelled from all Spanish territories, 261; Christopher Cullen, 295; Karl Rahner, 302.

Jews, against Paul, 103, 123; Gamaliel, 106; animosity between Samaritans and, 117; lack of toleration toward Jesus, 117; Aquinas r.e. toleration towards, 148, 154; subject to persecution through Sunday laws, 209; lack of religious freedom in Spain, 249.

John of Paris, Murray's appeal to, 64, 66-67, 68, 83, 99; historical context of, 71, 83; key ideas r.e. church and state, 71, 82.

John Paul II, and U.S. covert operations, 24; man's moral nature, 43; in defense of religious freedom, 98; and the Inquisition, 125; Magisterium declares the norms for society, 162; and *Dies Domini*, 198, 208; reforms of now continued by Benedict XVI, 241; interpretation of *DH* allows for Concordats, 246; associates the limitations of religious freedom with the common good, 295.

John XXIII, helped formulate modern concepts of Catholic religious freedom, 12, 98; echoes Pius XII on religious freedom and human rights, 65; cited in footnotes of *DH*, #1-5, 318, 319, #37, 321.

Joint Declaration on the Doctrine of Justification, 33.

Jones, A. T., 177.

Jurisdiction(al), authority defined, 41; France challenged the Church's, 58; state-to-state is horizontal, 70; state recognition of Vatican's, 71; of Constantine in ecclesial affairs, 84; civil authority has none r.e. religious convictions of individuals, 110, 111, 123, 124; Church's toward society, 127; authority of *Ad Extirpanda*, 128; during the Reformation, 139-142; of Trent, 144; Protestants validly baptized fall under the Church's, 146; those outside of Church's, 144; authority of the Church to compel, 145; r.e. toleration and immunity from, 157; Murray r.e. the Christian's conscience toward the Church's, 167, 171; civil authority has none r.e. first 4 Commandments, 198; of the Church toward her members, 208; in Spanish society, 239; and Concordats, 274.

K

Kattolica: Iva Ghax Dritt (Catholic: Yes, because it is a right), 37.

Konig, Francis Cardinal, in footnotes, 23, 24, 29, 49, 53, 63.

L

Laicism, Lefebvre argues that *DH* produces, 60; Winters argues the development of, 85; Founding Fathers did not concern themselves with, 86; Traditional Catholics and, 98.

Laodicea, Council of, 203-204.

Latitude, Catholic Church has shown more toward indigenous religious practices, 219.

Law of Nature, defined, 95-96; in Scripture, 109; Enlightenment concepts of, 98; Pope Leo XIII equates it with the eternal law, 186.

Law of Religious Liberty, Spain, 254.

Lefebvre, Marcel, horrified at *DH*, 48; attended Vatican II, but desired to preserve Traditional Catholicism, 48; viewed *DH* as a departure from the historical stance, 50; argued that *DH* contains no concept of the Catholic State, 59-60; calls for a repeal of *DH*, 60; argues that *DH* has no reference to a true religion, 60-61; Catholic Christian social order, 61; describes the moral rights of a state under traditional Catholic concepts, 62; argues for the right of government to coerce, 158.

Leo XIII, denounced separation, freedom of conscience, and free speech, 12; and the traditional role of the church and state, 57; concern r.e. democracy and the American Catholic Church, 57; proper function of church with state, 54-56, 58; and freedom of the Church, 65; Murray appeals to, 68; Progressive claims r.e. writings by, 69; Murray manipulates writings by, 76, 77; Gilson and writings by, 78; writings by and dissonance with Murray's interpretation, 78; and historical context, 78; Murray's interpretation of writings by, 80; and democracy, 80, 81; and social contract philosophers, 81; and limits to civil jurisdiction, 110; and bull of excommunication, 133; and Diet of Worms, 134-135; and Hildebrand, 152; on temporal order, 184; and natural law, 186; in relation to civil authority, similar to Vatican II, 190.

Letters Concerning Toleration, in footnote, 88.

Libertas ecclesiastica, *DH* enables the Church to fulfill and to challenge totalitarian regimes, 20, 298; during Speyer II (1529), 139; and *DH*, 140, 142; conflicts with individual rights, 152; Murray delimits the concept r.e. a Catholic State, 164; enters negotiations with other countries, 188; Church in Spain asserted to gain recognition in the Constitution, 257; used by Mexican Catholic hierarchy, 277; used to impose Catholic teachings upon society, 284, 290; central to *DH* and current times, not future, 301.

Libertas Praestantissimum, 12, 186.

Locke, John, and social contract theory, 81; no toleration for atheists and Catholics, 88; Bayle goes beyond r.e. freedom of conscience, 88; influenced Madison and Jefferson, 88; how natural law modified by, 95; UNDHR goes beyond, 96; distinct from *DH*, 160.

Lori, Bishop William, head of Ad Hoc Committee on Religious Freedom, 284.

Lubac, Henri de, arguments for Sunday worship, 208.

Luther, Martin, as Reformer, 16; formally excommunicated, 16; followers in conflict with Catholics, 135; followers and religious freedom, 136; to be put to death, 137.

Lutherans, and signing of The Joint Declaration on Salvation, 33; at Diet of Speyer II, 136, 138, 139, 140, 142; and Catholics opposed to anti-Sunday movement, 199; in Latvia, 323.

M

Madison, James, influenced by Baptists, 87; influenced by Jefferson, 87, 88; *DH* at odds with concepts of r.e. religious freedom, 89-90; and freedom of conscience, 91; r.e. Congress and coercion, 92-94; concept of church-state relations, 96; influenced by Locke, 111; separationism and health care, 290.

Magisterium, the Church & enlighten erroneous consciences, 35; teachings of are to be taken in the historical process of maturation, 78; norms of are for society, 162; the populace are to vote policies in harmony with, 192; most American Catholics are at odds with r.e. birth control, 285.

Malta, Catholic influence in, 36; usage of *DH* to protect non-Catholics, 38; example of , 41; Catholic Church treaties with, 322.

Maritain, Jacques, history of, 27; vision for societal construct, 27; dilemma of religious pluralism and democracy, 81; argued for the right of the Church to coerce, 226, 228.

Memorial and Remonstrance, 88-90.

Méndez, Hugo, former SDA student, 32; converted to Roman Catholicism, 214.

Metaphysical, jurisdiction of the Church based on concepts, 40; Pope Benedict XVI's critique of a misapplication of, 76; coercion can be part of the freedom of the will, 145-146; of the freedom of the will, 171; definition of, in footnote, 226; nebulous concept to relate to religious freedom, 228.

Morgan, Douglas, in footnotes, 8, 9.

Moses, some principles of the Ten Commandments, 110; on Mount Sinai, 185.

Moore, Marvin, editor of *Signs of the Times* and challenged by David Pendleton r.e. views on Catholicism, 214; in footnotes, 8, 9, 215.

Murray, John Courtney, S.J., dialogue r.e. religious freedom cases, 2-4; "equality before the law" argument, 4; possible rationale for support of *Everson*, 5, 6;

argument hints at subtle Catholic hegemony, 6; flaws in "equality before the law" argument, 6, 7; acknowledged the need to develop a theological continuity for religious freedom, 13; recognized that religious plurality was a part of democracy, 23; Maritain's societal construct similar to, 27; *DH* clears up ambiguity, 29; faulted for dismantling Catholic confessional states, 35; discontinued publishing on church-state, 40; critique of by Davies and Lefebvre, 59-62; *DH* reflects contributions to religious freedom and then to church-state relations, 66; historical consciousness, 68-69; "political Americanism" in *DH*, 69-70; supports the right of the Church to fulfill its mission, 70; Public Church model envisioned by Murray, 64, 73; analysis of some papal encyclicals, 76-78; hermeneutic of doctrinal development, 78-80; concept of apolitical Catholicism advocated by, 80, 81; formulation of the modern nation state is not compatible with that needed to support religious freedom in *DH*, 81-82; analysis and application of Paris's model is one-sided, 82-84; claimed compatibility of Catholic religious freedom with that of democracy, 84; Carrol wrongly believes *DH* and Enlightenment concepts were reconciled by, 85; distinct differences between the First Amendment and *DH*, 87; right to religious freedom in *DH* not based on "freedom of conscience", 91; seems to distort the historical context of the free exercise clause, 91; attempted to Catholicize the First Amendment, or failed to synthesize them, 86, 94; failed to reconcile a Catholic concept of religious freedom with Enlightenment thought of the First Amendment, 99; selective and only presents half of the idea for a secular society, 99; goal was to revolutionize the thesis and hypothesis formula, 151; need to examine the philosophical rationale of the views of, 151; defined religious freedom as "immunity from coercion", 151; viewed religious freedom not as religious indifferentism, 152; views of in *DH* require a certain historiography of Leo XIII, 152; emphasized diarchy as solution to church-state dilemma, 152; some views of merit scrutiny, 153; detailed analysis of "immunity from coercion" as taught by, 157; argued for a political and legal clarification r.e. religious freedom, 157-158; in *DH*, balances all-powerful state with civil right to religious freedom, 158; views principles of *DH* as permanent, 164; in agreement with other Catholic scholars that *DH* restricts the coercive authority of the Church, 164, 171; *DH* limits the dominance of the Church, but also recognizes its special status, 165; admits that the conscience of the Christian is bound by the magisterial and jurisdictional authority of the church, 166, 167; *DH* supports the right of the Church to Christianize society, 167; ideas of r.e. the repositioning of the state, 173; implies that *DH* adapts to the societal context, 221; Pietro Pavan worked with, 221; interpretation of *DH* by Vatican differs from interpretation by r.e. concordats, 246; some have viewed the work of on a par with the First Amendment, 280.

N

Natural law, when Catholics are a minority, appeal to, 29; Catholic concepts of religious freedom defined by, 43; as used by Traditionalists, 49; as used in Catholic political philosophy, 51; equated with divine law, 55; differentiated from Locke's Law of Nature, 95-96; as a tool of persuasion used by the Church, 100; as part of a Christianized society, 298.

Neuhaus, John Richard, and the public square, 100; to avoid Islamic confessional state, 281-282.

Non-preferentialism, 305. Defined in footnote, 7.

Nostra aetate, 174, 208.

Nuncio, 133.

O

Obama, President, Catholic Bishops versus, 218, 279, 299; exemptions for religious institutions, 286; not arbitrary r.e. health care, 286.

Olsen, V. Norskov, in footnotes, 8, 141.

P

Papacy, attitude of toward Luther in bull *Exsurge Domini*, 131-132; Charles V dependent on, 135; religious freedom based on political demands of, 142-143; Arian tribes destroyed by, 212; warred with the saints, 213; religio-political power, 223.

Pastoral Formation for the Laity, 197.

Pavan, Pietro, attend Vatican II as expert, 30; explains the basis for religious freedom in *DH*, 153; worked with Murray to draft *DH*, 221; indicates that the religious freedom of *DH* evolves, 222; clarifies that erroneous conscience not mentioned in *DH*, 292; explains limits to religious freedom in *DH*, 295; explains the special nature of the Catholic Church expressed in *DH*, 302.

Peace of Augsburg, 17; in footnotes, 17, 52.

Peace of Westphalia, 52, 53.

Periti, defined, 7, 68; Murray as, 40, 66, 68; Congar as, 156.

Petrine doctrine of papal primacy, 84.

Philippines, Catholic Bishops Conference of the Philippines (CBCP), 34; some Catholics use *DH* to defend the rights of non-Catholics, 38; examples of *DH* in, 41;

Catholic hegemony in, 306.

Philosophes, French, influenced Jefferson, 88; Enlightenment views of allow for disbelief, 99.

Poland, solidarity of Catholics in, 24; religious freedom under Soviets, 25; greater respect for convictions of SDAs, 251; Catholic influence in public schools, 322-323.

Pontifical Council for the Promotion of the New Evangelization, 28.

Power of the keys, defined, 41; how heretics damage, 133.

Proselytism, religious liberty for Catholicism includes, 21; biblical toleration includes, 124; cornerstone of the Protestant Reformation, 138, 139; restriction of causes non-Catholic religions to die out within several generations, 145; *DH* does not allow, 172; Catholicism and World Council of Churches unite to oppose for other religions, 195; some priests resist by other religions, 196-197; in some countries the Church has allowed more respect for other religions, 219; restrictions of in Spain parallel the Diet of Speyer II (1529), 243, 244; law against illicit in Spain, 252-254; Catholic hegemony restricts other religions in, 300, 302, 306.

Protestantism, see Reformation.

Public Church Model, defined, 19, 64, 100; a.k.a. Vatican II Model of *DH*, 96; Murray modified Paris' model, 99; very similar to the coercive model, 168.

Q

Quanta cura, in footnote, 207.

Quas primas, 58.

R

Rahner, Karl, 302.

Reform Package, in Spain, aided in transition to democracy, 234.

Reformation, Protestant, conditions in Western Europe prior to, 15; how it changed the religious dynamic, 16; Catholics and Lutheran World Federation united on salvation, a key doctrine of, 33; changed the *Corpus Christianum* , 52; Catholic Church became more aggressive since because of religious competition, 53; how it survived and became established, 121; established civil guarantees for religious freedom, 125; and struggles for freedom of conscience, 131; Seventh-day

Adventists as heirs of, 175.

Reformers, Magisterial, 168.

Reformers, Radical, persecuted by Catholic and Magisterial Reformers, 168; Heilke gives critique of *DH* from perspective of , 223.

Reinach, Allen, in footnote, 8.

Reiser, William, S. J., 221; in footnotes, 148, 221.

Relajado, 291.

Rousseau, Jean Jacques, 81, 87.

S

Sabbath, seventh-day, Saturday, 1, 201; Adelle Sherbert and, 2; Murray's understanding of, 6; in discussions with Catholics, 174; center of debate between SDAs and Catholics, 197; sign of salvation, 202; Catholic Church rejects and wants a distinct break with, 202, 205-206; moral duty to observe, 205-206; observers of biblical, tortured, 204; ceremonial, 205; condemned at the Council of Florence, 206; observers of biblical, named Judaizers by the Church, 207; persecution because of differences, 207; will be focal point in the end of time, 220; misperceptions of versus Sunday, 220; complex issues in Spain, 251-252.

Saxony, 135.

Secular(ism), *DH* confronts rampant, 26-28; versus the Church, 28, 45; Pope Benedict XVI and aggressive in Spain, 28, 230; through *DH* the Church does not deal with a double standard, 29; accusations against *DH* r.e. the Church and, 35; influence of the Church in, 41; since the 19th century, a societal shift toward, 68; UNDHR is purely, 96; the Church mandates laws to conform to divine laws, 127; state was the arm of the Church, 126, 130; all authority to banish Luther, 131; Luther to be tried only before a religious court and not a, 133; the Diet was, and comprised of laity, 134; heretics were delivered to a tribunal, 149; the Church solicited support from power for religious orthodoxy, 161; efforts to counteract may threaten minority religions, 168; *DH* and powers, 171; if no threat from, then what of religious groups and the Catholic Church, 173; -minded states with no overtones in society, 190; how the principle of Protestant Christianity is sacrificed by, 191; both religious and authorities to enforce human laws in defiance of God's, 191; banning of all public and private activities on Sunday, 204-205; the Church applies its principles in different ways in the modern state, 226; pre-Vatican II stance of the Church toward secular powers, 228; SDAs believe it is the duty of governments to defend freedom of conscience, 228; defined and defended by

Spanish news editors, 230; the Spanish Constitution adopts a society and a pre-eminent role for the Church, 238; in 2006, Spain is not wholly a state, 247; the Church wants an aconfessional state, but not a, 248; Cardoso defines it as absolute separation, 248; growing tide of in Spain, 254-258; the Mexican state of the 1830s provides for education and state, 263; cemeteries were –ized in Mexico, 263; Article 3 of the Mexican Law of Religious Associations fosters, 272; or separationist, 280, 303; Spain not wholly, 303; and atheistic state, 305.

Separation(ism), condemned in *Libertas Praestantissimum*, 12; Murray diminished to make it compatible with Roman Catholicism, 77; incompatible with a confessional state, 82; as part of the American heresy, 85; Madison foundational to the American concept of, 89; Monsignor McElroy maligns, 101; advocates of, 102; remove the concept of, 173; American Bishops opposed Kennedy who supported, 218; Catholic Church defines it as an evil, 227; President Kennedy supported, 227; not correctly defined, 230; strictly applied in Spain, 238; applied in Spain during constitution making, 239; strictly applied, 248; Pope Benedict XVI blames for the troubles in Spain, 256; strictly implemented in Mexico, 263; the Mexican Constitutions of 1857 and 1917 uphold, 269; versus religious freedom, 271; Article 24 of the Mexican Constitution favors, 273; in Mexico the Law of Religious Associations upholds, 275; in the Mexican context, 277; Farr opposed to in Islamic countries, 280; disallowance of federal funding to federally non-compliant institutions, 290; classical church-state model, 303; current U.S. church-state trend is a morphing from to an accommodationist form, 304; as a factor in future religious freedom, 305.

Seventh-day Adventist(s), 1963 was significant for Catholics and, 1; Murray's principle of universal equality before the law produces great disparity between Catholics and, 6-7; views of Murray possibly harmful to, 7; historical relations with Catholics, 8; long historical record as advocates of religious freedom, 43; ecumenical discussions with Catholics, 174; religious freedom central to identity, 175; commissioned A. T. Jones r.e. the Blair Bill in Congress, 177; chartered IRLA in 1893, 177; believe that the principles of God's government should guide all relationships, 178; believe that the use of force is contrary to God's government, 178; and civil authority, 180; interpretation of Revelation 13 as time of trouble, 181; similarities and differences with Catholics on religious freedom concepts, 181; believe that God is the Author of civil authority, 182; transcendental principles are reflected in civil authority, 183-185; believe humanity has a nature subject to God's Law, 185; believe in an objective moral order, 186; consider the world as their mission field, 187, 194; limits of civil authority r.e. religious matters, 189, 190-191; stand with Protestant Reformers and statesmen from the Founding Era, 191; do not believe government has the power r.e. the first four of the Ten Commandments, 193, 198; engage government leaders to defend religious freedom, 194; and Catholics differ r.e. proselytism, 195; observe that Catholic leaders do not allow their members to follow their conscience, 195; and Roman Catholicism have a common belief in law, 197-198; can face persecution through Sunday laws, 209; interpret Daniel 7 and Revelation 13 to refer to the Papacy, 209, 211, 212, 223; interpretation of Daniel 7:25, 213; Progressive's believe the historical interpretation is untenable, 213; Administrative Committee (ADCOM) statement r.e. Roman Catholicism, 215; responsibility toward other Christians, 216; take positive approach to other faiths, 216; Seibold questions historic interpretation of, 217; convinced of the validity of their prophetic views, 220; with Catholics r.e. religious freedom, have common principles, but different practices, 228; secular governments must respect freedom of conscience, 228; depend upon the Bible and the Holy Spirit for religious compliance, 229; do not rely upon force or legislation for religious compliance, 229; at odds with Catholics r.e. religious freedom, 229; view as definitive Catholic hegemony through *DH*, 229; promote religious liberty through seminars and rallies, 228, 229; prejudice against by members of FEREDE in Spain decreasing, 250; members of FEREDE in Spain, 250; in Spain, 251-252; decreased cases of Sabbath work conflict in Spain, 252; and other religions suffer government discrimination in Spain, 257.

Shariah law, defined, 283; in an Islamic state, the supreme law is, 282.

Shea, William, in footnote, 212.

Seibold, Loren, SDA pastor, 214; misperception of SDA eschatology and attempts to revise American history r.e. the Catholic Church, 217; argues that religious liberty in Catholic countries has improved, 218, 219; persecution of Christians, 218; refers to President Kennedy, 218; fails to consider other characteristic of the Little Horn in Daniel 7, 219; does not identify the Catholic Church as the Revelation 13 Beast, 219, 220.

Solidarity, in Mexico, 269.

Stokes, Anson Phelps, makes distinction between toleration and religious freedom, 154; distinguishes between revocable concession or defensible right in religious matters, 155.

Suarez, freedom of the will whether under direct or indirect coercion, 144, 171; no member has the right to leave the Church, 145; those born into heresy are under the Church's jurisdiction, if validly baptized, 146; position r.e. heretics, parallel to Vatican II, 146.

Sunday, in discussions between SDAs and Catholics, 174, 197; and debate in Europe and European Union, 198-200; John Paul II, *Dies Domini*, and, 198, 208; existing laws must be seen in light of the past, 201; and Christ's resurrection, no commandment to observe, 202; historical record during Christianity, 202;

observance and Constantine, 202, 203, 205; at Council of Laodicea, 203, 204; Council of Trent and, 206; Church claims substitution for biblical Sabbath, 206, 208, 209; rest on, leads to worship on, 207; conflicts with Sabbatarians, 208; rationalization for observance of, 208; law in Croatia, 209, 306; Catholic Church promotes worship on, 209; Seibold's misunderstanding of debate r.e. Sabbath and, 220; legislation by Catholics, overt hegemony, 228; Bishops use to rally members, 268; laws at the Founding Era, 298.

Sweeney, James, argues that *DH* allows the Church to fulfill its mission by Christianizing society, 167; interprets *DH* to deny coercive authority to the Church, 171.

T

Ten Commandments, distinction between 1st and 2nd tables of, 123-124; objective moral order based on, 192-193; distinction between ceremonial and moral Sabbath of, 205-206; God's moral Law for humanity, 206; persecution of followers of, 207.

Testem benevolentiae , 57.

Theocratic, challenge facing Traditional Catholics, 74; Old Testament model, 118; shift from to apolitical model, 119; classical church-state model, 303.

Toleration, pre-Vatican II none to a general, shown to all non-Catholics, 42, 151; apparently superseded by Vatican II's "immunity from coercion", 43; Traditional Catholics and, 44; *DH* does not include the word, 62; Bayle's views of, 88; Locke argued for, 88; civil sphere includes toward other Christian groups and non-Christian religions, 116, 117, 119, 120, 124; biblical approaches more unto a modern concept of religious freedom, 116, 120, 124, 125; variety of Scriptural interpretations necessitates, 117; biblical is more restrictive within the faith, 121, 124; biblical includes proclamation and proselytism, 124; at Diet of Speyer II, 143; philosophical parallels between Vatican II formulation and pre-Vatican II, 153-154; defined by Stokes as different from freedom, 154-155; Latin root, 156; *DH* similar to pre-Vatican II, but also different from it, 157; in Spain, non-Catholics receive mere, 243.

Torture, options of those subjected to, 144; no religious organization has the right to, 171; instigated by Satan, 179; fate of Judaizers during the Inquisition, 204, 207.

Totalitarian, nature of some modern regimes, 20; prior to and after Vatican II, 21;*DH* in relation to regimes, 23, 24, 26, 292; during 20th and 21st centuries, confessional states and semi- regimes, 30; Murray claims American democracy is different from, 76-77; Church confronted regimes, 190; strategy of the Church r.e., 300, 301.

Transubstantiation, in footnote, 197.

Trent, Council of, juridical authority of, 42; political bargaining granted tolerance to Protestants, 142; Pink argues for a jurisdiction-centered view of, 144; and Vatican II, 78, 80, 146; formulated a response to Protestant heresies, 206; and Sunday sacredness, 206.

Two swords theory, in footnote, 56.

U

Unam Sanctam, 74.

UNDHR 18, as modern document on religious freedom, 50; as comparative document on *DH*, 291.

Unitatis Redintegratio, 75.

United Nations, address of Pope Paul VI to, 65; International Religious Liberty Association (IRLA) represented at, 177; actual countries recognized by, 187; influence of *DH* upon, 296.

United States, ecumenical efforts in, 32; Catholic politicians in face strong opposition from Bishops, 38; as an example of a pluralistic society, 45; *DH* contrary to the First Amendment in the Bill of Rights, 50; Progressive Catholics re-interpret historical understanding of the Americanist controversy in, 69-70; *DH* attempts to parallel the Constitution of and democracy, 84-85; Seibold's eschatological views r.e., 220; foreign priests studying in exposed to democracy, 268; relations with Mexico r.e. Protestants, 276; Catholic-Muslim dialogues in, 283; Catholic Church claims violation of religious freedom in, 284; Catholic Church adopts different strategy in, 299.

United States Conference of Catholic Bishops (USCCB), website on religious freedom, 284; claims to a violation of religious freedom unfounded, 285-286; interprets the First Amendment in different ways to suit its hegemony, 288; attempts to impose moral teachings upon non-Catholics, 290; appeals to *DH*, 290; challenging the Obama administration, 279, 299; differences between Spain (CEE) and America, 300.

United States Commission on International Religious Freedom (USCIRF), in contact with the Dignitatis Humanae Institute, 279.

V

Vatican I, should be evaluated in light of Vatican II, 42.

Vatican II, *DH* and views on religious freedom may harm SDA's and others, 7; some SDA's consider the Church to uphold a traditional, pre- position on religious freedom, 9; historical events during the decade of, 21; Maritain's students contributed to documents at, 27; charges against the Church prior to, 21, 35; ecumenical relations in a post- context, 31; innovations arising from some interpretations of, 34; some blame for liberal moral condition, 35; Trent and Vatican I need to be re-evaluated in light of, 42; and immunity from coercion, 42, 43; the Church uses *DH* to dispel shadows of its pre- history, 45; Traditional Catholics and views of, 49; Lefebvre upholds a pre- stance, 48, 50; Traditional Catholics and a pre- concept of church and state relations, 50-59; pre- position of the Church and state, 58, 59; Lefebvre signed *DH* at, 59; public order from does have some restrictions, 62; how Progressive Catholics view, 63; post- relations and the Public Church Model, 64; intent of was to express the Church's position on various reforms, 64, 66; various Popes expressed the need for religious freedom prior to, 65; Progressive Catholics argue historical context for some encyclicals prior to that seem to contradict *DH* , 67, 68; by the time of, Murray viewed sacrality of society and state as archaic, 68; Murray's contributions at, 68; some theological aspects of a pre- stance on religious freedom are still valid, 75; Council of Trent and not compatible in many areas, 79-81; pre- argument that Catholicism was compatible with democracy, 81; Public Church Model of, 96, 99, 100; Diet of Speyer II (1529) similar to *DH* at, 141; aligns Trent within the Tradition of the Church, 146; pre- concept of tolerance, 147-151; comparison of pre- and ideas r.e. religious freedom, 153; *DH* resembles pre- concept of toleration, 156, 157; "separated brethren" is the language used for Protestant, 146, 173; civil authority from God emphasized at, 183; mission of the Church since, through *Ad Gentes*, 188; the Church's stance toward civil authority since, 190; Church confronted Communist states, 190; social teachings given a Scriptural foundation at, 193; natural law was given a Christological dimension at, 193; concordats prior to and after, 195; (1962-1965) introduced dramatic reforms within the Church, 207; promoted Sunday worship, 208; Murray argues against the possibility of a future Catholic confessional state similar to pre- , 221; conciliar teaching of is authoritative and also capable of further development, 221; Maritain argues that the coercive authority prior to, always retains, 228; debates at , which defined Catholics religious freedom, 242, 243; fostered transition to democracy in Spain, 256-257; influence the social doctrine in Mexico, leading to Liberation Theology, 268.

Vehementer nos, 57.

Voltaire, Francois Marie de, 87.

Vouchers, 288-289.

W

Were, Louis, diagrammatic outline of Revelation 13, 225; in footnote, 224.

White, Ellen G., views of in relation to civil authority and religious liberty, 175, 180, 184, 185, 189, 191, 215; Seibold's claims regarding the Catholic Church during the time of, 217-218.

Wittenburg, nailing of 95 Theses, 131; burning of papal bull, 132.

X

Xavier, University of, professor Thomas Bokenkotter, explains Christianization of Roman society and Sunday laws, 204.

Y

Ya (Spanish periodical), 242.

Z

Zaragoza, University of, Spain, SDA student denied enrollment because of Sabbath, 251.

Zoroastrian, commonality of ethical laws with Hindu, Buddhist, Confucian, Greek, Judeo-Christian, and Islam, 110.

ABOUT THE AUTHOR

Dr. Edwin Cook earned a Ph. D. in Church-State Relations from the J. M. Dawson Institute of Church-State Studies, Baylor University, Waco, TX, in August 2012. He has written numerous articles related to religion, politics, and society, many of which have been published in *Liberty* magazine. He has also given lectures on these topics in various countries, such as Ukraine, Romania, Spain, Dominican Republic, Mexico, Canada, and the United States. He currently serves as the pastor of the Waco English and Spanish Seventh-day Adventist Churches. He is the founder and Director of Liberty 21st Century, Inc. (www.liberty21stcentury.com), a corporation dedicated to defending and promoting religious freedom for people of all faiths whose actions are non-violent.

www.ingramcontent.com/pod-product-compliance
Lightning Source LLC
Chambersburg PA
CBHW071647160426
43195CB00012B/1384